African Americans
on the Great Plains

African Americans on the Great Plains

AN ANTHOLOGY | *Edited and with an introduction by*
Bruce A. Glasrud &
Charles A. Braithwaite

University of Nebraska Press
Lincoln & London

© 2009 by the Board of Regents of
the University of Nebraska
All rights reserved
Manufactured in the United States of America

Publication information for material originally
published in the *Great Plains Quarterly* appears on
pp. 339–40, which constitutes an extension of the
copyright page.

Library of Congress Cataloging-in-Publication Data
African Americans on the Great Plains : an
anthology / edited and with an introduction by
Bruce A. Glasrud and Charles A. Braithwaite.
   p. cm.
Includes bibliographical references and index.
ISBN 978-0-8032-2667-8 (pbk. : alk. paper)
1. African Americans—Great Plains—History.
2. Frontier and pioneer life—Great Plains.
3. Great Plains—Race relations—History.
I. Glasrud, Bruce A. II. Braithwaite, Charles A.
E185.925.A56 2009
305.896073078—dc22
2009008137

Set in Dante by Bob Reitz.

CONTENTS

Acknowledgments | vii

Introduction: *African Americans on the Great Plains* | 1
  BRUCE A. GLASRUD & CHARLES A. BRAITHWAITE

1. Black Soldiers at Fort Hays, Kansas, 1867–1869: *A Study in Civilian and Military Violence* | 24
  JAMES N. LEIKER

2. "Pap" Singleton's Dunlap Colony: *Relief Agencies and the Failure of a Black Settlement in Eastern Kansas* | 47
  JOSEPH V. HICKEY

3. Vengeance without Justice, Injustice without Retribution: *The Afro-American Council's Struggle against Racial Violence* | 71
  SHAWN LEIGH ALEXANDER

4. Prelude to Brownsville: *The Twenty-fifth Infantry at Fort Niobrara, Nebraska, 1902–1906* | 103
  THOMAS R. BUECKER

5. Black Enclaves of Violence: *Race and Homicide in Great Plains Cities, 1890–1920* | 124
  CLARE V. MCKANNA JR.

6. A Socioeconomic Portrait of Prince Hall Masonry in Nebraska, 1900–1920 | 144
   DENNIS N. MIHELICH

7. Diplomatic Racism: *Canadian Government and Black Migration from Oklahoma, 1905–1912* | 162
   R. BRUCE SHEPARD

8. "This Strange White World": *Race and Place in Era Bell Thompson's American Daughter* | 184
   MICHAEL K. JOHNSON

9. The New Negro Arts and Letters Movement among Black University Students in the Midwest, 1914–1940 | 204
   RICHARD M. BREAUX

10. Great Plains Pragmatist: *Aaron Douglas and the Art of Social Protest* | 233
    AUDREY THOMPSON

11. Frompin' in the Great Plains: *Listening and Dancing to the Jazz Orchestras of Alphonso Trent, 1925–1944* | 256
    MARC RICE

12. Early Civil Rights Activism in Topeka, Kansas, Prior to the 1954 *Brown* Case | 273
    JEAN VAN DELINDER

13. The Great Plains Sit-In Movement, 1958–1960 | 302
    RONALD WALTERS

14. The Omaha Gospel Complex in Historical Perspective | 320
    TOM JACK

Source Acknowledgments | 339
Selected Bibliography | 341
Contributors | 375
Index | 379

ACKNOWLEDGMENTS

We received considerable help in preparing and publishing this book, and for that assistance we wish to thank a number of people. We are grateful for the cooperation of the fourteen authors whose studies are featured here. Without their scholarship and abilities, of course, this book would not have been feasible. We acknowledge members of the staff at the *Great Plains Quarterly*, who aided and supported us. Since all of the articles originally appeared in the *Great Plains Quarterly*, we owe a debt to the Center for Great Plains Studies for granting us permission to reprint. Roger D. Cunningham, historian and colleague, read the introduction and made it stronger; thanks, Roger. Two outside readers asked pertinent questions, made a few suggestions, and helped us consider what constituted the geographic boundary of the Great Plains; we appreciate their support of publication. Thanks also to the staff at the University of Nebraska Press, especially Heather Lundine, editor in chief, who provided initial acceptance and encouragement; Bridget Barry, who guided the final manuscript's preparation; and the many others who helped turn the manuscript into a book. For the rest we remain responsible.

INTRODUCTION | African Americans on the Great Plains

BRUCE A. GLASRUD &
CHARLES A. BRAITHWAITE

P rior to the late twentieth century, the predominant histories of the West and the Great Plains included little evidence of the presence of African Americans. Nevertheless, African Americans have a long history of living in the West and evidence of this could be found in the works of two pioneering historians: Kenneth Wiggins Porter's *The Negro on the American Frontier* and W. Sherman Savage's *Blacks in the West*. Porter, a white historian, published his book in 1971; Savage, an African American, in 1976. But prior to the appearance of those two works, scant information was available. Walter Prescott Webb, in his classic *The Great Plains*, made little mention of blacks on the Great Plains: he commented on slavery but not actual slaves, and he mentioned the Dred Scott court decision but not Dred Scott the man. Similarly, Ray Allen Billington, in his oft-used textbook, *Westward Expansion*, did not discuss Estevan, although he included a chapter entitled "The West and Slavery," where he, too, wrote of the institution but nothing about slaves. Billington did reference the name of Dred Scott, but he revealed nothing about him. As Oklahoma black novelist Ralph Ellison later phrased it, to these and other historians, African Americans in the West were *The Invisible Man*.[1]

Fortunately, by the twenty-first century historians acknowledged the presence and role of black westerners. More recent editions of Billington's textbook include African Americans, and in a pivotal development, Quintard Taylor provided us with an excellent history of the black experience in the West: *In Search of the Racial Frontier: African Americans in the American West, 1528–1990*. Although Taylor's study has a considerable amount of information about black life and history on the Great Plains, and one can find several significant book-length state studies of African Americans on the Plains—including studies of Texas, Oklahoma, Kansas, Nebraska, South Dakota, Minnesota, Iowa, and New Mexico—still, no overall study of the black experience on the Great Plains exists.[2]

A first of its kind, *African Americans on the Great Plains* fills that gap and, it is hoped, will stimulate other writers to pursue studies of the black experience on the plains. The fourteen articles in this anthology, all originally published in the *Great Plains Quarterly*, cover the Great Plains as broadly but inconsistently defined. The Center for Great Plains Studies at the University of Nebraska, for example, defines the Great Plains as including the states of Colorado, Kansas, Montana, Nebraska, New Mexico, North Dakota, Oklahoma, South Dakota, Texas, and Wyoming, and the Canadian provinces of Alberta, Manitoba, and Saskatchewan. To that list we add Minnesota, Iowa, Missouri, and Arkansas. Yet definitional difficulties still intrude; it is troublesome, for example, to label the Texas Gulf Coast and the cities of Austin and Houston as belonging in the Great Plains, although they certainly are located in a Great Plains state.

This book is about African Americans and the making of black communities on the plains. It is about race relations. It is about discrimination and violence. It is about the struggle for civil rights and against Jim Crow. It depicts African American cultural growth and contributions and it includes the many and varied economic and political aspects of those contributions. The fourteen articles are arranged chronologically and cover key topics of the black experience on the Great Plains—organizations, employment opportunities, cultural contributions, family and gender issues, the military, prejudice and discrimination, rural and urban life, and violence. The book is intended for a broad readership that includes students, teachers, scholars, and the general reading public. Every essay is well-documented and packed with information, showcasing the resiliency and spirit of African Americans on the Great Plains of the United States.

African Americans first entered the Great Plains in 1528 when Estevan came to Texas with Spanish explorer Cabeza de Vaca. Killed while exploring New Mexico (1539), Estevan was the first in a long line of blacks who entered or settled on the Great Plains, either as slaves or as soldiers with Spanish explorers (some accompanying Coronado in 1540 and 1542 and others who aided the colonization of New Mexico in 1598). Black growth and settlement continued in succeeding years, albeit sparsely; in fact, by 1717 San Antonio's black population stood at 151. Black women were part of these numbers as well: in 1600 a black woman, Isabel de Olvera, journeyed to Santa Fe to work as a servant while other black women in the northern Spanish province were fighting to protect their rights, to file lawsuits, and to establish families and networks. Although much of the early exploration of the plains took place on the Spanish northern frontier, one slave, York, crossed the plains with the Lewis and Clark expedition and another, Jacob Dodson, accompanied John C. Fremont's expedition in 1843. Blacks became fur trappers and traders as well: two well-known examples were Edward Rose and James Beckwourth. In Minnesota, George and Stephen Bonga engaged in the fur trade and lived among the Obijway as late as 1866.[3]

Although slavery did not exist over the entire Great Plains, it was entrenched in Texas and in the Indian Territory. Slavery, as Paul Lack reminds us in *The Texas Revolutionary Experience: A Political and Social History*, was a major factor in precipitating the Texas Revolution.

The possibility of allowing slavery affected Kansas deeply and was responsible for "bleeding" Kansas in 1855. And while there were no "natural limits" to slavery's expansion, it failed only when people orchestrated its demise through legislation such as the Missouri Compromise (1820) and the Kansas-Nebraska Act (1854). Affirming the right of slavery to exist on the Great Plains was the Dred Scott decision. Scott, a Missouri slave, had resided temporarily in both Illinois and Minnesota and sued for his freedom on the basis of the fact that he had lived in free territory. The U.S. Supreme Court ruled against him, however, by declaring the Missouri Compromise unconstitutional (1857). The relationship between slavery and politics is clearly articulated in James A. Rawley's superb book *Race and Politics: "Bleeding Kansas" and the Coming of the Civil War*. Ultimately the Civil War settled the issue: slavery would not be allowed anyplace in the United States or its territories.[4]

The Civil War created a "Black Kansas" whose population in 1860 was 627 but, as author Frank Yerby noted in one of his novels, grew to over 12,500 by 1865. By the 1870s black Kansans had established small communities and resisted discrimination, though not always successfully. During the Civil War black regiments from Kansas volunteered and fought for the Union, including engagements in Arkansas and the Indian Territory (later named Oklahoma). African Americans from Iowa also enlisted in the U.S. Colored Troops; during the war 440 fought for the Union. White Texas soldiers, as Yerby also noted, massacred black soldiers and black civilians who resided in close proximity to military engagements. Although black soldiers jubilantly entered military service, their war experiences with white Confederates were filled with normal military danger and racism as well.[5]

A federal military presence in the two slave-holding regions of Texas and Oklahoma were used to enforce national laws, to help recently freed African Americans, and to reconstruct the southern states from 1865 to 1874. Overall, passage of the Thirteenth, Fourteenth, and Fifteenth amendments to the constitution had a profound and lasting effect on African Americans on the Great Plains. They were free, they were enfranchised, and they began to vote. In Colorado, Kansas, Texas, and Wyoming, voters elected black officeholders. At the same time, however, violent white opposition to African American freedom existed, particularly in Texas.[6]

One employment opportunity that was open to black males after the Civil War was enlistment in the U.S. Army. Primarily engaged on the Great Plains, the black soldiers' deployment ranged from Texas and New Mexico to South Dakota and Wyoming. Though all served under white officers, the military offered a measure of economic security and a level of respect from society not easily gained in the postwar years. Nicknamed "buffalo soldiers" by Plains Indians, from the outset the black soldiers faced considerable opposition and antagonism, even from those under their protection. In addition to the black regulars, black citizen-soldiers in the militias of Iowa, Kansas, and Texas performed largely ceremonial functions. They were, however, activated on at least two occasions during instances of domestic disorder. Many of these men later enlisted in the black volunteer regiments that were organized for the Spanish-American and Philippine-American wars.[7]

To some extent African American soldiers played their own role in the racial strife that often resulted when black garrisons were located near white communities. As James N. Leiker shows in Chapter 1, "Black Soldiers at Fort Hays, Kansas, 1867–1869: A Study in Civilian and Military Violence," Fort Hays in Kansas provides "an example of how civilian/military interaction helped to transfer racial hatreds to the newly conquered region." Relationships between soldiers from the fort and white civilians in Hays City were filled with conflict and violence. Black soldiers did not respond passively but instead retaliated to wrongs perpetrated upon them by white racists. In their search for protection and their struggle for acceptance these soldiers became a community. Similar civilian-military conflicts occurred in Texas and Oklahoma as well.[8]

One other attractive employment opportunity for black males on the Great Plains was that of a cowboy. Black cowboys lived and worked generally in Texas but also in the Dakotas, New Mexico, Kansas, and, occasionally, ranged as far west as Wyoming. Some black cowboys became successful ranchers, such as Daniel Webster "80 John" Wallace, who owned ranch land in Mitchell County, Texas. Unfortunately, for many years the black cowboys were "invisible" (just like many other blacks on the Great Plains). Contrary to the picture that one received from the movies and from television, black cowboys actually comprised around 40 percent of the total number of ranch hands.[9]

African Americans ventured westward for numerous reasons other than in search of employment or to serve in the military. Some were seeking an escape from the South, taking railroads, boats, or simply by walking. Some sought free or inexpensive land on the Great Plains. Others headed to Oklahoma in an effort to establish all-black towns and make Oklahoma a predominantly black state. Some moved westward from the North and entered Nebraska or the Dakotas. A search for freedom and economic opportunity, to escape violence and intimidation, and a taste for adventure all propelled the African American westward movement. Countless black women also enjoyed the West's opportunities. South Dakotan Kate Chapman encouraged everyone "for the sake of health, wealth and freedom, come west."[10]

In 1877 a massive migration to Kansas, led and encouraged by a black man from Tennessee, Benjamin "Pap" Singleton, began. Two years later a larger, unorganized, and leaderless mass migration occurred from the southern states of Tennessee, Mississippi, Kentucky, Louisiana, and Texas. Though the numbers are murky, between 1877 and 1880 over twenty-thousand African Americans migrated to and settled in Kansas; the African American population of Kansas grew by over twenty-six thousand between 1870 and 1880. These migrants became known as the "Exodusters." Buoyed by the chance for free land, by the spirit of John Brown, and by an opportunity to live apart from whites in separate black communities, the Exodusters established over a dozen towns such as Nicodemus and Dunlap. In the end the movement suffered from false promises and eventually failed; some of the migrants returned to their homes in the South while others moved to cities on the Great Plains. As Joseph V. Hickey notes in "'Pap' Singleton's Dunlap Colony: Relief Agencies and the Failure of a Black Settlement in Eastern Kansas," the movement to Dunlap, Kansas, had great potential for success. Dunlap Colony was carefully planned, received considerable financial support, and attracted about a thousand residents, yet it declined within twenty years. Local racial prejudice and discrimination created problems that plagued the community; more important, the failure of good-hearted relief agencies led to its downfall.[11]

The Exodusters were not the only African Americans on the Great Plains who moved to the region's larger towns and cities. Despite the romance connected with many black occupations and settlements during the nineteenth century, a large number of blacks migrated to the urban centers—Denver, Kansas City, Topeka, Omaha, Dallas, Houston, and San Antonio. Blacks worked as personal servants, hotel waiters, railroad porters, cooks, and janitors. They operated barbershops and restaurants, served as newspaper editors, and included a small but important professional class. Black women discovered opportunities for networking, for employment such as teaching, for religious endeavors, and for family matters. In one late nineteenth-century example, African American women in Great Falls, Montana, joined forces to establish and maintain their church, the African Methodist Episcopal Church. In some places, however, it was difficult for black women to obtain teaching positions; Ruth Flowers, the first black woman to graduate from the University of Colorado (in 1924), was forced to leave Boulder for South Carolina to secure a teaching job. In general, jobs for black women in Denver were difficult to find and hard to keep, leading to the often-repeated comment to "try being a black woman!"[12]

In these Great Plains cities, African Americans realized that they had to work together to make their communities viable and to protect themselves from racists and racial violence. Principal among their problems were the actions of their white neighbors. Shawn Leigh Alexander's "Vengeance without Justice, Injustice without Retribution: The Afro-American Council's Struggle against Racial Violence," focuses on the 1901 case of Fred Alexander, a black man who was lynched in Leavenworth, Kansas. Previously, blacks on the Great Plains organized local Afro-American leagues and ministerial alliances to protest white brutality as well as Jim Crow society. By 1901 the League had vanished and in its place the Afro-American Council emerged. Supported by and working with the council, blacks on the Great Plains strongly protested Fred Alexander's lynching and sought the imprisonment of those responsible. Later, a 1919 brutal lynching and race riot in Omaha, Nebraska, and a 1920 lynching in Duluth, Minnesota, led to the growth and influence of the National Association for the Advancement of Colored People (NAACP).[13]

Race riots and lynchings were not the only instances of violence faced by African Americans in the cities during the first decades of the twentieth century. Clare V. McKanna Jr., in "Black Enclaves of Violence: Race and Homicide in Great Plains Cities, 1890–1920," examines racial violence from one other perspective, pointing out that high interracial homicide rates were prevalent on the Great Plains during the years from 1890 to 1920. Racial violence in Coffeeville and Topeka, Kansas, as well as in Omaha, resulted from "enclaves of violence" where males, alcohol, cheap guns, idle time, and a convenient place came together. Around 80 percent of blacks who were charged were convicted; whites so charged received lesser sentences or were acquitted.[14]

Black soldiers stationed along the Texas-Mexico border also were involved in racial incidents during the last years of the nineteenth century and continuing into the twentieth century. The most explosive incident took place in 1906 at Brownsville, Texas, when black soldiers allegedly rioted in the town. The black soldiers were summarily discharged from the army, though little evidence and no confessions emerged. In "Prelude to Brownsville: The Twenty-fifth Infantry at Fort Niobrara, Nebraska, 1902-06," Thomas R. Buecker argues that these black soldiers, members of the well-regarded 25th Infantry, had fought in the Spanish-American and the Philippine-American wars; in their previous posting in Nebraska they had been treated well and had acted as model troops, gaining the respect of the Nebraska communities in which they resided. Yet those same black soldiers encountered a very antagonistic society in Texas and the congenial treatment they had received in Nebraska made the behavior of Texans seem even worse; the disparity was virtually impossible to accept and violence broke out. White Texans did not change their behavior, and later in 1917 a riot with black soldiers and white townsmen occurred in Houston.[15]

Race riots on the Plains were not limited to black military–white civilian episodes during the first years of the twentieth century. Although a riot in 1910 had decimated the black community in Anderson County, Texas, in 1919 race riots broke out in Elaine, Arkansas, Longview and Port Arthur, Texas, and Omaha, Nebraska, as black soldiers returning home from World War I refused to submit to Jim Crow treatment. Other racial riots took place in Tulsa, Oklahoma, in 1921, in Sherman, Texas, in 1930, and in Beaumont, Texas, in 1943.[16]

Not all African American twentieth-century history on the Great Plains is filled with violence. Black life was affected by and had an effect on urbanization: African Americans, to borrow a phrase from Darlene Clark Hine, were engaged in "making community."[17] They played a part in the Harlem Renaissance, fought in and supported World War I and World War II, and suffered through the ravages of the Great Depression of the 1930s. Bent on creating a better, more equitable, and more humane society, they participated in the civil rights movement and focused on closing fissures in the glass ceiling, on expanding their opportunities, and on living in a Plains society without Jim Crow segregation. By the twenty-first century African Americans could take pride in what they had accomplished but nevertheless continued their efforts toward a fairer share in that society.

As blacks on the Great Plains organized and challenged racism through organizations such as the Afro-American League and the National Afro-American Council, they also aided in developing their communities through self-help, economic betterment, and racial uplift programs with group emphasis. As Dennis N. Mihelich points out in "A Socioeconomic Portrait of Prince Hall Masonry in Nebraska, 1900–1920," the black Masons were a group of individuals and clubs who worked together to create a better community. What Mihelich also discovered was that membership in the Prince Hall Masons crossed class boundaries and resulted in "a multiclass fraternity." By working together the Masons survived the lynchings and race riot crisis of 1919, owned their own homes, and in general were young and socially mobile.[18]

As noted earlier, one goal of many African Americans on the Great Plains was to create predominantly black towns and communities in Oklahoma. As R. Bruce Shepard explains in "Diplomatic Racism: Canadian Government and Black Migration from Oklahoma, 1905–1912," blacks discovered that the movement to create black towns and communities in Oklahoma led to fierce white resistance and anti-black discrimination that culminated in Jim Crow legislation as soon as Oklahoma became a state in 1907. Three years later the state legislature disenfranchised black Oklahomans by use of a literacy test and a grandfather clause, the latter of which insured that whites owned the right to vote. As a result of *de facto* and *de jure* discrimination, a significant migration effort by black Oklahomans to move to Canada emerged. White Canadians reacted negatively to this migration and supported a successful diplomatic effort by their government to keep blacks out of their country. Black Oklahomans realized that discrimination was manifold—they escaped vicious anti-black behavior in the South and settled in Oklahoma, only to face increased discrimination when they tried to move to a potentially desirable new country and were met with stiff resistance. Most black Oklahomans remained in Oklahoma, eventually owning their own homes and achieving gainful employment despite the growing discrimination.[19]

Changes beginning with the end of World War I, gradually became apparent in the ability of blacks on the Great Plains to reduce the number of physical threats and create more viable communities, even in Texas. This was the advent of the "New Negro." For the remainder of the twentieth century the history of African Americans on the Great Plains revolves around six themes, each partially visible in previous years as well: (1) increased political activity; (2) protest and resistance to discrimination and violence, e.g., in Texas blacks led the attack on the white primary, and in Kansas on segregated public education as well as demonstrating a commitment to civil rights; (3) racial cohesiveness; (4) search for freedom; (5) significant cultural contributions, including a close relationship with the Harlem Renaissance; and (6) representative and responsible roles for black women.

Era Bell Thompson epitomized these and other aspects of black life on the Great Plains in the years after World War I. Born in 1906 in Iowa, Thompson's family moved to North Dakota in 1914 because her father believed they would encounter less prejudice and more opportunity there. Thompson was raised with few other African Americans in her circle of friends and acquaintances. In fact, the entire black population of North Dakota in 1920 was only 467. Thompson attended the University of North Dakota, later graduated from Morningside College in Iowa, and enrolled in graduate coursework at Northwestern University. She moved permanently to Chicago in 1931 and published her autobiography, *An American Daughter*, in 1946. Thompson's book detailed her experiences in North Dakota, noting that gatherings with other African Americans brought "a feeling of brotherhood, of race consciousness, and of family solidarity." She later was hired by John H. Johnson as editor for *Negro Digest* and then for *Ebony*. She died in 1986. Michael K. Johnson's article, "'This Strange White World': Race and Place in Era Bell Thompson's *American Daughter*," examines the effects of growing up in "this strange white world" of white people and white snow. Amid what W. E. B. Du Bois referred to as "double consciousness," Thompson and her family created their own African American culture on the North Dakota frontier.[20]

Other African Americans on the Plains, cognizant of the spirit of the "New Negro," also worked to develop their own culture on the Plains. In a singularly comprehensive overview entitled, "The New Negro Arts and Letters Movement among Black University Students in the Midwest, 1914–1940," Richard M. Breaux describes the effect of those ideas on university students in the Midwest in a cultural explosion that overlapped the Harlem Renaissance. Breaux explains that black students at the universities of Iowa, Kansas, Minnesota, and Nebraska made many contributions to the spirit and actuality of the New Negro movement. The students were involved politically and produced literature and art as well as music. As Breaux concludes, "blacks with a variety of talents and political views deserved the title New Negroes."[21]

The New Negro movement, also referred to as the Negro

Renaissance or the Harlem Renaissance (due to the significance of its locale), fostered a large number of African Americans who ventured to Harlem in the 1920s and 1930s to participate in that exciting moment in black social and cultural history. Many of them were originally from the Great Plains and this movement captured the spirit of the Great Plains, as Richard Breaux depicts so well. It was even more wide spread than Breaux's analysis. The Harlem Renaissance existed on the Great Plains outside the major universities, in its urban centers such as Houston, Dallas, Oklahoma City, Kansas City, Wichita, and Omaha, and in smaller communities such as Marshall, Texas, where two black colleges, Wiley and Bishop, were located.[22]

Representatives of the movement included Oscar Micheaux, a South Dakota homesteader and later writer and filmmaker whose autobiographical novels, *The Conquest* and *The Homesteader*, told us much about black life in South Dakota; singer Taylor Gordon, who in *Born to be Free* described growing up in Sulphur Springs, Montana; author Langston Hughes, whose novel, *Not Without Laughter*, describes growing up in Kansas; and writer and editor Frank Marshall Davis, who was raised in Arkansas City, Kansas, and matriculated at Kansas State University in Manhattan. All were important figures in the Harlem Renaissance.[23] From Texas came Bernice Love Wiggins, a black poet from El Paso, who in 1925 published her book of poems, *Tuneful Tales*. Lillian B. Horace, another black Texan, published her first novel, *Five Generations Hence*, in 1916 (it was also the first novel published by a black woman on the Great Plains). Wiley College professor and poet Melvin B. Tolson joined the renaissance in Harlem during the summers, and eventually wrote his master's thesis on the Harlem Renaissance, the first scholarly work on this significant movement. J. Mason Brewer (the Alain Locke of Texas) collected black Texas poetry and published *Heralding Dawn*, a great contribution to our knowledge of Texas writers of that era.[24]

These figures were not alone. From New Mexico came Mexico-born Anita Scott Coleman, who went on to publish more than thirty short stories in national magazines and journals during the period of the renaissance.[25] Other blacks on the Great Plains were influenced by the New Negro movement or gained a beginning during the later part of the period. Era Bell Thompson was affected by the spirit of the New Negro, and Margaret Walker, who attended college during the Harlem Renaissance, had her most inspired writing come out after World War II.[26]

The Harlem Renaissance, whether in New York City or on the Great Plains, was not solely about literature, vital as that was. As Richard Breaux reminds us, the visual arts were important as well. The most prominent of the visual artists undoubtedly was Aaron Douglas. Born in 1899 in Topeka, Kansas, Douglas attended the University of Nebraska, graduating in 1922. Douglas moved to Harlem in 1925 and became acquainted with and influenced by Alain Locke and W. E. B. Du Bois. Audrey Thompson, in "Great Plains Pragmatist: Aaron Douglas and the Art of Social Protest," refers to Douglas as the Harlem Renaissance's "leading visual artist." Depicting Douglas as a pragmatist, Thompson points out that Douglas used his art as social protest and emphasized and portrayed race as being an important and valuable experience for blacks, an experience that was diverse and complex.[27]

Along with the literary and visual arts, music was a hallmark of the Harlem Renaissance. Music was a vital element of black plains life during the 1920s and 1930s. Whether in Kansas City, Omaha, Tulsa, Oklahoma City, Dallas, Houston, or San Antonio, jazz and the blues precipitated the emergence of singers, groups, and bands. One of the best known bands was Alphonso Trent's Orchestra. In "Frompin' in the Great Plains: Listening and Dancing to the Jazz Orchestras of Alphonso Trent, 1925–44," Mark Rice calls Trent one of the most popular and influential band leaders. One of the "territory bands," that is, one that had a particular city as a base, Trent's band performed throughout the Southwest and the Great Plains. At one time or another Trent was based in Dallas, Texas, Kansas City, Missouri, and Deadwood, South Dakota. In general, Trent and other African American bands performed for engagements at extravagant white hotels and then, if time and schedules allowed, performed for the black communities. They were aided in getting their music out by the growth of public radio. In addition to Trent, other contemporaneous black bands on the Great Plains were the Bennie Moten Orchestra (based in Kansas City), Troy Floyd (in San Antonio), and the George E. Lee Orchestra (also in Kansas City). Kansas City was a pivotal locale for music and bands though it was not the only focal point of jazz and the blues on the Great Plains. Omaha, Houston, and Dallas also were meccas.[28]

Music served not only as a cultural and entertainment venue for the African American community, it also provided relief and a voice for reform efforts in the struggle for freedom and the more specific civil rights movement. Music could and did emphasize improvement in black society and reform of white society. Despite the national notice on civil rights actions and activities in the South in the two decades after 1954, early civil rights and freedom-seeking efforts in the western United States began on the Great Plains in the Afro-American Council and through the NAACP.

It was on the Plains that additional civil rights activities were initiated. From Oklahoma came a successful effort to challenge the grandfather clause in *Guinn v. United States* (1915). An El Paso physician, Lawrence A. Nixon, with support from the NAACP, led the fight to overturn a whites-only voting primary in Texas. Winning U.S. Supreme Court victories in *Nixon v. Herndon* (1927) and *Nixon v. Condon* (1932), however, was not enough to prevent the denial of black participation in the primary that determined elections in a one-party state. Not until 1944 did a Texas case (*Smith v. Allwright*) succeed in eliminating a whites-only primary. As a result of the ruling that came from *Sipuel v. Board of Regents of the University of Oklahoma* (1948), graduate schools were forced to enroll black students in states where no separate but equal institution was provided. In *Sweatt vs. Painter* (1950) the law school at the University of Texas could not exclude qualified African Americans.[29] Clearly, black legal challenges to discriminatory state legislation centered on the Great Plains.

African Americans on the Plains also were involved in other types of civil rights challenges before they were used elsewhere in the country. The major 1954 *Brown* decision, overturning public school segregation, came from Topeka, Kansas. As Jean Van Delinder, in her thorough article, "Early Civil Rights Activism in Topeka, Kansas, Prior to the 1954 Brown Case," points out however, it was no surprise that the 1954 case originated in Topeka. As of 1954 African Americans in Topeka had been challenging segregated and unequal schools for nearly a century. A particularly important challenge occurred in 1903, in the decision *William Reynolds v. Board of Education of Topeka*, and by the late twenties three other challenges—*Rich* (1928), *Wright* (1929), and *Foster* (1929)—had fought the color line in Topeka. Junior high schools in Topeka were desegregated in 1941 as a result of a successful court challenge, supported by the NAACP, for Oaland Graham, a black youth.[30]

Overall, African Americans on the Great Plains supported and encouraged the attacks on Jim Crow society. In many instances they were successful, but much was still to be accomplished since public accommodations remained segregated. University of New Mexico students successfully boycotted nearby restaurants for refusing to serve African Americans in 1947; the process culminated with the passage of a city nondiscriminatory public accommodations ordinance in 1952 and a similar statewide measure in 1955. Black students in Oklahoma and Kansas first used strategies such as the sit-in to achieve desegregation in public accommodations. Ronald Walters, an activist as well as an academician, reported on the sit-in movement on the Great Plains in his article, "The Great Plains Sit-In Movement, 1958–60." These sit-ins took place in 1958 within a week of each other in Wichita and Oklahoma City. Walters explains that the sit-ins on the Great Plains had "their proximity to the modern civil rights movement, their linkage to the sit-ins that did occur beginning in 1960, and their engagement of post–World War II youth in the process of social change." These sit-ins, as Walters noted, occurred before those in North Carolina and other places in the South that frequently have been recognized as the first efforts.[31]

By the end of the civil rights era African Americans on the Great Plains could take pride in their contributions to the civil rights movement. They participated in the movement and blacks on the Great Plains benefited from the results. One example is that of Texas political leader Barbara Charline Jordan. By 1974 (an obvious end to the civil rights movement) Congresswoman Barbara Jordan served on the important House Judiciary Committee, and as an impressive spokeswoman argued persuasively that President Richard M. Nixon should be impeached. Rather than risk impeachment, Richard Nixon resigned. Barbara Jordan grew up in Houston, Texas, and was elected to the Texas Senate in 1966 (the first black so elected since Reconstruction). She was elected to the U.S. Congress as the first black woman from Texas in 1972. Jordan delivered overwhelmingly positive keynote addresses to the national Democratic Party conventions in 1976 and in 1992. Although she chose to resign from Congress in 1978, Jordan's career illustrated how important the civil rights movement had been and showed how much valuable expertise the nation had missed during the previous century by seldom allowing blacks or women to hold public office.[32]

One other aspect of the maturation of African American society on the Great Plains can be noticed by the emergence of the black community in Omaha, Nebraska. For many years Omaha maintained one of the largest, most active, and most vibrant African American communities in the West. However, by the 1970s a decline in the meatpacking industry, in the railroads, and in other employment options for blacks in Omaha led to an exodus of over ten thousand African Americans from that city. Even today the decline is marked: Omaha blacks comprise one of the five most poverty-stricken communities in the nation. One result of the poverty was that Omaha's well-known Great Plains Black History Museum, the brainchild of Bertha Calloway, closed for lack of money. As part of her interest in the museum, Calloway (with Alonzo N. Smith) prepared a first-rate portrait of the African American experience in Omaha and in Nebraska in *Visions of Freedom on the Great Plains: An Illustrated History of African Americans in Nebraska*. The spirit of the black community is still alive, as Bertha Calloway signaled, and as Tom Jack demonstrates in "The Omaha Gospel Complex in Historical Perspective." Gospel music overcame religious boundaries and was carried forward by 116 black churches in Omaha. More recently, gospel music has transcended the churches and is presented by educational institutions and by the Omaha Mass Choir. Jack focuses on the narrower issue of gospel music in Omaha, but one can only be struck by the resilience and influence of the black community in Omaha's prominence during the major portion of the twentieth century.[33] To celebrate the glory, spirit, and resilience of Omaha's music history, the black community established the Omaha Black Music Hall of Fame.

The black community spirit that Tom Jack depicts in his description of Omaha is also present in the other African American communities, both large and small, on the Great Plains. Whether Deadwood, South Dakota; Lincoln, Nebraska; Cheyenne, Wyoming; Tulsa or Oklahoma City, Oklahoma; Leavenworth, Topeka, or Kansas City, Kansas; Texas cities large and small; or alone in North Dakota, all possess African American communities that have been created and nurtured by blacks, sometimes with white support, sometimes despite vicious white opposition and resentment.

The African American presence on the Great Plains, especially in the twentieth century, depended upon and succeeded by use of increased political activity, protest and resistance to discrimination and violence, race cohesiveness, a search for a better, more secure life, significant cultural contributions, and responsible roles for black women. Furthermore, African Americans on the Great Plains aided in the creation and continuation of a multicultural society, an important contribution as well as style of life. From Estevan to Dred Scott to "Pap" Singleton to Aaron Douglas to Barbara Jordan to Bertha Calloway to Barack Obama, the struggle for freedom and opportunity on the Great Plains has endured.

Notes

1. Kenneth Wiggins Porter, *The Negro on the American Frontier* (New York: Arno, 1971); W. Sherman Savage, *Blacks in the West, 1830–1890* (Westport CT: Greenwood, 1976); Walter Prescott Webb, *The Great Plains* (Boston: Ginn, 1931); Ray Allen Billington, *Westward Expansion: A History of the American Frontier*, 2nd ed. (New York: Macmillan, 1960); Ralph Ellison, *The Invisible Man* (1952; rpt. New York: Vintage, 1972).

2. Quintard Taylor, *In Search of the Racial Frontier: African Americans in the American West, 1528–1990* (New York: W. W. Norton, 1998). The state studies include: Alwyn Barr, *Black Texans: A History of African Americans in Texas, 1528–1995*, 2nd ed. (Norman: University of Oklahoma Press, 1996); Bruce A. Glasrud and James M. Smallwood, eds., *The African American Experience in Texas: An Anthology* (Lubbock: Texas Tech University Press, 2007); Jimmie Lewis Franklin, *Journey toward Hope: A History of Blacks in Oklahoma* (Norman: University of Oklahoma Press, 1982); Jacob U. Gordon, *Narratives of African Americans in Kansas, 1870–1992* (Lewiston NY: Edward Mellen, 1993); Bertha W. Calloway and Alonzo N. Smith, *Visions of Freedom on the Great Plains: An Illustrated History of African Americans in Nebraska* (Virginia Beach VA: Donning, 1998); Betti Carol Vanepps-Taylor, *Forgotten Lives: African Americans in South Dakota* (Pierre: South Dakota State Historical Society, 2008); David Vassar Taylor, *African Americans in Minnesota* (St. Paul: Minnesota Historical Society, 2002); Bill Silag, Susan Koch-Bridgford, and Hal Chase, eds., *Outside In: African-American History in Iowa, 1818–2000* (Des Moines: State Historical Society of Iowa, 2001); Leola Nelson Bergmann, *The Negro in Iowa* (1948; rpt. Iowa City: State Historical Society of Iowa, 1969); and Barbara J. Richardson, *Black Pioneers in New Mexico: A Documentary and Pictorial History* (Rio Rancho NM: Panorama, 1976).

3. Taylor, *In Search of the Racial Frontier*, 27–52; Dedra S. McDonald, "To Be Black and Female in the Spanish Southwest: Toward a History of African Women on New Spain's Far Northern Frontier," in *African American Women Confront the West, 1600–2000*, ed. Quintard Taylor and Shirley Ann Wilson Moore, 32–52 (Norman: University of Oklahoma Press, 2003).

4. Paul D. Lack, *The Texas Revolutionary Experience: A Political and Social History, 1835–1836* (College Station: Texas A&M University Press, 1992), 238–52; Taylor, *In Search of the Racial Frontier*, 53–80; James A. Rawley, *Race and Politics: "Bleeding Kansas" and the Coming of the Civil War* (Philadelphia: J. B. Lippincott, 1969).

5. Dudley Cornish, *The Sable Arm: Negro Troops in the Union Army, 1861–1865* (New York: W. W. Norton, 1966); Joseph T. Glatthaar, *Forged in Battle: The Civil War Alliance of Black Soldiers and White Officers* (New York: Macmillan, 1990). On white soldiers' treatment of blacks, see Anne J. Bailey, "A Texas Cavalry Raid: Reaction to Black Soldiers and Contrabands," *Civil War History* 35 (1989): 138–52; and Anne J. Bailey, "Was There a Massacre at Poison Spring?" *Military History of the Southwest* 20 (Fall 1990): 157–68.

6. Taylor, *In Search of the Racial Frontier*, 103-29; and Eugene H. Berwanger, *The West and Reconstruction* (Urbana: University of Illinois Press, 1981).

7. William A. Dobak and Thomas D. Phillips, *The Black Regulars, 1866–1898* (Norman: University of Oklahoma Press, 2001); Bruce A. Glasrud and Michael N. Searles, eds., *Buffalo Soldiers in the West: A Black Soldiers Anthology* (College Station: Texas A&M University Press, 2007). On the volunteers and militia, for example, see Roger D. Cunningham, "'A Lot of Fine, Sturdy Black Warriors': Texas's African American 'Immunes' in the Spanish-American War," *Southwestern Historical Quarterly* 108.3 (2005): 345–67, and Willard B. Gatewood Jr., "Kansas Negroes and the Spanish-American War," *Kansas Historical Quarterly* 37 (Autumn 1971): 300–313.

8. James N. Leiker, "Black Soldiers at Fort Hays, Kansas, 1867–1869: A Study in Civilian and Military Violence," *Great Plains Quarterly* 17 (Winter 1997): 3–17, quote at 14–15; James N. Leiker, *Racial Borders: Black Soldiers Along the Rio Grande* (College Station: Texas A&M University Press, 2002); and Garna L. Christian, *Black Soldiers in Jim Crow Texas, 1899–1917* (College Station: Texas A&M University Press, 1995).

9. Philip Durham and Everett L. Jones, *The Negro Cowboys* (1965; rpt. Lincoln: University of Nebraska Press, 1983); Sara R. Massey, ed., *Black Cowboys of Texas* (College Station: Texas A&M University Press, 2000); C. Robert Haywood, "'No Less a Man': Blacks in Cow Town Dodge City, 1876–1886," *Western Historical Quarterly* 19 (1988): 161–82.

10. Willard B. Gatewood Jr., "Kate D. Chapman Reports on 'The Yankton Colored People,' 1889," *South Dakota History* 7 (Winter 1976): 32–35, quote at 35.

11. Joseph V. Hickey, "'Pap' Singleton's Dunlap Colony: Relief Agencies and the Failure of a Black Settlement in Eastern Kansas," *Great Plains Quarterly* (Winter 1991):

23–36, quote at 24; Robert G. Athearn, *In Search of Canaan: Black Migration to Kansas, 1879–80* (Lawrence: Regents Press of Kansas, 1978); and Nell Irvin Painter, *Exodusters: Black Migration to Kansas after Reconstruction* (New York: Alfred A. Knopf, 1977).

12. Taylor, *In Search of the Racial Frontier*, 192–250; Peggy Riley, "Women of the Great Falls African Methodist Episcopal Church, 1870–1910," in *African American Women Confront the West, 1600–2000*, ed. Quintard Taylor and Shirley Ann Wilson Moore, 122–39 (Norman: University of Oklahoma Press, 2003); Susan Armitage, "'The Mountains Were Free and We Loved Them': Dr. Ruth Flowers of Boulder, Colorado," in *African American Women Confront the West, 1600–2000*, ed. Quintard Taylor and Shirley Ann Wilson Moore, 165–77 (Norman: University of Oklahoma Press, 2003); Moya B. Hansen, "'Try Being a Black Woman!': Jobs in Denver, 1900–1970," in *African American Women Confront the West, 1600–2000*, ed. Quintard Taylor and Shirley Ann Wilson Moore, 207–27 (Norman: University of Oklahoma Press, 2003).

13. Shawn Leigh Alexander, "Vengeance without Justice, Injustice without Retribution: The Afro-American Council's Struggle against Racial Violence," *Great Plains Quarterly* 27.2 (Spring 2007): 117–34; and Michael Fedo, *The Lynchings in Duluth* (St. Paul: Minnesota Historical Society Press, 2000).

14. Clare V. McKanna Jr., "Black Enclaves of Violence: Race and Homicide in Great Plains Cities, 1890–1920," *Great Plains Quarterly* 23.3 (Summer 2003): 147–60. For the broader picture of homicide and race in the West see Clare V. McKanna Jr., *Homicide, Race, and Justice in the American West, 1880–1920* (Tucson: University of Arizona Press, 1997).

15. Thomas R. Buecker, "Prelude to Brownsville: The Twenty-fifth Infantry at Fort Niobrara, Nebraska, 1902–06," *Great Plains Quarterly* 16.2 (Spring 1996): 95–106; Ann J. Lane, *The Brownsville Affair: National Crisis and Black Reaction* (Port Washington NY: Kennikat, 1971); John D. Weaver, *The Brownsville Raid* (New York: W. W. Norton, 1970); and Robert V. Haynes, *A Night of Violence: The Houston Riot of 1917* (Baton Rouge: Louisiana State University Press, 1976).

16. Bruce A. Glasrud, "Enforcing White Supremacy in Texas, 1900–1910," *Red River Valley Historical Review* 4 (Fall 1979): 65–74; Arthur I. Waskow, *From Race Riot to Sit-In: 1919 and the 1960s* (Garden City NY: Doubleday, 1966), 1–11, 105–20; Alwyn Barr, *Black Texans: A History of African Americans in Texas, 1528–1995*, 2nd ed. (Norman: University of Oklahoma Press, 1996), 138–39; Scott Ellsworth, *Death in a Promised Land: The Tulsa Race Riot of 1921* (Baton Rouge: Louisiana State University Press, 1982); Kenneth Durham Jr., "The Longview Race Riot of 1919," *East Texas Historical Journal* 18.2 (1980): 13–24; Edward Hake Phillips, "The Sherman Courthouse Riot of 1930," *East Texas Historical Journal* 25.2 (1987): 12–19; and James A. Burran, "Violence in an 'Arsenal of Democracy': The Beaumont Race Riot, 1943," *East Texas Historical Journal* 14.1 (Spring 1976): 39–51.

17. Darlene Clark Hine, *Hine Sight: Black Women and the Re-Construction of American History* (Bloomington: Indiana University Press, 1994), xxii.

18. Dennis N. Mihelich, "A Socioeconomic Portrait of Prince Hall Masonry in Nebraska, 1900–1920," *Great Plains Quarterly* 17.1 (Winter 1997): 35–48, quote at 36.

19. R. Bruce Shepard, "Diplomatic Racism: Canadian Government and Black Migration from Oklahoma, 1905–1912," *Great Plains Quarterly* 3.1 (Winter 1983): 5–16. On the African American experience in Canada see Robin W. Winks, *The Blacks in Canada: A History*, 2nd ed. (Montreal: Mc-Gill-Queen's University Press, 1997); and Rinaldo Walcott, *Black Like Who? Writing Black Canada*, 2nd ed. (Toronto: Insomniac, 2003).

20. Kathie Ryckman Anderson, "Era Bell Thompson: A North Dakota Daughter," *North Dakota History* 49 (1982): 11–18; Era Bell Thompson, *American Daughter* (1946; rpt. St. Paul: Minnesota Historical Society, 1986), quote at 74; and Michael K. Johnson, "'This Strange White World': Race and Place in Era Bell Thompson's *American Daughter*," *Great Plains Quarterly* 24.2 (Spring 2004): 101–12.

21. Richard M. Breaux, "The New Negro Arts and Letters Movement Among Black University Students in the Midwest, 1914–1940," *Great Plains Quarterly* 24.3 (Summer 2004): 147–62, quote at 159.

22. Cheryl R. Ragar, "Harlem Renaissance in the United States—Kansas and the Plains States," in *Encyclopedia of the Harlem Renaissance*, ed. Cary D. Wintz and Paul Finkelman, 512–14 (New York: Routledge, 2004); and Bruce A. Glasrud, "Harlem Renaissance in the United States—Texas and the Southwest," in *Encyclopedia of the Harlem Renaissance*, ed. Cary D. Wintz and Paul Finkelman, 521–25 (New York: Routledge, 2004).

23. Kenneth Wiggins Porter, "Micheaux, Oscar," in *Dictionary of American Negro Biography*, ed. Rayford W. Logan and Michael R. Winston, 433–34 (New York: W. W. Norton, 1982); Taylor Gordon, *Born to be Free* (1929; rpt. Lincoln: University of Nebraska Press, 1995); Langston Hughes, *Not Without Laughter* (New York: Alfred A. Knopf, 1930); and Frank Marshall Davis, *Livin' the Blues: Memoirs of a Black Journalist and a Poet*, ed. John Edgar Tidwell (Madison: University of Wisconsin Press, 1992).

24. Bernice Love Wiggins, *Tuneful Tales*, ed. Maceo C. Dailey Jr. and Ruthe Winegarten (1925; rpt. Lubbock: Texas Tech University Press, 2002); Lillian B. Horace, *Five Generations Hence* (privately published, 1916); Robert M. Farnsworth, *Melvin B. Tolson, 1898–1966: Plain Talk and Poetic Prophecy* (Columbia: University of Missouri Press, 1984); and J. Mason Brewer, ed., *Heralding Dawn: An Anthology of Verse* (Dallas: June Thomason, 1936).

25. Bruce A. Glasrud, "Anita Scott Coleman," *BlackPast Online Encyclopedia* (http://www.blackpast.org); and Laurie Champion and Bruce A. Glasrud, eds., *Unfinished Masterpiece: The Harlem Renaissance Fiction of Anita Scott Coleman* (Lubbock: Texas Tech University Press, 2008).

26. Johnson, "'This Strange White World,'" 101–12; Breaux, "New Negro Arts and Letters Movement," 147–62.

27. Audrey Thompson, "Great Plains Pragmatist: Aaron Douglas and the Art of Social Protest," *Great Plains Quarterly* 20.4 (Fall 2000): 311–22, quote at 311; and Amy Helene Kirschke, *Aaron Douglas: Art, Race, and the Harlem Renaissance* (Jackson: University Press of Mississippi, 1995).

28. Marc Rice, "Frompin' in the Great Plains: Listening and Dancing to the Jazz Orchestras of Alphonso Trent, 1925–44," *Great Plains Quarterly* 16.2 (Spring 1996): 107–15; Ross Russell, *Jazz Style in Kansas City and the Southwest* (Berkeley: University of California Press, 1968); Frank Driggs and Chuck Haddix, *Kansas City Jazz: From Ragtime to Bebop—A History* (New York: Oxford University Press, 2005); and Roger Wood and James Fraher, *Down in Houston: Bayou City Blues* (Austin: University of Texas Press, 2003).

29. Taylor, *In Search of the Racial Frontier*, 278–310; Bruce A. Glasrud and Laurie Champion, "A House Divided: Short Stories and the Civil Rights Movement in the West," *Journal of the American Studies Association of Texas* (2000): 1–18.

30. Jean Van Delinder, "Early Civil Rights Activism in Topeka, Kansas, Prior to the 1954 *Brown* Case," *Great Plains Quarterly* 21.1 (Winter 2001): 45–61.

31. George Long, "How Albuquerque Got Its Civil Rights Ordinance," *The Crisis* 60 (November 1953): 521–24; Ronald Walters, "The Great Plains Sit-In Movement, 1958–1960," *Great Plains Quarterly* 16.2 (Spring 1996): 85–94 quote at 86; and Taylor, *In Search of the Racial Frontier*, 278–310.

32. Barbara Jordan and Shelby Hearon, *Barbara Jordan: A Self-Portrait* (Garden City NY: Doubleday, 1979); and Mary Beth Rogers, *Barbara Jordan: American Hero* (New York: Bantam, 1998).

33. "African Americans in Omaha, Nebraska," *Wikipedia, the Free Encyclopedia (http://en.wikipedia.org/wiki)*; "Great Plains Black History Museum," *Wikipedia, the Free Encyclopedia (http://en.wikipedia.org/wiki)*; Calloway and Smith, *Visions of Freedom on the Great Plains*; and Tom Jack, "The Omaha Gospel Complex in Historical Perspective," *Great Plains Quarterly* 20.3 (Summer 2000): 225–34.

CHAPTER 1 | Black Soldiers at Fort Hays, Kansas, 1867–1869: *A Study in Civilian and Military Violence*

JAMES N. LEIKER

Historians of the western army contend with many romanticized myths. Few of those myths, in recent years, have held the popular consciousness as has that of the army's first black regulars, known as "buffalo soldiers." By now, the origins of the segregated regiments are quite familiar. In 1866, with the nation's acting military force having dwindled to a fraction of its Civil War size, the Republican Congress encouraged the enlistment of newly freed slaves and northern free blacks. Assigned to remote western areas, black units played an instrumental role over the next few decades in opening the West for white settlement. Despite their important functions, uniformed African Americans continually suffered racism and discrimination from frontier civilians and even from some of their own white officers.[1]

For much of this century, both popular culture and professional historians overlooked the buffalo soldiers. The gallant stereotype of patriotic, blue-jacketed warriors bringing civilization to the plains failed to accommodate the presence of armed blacks. Although scholars began to draw public attention toward black soldiers as early as the 1960s, the dedication of a buffalo soldiers monument at Fort Leavenworth in 1992 fully captured the popular imagination, partly because of Colin Powell's visible involvement. The Leavenworth project was accompanied by a veritable explosion of buffalo soldiers commemorations including museum displays, documentaries, newspaper and journal articles, and reenactment societies. Where once the public imagined the West only in terms of white soldiers and red Indians, the present fascination represents a positive step in defining the region as a meeting ground for numerous races and cultures, a step that scholars should applaud.

Yet not all have been enthusiastic about proclaiming buffalo soldiers' contributions to western conquest. From a Native American standpoint, lionizing the black regiments to redress historical neglect appears no more just nor progressive than the Anglo myths that excluded them. When the U.S. Postmaster General announced a commemorative buffalo soldiers stamp in 1994, representatives of the American Indian Movement demanded both the stamp's withdrawal and a public apology.[2] For all the topic's recent attention, few grasp its frustrating irony: that black males, themselves victims of white prejudice, voluntarily aided the subjugation of Native peoples for the benefit of Anglo expansion. This scenario illustrates the complicated, even paradoxical, nature of American race relations. Unfortunately, significant questions are overshadowed by the topic's "contribution" aspects, helping to provide a focus for national and racial pride, a cry of "we were there too." Nor have academic historians pursued the more difficult questions as aggressively as they should. New Western History, which has debunked many myths surrounding white occupation and shown its catastrophic consequences for minorities, generally ignores the army's role in western conquest. Military histories have added tremendously to knowledge about the subject but most employ traditional approaches that are more event-centered and descriptive than analytical and interpretive.

The time appears right for a serious reappraisal of the army's first black regulars, one that resists the temptation to cast them either as villainous enforcers of white oppression or heroic subjects of injustice. The former depiction rests on the questionable assumption that blacks shared whites' racist attitudes toward Indians; the latter, more common view treats them as passive victims, stoically enduring discrimination. Both rob the buffalo soldiers of conscious agency, seeing them not as historical actors but merely as "acted upon." In fact, when uniformed blacks entered the hostile racial climate of western towns, some acquiesced to white racism but others violently resisted. Although holding limited options, buffalo soldiers' individual reactions to civilian antagonism played a vital role in local race relations.

Setting the Scene

Fort Hays, located in northwest Kansas, serves as an example of black agency. Active from 1865 to 1889, its garrison protected stagecoach and railway traffic along the Smoky Hill River to Denver.[3] Stationed there in the late 1860s, troops from the Thirty-eighth Infantry and Tenth Cavalry (both consisting entirely of black soldiers) comprised the majority of the post's enlisted men up to 1869. Though engaged in several Indian battles, the average black soldier had more reason to fear civilians or even comrades than Indians; more injuries and killings resulted from altercations in camp or nearby Hays City than from combat. While Fort Hays's troubles were not unique, the unusual mingling of a predominantly black military with growing numbers of white civilians led to racial violence that mirrored and even surpassed that in other western communities.[4]

Given Kansas's early reputation among African Americans as a safe haven for freedmen, such an assertion might seem surprising. After all, Kansas had been among the first states to muster black volunteers into Union service.[5] Even after the Civil War, images of "Bleeding Kansas" and John Brown enhanced the state's prestige among southern blacks as a place of opportunity and freedom. In the late 1870s, thousands of "exodusters"—emigrants fleeing the South after Reconstruction—chose Kansas as their destination. While most exodusters found only disillusionment in the so-called "Canaan of the Prairies," active state charity organizations worked diligently to ease the refugees' plight.[6] In addition, Kansas claimed several black communities, among them Nicodemus, established in 1877 only fifty miles northwest of Hays City. If any state could have been expected to tolerate a high population of black soldiers, it should have been Kansas.

While the legacies of abolition and the Civil War may have encouraged relative openness in the state's eastern communities, however, isolated locales like Fort Hays initially shared little with Lawrence and Leavenworth. During the black units' peak enlistment in the late 1860s, the new forts and towns truly epitomized the "frontier," the peripheral edge of white settlement socially and geographically. While "frontier" as an analytical concept has been criticized for its ethnocentric connotations, the term retains usefulness for discovering how racial hatreds were transferred to the developing region.[7] By examining how the civilian community perceived and interacted with black soldiers, we can draw a clearer picture of how the black military experience helped to shape western race relations.

Understanding the reception of black soldiers in Hays City first necessitates an examination of the military and social atmosphere at Fort Hays. As Indian raids diminished by late 1867, three Tenth Cavalry companies were recalled for winter rest at Fort Riley, leaving Fort Hays largely under the protection of black infantry.[8] Because of its central location and proximity to the railroad, Fort Hays served as General Philip Sheridan's administrative headquarters and a depot for goods arriving by rail during the 1868–69 campaign. Although small cavalry detachments remained until 1871, infantry comprised the garrison's majority. Thus, if Fort Hays could claim a "semi-permanent" black population up to 1869, the Thirty-eighth Infantry fit that role better than the more transient Tenth Cavalry.

Narratives often focus on the cavalry's dramatic offensive campaigns and overlook infantrymen, who performed the more routine tasks of escorting surveying parties, military prisoners, and payroll and supply shipments. Infantry also received a disproportionate share of kitchen and hospital duties and sanitation detail. Although their activities attracted less attention, they nonetheless performed hazardous tasks in isolated groups of four or five that were vulnerable to surprise attacks. Troopers knew full well the perils of their work. Complaints reached the fort commander in July 1868 about five soldiers from the Thirty-eighth assigned to protect railroad water tanks. Housed in small shelters with ten-day rations, the troops fired indiscriminately at anyone—white, black, or Indian—who ventured too close. Lest the frightened infantrymen fire on peaceful Native people and provoke conflict, officers ordered them to deal cautiously with anyone who approached rather than resorting to gunfire.[9]

Black soldiers often are depicted as victims, thereby emphasizing the army's racial prejudice. Indeed, discrimination did occur; troops frequently suffered abuse by bigoted officers and received harsher punishments than white soldiers for disciplinary offenses. The prohibition against blacks serving as officers even in their own regiments indicates the army's low initial regard for their abilities.[10] Yet deplorable conditions awaited all of the western army's enlisted men, no matter their color. None would have asserted "equality" as a goal; the military, after all, constituted a system of institutionalized inequality. But that did not negate the possibility of fair treatment from officers who interacted with the men on a daily basis. In fact, at Fort Hays, white commanders often became their troops' greatest partisans, even protecting them from hostile civilians. In a macabre way, blacks and whites stationed there achieved a certain degree of equality: both lived abominably.

Fort Hays differed little from most outposts during its first few months, consisting merely of several tents and crude huts. Its isolated location limited the range of leisure activities—not that much leisure time was available. Poor hygiene and sanitation rendered soldiers vulnerable to disease. Beginning in July 1867, a devastating cholera epidemic swept the western forts, striking the black units especially hard. Cholera killed seven men of the Thirty-eighth Infantry that summer but the Tenth Cavalry lost more than twenty men, more than half the regiment's total number of combat deaths up to 1918.[11] Conditions gradually improved after the Union Pacific Railroad reached Hays in October 1867, particularly because it brought fresh supplies and materials for building permanent structures. Yet poor health continued to sap the garrison's strength. Despite their dangerous duties, soldiers obtained medical treatment more frequently for pneumonia and other ailments than for combat injuries. Gastrointestinal illnesses were especially common; nearly a third of the post's black soldiers received treatment for diarrhea.[12]

Health officials knew that improved hygiene and fresh food would decrease these problems yet found implementing such simple improvements difficult. Quartermasters unsuccessfully tried to provide unspoiled meat, while either insects or neglect doomed the post's paltry attempt at growing its own vegetables.[13] Most enlisted men, regardless of color, cared little for personal cleanliness. Assistant surgeon William Buchannon complained that Tenth cavalrymen stacked all their dirty clothes and muddy stable equipment under the bunks, attracting flies to an already crowded and improperly ventilated barracks.[14]

Constant guard and escort duty, as well as the transient nature of army life, makes such apathy seem understandable. Similarly, Fort Hays' hectic work load left enlisted men little time or inclination to attend the post school that taught reading and writing, addition and subtraction. What leisure time existed was spent enjoying the benefits of steady pay. Earnings ranged from thirteen dollars a month for new privates to thirty dollars for noncommissioned officers. Although some men sent money to families back east, most wages purchased necessities from the post sutler's store or from local civilian merchants. A considerable amount ended up in the town's many taverns and brothels.

Drunkenness affected all troops at Fort Hays, including buffalo soldiers. Post records include many accounts of privates charged with neglecting duty or engaging in disorderly conduct while under the influence of alcohol. Perhaps because their isolated work made it easier and more tempting to sneak a drink, the Thirty-eighth Infantry seemed particularly prone to such problems. In February 1868 the commander placed pickets to arrest all personnel who were intoxicated, created a disturbance, or lacked passes signed by a superior officer. Typical punishment for drink-related offenses involved a fine, brief incarceration, or a reduction in rank.[15]

Why the high frequency of alcohol use? The combination of disease, separation from family, fear of Indian attack, and general loneliness likely inspired many to seek solace from a bottle. Frontier racism made intoxication particularly dangerous for black soldiers. Since the white public perceived the black units as experimental at best, charges of drunkenness and immorality could easily taint black regiments' reputations. At Fort Hays, the picket guard decreased alcohol-related offenses but did not necessarily increase sobriety. When getting drunk on the fort became too risky, soldiers waited until payday and visited taverns in Hays City. This proved dangerous for the black soldier since he was subject to civilian law, not military, and white locals had extremely little patience with unruly armed blacks.

The violent atmosphere and miserable, disease-ridden conditions encouraged many desertions from the frontier military. In 1867 more than 14,000 men deserted the United States Army, nearly a quarter of its total strength.[16] Most deserters disappeared successfully into civilian populations; the military simply lacked the time and manpower to pursue runaways. Cavalrymen especially were likely to make clean breaks since they took their horses and all the army property they could carry, including food, mules, wagons, and firearms. Elizabeth Custer described how forty men deserted Fort Hays in one night, leaving officers fearful that the garrison would soon lack sufficient protection.[17]

Romanticized works on buffalo soldiers point proudly to their low desertion rates, a claim partly supported by statistics from Fort Hays. While more than half of the Seventh Cavalry deserted in only one year, a mere fourteen deserters were reported from Fort Hays' black regiments during its first five years.[18] Although drunkenness and insubordination were common among all enlisted men, desertion appeared primarily to be a white phenomenon. The dearth of black western settlers, and black soldiers' distinct appearance, made it difficult for potential deserters to blend into nearby communities. One should not, however, discount the more idealistic explanation that blacks' group identity and pride discouraged desertion. Despite its pitfalls, military service offered African American males opportunities for self-respect seldom matched in Reconstruction America.

Desertion rates remained high throughout the post–Civil War period but peaked in 1871.[19] By then Indian resistance in the Hays vicinity had nearly disappeared, even though the fort remained a valuable transportation depot and winter quarters. As white settlement increased, a reciprocal relationship developed between the post and nearby Hays City. Town merchants provided needed goods and services while the army employed civilian laborers on construction projects. Likewise, the thousands of dollars of army pay spent in Hays City fertilized a prosperous local economy.

Beneath this symbiosis lay major currents of hostility. Hays City resembled other western communities where violence between soldiers and civilians contributed to the region's reputation for bloodshed. If Civil War veterans were praised as heroes, federal regulars, often immigrants and displaced industrial workers, were often seen as rabble.[20] The proliferation of saloons and brothels which sprang up around every military post offended new settlers' puritanical values.[21] In addition, many westerners dismissed the federal regulars as ineffective Indian fighters, even resenting their presence. One Kansan, explaining why the state militia could deal with local hostilities more effectively, ridiculed the army's ceaseless bugling, alerting enemies as soldiers prepared to attack, retreat, awake, or go to bed.[22] Uniformed soldiers frequently elicited jokes or insults from civilians, not respect. In the case of a uniformed freedman, reactions could be openly hostile, especially among former Confederates for whom buffalo soldiers provided a visible reminder of southern defeat.

These charged emotions played out in the chaos of western communities during early years of development. Although scholarship on Kansas cattle towns emphasizes the exaggeration of violence in popular myth, Hays City, established in October 1867 as a Union Pacific terminus, lay beyond most major cattle trails, and its violence came not from rowdy Texas cattle drovers but from transients looking for profits from the railroad.[23] An eastern Kansas newspaper described Hays' citizenry in unflattering terms:

> Gamblers, pimps, prostitutes, and dead beats, run the town, and the most unblushing defiance of everything that is decent is the prevailing sentiment. One year ago, for the joke of the thing, they elected a prostitute as one of the School Board, and another Street Commissioner. How it is to be expected black or white soldiers will act any other way when they get a taste of the lightning poison vended there is a mystery to us. We hope the authorities of the State will incur no expense in protecting any such a class as runs Hays City.[24]

Observers did not exaggerate the town's horrific level of violence; from 1867 to 1874, Hays City saw more than thirty recorded homicides.[25] During periods of ineffective civilian law enforcement, black troops served as the town guard. In late 1867, a visitor recorded that:

> Hays City is really under martial law, the town being policed by soldiers from the fort; and, what makes it trebly obnoxious to some, the soldiers are colored. They certainly have the credit, however, of maintaining quiet and general good order throughout the day and night: that is, quiet for a frontier town.[26]

Actually, the presence of federal regulars exacerbated more violence than it prevented. Nearly half of all homicides up to 1874, thirteen, resulted from altercations between soldiers and civilians.[27]

Considering the color of the troops involved, a problem arises in trying to separate "racial" violence from the larger pattern of civilian-military violence everywhere, regardless of race. Simply because an episode involved a black participant did not mean it had racial causes. The key distinction rests on whether an incident originated from some discriminatory behavior based on skin color. By that criteria, not all violence involving blacks during Hays City's first three years can be classified as "racial." But the Fort Hays experience certainly shows a hardening of white opinions toward armed African Americans, reflected not only in the callous actions of local toughs but in how state newspapers reported such activity.

Black soldiers did not behave like passive victims of prejudice. The same group cohesion that discouraged black desertions encouraged a search for vengeance when a soldier was wronged or insulted. White troops shared the feud mentality that characterized fort-town relations; if an individual returned to the post bruised or bloodied, comrades shielded him from discovery until they could get revenge on his assailants.[28] For buffalo soldiers, however, the drive to retaliate appeared especially strong. During a national age of violent racism, the army's black frontiersmen upheld the doctrine of "eye for an eye." Their refusal to tolerate abuse certainly deserves a measure of admiration, but their actions ultimately intensified white prejudice, creating a cycle of hatred that resembled an ongoing blood feud.

The First Violent Encounter

The first violent encounter, initiated by townspeople, illustrates how officers generally sided with their men. Prior to the picket guard's establishment in February 1868, post commanders had to deal with the habitual problem of troops leaving the fort without permission. On December 21, 1867, a small detail was sent to retrieve all those absent without leave, most of whom were imbibing in civilian saloons. Privates Charles Allen, Thirty-eighth Company E, and John Washington, Tenth Cavalry Company I, demanded admittance to an establishment where AWOL soldiers reportedly languished. When they were refused, Allen began beating the door with his weapon. The saloonkeeper, Matthew "Red" Flinn, fired several shots, killing Allen and severely wounding Washington. The town guard, Allen's fellow infantrymen, immediately began searching for Flinn. Later the same evening a local named Cornelius Doyle accosted Corporal Albert E. Cropper, Thirty-eighth Company G, cursing him and shouting that "any damned nigger soldiers hunting Red" would be killed. The argument ended when Doyle apparently attempted to draw his pistol and Cropper fatally shot him with his rifle.[29]

While Allen's death produced no great uproar, talk immediately filled the streets about lynching Cropper. Civilian newspapers described Doyle's shooting far differently than the official military report. *The Hays City Railway Advance* claimed Doyle gave Cropper no "provocation whatever," a charge repeated by a Hays resident in a hearsay letter to the *Lawrence Tribune*.[30] Following his arrest and preliminary hearing, Cropper was transferred to the post guardhouse for his own protection. Meanwhile, fort commander Captain Samuel Ovenshine had arranged with county authorities to offer a reward for Red Flinn, who had left the county and later was located near Leavenworth.[31]

Whether Cropper really acted in self-defense cannot decisively be determined from the disparate accounts, even though his record shows no history of similar trouble.[32] Yet the fact that disparate accounts exist at all reveals how differently the civilian and military communities perceived the incident. Already suspicious of the patrol guard, residents now thought the army had protected a murderer. To prevent further hostility, Ovenshine withdrew the patrol and returned Hays City to the jurisdiction of civil law, the inefficiency of which only contributed to Cropper's eventual acquittal. By the time the District Court reconvened after a six-month hiatus, only one witness to Doyle's shooting remained in the county, and Cropper's case was dismissed for lack of suitable jurors.[33]

The killings of Allen and Doyle commenced years of hostility between the fort and town. While Cropper awaited trial, minor conflicts between black soldiers and white townsfolk continued through 1868, the same year Hays City came under control of an organized vigilante group. The vigilance committee visited perceived troublemakers and ordered them to leave town. Despite their stated purpose of establishing peace, vigilantes only increased local violence; thirteen documented murders occurred in 1869, the town's peak year for homicides.[34] While most eastern Kansas newspapers denounced the situation, at least one, the Lawrence *Tribune*, partly defended vigilante activity by declaring that lax law enforcement required citizens to protect themselves. In recalling the army's protection of the "murderer" Cropper, the writer implied the committee's real purpose was to defend the community from black soldiers.[35] In a state known for its supposed racial liberality, press coverage of events in Hays City paralleled what Democratic newspapers said about Southern race relations: armed, aggressive blacks, protected by a disliked federal military, posed threats to public safety. *The Leavenworth Daily*

Commercial even likened the violence to southern "black outrages" provoked by Radical Republicans.[36] Attitudes became even more "Confederate sounding" after a murder by black soldiers in early 1869 led to one of Kansas's few known racial lynchings.

Leading to a Lynching

Civilian and military accounts concur that the events of January 5–7 began when Privates Luke Barnes, Lee Watkins, and James Ponder were refused admission into a local brothel. Prostitutes, in Hays at least, rarely discriminated on skin color, so more than likely the men's disruptive behavior prompted the refusal. All three belonged to the Thirty-eighth Infantry, Company E, and at least two, Watkins and Ponder, had enlisted together in Nashville and spent detached service away from the post, protecting railroad camps.[37] Later that evening, the trio invaded the shop of a black civilian barber named John White. Hiding from the men's rage while they drunkenly smashed his shop, White heard the troops boast that they planned to get revenge for the deaths of their comrades by killing the next white man they saw. Wandering into the street, the trio opened fire on a Union Pacific watchman named James Hayes, a citizen of Leavenworth. Shot in the stomach, his spine severed, Hayes lived until the following morning, describing his assailants only as "two niggers."[38]

Evidence against Barnes, Watkins, and Ponder would have been extremely meager without John White's testimony. Accompanied by the county sheriff and a federal marshal on January 6, White identified the three out of a line-up of the entire garrison, explaining the vandalism to his shop and their stated intent to kill a white person. The barber's testimony placed the post commander, Lieutenant Colonel Anderson Nelson, in a precarious position. Authorities insisted Nelson release the three to civilian custody rather than placing them under military protection like Cropper. Besides the resentment such an action would generate among his troops, Nelson must have known about the defendants' tenuous safety in a Hays jail cell, especially with the vigilance committee in operation. With tensions between soldiers and civilians running high, Nelson decided on a conciliatory gesture and permitted county police to assume custody of the privates, who were arraigned later that day before a justice of the peace and placed under overnight guard.

Luke Barnes, Lee Watkins, and James Ponder never saw their case brought to trial. During the evening of January 6–7, a mob stormed the jail, overpowered the guards, and seized the prisoners from their cells. One account reported the mob's size as between seventy-five and one hundred, all with masks or darkened faces. The vigilantes hanged the men from the ties of a railroad bridge half a mile west of town. Union Pacific employees discovered their bodies the next morning.

Eastern Kansas newspapers, long contemptuous of Hays City's vigilante tradition, suddenly applauded the lynching. In James Hayes' hometown of Leavenworth, the *Daily Commercial* delighted in providing a detailed and hearsay version of the hanging:

> Sometime during the night the vigilantes released the mokes from prison and indulged them in a dance in mid-air, in which they executed a treble shuffle, something of a novelty in negro breakdowns which are chiefly remarkable for merely a double shuffle. No doubt existed of the guilt of the parties, as they sloshed around extensively brandishing their Springfield rifles, and threatening vengeance on the whites. The men and brethren appear to be rather airy out on the plains, . . . Let us have peace![39]

The likelihood that Barnes, Watkins, and Ponder would have been convicted and executed anyway illustrates this incident's strong racist motives. Hays City's high number of homicides shows remarkable tolerance for violence—except when perpetrated by blacks. Rather than simply hanging three killers, the lynching issued a statement that racial norms concerning troublesome blacks would be enforced illegally if necessary.

Retaliation for Lynching

Unlike other racial lynchings, however, the January 1869 episode involved United States soldiers, not usually known for meekness in the face of violence. Troops of the Thirty-eighth Infantry performed the unpleasant task of retrieving their comrades' bodies and preparing them for burial.[40] Rather than intimidating soldiers, the lynching only enraged both the officers and enlisted men. Lieutenant Colonel Nelson, whose disastrous decision had placed the three within vigilante reach, responded with his own retaliatory measures. On January 14 Nelson sent a Thirty-eighth detachment into Hays City to arrest all persons out after curfew. Black soldiers raided a ballroom and arrested fifty-one people, jailing them overnight at the fort guardhouse. Nelson later wrote Governor James Harvey that because of the rumored plots against his men, he intended to close the saloons and livery stables and even declare martial law if necessary.[41]

Such drastic steps became unnecessary as a short-lived calm ensued following the lynching. In late January, rustlers stole several head of livestock from the post herd. The troops—their tempers running high—blamed locals for the theft. On February 6 Tom Butler, a white ex-quartermaster's employee who had been fired on suspicion of stealing, left town following the Union Pacific tracks east. When a mule was reported missing the next day, officials dispatched a search party which consisted of the quartermaster and post surgeon, a civilian detective and numerous employees, and ten soldiers from the Thirty-eighth Infantry. Tracking and cornering Butler at a water tank, the group choked him with a rope until he confessed to participation in a rustling gang. The party then divided, with fort officials and employees in one group and the black troops escorting Butler in another. Likely recalling their friends' treatment a month earlier, the soldiers shot Butler and left his corpse in an abandoned house. The mule he supposedly had stolen turned up wandering a few miles from the fort.[42]

Clearly an act of revenge, Butler's murder illustrates the complicity of white military authorities. Tired of incessant attacks on the army's men and property, white officers willingly sided with black troops in using Butler as an example, frustrating any designation of the violence as purely racial. A Hays citizen summarized the situation: "There has been for some time much unpleasant feeling existing between the authorities of Hays City and Ft. Hays, commenced by the hanging of the three negro soldiers by the Vig's."[43] Indeed, the bad blood between fort and town transcended race, reflecting a larger pattern of antipathy characterizing civilian-military relations. In April, during the Nineteenth Kansas Cavalry's station at Fort Hays, white troops congregated nightly in Hays City, engaging in brawls and shootings with locals. As both the size and number of violent episodes increased, large gangs of black and white soldiers marched the streets armed *en masse*. Meanwhile, fort officials exercised little control over the troops' nightly sojourns.[44]

Shootout and Rampage

In May 1869 two years of animosity climaxed in an armed confrontation that shared many features with modern race riots. Newspapers claimed that black soldiers planned to burn Hays City to the ground, a possibility in the wake of the lynching. Yet because the troops had just been paid and drunkenness and fighting often accompanied receipt of wages, it appears the violence began with the alcohol. According to admittedly biased civilian sources, several black infantrymen tried to break into a brothel from which they earlier had been refused admission. A scuffle began, with troops lining up in battle formation and opening fire into nearby homes and businesses. Townspeople returned the fire, shooting from doors and windows and exchanging more than four hundred shots in about half an hour.[45]

At this point, fort officials finally took decisive action, dispatching soldiers from the Fifth Cavalry to quell the disturbance and ordering all infantrymen back to the post.[46] As white cavalrymen attempted to break up the melee, several residents embarked on a rampage against Hays City's few black civilians. Vigilante ruffians ordered all black families out of town and murdered two African American barbers. Of the newspapers that reported the atrocities, only the *Kansas Daily Commonwealth* voiced contempt for the deed:

> Hays City has added another laurel to its garland of infamy. The other night—after the affray—a full account of which appeared in our special dispatches—was ended and the soldiers had been withdrawn, a party of roughs deliberately hunted down and murdered two peaceful and unoffending barbers, who were citizens of the town, and as quiet and harmless men as it afforded. Honest and decent men will want for language to express their indignation at this brutal and cowardly outrage.[47]

Apparently, the two barbers became the only fatalities during the evening's chaos. The post surgeon recorded no gunfire injuries but newspapers reported six wounded civilians, including a U.S. Deputy Marshal, and a white trooper from the Seventh Cavalry.[48]

While the events of May 3 definitely had racial motivations, classifying them as a "race riot" is not quite accurate, occurring as they did during a period of vigilante activity. In its coverage of the incident, the *Commonwealth* even pointed out that not all the discord derived from blacks' or even the military's proximity:

> it is certain that human life and limbs are altogether too unsafe in that locality. Every trifling dispute is settled by an instantaneous appeal to

the pistol or the knife. All things considered, Hays City is one of the best places to move away from that can be found upon the globe.[49]

Buffalo soldiers proved a contributing but not determinative factor in the town's history of conflict. In late April and early May, the Thirty-eighth companies relocated to new assignments on the Mexican border, leaving Fort Hays with fewer than a hundred troops by summer of 1869.[50] Even so, the community's reputation for bloodshed continued, with friction between soldiers and civilians remaining a constant. In 1871, a saloon brawl involving white troops escalated into gunfire, resulting in the death of the county sheriff.[51]

One should not isolate racial tensions from their larger social context and exaggerate their importance over other causes of violence. Yet the buffalo soldiers' presence did produce long-lasting hostility toward the black population. As the *Daily Tribune* stated, "Hays City seems to have many of the same ideas that unreconstructed rebels have, to wit: that negroes have no rights which a white man is bound to respect."[52] Following their eviction in May 1869, some black families were permitted to return, a decision most later regretted. In March 1871, four residents were arraigned for invading the home of an elderly black woman and raping her. Whites expressed disgust that the men were arrested on the word of "colored people." Fearing for their safety, the fort commander permitted all black families to relocate into dugouts on the post for protection, with troops once again sent into town to restore order.[53] The 1869 lynching and other such episodes firmly established the area's reputation as an unsafe place for African Americans. An observer in 1909 commented on the community's white homogeneity:

> no negro has ever ventured to make Hays a place of residence. An occasional straggler has worked a few days in town, but the history of the place has appealed too strongly to his imagination for him to remain.[54]

Conclusion

Fort Hays's predominantly black garrison and its hostile relationship with citizens in Hays City provide an example of how civilian/military social interaction helped to transfer racial hatreds to the newly conquered region. The years from 1867 to 1869 saw African Americans' introduction to regular army life, the beginning of a twenty-year process in which they would forcibly help to seize western lands from American Indians. Prejudice always remained a factor in their lives but as the Hays City experience indicates, their active involvement in a local cycle of hatred obscured whatever achievements whites might have recognized and intensified racist paranoia.

Whether black soldiers' participation in an occupying army deserves praise or criticism, of course, remains a matter of individual perspective and moral judgment, an arena in which the historian can claim no particular authority. Yet if history teaches any lesson, it is that one group's pride may be another's tragedy. As Vernon Bellecourt has asked, "Which do we value more, a wildly bastardized fable of progress and equality, or truth? Justice is the act of conscious, informed human beings."[55] In the recent rush to reveal the buffalo soldiers' past, historians should not forget the dual importance of understanding their legacy, lest new myths be created similar to those that once depicted white soldiers like Custer as heroes. Furthermore, the buffalo soldiers existed not only as enlistees in the fight against Indians but as actors in a complex theatre of negotiations framed by civilian whites' racism and the usual conflicts between army and civilians in a garrison town. Just as ethnocentric interpretations once regarded black history as insignificant, romanticizing the buffalo soldiers' experience not only perpetuates distortion, but it also robs them of the right to be judged not as representatives of an entire race but as human beings capable of human error.

Notes

1. For an overview of the black cavalry's official duties, William H. Leckie's *The Buffalo Soldiers: A Narrative of the Negro Cavalry in the West* (Norman: University of Oklahoma Press, 1967) has become a classic. Arlen L. Fowler's *The Black Infantry in the West, 1869–1891* (Westport CT: Greenwood, 1971) and John M. Carroll's edited collection, *The Black Military Experience in the American West* (New York: Liveright, 1971) also provide valuable descriptive information. For more recent works that deal with black soldiers' reception in civilian communities and their relationships with white officers, see Monroe Lee Billington, *New Mexico's Buffalo Soldiers, 1866–1900* (Niwot: University Press of Colorado, 1991), and Frank N. Schubert's *Buffalo Soldiers, Braves, and the Brass* (Shippensburg PA: White Mane, 1993).

2. Vernon Bellecourt, "The Glorification of Buffalo Soldiers Raises Racial Divisions between Blacks, Indians," *Indian Country Today*, May 4, 1994, 5A.

3. For general information on Fort Hays, see Leo Oliva, *Fort Hays, Frontier Army Post, 1865–1889* (Topeka: Kansas State Historical Society, 1980). Robert M. Utley's *Frontier Regulars: The United States Army and the Indian, 1866–1891* (Lincoln: University of Nebraska Press, 1973) provides a thorough discussion of the late 1860s campaigns.

4. Studies of the buffalo soldiers' impact on local race relations commonly focus on specific forts and communities. For useful examples, see Monroe Lee Billington, "Black Soldiers at Fort Selden, New Mexico, 1866–1891," *New Mexico Historical Review* 62 (1987): 65–80; Thomas R. Buecker, "Confrontation at Sturgis: An Episode in Civil-Military Race Relations, 1885," *South Dakota History* 14 (Fall 1984): 238–61; Michael J. Clark, "Improbable Ambassadors: Black Soldiers at Fort Douglas, 1896–99," *Utah Historical Quarterly* 46 (1978): 282–301; and Ronald G. Coleman, "The Buffalo Soldiers: Guardians of the Uintah Frontier, 1886–1901," *Utah Historical Quarterly* 47 (1979): 421–39.

5. Dudley Taylor Cornish, "Kansas Negro Regiments in the Civil War," *Kansas Historical Quarterly* 20 (May 1953): 417–29. For a more detailed discussion of the black volunteers, see Cornish, *The Sable Arm: Black Troops in the Union Army, 1861–1865* (Lawrence: University of Kansas Press, 1956); and Joseph T. Glatthaar, *Forged in Battle: The Civil War Alliance of Black Soldiers and White Officers* (New York: Free Press, 1990).

6. Robert Athearn, *In Search of Canaan: Black Migration to Kansas, 1879–80* (Lawrence: University Press of Kansas, 1978); and Nell Irvin Painter, *Exodusters: Black Migration to Kansas after Reconstruction* (New York: Alfred A. Knopf, 1977).

7. For discussion of the frontier concept, see Patricia Nelson Limerick, Clyde A. Milner II, and Charles E. Rankin, eds., *Trails: Toward a New Western History* (Lawrence: University Press of Kansas, 1991).

8. December 1867 monthly returns show Companies E and G, Thirty-eighth Infantry, and Companies F and I, Tenth Cavalry, to be present. Of the 435 enlisted men,

285 belonged to black regiments. Headquarters, Tenth Cavalry, Special Order No. 139, Fort Riley, Kansas, 26 November 1867, Letters Received (LR), Fort Hays (FH), National Archives Microfilm Publication (NAMP), T-837, roll 5; and Post Returns, Fort Hays, December 1867, Adjutant General's Office (AGO), Record Group (RG) 94, NAMP, roll 3.

9. Brev. Maj. E. A. Belger to Maj. John Yard, Tenth Cavalry, Post Commander of Fort Hays, July 16, 1868, LR, FH, NAMP, T-713, roll 5.

10. Descriptions of prejudice are available in Billington, *New Mexico's Buffalo Soldiers*, pp. 181–201, and Fowler, *Black Infantry in the West*, pp. 114–39. Jack D. Foner's *The United States Soldier Between Two Wars: Army Life and Reforms, 1865–1898* (New York: Humanities Press, 1970), pp. 127–47, describes army and civilian attitudes toward the black units and attempts to replace them with integrated regiments.

11. James N. Leiker, "Voices from a Disease Frontier: Kansans and Cholera, 1867," *Kansas History* 17 (Winter 1995): 236–53; and Roman Powers and Gene Younger, "Cholera on the Plains: The Epidemic of 1867 in Kansas," *Kansas Historical Quarterly* 37 (1971): 351–93; Post Returns, FH, July and August 1867, AGO, RG94, NAMP, roll 3; Maj. Edward Glass, ed., *The History of the Tenth Cavalry* (Fort Collins: Old Army Press, 1972), p. 95.

12. Monthly Registers of the Sick and Wounded, FH, NAMP, T-713. Dysentery, rheumatism, bronchitis, syphilis, and gonorrhea were also prevalent.

13. Oliva, *Fort Hays*, p. 57.

14. Report of William Buchannon, Assistant Surgeon, 14 July 1868, Monthly Surgeon's Reports, FH, NAMP, T-837, roll 3.

15. General Order No. 8, February 21, 1868, General Orders, FH, NAMP, T-713, roll 20.

16. For a discussion of army desertion rates in the post–Civil War period and their causes, see Foner, *United States Soldier*, pp. 6–10, 222–24.

17. Elizabeth Bacon Custer, *Tenting on the Plains* (New York: Charles L. Webster, 1887), pp. 695. This edition is not to be confused with the 1895 abridged version, which contains no reference to the forty deserters.

18. Monthly Post Returns, FH, 1866–71, AGO, RG94, NAMP.

19. Foner, *United States Soldier*, pp. 222–23.

20. For public perceptions of federal regulars, see Foner, *United States Soldier*, pp. 59–75.

21. Billington, *New Mexico's Buffalo Soldiers*, pp. 181–82.

22. *Leavenworth Daily Conservative*, July 10, 1867.

23. For the myth of violence, see Robert R. Dykstra, *The Cattle Towns* (Lincoln: University of Nebraska Press, 1966). For a more recent revisionist example, see Ty Cashion's "(Gun)Smoke Gets in Your Eyes: A Revisionist Look at Violent Fort Griffin," *Southwestern Historical Quarterly* 99 (July 1995): 81–94.

24. *Junction City Weekly Union*, 8 May 1869.

25. James D. Drees, "The Hays City Vigilante Period, 1868–1869," Master's thesis, Fort Hays State University, 1983, pp. 105–7.

26. *Kansas Daily Tribune*, November 26, 1867.

27. Drees, "Hays City Vigilante Period", p. 8.

28. Elizabeth Custer, *Following the Guidon* (New York: Harper and Brothers, 1890), pp. 155.

29. Capt. Samuel Ovenshine, Fifth Infantry, Post Commander, FH, to Brev. Capt. M. Howard, Fort Harker, February 2, 1868, Letters Sent (LS), FH, NA, RG393 (Continental Commands), part 5; *Atchison Daily Free Press*, January 4, 1868 (quoted).

30. *Kansas Daily Tribune*, December 25, 1867; *Railway Advance*, December 24, 1867.

31. Ovenshine to J. M. Soule, Esq., Justice of the Peace, and J. E. Walker, Pres. of Ellis Co. Board of Commissioners, January 30, 1868, LS, FH, NA, RG393, Continental Commands, Part 5; Ovenshine to Howard, February 2, 1868, LS, FH, NA, RG93.

32. Muster rolls show Cropper as being born in Baltimore, aged twenty-one at time of enlistment in May 1867, and having been promoted to corporal within six months. He was discharged in 1870 at expiration of service and reenlisted twice, joining the Ninth Cavalry in 1875. Enlistment records describe his character as "excellent." Unit Muster Rolls, Thirty-eighth Infantry, Company G, 1868, RG94, NA; and Enlistment Papers, RG94, NA.

33. *Railway Advance*, December 24, 1867; *Kansas Daily Tribune*, January 10, 1869.

34. Drees, "Hays City Vigilante Period," p. 8. Of many local histories of Hays City's "gunfighter period," this provides the most thorough discussion of vigilante violence and its causes.

35. *Kansas Daily Tribune*, January 10, 1869.

36. The *Leavenworth Daily Commercial*, January 9, 1869.

37. Information on Barnes, Watkins, and Ponder was obtained from Unit Muster Rolls, Thirty-eighth Infantry, Company E, 1868–69, NA, RG94.

38. Lt. Col. Anderson Nelson, Fifth Infantry, Post Commander, FH, to Gov. James Harvey, 18 January 1869, LS, FH, NA, RG393, part 5. This contains the first official mention of the lynching by military personnel but since Nelson did not elaborate, detailed information in this and the following paragraphs derives from civilian newspapers. The *Leavenworth Times and Conservative*, 9 January 1869, provided a very brusque summation. The *Leavenworth Daily Commercial*, January 9 and 12, 1869, delivered the most factual details but also the most editorial comment, praising civilian law officers' handling of the matter. Though the papers vary in their reporting, all agree, including *The Kansas Daily Tribune*, January 10, 1869, on the points presented here.

39. *Leavenworth Daily Commercial*, January 9, 1869.

40. *Kansas Daily Tribune*, January 10, 1869.

41. *Leavenworth Times and Conservative*, January 16, 1869; Nelson to Harvey, January 18, 1869, LS, FH, NA, RG393, part 5.

42. *Kansas Daily Tribune*, February 19, 1869.

43. *Kansas Daily Tribune*, February 19, 1869.

44. Drees, "Hays City Vigilante Period," p. 42.

45. Both the *Leavenworth Times and Conservative*, 4 May 1869, and *Kansas Daily Tribune*, May 8, 1869, claimed the blacks had a predetermined plan to burn the town.

46. 1st Lt. Mason Carter to Capt. J. W. Clous, Thirty-Eighth Infantry, May 3, 1869; and Carter to Capt. Sam Ovenshine, May 3, 1869, LS, FH, NA, RG393, part 5.

47. *Kansas Daily Commonwealth*, May 6, 1869, reprinted in *Junction City Weekly Union*, May 8, 1869.

48. *Kansas Daily Commonwealth*, May 4, 1869; *Leavenworth Daily Times and Conservative*, May 4, 1869; *Kansas Daily Tribune*, May 8, 1869; and Monthly Register of the Sick and Wounded, May 1869, FH, NAMP, T-837, roll 3A.

49. *Kansas Daily Commonwealth*, May 4, 1869.

50. Post Returns, April 1869, FH, NAMP, T-713, roll 20.

51. *White Cloud Chief*, July 27, 1871.

52. *Kansas Daily Tribune*, May 8, 1869.

53. Maj. George Gibson to Acting Assistant Adjutant General, Headquarters, Department of the Missouri, Fort Leavenworth, March 4 and 5, 1871, LS, FH, NA, RG393, part 5.

54. James Beach, "Old Fort Hays," *Kansas Historical Collections* 11 (1909–10): 580.

55. Bellecourt, "Glorification of Buffalo Soldiers," p. 5A.

CHAPTER 2 | "Pap" Singleton's Dunlap Colony: Relief Agencies and the Failure of a Black Settlement in Eastern Kansas

JOSEPH V. HICKEY

There are gathered at Dunlap and vicinity at the present time between 275 and 300 families of colored people, all of whom are succeeding quite well and many of whom are on the road to prosperity. The plan of Dunlap Colony is very simple, the chief reason, probably, of the success met with, being the fact that every settler is compelled to own his property, no renting being permitted . . . as Mr. Atchison expressed it, "everyone is fat and happy."

So wrote the *Topeka Daily Capital* on October 19, 1882, describing the Dunlap Colony, one of more than a dozen "exoduster" settlements that blacks established in Kansas following the collapse of Reconstruction.[1] In the 1880s the Dunlap Colony may have represented one of the best chances for blacks to succeed as yeoman farmers in Kansas. Not only had the Dunlap Colony been carefully planned by Benjamin "Pap" Singleton, but in the spring of 1878 he and his business associates, Columbus Johnson and Alonzo DeFrantz, personally helped two hundred Tennessee transplants move to Dunlap and select and make down payments on their forty- to eighty-acre farms. In addition, during the Great Exodus in 1879, when twenty thousand blacks fled poverty and oppression in the south and relocated to Kansas, the Dunlap Colony received substantial financial support. The Kansas Freedmen's Relief Association (KFRA), a state organization founded in May 1879 and headed by Kansas Governor John St. John, provided some of the aid. Much of the rest came from the Presbyterian church, which not only helped destitute blacks purchase farms, livestock, and homes, but also established "The Freedmen's Academy of Kansas," a "Literary and Business Academy" that offered a free education to all former slaves and their children.[2]

Despite these promising conditions, the Dunlap Colony fared little better than other colonies in Kansas, including the well-known Nicodemus Colony and others in the semiarid western portions of the state. Like most exoduster settlements, Dunlap's population, which included ninety families in 1885, began to decline rapidly at the turn of the century, and by the end of the Great Depression only a small number of families remained. Today, of the more than one thousand black settlers that once called Dunlap their home, only one black remains, eighty-four-year-old London Harness, who lives on the farm his grandparents purchased in 1879—the year of the Great Exodus.

As with other rural settlements in Kansas, many factors contributed to the Dunlap Colony's death. Improved transportation, the mechanization of agriculture, and urbanization played significant roles. Because it was a black settlement, however, a number of other factors that were unique to exoduster settlements must also be considered. Although local racial prejudice and discrimination contributed to the colony's decline, another factor may have caused even more harm, and that was the misguided attempts of Dunlap relief agencies to transform as many exodusters as possible into landowners and independent farmers. I suggest that Pap Singleton's colony ultimately fell victim to the best intentions of relief agency and missionary workers, who, during the Great Exodus, decided that it was their duty to relocate as many destitute blacks from Topeka and other Kansas cities—where they had gathered to take advantage of temporary housing and relief aid—to the Dunlap countryside, and in so doing placed an impossible burden on the Dunlap Colony.

The Dunlap Environment

Pap Singleton's decision to locate a farming colony in Dunlap was strongly influenced by two factors: one was the nature of the physical environment, which to all appearances—and according to exaggerated claims of local boosters—was an idyllic agrarian environment. The other was cheap government lands that could be had for a small down payment and at very favorable interest rates. As did so many western promoters, however, Singleton and his followers soon discovered that there was a substantial gap between appearance and reality.

Dunlap is located in the extreme southeastern corner of Morris County in east central Kansas. During the 1870s and early 1880s, black settlements were created in Dunlap village, in the uplands above the village on the Morris County side, and in the neighboring Lyon County uplands three miles or so to the east and northeast of the village. Dunlap village itself is in the Neosho River valley, which contains rich and deep soils that during the last century have consistently produced excellent corn, sorghum, and wheat crops. To contemporary farmers, the Neosho valley's only serious flaw is that it periodically floods, which often delays planting and sometimes destroys crops and requires replanting. Four or five floods per year are not uncommon, and in 1973, when record floods occurred, the Dunlap townsite was covered by water on ten separate occasions.[3]

The uplands, where the exodusters established almost all of their farms, presented more formidable obstacles to small-scale farmers. The slope gradient, in many areas 15 to 20 percent, is subject to severe erosion when plowed. Limestone outcrops are common throughout the uplands, and in most areas the soil is too shallow for sustained cultivation. According to contemporary soil conservation agents, the uplands are "better suited to native range than to feed crops or tame pasture."[4]

When he scouted the Dunlap uplands in the 1870s, Pap Singleton may have recognized some of their limitations, but, like others in this period, it is likely he misjudged the area's climate. Dunlap receives an average of 33.59 inches of rainfall a year, an amount that would have seemed more than adequate for the kinds of crops that the exodusters preferred. What Singleton and others did not know, however, is that Dunlap is in a climatic transition zone and rainfall is highly erratic. Rains often come all at once or not at all, sometimes thoroughly soaking one locality and leaving another a few miles away parched and dry. In some years a rainless June may be interrupted by a three-day deluge during which five to ten inches of rain fall, only to be followed by a long summer drought. The erratic climate, thin soils, and rocky hillsides provided conditions that gradually favored a farmer-stockraiser emphasis, and from the 1880s until today the primary agricultural focus of the area has been the summer fattening and winter feeding of cattle, with livestock feed produced in the valleys and the uplands used for pasturage and hay.[5]

During much of the nineteenth century, Dunlap's social environment was no less turbulent than its physical environment. From 1846 to 1872 the land that would one day become Dunlap was part of the Kansa Indian Reservation, which initially covered 256,000 acres. In 1859, under considerable pressure from squatters, town-boomers, and railroad promoters, the government reduced the reservation to 80,000 acres in the southwest corner of the old reservation. Then in 1872, after officials had removed the Kansa Indians to Oklahoma, the government placed the remaining lands on the market to be sold to an army of squatters, who had taken up residence in the area long before the Indians had departed, and to other interested buyers. In 1874 Joseph Dunlap, a trader to the Kansa Indians in nearby Council

Grove, laid out the town that bears his name and built the first store near the Missouri, Kansas, and Texas (Katy) railroad tracks, which had been built through the Neosho valley in 1869.[6]

Pap Singleton's Dunlap Colony

Born a slave in 1809, Benjamin Singleton spent his childhood and young manhood in Nashville, Tennessee, where he worked as a carpenter and cabinetmaker. After he was sold to owners in the Gulf states, he repeatedly escaped back to Nashville until eventually he fled north to Canada. During the Civil War he moved to Detroit, where he ran a boarding house, and at war's end he once again returned to the Nashville area, this time to found the "Tennessee Real Estate and Homestead Association," which he organized to help poor Tennessee blacks purchase farms. After a fruitless search for reasonably priced lands in Tennessee, Singleton focused his attention on former Indian lands in Kansas, and in 1873 he visited the Baxter Springs area with the express purpose of securing for his clients "Cherokee Strip" lands that the government had recently made available to the public. Robert Athearn wrote that in 1875 Singleton helped 300 blacks relocate from Tennessee to Cherokee County in southeastern Kansas, where he founded "Singleton's Colony." Three years later the government placed large blocks of the Kansa Diminished Reservation in the Neosho valley on the open market, and Singleton's second and final planned settlement—"Dunlap Colony"—was born.[7]

In May 1878 Singleton, several of his associates, and about two hundred settlers moved to the Dunlap vicinity. Because squatters, the railroads, and speculators had taken the best farmland in the river and creek valleys and the bottoms that remained were priced at $7.00 or more an acre, almost all of the 7500 acres purchased by the black colonists were in the uplands. All colonists made small down payments on forty- and eighty-acre claims costing between

$1.25 and $2.00 an acre and agreed to pay the outstanding debt over a period of six years at 6 percent interest per year.[8]

Apparently a large block of land sufficient for the entire colony could not be found, so four distinct upland settlements, each with between four and a dozen households, were created. One, established seven miles or so north of Dunlap above Rock Creek in Morris County, became known as the "Rock Creek Colony." Two others, both roughly three miles east and northeast of Dunlap, were in Lyon County—one in Americus Township, the other in Agnes City Township. A final settlement was established in the village of Dunlap itself, where possibly as many as twenty families took claims on the north side of the Katy railroad tracks that extended from the valley floor northeast into the rocky uplands.[9]

Dunlap and the Exodus of 1879–80

Colony members had only begun to break out the prairie for farms and move from crude brush shelters—where they had spent the first winter in Kansas—to permanent homes when the Great Exodus of 1879 began. Benjamin Singleton later took credit for the Great Exodus, claiming his circulars inspired thousands of southern blacks to move to "Sunny Kansas." Certainly his promotional material, and fabled rumors that in addition to being the land of John Brown, Kansas promised every freedman $500, forty acres, a mule, first class hotels, apples as big as grapefruits, and complete equality, were powerful magnets that drew the poor and dispossessed to the state. But terrorism, poverty, and the loss of their civil and political rights following the end of Reconstruction in 1877 provided the "push" that inspired blacks to leave southern homes many had known for generations and take a chance on what was for most the complete unknown.[10]

From 1879 to 1880 more than 20,000 "exodusters" migrated to

Kansas, with many settling in Wyandotte, Leavenworth, Atchison, Parsons, and other towns in the eastern part of the state. Topeka, though, attracted by far the largest exoduster population of all. As Robert Athearn wrote,

> the municipality's apparent willingness to receive them as evidenced by the creation of a temporary relief committee and the construction of temporary housing facilities, put the city into the "Exoduster business" in a big way.[11]

The decision of Governor John St. John and his followers to establish the Kansas Freedmen's Relief Association in May 1879, to "aid destitute freedmen, refugees, and emigrants coming into the state," played an even greater role in making Topeka the Mecca of southern black hope. After it was organized, committee members began a large-scale effort to secure funds from philanthropists in America and England, and within a few months they had collected thousands of dollars worth of food and clothing. Shortly thereafter rumors began to circulate in the south that not only was food abundant in Topeka, but officials there were anxious to give every freedman a free government claim. At the same time, officials in many Kansas cities decided that Topeka was better able to care for impoverished blacks than they were, and they began to funnel "excess" populations to the capital.[12]

The day after the KFRA was organized, 180 impoverished blacks arrived in Topeka, and over the next few months the Association temporarily housed, fed, and clothed thousands of exodusters before finding them jobs and permanent homes in other areas. The KFRA's resettlement plan was complex and at various times included five major options. One strategy was to purchase tracts of land in "Tennesseetown," a black enclave located on the city's western perimeter, subdivide them into house lots, and resell them at cost to the refugees. Another was to find work for the refugees in other parts of the state by having Laura Haviland, a Quaker philanthropist who was secretary of the Association and operated the KFRA's employment bureau, print circulars and send them to prospective employers. The third was to funnel refugees to other states and the fourth to relocate poor blacks to western Kansas. A final plan sought to remove exodusters from Topeka and other cities and relocate them to rural areas in eastern Kansas—either to colonies that the state would help establish or to settlements that had been colonized in the mid-1870s. Since Dunlap already contained a viable black community, and a local relief agency had been organized there soon after the formation of the state body, it seemed ideally suited to the KFRA's needs.[13]

Two local agencies—the Presbyterian church, and the Freedmen's Aid Association of Dunlap, Kansas, a chapter of the KFRA—played major roles in relocating Topeka refugees to the Dunlap area. In 1879, during the Great Exodus, the Presbyterian Synod of North America assigned the Reverend John M. Snodgrass "missionary to the colored people of Dunlap, Kansas." He in turn was instrumental in encouraging the church to build the literary and business academy that opened in 1880 and was chartered in 1883 as "The Freedmen's Academy of Kansas" and known locally as the "Colored Academy." According to its charter, its mission was "to educate the colored youth for teaching, for business management, for mechanical industries, for an honorable social life; and to encourage the settlement of destitute colored families of the cities on cheap lands in the country." In 1880, the church also assigned two blacks to the school: Andrew Atchison as principal and Maggie Watson as primary school teacher.[14]

Although the Mission Board of the Associated Presbyterian church had secured the Academy's charter, its members apparently wanted the school to serve all blacks in Kansas, so the management of the school was placed in the care of "twelve directors who were chosen as representative men from different Christian denominations of the state." In 1883, the Academy's staff was comprised of Mr. Andrew

Atchison, principal; the Reverend John Snodgrass, instructor of music; Mrs. L. P. Fulton, instructor of woman's work (sewing); and primary teachers, Maggie Watson, Georgia Smith, and Mr. R. B. Atchison. In 1882, they served ninety male and eighty-five female students, of whom forty-five were listed as adult ex-slaves.[15]

From its formation in May 1879 to the spring of 1881, the KFRA relocated urban refugees to Dunlap and supplied them with food, clothing, and housing in the village. When the KFRA closed its Topeka headquarters on April 15, 1881, the Freedmen's Relief Association of Dunlap took charge of the refugees and their care. Founded in the spring of 1881 and legally incorporated the following September, the Freedmen's Relief Association was directly linked to the Academy and the Presbyterian church, for the president of the Association was John Snodgrass, and Andrew Atchison was its secretary. Columbus Johnson, Pap Singleton's former business partner in the "Tennessee Real Estate and Homestead Association," also was an officer; an 1882 Association pamphlet described him as "Soliciting Agent," a role that included two major duties: helping refugees move from Topeka and other cities to Dunlap; and soliciting charitable donations that were to be used to purchase farms for poor blacks.[16]

It is impossible to give the exact number of exodusters that the KFRA and the Freedmen's Relief Association relocated from Topeka and other urban areas to Dunlap. The initial wave of settlers in 1879–80 may have included one hundred people or more, but a report in the February 1880 *Morris County Times* suggests that many found conditions in Dunlap so bleak they were planning to "return to former homes in the future." Most of those who stayed took up residence at the edge of Dunlap village, and as the *Morris County Times* also observed, "the exodusters have built innumerable small dwellings, which give the town a decided 'band-box' air." In this early phase of refugee settlement only a few families appear to have settled in the countryside, and it is uncertain whether the KFRA gave them any assistance. Robert Athearn mentioned that one exoduster at least, a man named Henry Carter, paid for his own farm by working on local ranches in the Dunlap vicinity from 1879 to 1880.[17]

Whatever the number of actual settlers, the possibility that hundreds or even thousands of poor blacks might flood the area—and in the thinking of many whites, harm Dunlap's economic future—generated intense local hostility. The white population (which included approximately two hundred families in 1880) may have feared that the large black population would give blacks considerable influence in local politics, and some poor whites seem to have been concerned that the bountiful state aid that black farmers were rumored to have received gave blacks a competitive advantage. For example, an 1881 Freedmen's Aid Association pamphlet asked,

> What will be done with the colored refugees? . . . [I]t was difficult to answer because of their vast numbers, extreme poverty, . . . and because of the dislike of our white citizens to receive them as near neighbors.[18]

The Freedmen's Aid Association also bore some of the hostility. For example in 1882 Dunlap citizen T. R. Cannon wrote a letter to the *Dunlap Chief*, a Morris County newspaper, claiming funds given to the Freedmen's Aid Association were being misappropriated. Cannon also stated that "Poor white people should be cared for too."[19]

While the 1878 colonists were greeted with curiosity, the exodusters encountered various forms of prejudice and discrimination. For example, in September 1879, at a "donation and barbeque" for the benefit of exodusters that was attended by an estimated 1,500 blacks and whites, the editor of the *Morris County Times* wrote that everything went just right "with the exception of one negro boy who was inclined to be a little noisy because the colored people were not permitted to join in a quadrille with the whites . . ."[20] As more poor blacks arrived, discrimination intensified and clear social boundaries between whites and blacks were drawn and enforced.

On March 5, 1880 the *Morris County Times* reported that "There will be a meeting of colored citizens of Dunlap Township to take into consideration a graveyard, as [there is] a public objection to colored people being buried where good Republicans are buried." A short time later, blacks established their cemetery about a half mile north of the white one. Separate churches and schools also were established. For example, in March 1882 the editor of the *Dunlap Chief* wrote that School District No. 40 "is divided—the white children occupying the school house of the district, and the colored . . . one room of the Academy building." Residential areas were segregated as well, with blacks north of the tracks, and whites to the south. Some merchants barred blacks from entering their stores, and black and white social activities were reported separately by the local newspapers. For example during the early 1890s, local news and gossip about blacks in the *Dunlap Courier* and the *Dunlap Reflector* could only be found in columns entitled "Colored Folks" or "Colored Society News."[21]

Relief Agencies and Black Farmers in the Dunlap Uplands

At the height of the exodus in 1879–80, the Academy and the Kansas Freedmen's Relief Association were acutely aware of the suffering of the poor, and this clearly influenced their decision to relocate as many blacks as possible from urban areas to Dunlap. After the crisis had ended and black emigration had largely ceased in 1881, however, the Academy and the Freedmen's Relief Association of Dunlap continued or even increased their efforts to bring urban blacks to the area, apparently ignoring the fact that black villagers and farmers who had already settled in the area were having a difficult time succeeding.

While the original colonists and many of the exodusters had come from farming backgrounds, few were prepared for the conditions in the Dunlap area. At a time when the farms of their white neighbors averaged almost one hundred sixty acres, those of black settlers averaged but eighty-seven acres. Moreover, the farms of whites typically contained a mix of bottomlands and upland pastures. Those of blacks were located almost exclusively in the uplands and many contained such an abundance of rocks that London Harness, whose grandparents lived on such a claim, cannot understand how they ever could have plowed them. Confined to the uplands, few blacks had access to timber and water, and a lack of reliable water may have had particularly serious consequences because of their agricultural focus on corn and hogs. The agricultural strategy of J. A. Bridges of Americus Township in Lyon County is somewhat typical of his black neighbors. In 1885 twenty acres of his eighty-acre upland farm were in corn, and on the other sixty he kept five hogs, two horses, and two cows.[22]

In December 1879, black farmers in Morris and Lyon Counties, apparently struggling to meet the second installment on their loans, petitioned the KFRA for assistance. It is unlikely they received much help, however, for at that time the Association was preoccupied with resettling the urban poor. An Academy circular described the first two winters as particularly hard on the immigrants, and in an interview in the *Topeka Daily Capital* in October 1882, Andrew Atchison, the principal of the Academy, noted that, while everybody was fat and happy that year, "The crops of the previous year [1881] were somewhat disheartening." Census data for the years 1880–85 also suggest that black farmers experienced difficulties in the uplands; despite the efforts of relief agencies to expand the number of black farmers, few settled in any of the four settlements, and the number of black farmers in Agnes City Township in Lyon County actually declined in this five-year period from twelve households to five, probably because of farm failures.[23]

Despite these problems, the Academy and Freedmen's Aid Association continued to request aid from the state and from wealthy individuals so that additional poor blacks could be relocated to the Dunlap countryside. In a pamphlet distributed in the fall of 1881, the Freedmen's Aid Association stated:

> It is the desire of the Dunlap Freedmen's Aid Association to secure means to purchase some tracts of land near Dunlap to be sold to the Refugees on easy terms and the payments to be added to the school fund.

Several months later in its Quarterly Report, the Freedmen's Aid Association noted:

> The Association has resolved upon the purchase of a choice tract of land to be divided into five- and ten-acre lots for the accommodation of as many of the homeless families of refugees as possible . . . The land will be sold to the refugees on easy terms.[24]

Ann F. Jamison of Maine, "a supporter of John Brown and the abolitionist cause," seems to have responded to an Association request. In 1881 she bequeathed to the Association sufficient money to purchase 240 acres that were to be given to the Dunlap Colony "for the purposes of encouraging poor colored families who make a difficult living in the cities to remove to the country." Land was found, all of it in the uplands three miles southwest of Dunlap village, and in 1886 it was opened for settlement. According to the provisions of Jamison's will, each farm was to be sold to the poor for $1.00, provided that blacks "personally reside upon, improve and cultivate [it] . . . in a husband-like manner . . . , and that said premises shall not be sold . . . until the expiration of seven years."[25]

As they said they would do, rather than partition the land into forty- or eighty-acre farms—like those owned by the majority of black farmers who were at best marginally successful—Association members subdivided the 240 acres into twenty-eight lots, with each lot containing either five or ten acres of land. They called the property "A. B. Whiting's Subdivision."[26]

The following year Mark and Hannah Hillyer of Topeka, apparently wishing to take advantage of $3500 donated to the Academy to buy additional land for poor blacks, partitioned their land at the northern edge of the village into thirty-two five-acre lots. These lands, called Hillyer's Subdivision, were offered to black refugees for $160 each. Buyers (or the Academy on their behalf) were required to make a small down payment, pay 10 percent interest per year on the outstanding debt, and pay off the loan in a five-year period.[27]

By the early 1890s fifteen black families had taken claims in Whiting's Subdivision. The Academy seems to have provided each with a twelve-by-sixteen-foot cabin, a livestock pen, and possibly some livestock. That year's census shows that most cultivated about two acres of their five- or ten-acre farms, and despite their meager farm holdings, most owned two or more horses, a cow, and several hogs. In the same period, six families took claims in Hillyer's Subdivision. Their farm sizes, the amount of land in cultivation, and livestock holdings were so similar to those of people living in Whiting's Subdivision, that it appears likely that they too received money and assistance from the Academy Board.[28]

The Dunlap Colony's Failure

Given Dunlap's stock raising emphasis in the 1880s and the fact that by this time local farmers were fully aware that a minimum of 160 acres—including both bottomlands and upland pastures—was needed to sustain a viable farming operation, it is difficult to comprehend the actions of the Academy Board. It might be argued that Dunlap relief agencies were unaware of the limitations of the Dunlap uplands, but local understanding that this niche was primarily suited to pasture and hay had dominated farmer thinking for almost three decades. It is more likely that Association members considered it only a temporary measure when they placed poor black families on five- or ten-acre farms; when they secured additional funds they probably planned to increase the size of black farm holdings. But the charitable aid that trickled into the area in the early 1880s gradually diminished, and after 1886 benefactors became very hard to find. The loss of aid had the most serious consequences for those who had taken five- or ten-acre claims, but over the next decade several developments adversely affected the entire black community.[29]

One was a cattle bust that came in 1887 after six years of spectacular growth in Dunlap and in most other parts of the West. Prior to the bust, dozens of ranches had been established in the area, herds had been expanded, and Dunlap had become a major cattle shipping station on the Katy line. Black settlers derived a considerable portion of their incomes from working on local farms and ranches, and during the boom years employment opportunities were excellent. For example, London Harness noted that many early settlers worked on local stock farms for $.50 a day, baling hay and shucking corn. And, as noted earlier, by working on local ranches, Henry Carter not only was able to make a down payment on his forty-acre farm but also purchase a "horse and two cows."[30] While employment opportunities in stone quarries in Dunlap and in Strong City twenty miles to the west tempered the impact of the cattle bust, the loss of income from farm labor was keenly felt by all black settlers.

A few years after the cattle bust, Kansas and the nation entered a period of severe economic depression. Beginning in 1889, agricultural prices steadily declined. For example, in 1889 and again in 1896, corn prices fell to $.20 a bushel, and wheat at $.49 was not much better. Many Kansas farmers attempted to hold on to their farms by borrowing at annual interest rates of from 40 to 375 percent, but this tactic rarely succeeded; between 1880 and 1890 the number of tenant farmers in Kansas increased from 16.3 percent to 35.2 percent.[31]

In Dunlap the full impact of the depression does not appear to have been felt immediately, for Dunlap's black population declined only slightly, from ninety families in 1885 to eighty-six in 1895. Over the next decade, however, Dunlap's black population declined by more than 50 percent, from eighty-six families to forty.[32] Given its central role in the community, the closing of the Academy in the early 1890s must have been a particularly serious blow. Without its support, blacks not only lost valuable economic assistance but also a free education, which may have been a major reason many decided to leave the community.

In May of 1889 the Academy sold most of its real estate holdings to local businessmen, and a year later John Snodgrass moved to Iowa, where he retired. Andrew Atchison, the Academy's principal, seems to have left the area sometime during the same year, and a short time later the Academy ceased operation. The Academy building sat vacant until 1895, when Dunlap businessman Alfred Parrish purchased the neat two-story frame structure and moved it several blocks to Commercial Street, where it served as his family's residence for several decades. After Parrish's death it was left vacant, and eventually it burned to the ground.[33]

Soon after the Academy closed, blacks began to flee Dunlap, abandoning both their five- and ten-acre farms and their homes in the village. Between 1895 and 1905, the number of black families in the village declined from twenty-nine to nineteen, and only six of twenty-one farmers remained in Whiting's and Hillyer's Subdivisions. The rural black population in Valley Township, in Morris County, declined by more than 50 percent. Even in the three original 1878 settlements, where black farmers had the largest farms and seemingly the best chances of success, losses were heavy. In Americus Township in Lyon County, the black population declined from twelve families to five, in Agnes City only two of seven families remained, and in the Rock Creek Colony only five of thirteen families survived the decade.[34]

As happened throughout rural Kansas, Dunlap's citizens, both black and white, gradually left the farm and moved to cities. By the depression so few black families remained that they closed their schools and black children began to attend integrated schools. On September 22, 1931, blacks held their last Emancipation Day Ceremony, an event that had until that time celebrated their black heritage, their coming to Dunlap, and their sense of commitment to others in the Dunlap community. Two black churches remained open until the early 1950s, but in the end each was supported by only a handful of families. Today, London Harness is the final link to the past, the last reminder of the exoduster presence in the Dunlap area and of black efforts to succeed as yeoman farmers in eastern Kansas.[35]

In examining the actions of the Kansas Freedmen's Relief Agency, its local chapters, and various missionary aid groups, it is clear that during the exodus their primary goal was to assist and relocate destitute blacks from Topeka and other Kansas cities to the countryside. Politicians and religious groups joined forces to accomplish this goal, though both groups seem to have had motives of their own. Politicians wanted to remove blacks to the countryside to relieve overcrowding, reduce the possibility of civil disturbances, and contain the spread of disease. Religious groups may have had similar objectives, but their ideology also had a strong anti-urban bias which held that in cities the poor were inclined to laziness, moral laxity, and corruption. By contrast, missionary groups fervently believed that if poor blacks worked with their hands in the countryside they would be both economically and morally rewarded.[36]

Long-term plans by relief agencies to transform exodusters into yeoman farmers are much less in evidence in Dunlap; the support Dunlap farmers received was clearly inadequate. Dunlap was not the only colony in eastern Kansas that received KFRA and missionary aid. Singleton's Colony in southeastern Kansas and the Little Coney Colony in Chautauqua County also received some assistance. The KFRA also established the Wabaunsee Colony in the rugged Flint Hills uplands. There, as in Dunlap, blacks were given farms of forty acres or less, and as happened in Dunlap, they too failed and moved back to the city. The efforts of relief agencies to solicit funds were so vigorous that many Kansans may have concluded that black farmers had been given every opportunity to succeed, but the nature of that assistance shows that rather than helping blacks succeed as yeoman farmers, the efforts of relief agencies ensured that they would fail.[37]

I do not want to suggest that relief agencies had no benefits for black exodusters: clearly relief workers saved many lives and their humanitarian aid helped many find homes, receive educations and job training, and even get a start in farming. They had other unintended benefits as well. There is another side of the exoduster story that deserves to be told, and that is how Dunlap colonists and exodusters used the meager aid they were given not only to sustain the colony for more than half a century, but to build a social support system that stretched across Kansas and included most cities and many small rural communities as well.

The Dunlap Colony's Success

Local newspapers and most historic documents tend to emphasize the helplessness and vulnerability of the exodusters—in part to promote a greater appreciation for white generosity. But there are occasional newspaper accounts that mention black church groups and associations that blacks created to help themselves as well as to assist those with special needs. For example in 1879 the *Morris County Times* mentioned that the "'Colored Actual Settlers' had met to take into consideration the payments of their land," and near the turn of the century *The Dunlap Reflector* stated that blacks had a new organization called "The National Ex-Slave Pension Association."[38] Emancipation Day, as London Harness explained to me, however, was particularly important to black self-help and success.

Soon after they arrived in Dunlap, blacks began to celebrate Emancipation Day, an event that drew hundreds and sometimes more than a thousand people. Most of the people who attended the celebration were local blacks, but kin, friends, and former residents from other parts of Kansas were well represented, as were whites from the village and nearby towns, businessmen, and local and state officials. To most outsiders, Emancipation Day was little more than feasting, games, and inspirational speeches. For black families, however, it was not only a day to celebrate their freedom but also an opportunity to make social contacts with both blacks and whites across the state. It was a time for kin to pool their resources and help those in need. It also was a vital communication channel that alerted blacks to employment opportunities in various cities and on local farms and to prejudice and discrimination in various parts of the state. Contacts with white officials and local whites were also useful not only in helping blacks find jobs but also in resolving local problems in a rare forum where blacks—rather than whites—were the majority.

Many blacks even appear to have found a way to turn the colony's failure to their advantage. During interviews, London Harness told me that throughout his working life he knew where many former Dunlap families had moved, and when working in Manhattan, Abilene, Junction City, and other Kansas towns, he could always count on their providing him with housing, food, and other necessities. For blacks these were essential services, for until the 1950s in many Kansas towns and villages blacks were unwelcome in hotels and restaurants, and many whites either would not serve blacks or demanded that they take their meals and eat in segregated areas, or in some small towns, outdoors.[39] Thus while the Dunlap Colony was a failure in terms of establishing a persistent black farming community in the Kansas Flint Hills, it was a success in allowing individual black families to escape poverty and overcrowding in Kansas cities and in establishing an enduring social and economic network that enabled many generations of family members to live, work, and travel throughout the state.

Notes

The author gratefully acknowledges oral history information provided by Mr. London Harness. The assistance of Gail Graham and the staff at the Lyon County Historical Society is also much appreciated. Thanks are also due Professors Kenneth Hendrickson, Thomas Isern, William Thompson, and Kendall Blanchard, who read earlier drafts of the paper, and Virginia Cunningham, for her editorial comments. I also want to thank the reviewers for their insightful comments and recommendations. An earlier version of this paper was presented to the Western Social Science Association in Albuquerque, New Mexico, April 1989.

1. *Topeka Daily Capital*, October 19, 1882, Morris County clippings, vol. 1, 1874–1933, Kansas State Historical Society (KSHS), Topeka KS. Robert G. Athearn, *In Search of Canaan: Black Migration to Kansas 1879–1880* (Lawrence: Regents Press of Kansas, 1978), p. 167, noted that "the 1880 census figures show 43,107 blacks in Kansas, an increase of 26,000 since 1870."

2. Athearn, *In Search of Canaan* (note 1 above), p. 205. See also Lee Ella Blake, *The Great Exodus of 1879–1880 to Kansas* (Manhattan: Kansas State College of Agriculture and Applied Studies, 1928), p. 15. Nell Irvin Painter, *Exodusters: Black Migration to Kansas after Reconstruction* (New York: Alfred A. Knopf, 1977), p. 116, noted that "Singleton, W. A. Sizemore, and Alonzo De Frantz lived there [Dunlap Colony] from the middle of 1879 to the early part of 1880." Athearn, *In Search of Canaan*, p. 57, wrote that the KFRA asked for incorporation in May 1879, and that Governor St. John headed its thirteen member governing board. Presbyterian church efforts in founding the Freedmen's Academy of Kansas are discussed in H. C. Speer, *Fourth Biennial Report, Superintendent Public Instruction, 1883–84* (Topeka KS, 1885), p. 127, KSHS.

3. *Emporia Gazette*, May 3, 1962, "Dunlap"—"History of Dunlap Is Full of Excitement of Old West," Gilson Scrapbooks (newspaper clippings), Lyon County Historical Museum, Emporia KS. See also Fred Bernard in *Flint Hills Oral History Project* (Emporia: Emporia State University, 1974), p. 1. Bernard said that in 1973 ten floods occurred in Dunlap and that prior to that time, "five had been the record."

4. Wesley L. Barker, U.S. Department of Agriculture, Soil Conservation Service, *Soil Survey of Morris County, Kansas* (Washington DC, 1974), p. 12.

5. Joseph E. Van Riper, "Details of a Simplified Koeppen-Geiger System of Climatic Classification," *Man's Physical World*, 2nd ed. (New York: McGraw-Hill, 1971), pp. 626–30. The dividing line between Humid Continental Climate and Humid Subtropical is near Council Grove KS; Joseph V. Hickey and Charles E. Webb, "The Transition From Farming to Ranching in the Kansas Flint Hills," *Great Plains Quarterly* 7 (Fall 1987), p. 255n8; "Farm Facts 1974–75," *Kansas State Board of Agriculture, 58th Annual Report* (Topeka: State Printer, 1974–75), 19F. My figures are long-term rainfall averages for the twentieth century. Barker, *Soil Survey of Morris County, Kansas*, p. 50.

6. William E. Unrau, *The Kansa Indians: History of the Wind People, 1673–1873* (Norman: University of Oklahoma Press, 1971), p. 213. See also H. Craig Miner and William E. Unrau, *The End of Indian Kansas: A Study of Cultural Revolution, 1854–1871* (Lawrence: Regents Press of Kansas, 1978), p. 102; Morris County clippings.

7. Athearn, *In Search of Canaan*, p. 77; Orwal L. McDaniel, "A History of Nicodemus, Graham County, Kansas" (Master's thesis, Fort Hays State University, 1950), p. 12; Painter, *Exodusters*, p. 113; Roy Garvin, "Benjamin, or 'Pap' Singleton and His Followers," *The Journal of Negro History* 33 (January 1948): 8. Kenneth M. Hamilton, "Black Town Promotion and Development on the Middle Border, 1877–1914" (PhD diss., Washington University, St. Louis, 1978), p. 26, noted that the success of Singleton's Cherokee County Colony "prompted various Kansas railroads . . . to send immigration agents into Tennessee and Kentucky to recruit more blacks, in the process offering reduced fares from Nashville to Topeka."

8. Randall B. Woods, *A Black Odyssey: John Lewis Waller and the Promise of American Life, 1878–1900* (Lawrence: Regents Press of Kansas, 1981), p. 20. Athearn, *In Search of Canaan*, p. 77, gives an even larger black population for Dunlap, "eight hundred settlers." I determined homesite and settlement locations from tract records in Morris and Lyon counties and used Geological Survey maps to determine their upland nature. These records are in both Lyon and Morris counties; Register of Deeds Office, Council Grove KS, and Register of Deeds Office, Lyon County KS.

9. London Harness, *Flint Hills Oral History Project*, pp. 3, 27.

10. Painter, *Exodusters*, pp. 207, 158–59, 191–93. See also Athearn, *In Search of Canaan*, p. 81; Van B. Shaw, "Nicodemus, Kansas: A Study in Isolation" (PhD diss., University of Missouri, 1951), p. 86.

11. Athearn, *In Search of Canaan*, p. 57. Athearn discusses the various strategies for black removal from Kansas cities in chapter 9, pp. 155–71.

12. Athearn, *In Search of Canaan*, pp. 57, 167.

13. Thomas C. Cox, *Blacks in Topeka, Kansas 1865–1915, A Social History* (Baton Rouge: Louisiana State University Press, 1982), p. 62; Athearn, *In Search of Canaan*, p. 263; Blake, *The Great Exodus*, p. 60.

14. William M. Glasgow, *Cyclopedic Manual of the United Presbyterian Church of North America* (Pittsburgh: United Presbyterian Church Board, 1903), cited in Cheryl Romine, "The Freedmen's Academy Mystery," paper prepared for Flint Hills Folklife Class, Emporia State University, Summer, 1989; Andrew Atchison, "An Urgent Appeal in Behalf of a New and Important Charity," *Freedmen's Academy of Kansas*, pamphlet, 1884, KSHS; *The Dunlap Chief*, March 3, 1882. Under the heading "Dunlap Colored Academy," the newspaper noted that "Andrew Atchison and Miss Maggie Watson have since come [to the Academy] as auxiliary workers."

15. H. C. Speer, *Fourth Biennial Report Superintendent of Public Instruction, 1883–84* (Topeka: State Printer, 1885), p. 128; Doug Thompson, "A Historical Study of Dunlap, Kansas and the Negro Exodus," Social Science Research Project, Emporia State University, May 1974.

16. Kansas Colored Literary and Business Academy of Dunlap, Morris County KS, Business Report, November, 1881, cited in Thompson, "A Historical Study of Dunlap, Kansas," pp. 80–81.

17. *Morris County Times*, February 27, 1880; Andrew Atchison, *The Freedmen's Aid Association of Dunlap, Kansas*, pamphlet, vol. 1, 1881, KSHS. The pamphlet noted, "About forty families have settled in the village . . . [I]t is their desire to obtain small farms." The 1880 census also shows that most exodusters initially settled in or near the village. Atheam, *In Search of Canaan*, p. 278.

18. *The Freedmen's Aid Association of Dunlap, Kansas*, pamphlet, 1881; Andrew Atchison to John P. St. John, August 22, 1881, Governor St. John Letters file, KSHS. My count of white families includes those in Dunlap Village and in Valley Township, Morris County, that are listed in the 1880 federal census. The white population would have been considerably larger had I counted Agnes City and Americus townships in Lyon County as part of the area. Tenth United States Federal Census, Morris County KS, Valley Township and Dunlap Village, 1880, K-19, vol. 13, Reel 390.

19. T. R. Cannon, "True Freedom and How to Gain It," *Dunlap Chief*, April 28, 1882. Atheam quotes an E. D. Bullen, of Dunlap, who had written Governor St. John in 1882 and claimed "'the Association is doing a good work for the colored people . . . but [it is] so very obnoctious [sic] to the whites,'" *In Search of Canaan*, p. 271.

20. *Morris County Times*, September 26, 1879.

21. *Morris County Times*, March 5, 1880. *The Dunlap Courier*, July 11, 1891, listed under the heading "colored churches" Methodist-Episcopal, Baptist, and First Mount Zion Missionary Baptist. *Dunlap Chief*, March 10, 1882; Fred Bernard, p. 3, and London Harness, p. 6, *Flint Hills Oral History Project*. See also, *Morris County Times*, March 5, 1880; *Dunlap Courier*, July 11, 1891.

22. Kansas State Agricultural Census, Morris County, Valley Township, 1885, vol.

183, reel 93, KSHS. Farm sizes are based on a comparison of white and black farms in Agnes City Township in Lyon County, where black farm holdings were somewhat larger than those in other black settlements.

23. *Morris County Times*, December 19, 1879; Andrew Atchison, *Topeka Daily Capital*, October 19, 1882, Morris County clippings, KSHS; United States Federal Census, Lyon County, Agnes City Township, 1880, reel 390, schedule 2; Kansas State Agricultural Census, Lyon County, Agnes City and Americus townships, 1885, KSHS.

24. The Freedmen's Aid Association, "Quarterly Report of the Freedmen's Aid Association of Dunlap, Kansas," February 1, 1882, pamphlet, vol. 4, KSHS.

25. A. B. Whiting's Subdivision, Tract Records, Morris County, Register of Deeds Office, Council Grove KS. For example, see H. W. Watkins Grantee, Ann F. Jamison Grantor, May 1, 1889. The land was in Section 27, Township 17, Range 9 east.

26. "Quarterly Report," February 1, 1882.

27. Atchison, "An Urgent Appeal"; Hillyer's Subdivision, Plat Record No. 27, S. E. quarter of Section 12, Township 17, Range 9 east, Tract Records, Morris County, Register of Deeds Office, Council Grove KS.

28. Bernard, *Flint Hills Oral History Project*, p. 3. Kansas State Agricultural Census, Dunlap City, Morris County KS, 1895, vol. 250, reel 200, schedule 2. I came to this conclusion after determining the tenants of each subdivision and comparing their farms and livestock holdings as listed in the 1895 census.

29. The (Council Grove) *Republican and Democrat*, May 25, 1878, discussed folk notions about the bottoms and uplands; Hickey and Webb discuss Kansas pioneer perceptions of the bottoms and uplands in "The Transition From Farming to Ranching." After 1889 I found no record of any additional land purchases by the Academy. Moreover, in 1889 the Academy sold all of its holdings to R. A. Boyd, a local businessman. See also Romine, "Freedmen's Academy Mystery."

30. Robert W. Richmond, *Kansas a Land of Contrasts* (St. Charles MO: Forum Press, 1974), p. 125; Daniel Fitzgerald, *Ghost Towns of Kansas* (Holton KS: Bell Graphics, 1982), vol. 3: 228; Harness, *Flint Hills Oral History Project*, p. 16; Athearn, *In Search of Canaan*, p. 278.

31. Fred A. Shannon, *The Farmer's Last Frontier, Agriculture 1860–1897* (New York: Farrar and Rinehart, 1945), p. 235; Scott G. and Sally McNall, *Plains Families* (New York: St. Martins Press, 1983), p. 27.

32. Kansas State Agricultural Census, Valley Township and Dunlap City, Morris County, Kansas, 1885, Americas and Agnes City townships, Lyon County, Kansas, 1885, 1895, 1905, and Garfield Township, Morris County KS, 1895, 1905.

33. Romine, "Freedmen's Academy Mystery." See also Louis H. Douglas and Scott Shelley, *Community Staying Power: A Small Rural Place and Its Role in Rural Development* (Manhattan: Kansas State University, Research Publication 171, 1977), p. 27n7, KSHS.

34. Kansas State Agricultural Censuses, Americas and Agnes City townships, Lyon County KS, 1895, 1905, Garfield Township, Morris County KS, 1895, 1905.

35. London Harness, *Flint Hills Oral History Project*, pp. 16, 27. One of the Emancipation Day celebrations is mentioned in *The Americus Greeting*, September 19, 1890.

36. Athearn, *In Search of Canaan*, pp. 201; *Freedmen's Aid Association*, pamphlet, vol. 5, 1883, KSHS.

37. McDaniel, "History of Nicodemus, Graham County," p. 18; see also Athearn, *In Search of Canaan*, pp. 270, 156.

38. *Morris County Times*, December 19, 1879; *The Dunlap Reflector*, January 15, 1897.

39. Taped interview by author with London Harness, Emporia KS, August 1990.

CHAPTER 3

Vengeance without Justice, Injustice without Retribution: *The Afro-American Council's Struggle against Racial Violence*

SHAWN LEIGH ALEXANDER

"The Negro's friend has dwindled to a Smith & Wesson pistol, a Repeating Rifle, 50 rounds of ammunition for each, a good, strong nerve, a lesson in good marksmanship, and then use." That was the call from the editors of the *Wichita Searchlight* on January 19, 1901, just one week after the streets of Leavenworth, Kansas, witnessed the burning of Fred Alexander, a twenty-two-year-old black Spanish-American war veteran. The brutal murder of Alexander horrified many African Americans throughout the region, who decided that it was time to stand up and let their grievances be heard by argument and hot lead if necessary. It was in this environment that many black citizens banded together to create a state branch of the country's only national civil rights organization of the period, the Afro-American Council. This article highlights the activities of the Kansas Afro-American Council and its response to the lynching of Fred Alexander. In doing so it demonstrates that the Council, on the national and local levels, represented the persistence of a protest tradition in post–Reconstruction America and showed the desire among certain individuals for the creation and preservation of a national civil rights organization.[1]

To understand the desire of many within the African American community to create a national civil rights organization, it is important to know the social and political situation in which much of the community lived. Only a generation removed from slavery, African America remained locked in a brawl with white America over their very existence. Although many white Americans prospered during the Gilded Age and the Progressive Era, benefiting from limited political, social, and economic reforms, conditions for African Americans reached their lowest point in the post-Emancipation era. This was a time of political disfranchisement, segregation, sharecropping, mob violence, Social Darwinism, and pseudoscientific racism. In the economic sphere, laws were written and rewritten to restrain black mobility. In politics, beginning in 1890 with the Mississippi Plan, which used a combination of literacy tests, an "understanding" clause, and a poll tax, African Americans were systematically disenfranchised in much of the South and the border states. In the social realm, beginning with Tennessee in 1880, states steadily passed statutes that segregated African Americans on railroad cars, in depots, and on wharves. Then, after the Supreme Court declared the Civil Rights Act of 1875 unconstitutional in 1883, southern governments began banning blacks from public and private establishments, including hotels, restaurants, theaters, parks, and libraries. Within a few years numerous states also began instituting laws that segregated schools, and in little over a decade the Supreme Court, with its famous decision in *Plessy v. Ferguson*, legally sanctioned Jim Crow or racial segregation as long as the facilities provided were equal.[2]

De jure political and social segregation was only the symbolic result of a process and system that was being imposed by a reign of terror on black individuals and communities throughout the nation from virtually the end of the Civil War into the twentieth century. From 1880 through 1910 the visibility of racial violence assumed new proportions as violence beset and frequently consumed reform throughout the nation. The act of lynching and mob violence was used to intimidate blacks into submission in the political, social, and economic realms. These lynchings often became ritualistic affairs, where blacks of all ages and genders were slowly executed by mutilation and burning in a public forum, often with a carnival-like atmosphere.[3]

In the latter part of the nineteenth century, de facto and de jure discrimination, violence, and intimidation defined the racial order throughout the nation. The black community in Kansas was not protected from this situation. During the Civil War and in its immediate aftermath, a number of freed and free men and women moved to the state in search of political and economic opportunity. The migration continued throughout the 1870s, and as the racial climate deteriorated in the South following the collapse of Reconstruction, southern migrants developed what historian Nell Painter has called Kansas Fever. During the period between 1870 and 1880, the black population of Kansas increased to more than 40,000. Almost immediately Kansans of both races began trying to hammer out some sort of modus vivendi, and while the rigid Jim Crow system that became synonymous with southern states did not fully develop in Kansas, de facto and de jure discrimination was practiced in the region.[4]

When the Supreme Court overturned the Civil Rights Act of 1875 in 1883, one of the five cases they reviewed originated in Hiawatha, Kansas. Following the court's ruling, as in other regions of the country, discrimination in public accommodations arose throughout the state. Furthermore, racial violence reared its ugly head occasionally in the Sunflower State as the lynchings in Fort Scott (1881) and Topeka (1889) demonstrate. African Americans in Kansas and throughout the nation dealt with this assault on their political and civil rights and their personal safety by overwhelmingly turning inward, looking to the African American community, its institutions, organizations, and fraternal, mutual aid, and beneficial societies, for protection, solace, and guidance. One of these developing organizations was the Afro-American League and its successor, the National Afro-American Council.[5]

The architect of the Afro-American League was the unyielding radical journalist T. Thomas Fortune. As early as 1884 Fortune had used the editorial page of his paper, the *New York Globe*—subsequently renamed the *Freeman* and finally the *Age*—to promote the formation of a national organization to defend against the hostile conditions from which the black population suffered. In 1887, after the continued decline of African Americans' civil and political rights, support for Fortune's proposed civil rights organization gained strength. In that year, the young Booker T. Washington expressed his enthusiasm for the idea when he wrote, "Push the battle to the gate. Let there be no hold-up until a League shall be found in every village." John Mitchell Jr., the outspoken editor of the *Richmond Planet*, also showed his support in his paper when he called for black America to "follow words with action. . . . Let the cry for organization go forth until the country is girdled with organizations of colored men who will be able to demand recognition and force the respect due the law by all men." Mitchell was so encouraged by the prospects of the League idea that he created the first state League in Richmond, Virginia, on June 22, 1887.[6]

In Kansas, the African American community was also heeding Fortune's call for a race organization. Blacks in Topeka created a League during the fall of 1887, and over the next few years the idea of the League gained momentum throughout the state. Leagues formed in Kansas City, Wichita, and Leavenworth, and in the final months of 1889 supporters of the league idea called for a state convention of the new civil rights group.[7] With this support in Kansas and other locales, Fortune called for a nationwide meeting to formulate a national body that would coordinate the efforts of the local leagues. On January 15, 1890, 141 delegates from twenty-one states gathered to create the first national civil rights organization in the United States.[8]

Over the next three years of its existence, the Afro-American League challenged attempts to segregate schools in Ohio, discrimination in insurance rates in New York, and separate coach laws in Tennessee. The organization also tested discrimination in restaurants with the case of its second president, T. Thomas Fortune, versus the Trainer Hotel, which became a kind of embarrassing cause célèbre for the movement due to Fortune's reported fondness for drink. Despite these small instances of success, however, the national organization folded in the early months of 1893. Fortune cited the lack of funds as the reason for the quick demise of the group. Less than a year after proclaiming the organization defunct, he attempted, to no avail, to rekindle the League flame around the anti-lynching activities of Ida B. Wells, but ultimately the League quietly faded away on the national scene.[9]

The protest tradition, however, did not die. Among a certain cadre of individuals, the desire for an active civil rights organization continued to be a goal. In September of 1898, two years after the Supreme Court's *Plessy v. Ferguson* decision had declared the doctrine of "separate but equal," and the year the court upheld Mississippi's disfranchisement legislation in *Williams v. Mississippi*, this desire became a reality, as the Afro-American League was reborn on the national level as the Afro-American Council. Among the leadership of the new organization was Bishop Alexander Walters, president; Ida B. Wells-Barnett, secretary; and T. Thomas Fortune, director of the executive committee.[10]

In its first year of activity, the organization solidified its Legal and Legislative Bureau and outlined its plan of attack on the growing Jim Crow system. The Legal Bureau, initially under the direction of Library of Congress librarian Daniel Murray, placed its attention, among other activities, on the increase of lynching and mob violence directed toward the black community. Such action became increasingly important following the horrible lynching of Sam Hose in Georgia. Following the brutal murder of Hose, the Council planned a day of prayer and fasting and organized ministers of all denominations to address the issue from the pulpit on June 4, 1899. Furthermore, the Literary Bureau of the Council sent out an appeal to all southern governors demanding that they use their offices to see that all citizens in their jurisdiction received justice.[11]

Two months later the Council held its first annual convention in Chicago. At this meeting the delegation agreed, among other things, to have the Anti-Lynching Bureau, under the leadership of Ida B. Wells-Barnett and John Mitchell Jr., investigate all lynchings and have their findings published. Moreover, the group agreed to have the Legal and Legislative Bureau draft an anti-lynching bill that Council member and North Carolina representative George H. White would introduce to Congress.[12]

Black communities throughout the nation, including those in Kansas, supported this action. While the Council was in session, the editors of the *Parsons (Kansas) Weekly Blade* applauded the actions of the Council and the principal participants, Daniel Murray, George White, and Edward Brown, in drafting the proposed national anti-lynching legislation. They also celebrated the action of Nebraska Council members who were advocating the passage of a state anti-lynching bill. They did not believe, however, that such a measure was necessary in Kansas at the time, despite the occasional incidents of racial violence in the region. Such sentiment would change in Kansas in the coming year and a half.[13]

Over the next year, the Council worked on its proposed objectives. Brown, Murray, and White drafted the organization's anti-lynching bill, and the group also raised money for its proposed case against Louisiana's grandfather clause. In other activity, Ida B. Wells-Barnett went on a speaking tour throughout the Midwest and the upper East Coast to solicit funds for the Anti-Lynching Bureau. The organization also continued to promote the formation of local and state branches throughout the country.[14]

By the second year of its existence, the organization began to gain some strength. This strength was especially demonstrated by the actions of the local councils that became more active around regional issues. In previous studies of the Afro-American Council and African American civil rights organizing during the period, scholars have remained focused on the national organization and the activities of the national leadership rather than on local activities of the group, preventing many from recognizing the extent to which the locals took matters into their own hands and defended their rights without the guidance or support of the national organization. Such is the case with the growth of the Kansas Afro-American Council and its activities around the lynching of Fred Alexander.[15]

In October 1900 the town of Leavenworth witnessed the first of a series of disturbing headlines that made the area newspapers over the next several months. On October 18 the *Leavenworth Times* warned the community that there was a black male "lurking around." The paper ran an article on the fourth page entitled "Negro Attempts to Assault White Girl." In the piece the journalist explained that a young woman had been followed and attacked on her walk home. Though she could not describe the assailant, she was certain that it was an African American male.[16]

Over the next few weeks, the local papers reported assaults on several other women in the city. Then, on November 7, Bessie Dougherty, a twelve-year-old African American girl, found the body of a young white woman in a ravine near Lawrence Avenue. Frightened, Bessie ran to tell her aunt what she had seen. They returned to the ravine and were unable to identify the girl. Shortly after, a crowd gathered and a white male, William Forbes, came forward and sadly identified the young woman as his nineteen-year-old daughter, Pearl. According to reports, William Forbes explained that his daughter must have been attacked when she was walking home from her job at the chocolate department of a cracker and candy factory on the evening of November 6. The family was not alarmed when she did not return from work the previous evening because she sometimes spent the night with a coworker, Mary Johosky.[17]

The police and Coroner Harry W. Koohler quickly came to the ravine and began investigating the crime. Everyone on the scene immediately feared that she had been sexually assaulted, but despite the fact that her underclothing was torn, the coroner concluded that no sexual contact had taken place. There apparently had been a struggle, however, since the weeds were trampled down, her hair was disheveled, and there was a contusion above her right eye in addition to the visible hand marks on her throat. In his final report the coroner determined that Pearl was strangled during the affair.[18]

Though the assailant had done very little to conceal the crime, there were few clues as to who actually perpetrated the act. The attention, however, immediately fell on the African American community. The white community was also quick to connect the previous assaults to the Forbes murder and to promote the idea that a black incubus was lurking around waiting to pounce on any innocent young white female who happened across his path. In its discussion of the Forbes murder, the *Leavenworth Times* stated, "Although it is not known whether it was a white or colored man who committed the deed it is strongly suspected that it was one of the latter class because of the fact that the man who made all of the assaults was a Negro." With such sentiment in the air, it was not long before the idea of a lynching bee was posited in the minds of the community. As the editors of the *Times* cried out, "[I]f the people of the city have their way, he will be summarily dealt without due recourse to the law."[19]

Uncharacteristically for the turn of the century, however, the white community of Leavenworth did not lynch the first African American male who happened to stumble into the wrong area. Despite the fact that a number of suspects, all black men, were questioned in relation to the Forbes murder, none were charged and the crime remained unsolved for several months. Surprisingly, as tensions and frustrations continued to rise, the community did not call for the immediate execution of any of the suspects without due process of law.[20]

The relative calm of the community is even more surprising since, in addition to the Forbes murder remaining unsolved into the winter months of 1900 and 1901, the assaults on young white women also continued. Less then a month after Bessie Dougherty found the body of Pearl Forbes, the *Times* reported that several more assaults had occurred near the ravine on Lawrence Avenue. Interestingly, according to a report on December 5, the assailant was not African American but a white male wearing a dark, short overcoat and a black cap pulled down over his face. A few days later the *Times* again reported on a series of assaults in the general vicinity of the Forbes murder. This time the reporter explained that two of the victims described their assailant as a large white man, and one described her attacker as a slight black man. Despite these varying descriptions, the community continued to look to the African American community as the source of the crimes. Less than two weeks into the new year, the community would have its incubus.[21]

On Saturday evening, January 12, Eva Roth was walking home from her job when she noticed Fred Alexander following her down Cherokee Street. According to the twenty-two-year-old Eva, she was not at first frightened since she had known Mr. Alexander from childhood. They had both grown up in the same neighborhood. When she turned on Broadway and Alexander turned in the same direction, she became frightened, despite her early calmness. She crossed the Broadway Bridge and went up to the Clark house to wait for him to pass. Once he did, seemingly without noticing her—according to Roth, Alexander passed by whistling and very relaxed—she told herself that she was overreacting and continued down Broadway Avenue. A few moments later she explained that she again felt she was being followed, and when she turned around she was surprised to find that it was for a second time Alexander. This time he was much closer and was able to reach out and grab her. She screamed and Alexander ran off.

William A. Evans, the principal of the local high school and the first on the scene, said that he found Roth lying in the snow and mud. When he asked her what had happened, she claimed that she was attacked by "a darkey that had followed her." She did not name Alexander as her assailant as she later clearly claimed in her recounting of the event. According to Principal Evans, Nona Rollins, a young African American girl who was part of the growing crowd around Ms. Roth, listened to the woman's story and exclaimed, "I know who it was. It was Fred Alexander. He just now ran down the street and into our house." Upon this news the call was put out for Alexander's arrest.[22]

Officer Mike McDonald arrested Alexander within twenty minutes without incident. McDonald took the accused to the police station where he was questioned. Despite Alexander's insistence that he was innocent, he was held in custody. Unlike the previous incidents when individuals were brought in for questioning for the attacks over the past months, many in the community began thinking that they had the person who was responsible for all of the attacks. A large crowd began gathering outside the city jail.

One citizen had gone to the local grocery store and purchased some rope before arriving at the scene. Holding his purchase aloft, he cried out to the gathering crowd, "I am here for the same purpose you men are. I want to feel that my wife and daughters are safe when they are walking along the streets of Leavenworth, no matter whether it be day or night." Then, without mentioning the word lynching, and holding the haunting symbol of the rope in the air, the man asked for all those who supported him and his mission to follow him into the jail to gather the accused.[23]

The mob moved as one toward the jail but was held off by police officers on the scene. Knowing that Alexander had been secretly swept off to another location, the officers, after some discussion, agreed to allow five members of the gang search the premises. After realizing that Alexander was not held at this location, the band of hooligans quickly surmised that he had been relocated to the county jail, and the group moved with "no noise except that of heavy walking" toward the new suspected confines of their villain.[24]

Upon arrival at the county jail, the group was allowed admittance and was shown throughout the premises from the cellar to the garret. They were also allowed to search the courthouse but were unable to locate Alexander. The crowd then realized that they had been outmaneuvered, and deduced that the prisoner must have been taken to the state penitentiary in Lansing. At 11:00 Saturday night, five and half hours after Fred Alexander had supposedly assaulted Eva Roth, the crowd disbursed. The group was not discouraged, however, as many of the men remarked as they were leaving, "Our time will come, he will have to be brought to the city for trial."[25]

During his interrogation on Saturday evening and throughout three hours of a "sweating process" on Sunday, Alexander declared his innocence in the affair. He also proclaimed his innocence in the murder of Pearl Forbes, which, once he was placed in custody, the community quickly assumed he was guilty of as well.

On Sunday, Ed C. Murphy, a city detective, declared that he had suspected Alexander for the Forbes murder long ago. Murphy and another detective had actually questioned the young war veteran one evening and "great beads of sweat oozed out of [Alexander's] forehead," but they did not have "sufficient evidence to arrest him." Moreover, the detective asserted that Roth had claimed that Alexander grasped her by the wrist and placed one hand on her throat. According to Murphy, that was the same manner in which the other girls claimed they were approached and that is how he believed Pearl Forbes was attacked. Murphy claimed that all evidence "points to Alexander as the fiend who attempted the several crimes."[26]

The same day, John Roth, father of Eva, stated that he would charge Fred Alexander with attempted criminal assault, and despite having no evidence, he would also charge Alexander with intent to commit rape. In a special Sunday session, a warrant was sworn out in the city court and placed in the hands of Sheriff Peter Everhardy. The sheriff, Chief of Police Joseph A. Cranston, Warden Joseph B. Tomlinson, and Leavenworth mayor Shaw F. Neeley held a meeting in the police station to arrange for Alexander's return to the city for arraignment.

During the afternoon many white citizens of Leavenworth also met in Bond's hall and formed the Leavenworth Vigilance Committee. The membership of the committee was kept secret, but it was announced that the group was formed for the "purpose of seeing that Alexander was lynched after his guilt had been positively established, especially for the Forbes murder." The group also vowed to work on removing a number of "objectionable characters" from the community. Following the meeting the committee placed "sentinels" on the road leading from the town to the penitentiary as well as at the police station, county jail, and courthouse, with orders to notify the group immediately if any action of moving Alexander was announced or seen.[27]

Leavenworth law enforcement officials could not decide on the best means of moving Alexander from the penitentiary in Lansing back to the courthouse for arraignment. At eight o'clock in the evening, a group of nearly 500 decided not to wait and went to Lansing to demand that Alexander be released to them. Warden Tomlinson refused. Despite the crowd threatening to use dynamite to gain entrance into the penitentiary, he held fast. After a few hours the group concluded that Alexander would have to be brought to the city in the morning for his preliminary hearing. They decided they could wait.

The following day was again full of chess moves between

government officials and the anxious whites of Leavenworth who were now even more determined to see Alexander brought to their form of justice. Crowds developed at the courthouse, the county jail, and the penitentiary in the afternoon. Sheriff Everhardy deputized over twenty individuals and left for the penitentiary. He did not return with the prisoner, as many had expected, and by evening the crowd once again fixed its attention on the penitentiary, since there was no sign that Alexander had yet been moved.[28]

While the mob formed around the penitentiary, rumors began to spread that the black community of Leavenworth was forming a rescue team for the young Alexander. The white community also began to issue threats against the life of county attorney Harry Michaels for his assistance in collecting the affidavits against the prisoner. These actions and rumors made the restless group outside the penitentiary believe that something needed to be done immediately. However, William Forbes, the father of Pearl Forbes, calmed the crowd. He told the anxious mob that the authorities were not moving Alexander on that evening because he had not yet confessed to the murder of his daughter. Once that confession was obtained, he assured them that Alexander would be transferred to Leavenworth, and at that time his fate would most certainly be in their hands. He proclaimed that when they get the confession, they would "then lynch the brute." Forbes and the authorities were convinced that Alexander would confess and were certain that he was the murderer despite only circumstantial evidence against him. Most important in the minds of Forbes and the local authorities, Alexander could "give no satisfactory account of his whereabouts" on that night nearly two months ago.[29]

On Tuesday morning Governor William E. Stanley contacted Sheriff Everhardy and explained that he had made available two companies of the Kansas National Guard for the protection of Alexander. The sheriff refused the assistance, however, and made certain that the governor understood that he, the sheriff, had the power and the will to protect the prisoner. The governor also contacted Warden Tomlinson and instructed him not to turn over Alexander unless the sheriff demonstrated enough strength to protect him.

Throughout the morning the sheriff and the prosecution worked to see if they had enough evidence to formally charge Alexander with the murder of Pearl Forbes. Two Leavenworth police detectives, Ed C. Murphy and Thomas Brady, had signed affidavits claiming that they had visited Alexander's home after midnight following the murder of Pearl Forbes. During their visit they stated that they believed he was guilty but did not have enough evidence to arrest him. A large amount of their suspicion was based on the fact that they found him asleep on his father's floor with only a thin sheet covering him on a night that was extremely cool and that when he was questioned he began sweating profusely. In addition to this signed affidavit, a number of other individuals produced evidence that accounted for Alexander's whereabouts for all but the forty-five-minute time frame when Pearl Forbes was attacked and killed. This circumstantial evidence and the sworn statements were combined with the fact that Eva Roth and fifteen-year-old Kate Gilson, another woman who claimed she was attacked a short time before Miss Roth on Saturday evening, had identified Alexander as the individual who assaulted them. Finally twelve other women implicated Alexander as the man who attempted to attack them over the course of the past few months. All of these incidents were held together by claims that in every incident, the individual following the victim was whistling, and that Alexander had a habit of whistling.[30]

The legal forces in the Leavenworth region believed that this was enough evidence, and on January 15, at 1:50 p.m., the State of Kansas formally charged Fred Alexander with the murder of Pearl Forbes. Sheriff Everhardy, Deputy Sheriff Stance Myers, and a number of special deputies went to the penitentiary to serve Alexander with the new charges. In addition, the group went with the intention to bring Alexander back to Leavenworth. Judge Miles Moore demanded Alexander's presence in his courtroom by the end of the afternoon for arraignment in the Eva Roth case. After some discussion about Alexander's protection, Warden Tomlinson turned the prisoner over to the sheriff's custody at 3:14 p.m. Shortly before 4:00 p.m., Alexander was safely transferred to the county jail.[31]

Within minutes of Alexander's arrival, a large mob of more than 5,000 people surrounded the jail. In less than thirty minutes the mob had gained entrance into the jail and had acquired keys to the cells. The gang grabbed Alexander and led him to the ravine where Pearl Forbes's body was found. Members of the group tied Alexander to a rail and covered him with kerosene from a Standard Oil tank wagon that stood nearby. William Forbes came forward and asked Alexander to confess to the murder of his daughter. Though his fate was certain, Alexander did not confess. Instead, he turned to the crowd and proclaimed, "People, you are killing the wrong man. Some day you'll run up against the right man, the man who killed the girl." These were his last words. Forbes struck a match. Alexander was set afire, only blocks from his family's home.[32]

The fire died down after Alexander's body had burned for nearly three hours. "The young men of Leavenworth, who considered the measure necessary for protection of their sisters, wives and sweethearts," carried off the "shriveled hands and ears of the victim . . . as mementoes. . . . [Men], Women and children [also] fought . . . for fragments of the boards which the fire left unconsumed. . . . One man secured the handcuffs and went away delighted with his good fortune."[33]

After eight o'clock, county coroner Koohler arrived and collected what was left of Alexander's remains. He placed the remains in a wooden coffin and took them to Sexton's undertaking for public viewing. According to reports, for more than an hour a "constant stream of people passed through and reviewed the charred and almost shapeless mass of burned flesh" with a "morbid curiosity."[34]

The following day, Coroner Koohler and a jury of six local representatives determined that Alexander had come to his "death by having been burned to death . . . by parties unknown." The coroner declared that he believed that everyone had become "unconscious about 4 o'clock yesterday afternoon." He reported that he had done all he could to secure evidence against someone, but nobody knows who was in the mob." After the inquisition was completed, the remains were turned back over to the funeral home, after which undertaker James Sexton requested the Alexander family to come and collect the remains of their son for proper burial. It was reported that only one member of the family, Fred's younger brother, came to view the body. The family refused to bury the body, and Alfred Alexander, Fred's father and a seventy-one-year-old exoduster, said, "The people have mutilated him, now let them bury him." The city unceremoniously buried Fred Alexander in Mount Muncie Cemetery during the afternoon of January 16. Only the driver accompanied the remains.[35]

Condemnation of the city of Leavenworth for the murder of Fred Alexander was strong and fierce. The *St. Joseph Gazette* exclaimed, "[S]hame, shame upon the people of Leavenworth." The *Kansas City World* thought that the "action of the mob at Leavenworth will be an everlasting disgrace that the Sunflower state will not recall." The editors believed that the actions of the mob put at "naught all that Kansas has ever done for the emancipation and elevation of the descendents of Ham." Finally, the *Detroit Journal*, like the *St. Joseph Gazette*, believed that Kansas had shamed itself. The editors exclaimed that Kansas had "violated all her traditions and covered herself with a disgrace that can never be washed away." Moreover, "that such a crime could be perpetuated in Kansas, the citadel of equal rights and the original forcing ground of abolition, only intensified the lawlessness of the atrocious proceeding."[36]

The Kansas Legislature and Governor Stanley agreed with the press coverage of the brutal murder of Fred Alexander. The legislature condemned the act and called for a thorough investigation, demanding that "the perpetrator of this monstrous proceeding shall be punished to the full extent of the law." Governor Stanley explained that he believed Sheriff Everhardy and Warden Tomlinson were responsible for Alexander's death. Despite his belief that both public officials were guilty, he reserved his harshest criticism for Everhardy. "The sheriff of Leavenworth is either a despicable scoundrel or a despicable coward," asserted Stanley. The sheriff had assured him that he could and would protect Alexander. Otherwise, the governor would have sent in the military force that he had at the ready. "The sheriff is to blame, and nobody else," explained the governor. Stanley proclaimed that he would reprimand him in some way and that he was considering a $500 reward for the apprehension of any of the ringleaders. The *St. Joseph Daily News* concurred with the governor and called for him to restore the death penalty and make the sheriff the first person to be arrested, tried, convicted, and hanged as an accessory to murder.[37]

While the blame game continued, Sheriff Everhardy expressed his innocence while isolating himself from the public, claiming that he had become ill after all the stress of the Alexander affair. In other activity, the Kansas Legislature introduced a symbolic resolution that called for the expulsion of Leavenworth from the state. The Missouri Legislature responded by announcing that they would adopt the city as part of Platte County. Finally, Albert Alexander went to the press and expressed his son's innocence, proclaiming that he and his family were calling upon the governor to issue a reward for the apprehension of the ringleaders of the lynching.[38]

Following the lead of the Alexander family, the black citizens of Kansas responded to the murder of Fred Alexander in a proactive manner. Many African Americans appealed for the community to turn inward and called for the use of self-defense if the white community continued to use such barbaric actions against the black citizens of the state. The *Wichita Searchlight* exclaimed that the African American community needed to arm themselves. Any black citizen of Kansas without a "Smith & Wesson pistol, a Repeating Rifle, [and] 50 rounds of ammunition for each . . . [was] foolish." The *American Citizen* believed that the burning of Alexander was "a solemn warning" to African Americans "all over the country to get together or stay apart and be exterminated."[39]

Amid these calls for self-defense and self-reliance, African Americans throughout the region began to hold conventions condemning the actions of the mob in Leavenworth and discussing the response the community should take. Five hundred blacks met in Kansas City under the auspices of the National Negro Business League on January 22. Supporters of the Afro-American Council throughout the region also began to organize. As the League was meeting in Kansas City, 300 Council supporters convened in Wichita. They condemned Alexander's burning and called upon the governor and the legislature to apprehend and punish the perpetrators. Moreover, in keeping with earlier sentiment, they believed that the culprits of the crime included "the cowardice of a set of weak officials who are unworthy of the offices they pretend to hold."[40]

During the final days of January, black Kansans also met in Arkansas City, Emporia, Edwardsville, and Topeka. In Topeka 150 concerned blacks converged in a hall on Kansas Avenue to discuss the necessary action. The principal speaker at the event was W. B. Townsend of Leavenworth, who called upon those in attendance and the black community of Kansas in general to assert their manhood and "attend to Negro Business."

In an address to the people of Kansas, the convention called for all citizens of the state to unite for the proper enforcement of all laws and urged the governor, the attorney general, and the Leavenworth county attorney to apprehend and convict the perpetrators of the Alexander murder. The group also called upon all black citizens of Kansas to unite under the Afro-American Council and apply pressure to the state's political machine to prevent Kansas from becoming "another Georgia." Similar sentiments were raised in the other meetings. Finally, they and the other local groups that met throughout the state agreed to hold a meeting in Topeka on February 22 to perfect the state Council. Moreover, Dr. William H. Hudson of Atchison, the chairman of the executive committee of the Kansas Afro-American Council, asked all charities and organizations to correspond with him in order to discuss the action the Council should take in response to the Alexander murder.[41]

In addition to the activity in Kansas, Council members in various places throughout the country met to show support for the Kansas organization and its burgeoning struggle. In Des Moines, Iowa, for instance, Council supporters gathered to celebrate Abraham Lincoln's birthday and to condemn the lynching of Fred Alexander. C. B. Woods, the president of the Des Moines Council, called the meeting to order and impressed upon the audience the necessity of uniting to end the so-called race problem. As he stated, "[Y]ou must not expect some other race to solve the question for you, but do it yourself and above all things, let your motto be, 'United we stand; divided we fall.'" Local attorney George Woodson also pushed the issue of unity and forcibly impressed upon the audience that only through unity of action within the Afro-American Council would the race be able to gain some method "to stop the burning of our fellow man."[42]

Throughout the month of February, the supporters of the Council continued to drum up support for the formation of a unified organization. A week before the proposed state conference, the group published a strong appeal urging all to attend, asserting that it was "better to drown unitedly [sic] trying to swim than to die with muscles and brain, either idle or disconcerted." According to Dr. Hudson and his cosigners, unity was necessary to prevent another "Fred Alexander burned in the state, just because he is black."[43]

In addition to the formation of a more permanent Afro-American Council in Kansas, a group of ministers from throughout the state were organizing the Ministerial Union. Nearly 200 concerned citizens gathered on February 17 in Kansas City. Albert Alexander was present at the meeting and asked for those in attendance to aid him and his family in finding and prosecuting the ringleaders of the crime. Moreover, he provided the audience with details of his son's prosecution that he claimed were not carried by the Associated Press. He described how detectives had come to his house after the Forbes murder, but despite the claims of the Leavenworth law enforcement, they were unable to find evidence that Fred was the murderer. Finally, in relation to the lynching, he declared that the Associated Press had sanitized the crime and had chosen not to publish all the gruesome details, including the attempts of the crowd to force his son to eat his own flesh prior to being set afire.

The Ministerial Union took up a collection to start a fund to aid in the capture and prosecution of the perpetrators of the Leavenworth burning. "Since Kansas unfortunately has a Governor who has not seen fit to offer a reward" that he had promised, explained Reverend Henry V. Plummer, president of the organization, "the appeal to every negroe's [sic] pocket book must be stronger." Finally, the group of ministers and their supporters agreed to assist the Council in any plans they developed in Topeka at the end of the week.[44]

Five days after the meeting of the Ministerial Union in Kansas City, African Americans converged on Topeka to form the Kansas State Afro-American Council. In the group's published resolutions, among other things, the more than one hundred delegates from about fifteen counties created an executive committee with the mission to call upon Governor Stanley, asking him to post the reward for the arrest and prosecution of the members of the mob. The delegates also agreed to urge Attorney General Aretaf A. Goddard to bring charges against the officers who were derelict in their duties and to implore the legislature to pass legislation to suppress mob violence. In addition, the delegates raised several hundred dollars of their own to combine with any reward that the governor might offer. Finally, the Council and the Ministerial Union agreed to join their activities.[45]

Council supporters understood that their activity was not going to be easy. White citizens throughout Kansas, but particularly in Leavenworth, were taking issue with the organizing activities of the black community. In Leavenworth on the eve of the Council meeting, W. B. Townsend's home was destroyed by a mysterious fire, the second such fire in the black community since the Alexander murder. Members of the Council understood that this was a deliberate attack on Townsend for his open support for the formation of the Council and for the push to prosecute the ringleaders of the lynching. The Council acknowledged this, declaring that the organization would not stand for such action against the black community and that they would defend their homes in any way necessary.[46]

The day after the convention, the Council's executive committee, led by attorney James H. Guy of Topeka, met with Governor Stanley and succeeded in convincing him to offer the $500 reward for the apprehension and conviction of Fred Alexander's murderers. According to the governor's published proclamation, he would only offer the reward for the apprehension and arrest of any of the killers for ninety days. If the Council could not apprehend the "unknown party" within ninety days, the reward would no longer be paid. With this limited yet successful start, the Kansas Afro-American Council hit the road running in their attempt to get blacks in the state the "same treatment that other races" received.[47]

Over the next month, the Kansas Afro-American Council continued to move quickly. At the end of March, Dr. William H. Hudson informed his constituents that eleven cities had formed branches and sent money for the Alexander case. Moreover, Hudson explained that the state council's executive committee had begun to negotiate with lawyers on how to proceed with the case and implied that the suit would include an investigation of the local sheriff's involvement in the lynching. Finally, not satisfied with the war chest the group had secured, Hudson and the other Council executives ambitiously called upon the organization's members to raise $10,000 to assist in the capture and conviction of the Fred Alexander mob and to bring to "justice any official whose derelection [sic] of duty aided and abetted" the crime.[48]

On April 13 Alfred Alexander and representatives of the Council approached County Attorney Harry Michael with evidence in the crime and asked him to issue a warrant for the arrest of William Forbes, one policeman, and one city official. The exact nature of the charges were not released nor was the response of the county attorney. In their coverage of the events, the editors of the *American Citizen* called upon African Americans throughout Kansas to not be deterred and to support the Council and Alexander in their actions. "If you have race pride you have an opportunity to show it," declared the editors.[49]

With this flurry of activity, the Kansas Afro-American Council demonstrated that they were prepared to fight for their rights. By mid-May, as the deadline of the governor's reward approached, the *Topeka Plaindealer* reported, "[S]everal lawyers have been seen [and] sworn depositions have been taken in the city which gloats of burning a live[sic] a 'nigger' like fiends of hell to a heart-rendering death. . . . [And] the details of procedure have been carefully planned." Now the editors assured their readers, the Council was "ready to take the next step in the open."[50]

The move did not take place quickly. County Attorney Michael dragged his feet on the Council's requests for warrants and ultimately concluded that the Council's evidence was insufficient. Because of Michael's apathy and negligence, the Council missed the governor's deadline for the reward. This, however, did not discourage the Council. During the first week of June, the *Topeka Plaindealer* again discussed the Fred Alexander affair, this time focusing on the legal case. J. H. Childers, chief editor of the *Plaindealer* and a Council member, informed his readers that reward or no reward, the Kansas Afro-American Council was laboring to "visit retribution upon the head of the cowardly sheriff of Leavenworth county, whose complicity in the recent outrageous crime . . . is conspicuous." Furthermore, Childers explained that the Council was compiling evidence to prove that the sheriff was actually "a party to this dastardly crime." What Childers and the Council asked their Kansas constituents to do at the moment was to continue to send donations for the legal case and aid the Council in advocating for the state legislature to pass anti-lynching legislation. The Kansas Council desired the passage of such legislation that existed in Ohio and South Carolina where the counties could be held responsible for injuries to persons and property committed by mobs.[51]

Within a month the Council, working in conjunction with the Ministerial Union, met with Kansas attorney general Goddard and asked him to remove Leavenworth sheriff Everhardy from office. The group had called upon the attorney general back in February, making a similar request, but he had told them they needed to collect the necessary evidence to have him consider such action. After five months of quietly gathering affidavits, the group presented the attorney general with twenty sworn statements accusing the sheriff of "neglect of duty and malfeasance in office." Upon receiving the evidence, Goddard told the group that he would survey the material and take the appropriate action. The Council, however, did not passively wait for him to act. In an attempt to prevent the attorney general from sweeping the case under the rug, they took their case to the press and had both the *Topeka Plaindealer* and the *Kansas City Journal* publish the evidence.[52]

When the evidence was made public, the *Leavenworth Chronicle* published the report of the Council's call on the attorney general under the headline

> One Lesson isn't enough. Colored people trying to stir up trouble over the Alexander affair. They want Sheriff Everhardy ousted and have filed a lot of papers with Attorney General Goddard. The people of Leavenworth settled the Alexander matter to their own satisfaction and any Negroes not satisfied can have another lesson if they wish.

The editors of the *Topeka Plaindealer* responded by proclaiming that "the Negroes of Kansas stand ready to meet the class of hudlums [sic] and pug-uglies," and they asserted that "the second lesson" would not "be such a one sided affair as the first."[53]

Unfortunately for the Council and its supporters, the Kansas political machine was not going to charge one of its officials for the murder of Fred Alexander no matter how much evidence they brought to the attorney general. Poet Sterling Brown years later hauntingly expressed the sentiments that surely were on the minds of the black citizens of Leavenworth and many throughout the country facing similar injustices:

> They got the judges
> They got the lawyers
> They got the jury-rolls
> They got the law
> They don't come by ones
> They got the sheriffs
> They got the deputies
> They don't come by twos

They got the shotguns
They got the rope
We git the justice
In the end
They come by tens.⁵⁴

The citizens of Kansas got word in mid-September that, after dragging his feet for a number of months, Attorney General Goddard did not deem the evidence sufficient to sue for the removal of Sheriff Everhardy from office. Many in the organization believed that the attorney general was acting out of political ambition, as he had "the supreme court judgeship bee buzzing in his political Stetson," but his refusal was still a setback. Following the decision, the Council referred its case to Governor Stanley, who had supported the activities of the organization with his offering of a reward for the apprehension of the murderous ruffians. The governor's support, however, did not include the removal of a public official despite the fact that he had implicated the sheriff directly following the murder of Alexander. Moreover, as the editors of the *Topeka Plaindealer* pointed out, Stanley had larger political goals, as he was "ambituous [sic] to be [a] United States Senator" and they did not believe that he would risk his political dreams on the prosecution of a white public official for the murder of an African American.⁵⁵

Ultimately, the *Topeka Plaindealer* was correct. Governor Stanley would not gamble away his political future and refused to step in and remove Sheriff Everhardy from office. Despite the setback, however, members of the Kansas Afro-American Council continued to organize for their social and political rights. Over the next few years, the Kansas branch of the Council became one of the group's strongest in the Midwest. Moreover, the organization's attempt to remove the guilty public official was a bold move for any group of African Americans living in the South or the lower Midwest at the turn of the century and foreshadowed an approach that the National Association for the Advancement of Colored People would use in the coming decades.

While the actions of the Kansas Afro-American Council in the Alexander affair are remarkable for the period, they were not alone in their attempt to defend their rights in the region. Local branches of the Council in the Midwest and Great Plains were active throughout the period, as was demonstrated in the Iowa branch's support for the Alexander case and the early activity of the Nebraska Council to pass an anti-lynching bill in their state. Moreover, in addition to the activity in these states, there were active councils throughout the region, including Colorado, Illinois, Minnesota, Missouri, Oklahoma, New Mexico, Texas, and Wisconsin. Furthermore, in addition to the activity of the Afro-American Council, black men and women in the region were lending their support to other developing African American organizations such as the National Negro Business League and the National Association of Colored Women's Clubs.

All of this activity is an example of African Americans throughout the country organizing for their self-help and self-defense during the period in which the promises of the Reconstruction era were being systematically stripped away. Moreover, setbacks or defeats such as the Alexander affair did not detour the cadre of individuals who knew their rights and had the courage to defend them. Throughout the early twentieth century the Council on the national and local levels continued to press forward with their own legal struggles. At the same time as the legal fight in Kansas, for example, the National Council instituted a challenge of the Louisiana "grandfather clause" as well as two suits challenging the changes to the Alabama suffrage laws. The Legal and Legislative Bureau also testified before congressional committees on the Irwin and Morrill bills, which called for the creation of a commission to investigate the condition of the race in the southern states and for an amendment to the Interstate

Commerce Law, respectively. Furthermore, the Council took on the lawsuit of H. T. Johnson, editor of the *Christian Recorder*, against the Pullman Company.[56]

These activities by the Afro-American Council and those by its predecessor, the Afro-American League, represent an important chapter in African American social and political thought. In a period increasingly dominated by the ideas of industrial education and accommodation, the League and the Council represented the persistence of a protest tradition. The group's platform of emphasizing civil rights and suffrage, along with promotion of racial solidarity, economic nationalism, and self-help, was an attempt to merge into one organization many of the political ideologies that dominated black intellectual thought at the time. The activities of the two groups between 1890 and 1909, and of the organizations that developed in their wake, represented examples of African America's various organizational responses to the growing Jim Crow system. More importantly, the activities of the League and Council demonstrate that there was agitation in the age of accommodation, which paved the road for many of the activities developed by the National Association for the Advancement of Colored People over the past century, especially their "go into the courts and fight it out" mentality.[57]

Notes

The author expresses his thanks to Ernest Allen Jr., John H. Bracey Jr., David W. Blight, Glenda Gilmore, David Goldberg, and James Smethurst for their guidance on this article, and to Kelly M. Farrell for her editorial comments, encouragement, and support.

1. *Wichita Searchlight*, January 19, 1901; Emma Lou Thornbrough, "The National Afro-American League, 1887–1908," *Journal of Southern History* 27 (November 1961): 494–512; Emma Lou Thornbrough, *T. Thomas Fortune: Militant Journalist* (Chicago: University of Chicago Press, 1972); August Meier, *Negro Thought in America: 1880–1915: Racial Ideologies in the Age of Booker T. Washington* (Ann Arbor: University of Michigan Press, 1963); Robert Factor, *The Black Response to America: Men, Ideals, and Organization from Frederick Douglass to the NAACP* (Reading MA: Addison-Wesley, 1970); Shawn Leigh Alexander, "'We Know

Our Rights and Have the Courage to Defend Them': Agitation in the Age of Accommodation, 1880–1910" (PhD diss., University of Massachusetts–Amherst, 2004).

2. Rayford Whittingham Logan, *The Betrayal of the Negro: From Rutherford B. Hayes to Woodrow Wilson* (1965; reprint, New York: Da Capo Press, 1997); August Meier, *Negro Thought in America: 1880–1915: Racial Ideologies in the Age of Booker T. Washington* (Ann Arbor: University of Michigan Press, 1963); Leon Litwack, *Trouble in Mind: Black Southerners in the Age of Jim Crow* (New York: Alfred A. Knopf, 1998); Wilson J. Moses, *The Golden Age of Nationalism, 1850–1925* (Hampden CT: Archon Books, 1978); Kevin K. Gaines, *Uplifting the Race: Black Leadership, Politics, and Culture in the Twentieth Century* (Chapel Hill: University of North Carolina Press, 1996); Factor, *Black Response to America*; Edward L. Ayers, *The Promise of the New South: Life after Reconstruction* (New York: Oxford University Press, 1992); C. Van Woodward, *The Strange Career of Jim Crow* (New York: Oxford University Press, 1966).

3. NAACP, *Thirty Years of Lynching in the United States, 1889–1919* (New York: National Association for the Advancement of Colored People, 1919), 29. See also Ayers, *Promise of the New South*, 301–4, 435–37; Herbert Shapiro, *White Violence and Black Response: From Reconstruction to Montgomery* (Amherst: University of Massachusetts Press, 1988), 65–75, 96–103, 104; and Michael J. Pfeifer, *Rough Justice: Lynching and American Society, 1874–1947* (Urbana: University of Illinois Press, 2004).

4. Thomas Cox, *Blacks in Topeka, Kansas, 1865–1915: A Social History* (Baton Rouge: Louisiana State University Press, 1982); Nell Irvin Painter, *Exodusters: Black Migration to Kansas After Reconstruction* (New York: W. W. Norton, 1977); William H. Chafe, "The Negro and Populism: A Kansas Case Study," *Journal of Southern History* 34 (August 1968): 402–19; Randall B. Woods, "Integration, Exclusion, or Segregation?: The Color Line in Kansas, 1878–1900," *Western Historical Quarterly* 14 (April 1983): 181–98.

5. Cox, *Blacks in Topeka*, 111–35; Chafe, "The Negro and Populism"; Woods, "Integration, Exclusion, or Segregation?"; August Meier and Elliott M. Rudwick, *From Plantation to Ghetto* (New York: Hill and Wang, 1970). There were nineteen African Americans lynched in the Kansas from 1882 to 1968. See *Chronological Listing of Lynching Victims, 1882–1968*, located in the archives of Tuskegee University in Tuskegee, AL.

6. *New York Freeman*, June 18, July 9, and September 17, 1887; Thornbrough, *T. Thomas Fortune*, 108. See also Louis R. Harlan and Raymond Smock, eds., *The Booker T. Washington Papers*, 14 vols. (Chicago: University of Illinois Press, 1972–1989), 2:357. For a discussion of Fortune's editorial career, see Thornbrough, *T. Thomas Fortune*, especially 35–135. For a short look at Fortune's career, see Cyrus Field Adams, "Timothy Thomas Fortune: Journalist, Author, Lecturer, Agitator," *Colored American Magazine* 4 (January–February 1902): 224–28; Donald E. Drake, "Militancy in Fortune's *New York Age*," *Journal of Negro History* 55 (October 1970): 307–22; William Seraile, "The Political View of Timothy

Thomas Fortune: Father of Black Political Independence," *Afro-Americans in New York Life and History* 2, no. 2 (1978): 15–28; and Jean M. Allman and David R. Roediger, "The Early Editorial Career of Timothy Thomas Fortune: Class, Nationalism and Consciousness of Africa," *Afro-Americans in New York Life and History* 6, no. 2 (1982): 39–52 [55]. For information on Booker T. Washington, see Meier, *Negro Thought in America*; Louis R. Harlan, *Booker T. Washington: The Making of a Black Leader, 1856–1901* (New York: Oxford University Press, 1972); and Harlan, *Booker T. Washington: The Wizard of Tuskegee, 1901–1915* (New York: Oxford University Press, 1983). For information on John Mitchell Jr., see Ann Field Alexander, *Race Man: The Rise and Fall of the "Fighting Editor" John Mitchell, Jr.* (Charlottesville: University of Virginia Press, 2002).

7. *Commonwealth*, August 31, 1887; *Benevolent Banner*, September 10, 1887; *Leavenworth Advocate*, November 23 and 30, 1889, and April 26, 1890; Cox, *Blacks in Topeka*, 134–35.

8. *Western Appeal*, December 22, 1888; *Official Compilation of Proceedings of the Afro-American League National Convention, January 15, 16, 17, 1890* (Chicago: J. C. Battles and R. B. Cabbell, 1890), 8.

9. *Indianapolis Freeman*, July 14, 1894; Alexander, "'We Know Our Rights,'" 1–152.

10. Alexander Walters, *My Life and Work* (New York: Fleming H. Revell, 1917), 98, 104–9; George Mason Miller, "'A This Worldly Mission': The Life and Career of Alexander Walters (1858–1917)" (PhD diss., State University of New York at Stony Brook, 1984), 165–68; Ida B. Wells-Barnett, *Crusade for Justice: The Autobiography of Ida B. Wells*, ed. Alfreda M. Duster (Chicago: University of Chicago Press, 1970), 255–56; Thornbrough, *T. Thomas Fortune*, 179, 185; Factor, *Black Response to America*, 128–29. For the Plessy decision, see *Plessy v. Ferguson*, 163 U.S. 537 (1896). For the Williams decision, see *Williams v. State of Mississippi*, 170 U.S. 213 (1898).

11. *Salt Lake Broad Ax*, June 6, 1899; *Colored American*, June 3, 1899; *Washington Post*, June 11, 1899. For information on the Sam Hose lynching, see W. Fitzhugh Brundage, *Lynching in the New South: Georgia and Virginia, 1880–1930* (Urbana: University of Illinois Press, 1993); and Philip Dray, *At the Hands of Persons Unknown: The Lynching of Black America* (New York: Random House, 2002). For the Council's response, see Alexander, "'We Know Our Rights,'" 170–84.

12. Cyrus Field Adams, *National Afro-American Council: A History of the Organization Its Objects, Synopses of Proceedings, Constitution and By-Laws, Plan of Organization, Annual Topics, Etc.* (Washington DC: Cyrus Field Adams, 1902), 6–8. For more descriptions of the Council's Chicago Convention's resolutions, see *Western Appeal*, August 19, 1899; *Colored American*, August 26, 1899; *Chicago Broad Ax*, August 26, 1899; and W. E. B. Du Bois, "Two Negro Conventions," *The Independent* 51 (September 7, 1899): 2426. See also Miller, "'A This Worldly Mission,'" 212–13; and Benjamin R. Justesen, *George Henry White: An Even Chance in the Race of Life* (Baton Rouge: Louisiana State University Press, 2001).

13. *Parsons Weekly Blade*, August 25, 1899. For information on *Parsons Weekly Blade*, see Arnold Copper, "'Protection to All, Discrimination to None': The *Parsons Weekly Blade*, 1892–1900," *Kansas History* 9 (1986): 58–71.

14. Adams, *National Afro-American Council*, 26–28; Alexander, "'We Know Our Rights,'" 153–213; and Shawn Leigh Alexander, "The Afro-American Council and Its Challenge of Louisiana's Grandfather Clause," in *Radicalism in the South Since Reconstruction*, ed. Chris Green, Rachel Rubin, and James Smethurst (New York: Palgrave, 2006), 13–38.

15. Thornbrough, "The National Afro-American League"; Thornbrough, *T. Thomas Fortune*; Meier, *Negro Thought in America*; Factor, *Black Response to America*. See also Alexander, "'We Know Our Rights,'" 214–61.

16. *Leavenworth Times*, October 18, 1900. It is not clear who Bessie Dougherty ran to; the *Times* indicates that she ran to her tell her aunt. At the time Bessie was living in the home of her grandparents, Henry and Anna Smith. Mary Johosky lived with her parents, John and Mary, at 353 Lawrence Avenue, a short distance from the scene of the crime.

17. *Leavenworth Times*, November 8, 1900.

18. *Leavenworth Times*, November 8, 1900.

19. *Leavenworth Times*, November 8, 1900. See also Amy L. Waters, "Alexander Burned: Burned at the Stake: The Fred Alexander Lynching in Leavenworth KS," unpublished paper, Leavenworth Public Library, 1998:3. For the term incubus being used this manner, see Glenda E. Gilmore, "Murder, Memory, and the Flight of the Incubus," in *Democracy Betrayed: The Wilmington Race Riot of 1898 and Its Legacy*, ed. David S. Cecelski and Timothy B. Tyson (Chapel Hill: University of North Carolina Press, 1998), 73–94.

20. For an example of historical work on lynching and mob violence during the period, see Brundage, *Lynching in the New South*; Dray, *At the Hands of Persons Unknown*; Shapiro, *White Violence and Black Response*; Pfeifer, *Rough Justice*; Pfeifer, "The Ritual of Lynching: Extralegal Justice in Missouri, 1890–1942," *Gateway Heritage* 13 (Winter 1993): 22–33; Stephen J. Leonard, *Lynching in Colorado, 1859–1919* (Boulder: University Press of Colorado, 2002); Clare V. McKanna, *Homicide, Race, and Justice in the American West, 1880–1920* (Tucson: University of Arizona Press, 2002); and McKanna, "Black Enclaves of Violence: Race and Homicide in Great Plains Cities, 1890–1920," *Great Plains Quarterly* 23 (Summer 2003): 147–59.

21. *Leavenworth Times*, December 5 and 8, 1900. See also Waters, "Alexander Burned," 4.

22. *Leavenworth Evening Standard*, January 14, 1901. Nona Rollins lived at 733 Chestnutt Street with her parents, John and Lisa, and her three brothers. Chestnutt Street intersected South Broadway Avenue, near William Evans's home at 715 South Broadway Avenue.

23. *Leavenworth Evening Standard*, January 14, 1901.

24. *Leavenworth Evening Standard*, January 14, 1901.

25. *Leavenworth Evening Standard*, January 14, 1901.

26. *Leavenworth Evening Standard*, January 14, 1901.

27. *Leavenworth Evening Standard*, January 14, 1901.

28. *Leavenworth Evening Standard*, January 14, 1901.

29. *Leavenworth Evening Standard*, January 14, 1901; *Leavenworth Chronicle*, January 15, 1901.

30. *Leavenworth Chronicle*, January 14 and 15, 1901; *Leavenworth Evening Standard*, January 14 and 15, 1901; Waters, "Alexander Burned," 8.

31. *Leavenworth Chronicle*, January 15 and 16, 1901; *Leavenworth Evening Standard*, January 16, 1901.

32. *Leavenworth Chronicle*, January 16, 1901; *Leavenworth Evening Standard*, January 16, 1901; *Leavenworth Times*, January 16, 1901; *American Citizen*, January 18, 1901.

33. *American Citizen*, January 18, 1901; *Leavenworth Times*, January 16, 1901.

34. *Leavenworth Evening Standard*, January 16, 1901.

35. *Leavenworth Evening Standard*, January 16 and 17, 1901. See also Records of the Leavenworth County Coroner: Death Records January 5, 1901, to April 14, 1906, "Copy Verdict of Jury Inquest Fred Alexander," and "Coroner's Death Record," Kansas State Historical Society, Topeka, KS.

36. *St. Joseph Gazette*, January 16, 1901; *Kansas City World*, January 16, 1901; *Detroit Journal*, January 16, 1901. See also *Evening Standard*, January 17, 1901.

37. *Evening Standard*, January 16, 1901; *Topeka Daily Capital*, January 17, 1901; *American Standard*, January 18, 1901.

38. *Evening Standard*, January 22, 1901; *Leavenworth Times*, January 22, 1901; *Leavenworth Chronicle*, January 23 and 26, 1901.

39. *Wichita Searchlight*, January 19, 1901; *American Citizen*, January 18, 1901.

40. *American Citizen*, January 24, 1901.

41. *Topeka Plaindealer*, February 1, 1901. Black citizens of Kansas also met and drew up similar resolutions in Arkansas City, Emporia, and Edwardsville.

42. *Iowa State Bystander*, February 15, 1901.

43. *Topeka Plaindealer*, February 15, 1901.

44. *American Citizen*, February 22, 1901.

45. *American Citizen*, March 1, 1901; *Topeka Plaindealer*, March 1, 1901; *Wichita Searchlight*, March 2, 1901. In a strange course of events, while the Council was forming in Kansas it was announced that John W. Forbes, brother of William Forbes, the man who lit the fire to burn Alexander, married a twenty-four-year-old African American woman in Shelbyville TN. See *American Citizen*, March 1, 1901, and *Topeka Plaindealer*, March 1,

1901. The *Topeka Plaindealer*, March 8, 1901, ran a satirical editorial commenting on the situation: "The white citizens of Leavenworth, who burned Alexander, in order to show that they are opposed to the mixing of the white and black races must feel very very proud of the indorsement [*sic*] their efforts have received from the Forbes family."

46. *Topeka Plaindealer*, March 1, 1901.

47. *American Citizen*, March 1, 1901; *Topeka Plaindealer*, March 1, 1901.

48. *Topeka Plaindealer*, March 22, 1901; *American Citizen*, March 22 and 29, 1901. Kansas Council secretary Fred Roundtree did say the organization would use some of the funds to aid the national organization in their activities. See *Topeka Plaindealer*, March 22, 1901.

49. *American Citizen*, March 29, 1901.

50. *Topeka Plaindealer*, May 10, 1901.

51. *Topeka Plaindealer*, June 7, 1901.

52. *Topeka Plaindealer*, July 19, 1901. See also *Iowa State Bystander*, July 26, 1901. One affidavit claimed, "Reddy McDonald, a deputy sheriff, rode into town ahead of the sheriff and party from the prison and told the crowd that Alexander was on the way." Along with the evidence collected by the Council and the Ministerial Union, many citizens of Leavenworth were convinced that the mob murdered an innocent man. A few days before the group met with the attorney general, 150 people held a vigil at the sight of Alexander's murder. During the vigil, the minister asked the Lord to show them his divine wisdom and let it rain in the next twenty-four hours if Alexander was guilty of the crimes he was accused. As the *Topeka Plaindealer* and the *Topeka State Journal* reported, twenty-four hours had passed and not a drop of rain had fallen in Leavenworth. See *Topeka Plaindealer*, July 19, 1901.

53. *Leavenworth Chronicle*, July 18, 1901; *Topeka Plaindealer*, July 19, 1901.

54. Sterling Brown, "Old Lem," in *The Collected Poems of Sterling Brown*, ed. Michael S. Harper (New York: Harper and Row, 1980), 170–71.

55. *Topeka Plaindealer*, September 18, 1901.

56. House Committee on Labor, *Commission to Inquire into the Condition of the Colored People*, House Report 2194, 57th Cong., 1st sess. (Washington DC: Government Printing Office, 1902), and House Committee on Interstate and Foreign Commerce, *Hearings before the U.S. Congress, House Committee on Interstate and Foreign Commerce of the House of Representatives*, 57th Cong., 1st Sess. (Washington DC: Government Printing Office, 1902), 437–454. See also Alexander, "'We Know Our Rights and Have the Courage to Defend Them,'" 289–476; and Shawn Leigh Alexander, "The Afro-American Council and its Challenge of Louisiana's Grandfather Clause," 13–38.

57. Alexander Walters, "The Afro-American Council and Its Work," *Colored American Magazine* 11 (September 1906): 207.

CHAPTER 4

Prelude to Brownsville:
The Twenty-Fifth Infantry at Fort Niobrara, Nebraska, 1902–1906

THOMAS R. BUECKER

Around midnight on August 13, 1906, gunshots suddenly rang out on the deserted streets of Brownsville, Texas. Unknown parties indiscriminately fired at a number of private residences, severely wounding a police officer, and into a nearby saloon, killing a bartender and slightly wounding a patron. Apparently all victims were Hispanics. When the ten-minute fusillade was over, witnesses claimed black soldiers from the Twenty-fifth Infantry stationed at adjacent Fort Brown were responsible for the outrage. Substantiation for their accusations seemingly came when civil and military authorities discovered expended military cartridges at the scene.[1]

The Brownsville citizenry had not been happy when they received word that the black Twenty-fifth was to be stationed at nearby Fort Brown and several race-related incidents had occurred between soldiers and white townspeople—Brownsville was a southern town and Jim Crow laws prevailed. After the shooting, anger against the alleged soldier assailants quickly spread across the country. Understandably, debate in the national press divided along racial lines. Although it was never proved in a military court who perpetrated the shooting, President Theodore Roosevelt ordered the First Battalion of the Twenty-fifth, the entire garrison at Fort Brown, dismissed from the

United States Army. The soldiers and their supporters fought those discharges for decades to come.

Three weeks before the shooting, the soldiers, described as an "exceptionally bad lot of disgraceful ruffians," who were accused of a "horrible atrocity . . . unparalleled for infamy," had been transferred from a fort in Nebraska.[2] There they had been seen as a "peaceable, orderly, well behaved set of soldiers."[3] Closer examination confirms that the experience of the Twenty-fifth Infantry at Fort Niobrara stands in stark contrast to what followed at Brownsville.

Setting the Scene

The Twenty-fifth Infantry was organized in 1866 as one of several regular army cavalry and infantry regiments to be composed solely of black enlisted men. The regiment served in Texas until transferred to the Department of Dakota in 1880. During the Spanish-American War it participated in the invasion of Cuba and again served overseas in the Philippine Insurrection. In 1902 the regiment was returned to the states as part of the regular rotation of overseas units.[4]

Fort Niobrara, in Cherry County in north-central Nebraska, had been established in 1880 to guard the Rosebud reservation just across the border in South Dakota. From the mid-1880s until 1898 it housed large troop components and became an impressive installation of more than seventy buildings. The nearby town of Valentine greatly benefited from the sizable military payroll and related subsistence and construction contracts.[5]

All of this changed with the Spanish-American War and subsequent Philippine Insurrection, when troops were mobilized for overseas deployment. The reduction of troops at the post, at one time down to twenty-seven men, brought corresponding financial despair to the local businesses. In 1901 another blow came when Fort Niobrara appeared on the abandonment list. As well as being deemed no longer vital to the safety of nearby communities, the old frontier posts in the interior were expensive to maintain.[6]

At the turn of the century the United States Army was in a state of flux in regard to size, function, and location of its garrisons. Even though larger and more centralized posts were being planned and built, garrisons were needed now for the large numbers of soldiers returning from the Philippines, and some of the older posts fit the bill. Regarrisoning the old posts of Forts Robinson and Niobrara in Nebraska would bring satisfaction to the impatient local communities and their congressional delegates.[7]

By the late summer of 1902, the Twenty-fifth Infantry arrived stateside. Regimental headquarters, band, and the First and Third Battalions were assigned to Fort Niobrara. The Second Battalion went to Fort Reno, Oklahoma. Just after arriving in the states, the soldiers received the "somewhat gloomy information" that their new home would be Nebraska. Service there was a distinct departure from the Philippines, where the soldiers enjoyed life among "its free-and-easy-going native society." In the words of the regimental chaplain, Nebraska was a dreary place.[8]

Black Soldiers, White Town

As was typical at many western duty stations on the upper Plains, the soldiers found themselves in a largely white society. By 1900 Valentine reported a population of 973, only twelve of whom were black. With hundreds of Valentine citizens at the depot to greet them, the First Battalion arrived in Valentine on August 17, 1902. Five days later the Third Battalion pulled in and marched the four and one-half miles southeast to the fort.[9] Because the post had been largely vacant, the new garrison found it overrun with rattlesnakes. It was several weeks before the reptile occupants were cleaned out.[10]

In addition to an overabundance of snakes, the soldiers found other immediate disadvantages. With the companies at full strength, the barracks were overcrowded. Buildings originally built for sixty men now housed one hundred. Most soldiers resolved to adjust to the desolation and inconvenience of their new station; but others could not. In September thirteen men of the regiment deserted, by far the largest number to desert in a single month.[11]

While the soldiers adjusted to their new situation, the local citizens sized up their new neighbors. The white community had had experience with black soldiers before. From 1885 to 1891 companies of the Ninth Cavalry had served at Fort Niobrara, garrisoned with a larger number of white troops. This time it was a different situation, with only black soldiers comprising the garrison.

Elsewhere, when word reached a white community that black troops were to arrive, fear and anxiety quickly arose and conflict often resulted.[12] Valentine did not protest—they welcomed the Twenty-fifth Infantry. Valentine was a post town, and its citizens keenly appreciated the benefit of a large garrison. Soldiers were soldiers, and they would bring a welcome boost to the sagging local economy. Generally speaking the manifestations of overt racism on the northern frontier were far less serious than those in the south and southwest.[13] By 1903 Chaplain Theophilus Steward, an African American, reported, "our men enjoy the very high favor of the people of the vicinity so far as I hear any expression."[14] In Valentine, the townspeople realized the days of Fort Niobrara were numbered and wanted to take advantage of a large garrison regardless of race.

The bottom line for a "post town" was money from the soldiers. Understandably, the merchants' business flourished after the monthly payday. Soldier pay brought more than twelve thousand dollars into Valentine's economy each month. After the first payday for the Twenty-fifth, a local paper noted, "Since then they have been making business lively in town which is fully appreciated by every citizen of Valentine, reminding them of the good old days before the recent Spanish-American War."[15] Not only did soldiers spend their pay, but local building contractors received construction and repair contracts. The post absorbed thousands of dollars worth of locally procured food, grain, hay, and wood each year.

During this period of American history, race relations were at a very low point, but in many parts of the west, including Valentine, the color line had not been drawn. The black regimental chaplain, Theophilus Steward, was frequently invited to deliver sermons in Valentine churches, something not generally seen in other parts of the country.[16] On one occasion, arrangements were made for an "Emancipation Day" commemoration in town. Discharged soldiers confidently sought employment with local ranchers and businessmen. George Schuyler, long-time editor of the black weekly *Pittsburgh Courier*, noted, "in those few places where people treated the Black soldiers as human beings, relations were usually harmonious."[17] To the Twenty-fifth Infantry, Valentine proved the rule rather than the exception.

Much of the racial climate of a community was expressed in its local press. As in other localities, one Valentine paper tentatively approved and yet put the soldiers on probation:

> A more gentlemanly or better behaved lot of men never garrisoned Fort Niobrara than they have thus far proven themselves to be and may it be said to their credit they show a disposition to create less disturbance and noise than did many white soldiers who have been stationed here. They are evidently from the best class of their race and so long as they conduct themselves in the commendable way set out they will have the confidence and good will of our people as a whole.[18]

The regiment never flunked its probation at Niobrara.

Another factor for racial harmony was the closeness of an Indian population. Valentine was only seven miles south of the Rosebud Sioux reservation, and the old fears of uprising dating back to 1890 remained fresh. As late as 1904 a Valentine paper wrote that Nebraska needed its military posts "because of the Indians and the thinly populated districts adjoining."[19] Frank Schubert, a historian of the black military, has pointed out that close proximity to Indian reservations was fundamental to shaping the attitudes of local whites. He identified a two-category racial system in which reservation Indians were the lower of the two categories. The townspeople would then accept Black soldiers in order to maintain that dichotomy. Schubert also noted that the "reservation may well have exerted a greater positive influence on black and white relations than American egalitarian rhetoric or the frontier itself."[20]

The soldiers of the Twenty-fifth Infantry quickly became an accepted and valued segment of life in Valentine. The soldiers "were on the most friendly terms" with the citizens there.[21] In Valentine there was no discrimination against the soldiers either in local businesses or in state law. As a result, soldiers at Fort Niobrara received better treatment from whites than most were accustomed to in civilian life.[22]

Soldier Life

Since Fort Niobrara was a regimental headquarters post, staff officers were assigned there. One of the most valuable and influential was Chaplain Steward, the third African-American U.S. Army chaplain, who was responsible for the moral, educational, and spiritual interests of the command. The Twenty-fifth Infantry Band provided entertainment for the local community. Besides the soldiers, the post was home to seventy-five to one hundred dependents—wives, children, and other relatives of enlisted men and officers. Other camp followers gradually joined the off-post community in and around Valentine.

The service of the infantrymen was typical for the army in

peacetime—stateside garrison duty in the zone of the interior. Soldiers participated in large-scale maneuvers, which came into vogue after 1900 to give officers training in handling large bodies of men and to provide field experience for the National Guard. While the Twenty-fifth was at Fort Niobrara, department maneuvers were held at Fort Riley, Kansas. Other than this, there was little detached service away from the post. In 1903 several companies went to Fort Des Moines, Iowa, for temporary duty. In April 1906 Company A changed station to Fort Washakie, Wyoming. Part of the Wind River Reservation had been opened for settlement, and extra troops were called in to settle any unrest among the Indians there. Along with an un-ending routine of drill and fatigue duty, the soldiers participated in annual practice marches. These lasted a week, with field exercises in defense and reconnaissance. Other military activity included annual inspections.

Changes came with uniform and ordnance improvements. The army converted from the old blue field uniform to the more functional khaki. Early in 1906 the soldiers received the new model 1903 Springfield rifle, and a main part of their military training was work on the target range. The regular season ran from May 1 through July 31, with an extra month in the fall. Soldiers received preliminary small arms instruction and fired in the indoor gallery before moving on the range for company and battalion competition.[23]

As was usual with soldiers in garrison duty, morale was a prime consideration. In the fall of 1902, the army was reduced in strength, resulting in the loss of nearly 250 men at the fort. Average company size dropped from ninety to sixty-five. Many men were discharged when their terms ran out, with more than three hundred leaving in 1905 alone. Large turn-over frequently left "the garrison unsettled" when experienced men left.[24]

Desertion could serve as an indicator of morale. Historically, desertion was extremely low in the black regiments compared to the white units and the desertion rate at Fort Niobrara—1.7 men per month for a garrison averaging six hundred men—was low even for black regiments. Only eighty-one soldiers deserted during the four years the regiment was at Fort Niobrara. Black soldiers found army life a good alternative to that in the civilian world.[25]

Post morale must have been affected by new men coming into the regiment "who have not settled down into regular ways."[26] Recruits generally arrived at their stations with little training or discipline. Most were young men from the South who undoubtedly suffered "culture shock" when they arrived in the desolation of north-central Nebraska. The severity of winter was hard on recruits and veterans alike. As one soldier recalled, "Worst of all, the privy was outside the barracks . . . a picture of a fellow making that run at night in zero weather would be amusing indeed ."[27]

The relationship between the enlisted men and the officers of the Twenty-fifth regiment was good. Major Charles W. Penrose recalled his troops were "well drilled—I considered it [his battalion] one of the best that I have ever seen." He added, "The men were easy to discipline."[28] Other officers favorably compared the black soldiers to any other troops they served with. Some felt the enlisted men took great pride in their officers, and apparently most enlisted men got along with the officers and actually liked them.[29]

At this time, however, white society was growing increasingly hateful toward blacks, and white officers who commanded black soldiers bore a stigma. White officers considered service in black regiments a poor career choice.[30] The turnover rate of officers in the Twenty-fifth was high, and by 1906 most had served two years or less with the regiment. Many of the lieutenants were enlisted men commissioned into the regular army after the Spanish war or West Point graduates with low class rankings. The only black officer with the regiment was Chaplain Steward, who joined in 1891. Colonel Alpheus Bowman, who commanded the regiment when it arrived at Niobrara, was a Civil War veteran. Colonel Ralph W. Hoyt, who assumed command in 1904, had at that time thirty-two years service as a commissioned officer. Neither had had any previous service with black troops until he was promoted by grade into the regiment. As was typical in the old army, company officers left most of the management of their soldiers to veteran non-commissioned officers.[31]

Off Duty

Reports of violence committed by soldiers on leave in Valentine were no more numerous and perhaps fewer than at other post towns of the era. Soldier related intrusions and beatings involving civilians were occasionally reported. No shooting incidents involving whites were ever reported, although several shootings between blacks happened. One evening in November 1903 two quarreling soldiers started a shooting scrape, one wounding the other three times. The newspaper did comment, "three of the shots were wild and had the usual number of people been on the streets, some innocent party might have been killed."[32]

Another problem arose when, after an evening on the town, soldiers "borrowed" horses from private barns and used them to return to the fort. At the post the horses were merely turned loose. But all this was relatively tame when compared to conduct of white Twelfth Cavalrymen in Crawford while that regiment was stationed at Fort Robinson.[33]

Activities and entertainments for off-duty enlisted men were much the same as at other isolated western posts, although there was little official consideration given to off-duty recreation and entertainment. At the same time, there were few restrictions on how the soldiers spent their free time.

Sports

Athletics proved the main sanctioned off-duty diversion for the soldiers, and team sports entertained both soldiers and local spectators.

There was no color line, as most competitors were white civilian teams. Baseball was by far the favorite soldier sport. Early in 1903 post athletic officers carefully selected a regimental baseball team and organized company and battalion level teams for inter-regimental and local competition. The regimental nine played civilian teams from Gordon, Valentine, Ainsworth, and other western Nebraska communities, as well as Tenth Cavalry teams from Fort Robinson. Large numbers of eager Valentine residents attended games in town, while for one contest at the fort, "Every available rig in town was brought into service to convey our townspeople to the scene of the ball game."[34] During the Twenty-fifth's stay at Fort Niobrara, the regimental team lost only three ball games, one to a Deadwood team and two to Gordon.[35]

Boxing both in town and at the post was likewise popular. Regimental champions frequently met challengers from as far off as Omaha in matches before hundreds of spectators. In January 1904 the hall was packed when Hamp Ireland, champion of the Twenty-fifth, defeated John Brown of the Eleventh Infantry. White civilian boxers came from Hot Springs to spar with soldier contenders. Before one match, the paper accurately predicted, "It is quite likely that Valentine will be deserted tonight by its male population—the attraction being a boxing contest at Fort Niobrara."[36]

Other activities included hunting in the surrounding prairies for grouse, prairie chickens, and ducks. Soldiers occasionally played football, though it was not especially popular, particularly after the Fort Robinson eleven defeated the 1904 post team 41–0. Throughout much of the year, the training process for all enlisted men included monthly "field day" exercises. Large numbers of interested civilian spectators usually watched field day competitions in track and field and other team events as well as the drills and exercises put on by the garrison for senior inspecting officers.[37]

Arts and Entertainment

The Twenty-fifth Infantry band was an immensely popular source of entertainment for both the soldiers and Valentine citizens. During the years at Fort Niobrara, the band played in numerous concerts. One program featured the overture from "The Bohemian Girl," followed by a Caprice from the "Midway Plaisance," selections from "The Red Hussar," winding up with a medley of songs, "Salute to Erin." During summer months open air concerts were presented weekly on the post parade ground. In 1904 the band toured several towns along the railroad, where dances usually followed their concerts. For one 1903 concert, the Valentine citizenry was promised "a musical treat such as is only heard in the large cities."[38]

In keeping with the times, soldier minstrel shows also entertained the post and local community. One show featured a farcette called "An Elephant on His Hands," songs, stump speech, dance sketch, and an encore, "Dr. Hipp, the Hypnotist." Late in 1903 a group of soldiers presented vaudeville shows in town featuring "Edison's Exhibition Kinetoscope." Also that year the garrison furnished a quartette for joint G. A. R. Memorial Day observances. And in the winter of 1905 the Fort Niobrara Minstrels gave a benefit performance at the county courthouse for the rectory fund of St. John's Church.[39]

At Fort Niobrara the black enlisted men had at least some opportunity for educational and spiritual enrichment. Chaplain Steward conducted day school for the children and enlisted men's school in afternoons and evenings. By December 1902 his soldier school had seventy students, instructed by four assistant teachers. At least once a week Steward lectured on U.S. history and civil government. Although educational work took time away from his chaplaincy duties, he found "the interest manifested by the enlisted men in the main is good."[40]

Throughout his tour at Fort Niobrara, Steward worked constantly to fill his combination chapel-school house. He was "convinced that our religious work contributes an important share to the contentment of the garrison."[41] During the first years in Nebraska, the soldiers supported a YMCA group that had been organized in the Philippines and received traveling libraries from the YMCA international committee.

The Sporting Life

Off-reservation entertainments also proved identical to those at other western posts. Lax law enforcement that tacitly acknowledged worldly desires led to the "happy go easy way" familiar to post town morality and not restricted by the color line. Soldiers frequented local saloons where they drank alongside white patrons with no objection. Blacks were also freely served in eating places and patronized local stores and businesses. Soldiers remarked on how well they were treated by the white population whenever they came into town.[42]

Nevertheless, the soldiers operated in white surroundings; while in town they were expected to keep in line. Shortly after the regiment arrived in Valentine, Colonel Bowman issued a circular that complimented the soldiers' conduct yet warned: "It rests with the enlisted soldiers of the regiment to proudly maintain their well-earned reputation for gallantry in their sober, self-respecting, manly conduct among our Nebraska friends."[43]

Not all their needs could be met within the city limits. Enterprising individuals opened up several "resorts" or "sporting houses" that catered to the black soldiers. These resorts were located outside town along the Niobrara River between one and one-half and four miles from the post. By 1903 Charlie Price's Harris House, and Stratton & Kline flourished as combination bar-gambling-dance hall-brothel operations.

The river resorts mushroomed because the black soldiers needed places where they could gather and socialize freely away from the predominately white society. Operated by blacks, some of whom were discharged soldiers, the resorts were located close to the fort, actually within the military reservation, on land homesteaded before the reservation was declared. Besides liquor and gambling, "vile picture machines" and female companionship were readily available. The soldiers often referred to the resorts as "hooks" and the soldier patrons as "hookers." One veteran recalled "there were some habitues of the 'dives' who would brave the bleak cold and drifting snow to have their nightly whirl with the denizens in their abodes of debauchery."[44]

Resort operations openly sold liquor without proper licenses. Some local citizens protested that although the "hooks" were outside the city, they were still under county jurisdiction, but the "hooks" continued their profitable operation. Between 1902 and 1906, however, fifteen of the twenty-one incidents of serious violence involving soldiers that occurred, originated at the resorts. Eleven of the incidents involved shooting injuries, including four deaths. Petty bickering, jealousy over female affection, and inter-regimental bad blood appear to have been the main causes. By 1906 nearly all county court prosecutions grew out of crimes originating at the resorts.[45]

Prostitution, both at the resorts and in houses in town, was another vice available to soldiers. In Valentine, "Auntie" Deliah Cole ran a popular boarding house used by local prostitutes, and by 1905 four or five similar houses were operating in the Valentine vicinity. At the post hospital, the number of cases of venereal disease treated monthly grew three-fold to sixteen by the fall of 1905.[46]

For those short of funds for gambling, women, or liquor, Private John Hollomon was the "financial man." He loaned money at twenty-five percent per month and arranged credit for soldiers with saloon owners and merchants in town. He was captain of the regimental baseball team, and his henchmen, known as the "dirty dozen," rounded out the team.[47]

Cleaning Up the Joints

Immorality was continually under fire from both the post and the town. In December 1902 Chaplain Steward reported that he had been able to shut down "a miserable den of vice." He lamented the "disreputable houses" well-advertised in the post and the many "bad women domiciled" near the post who were "wielding a very strong influence." In 1903 leading citizens unsuccessfully attempted to close down gambling houses in Valentine.[48]

On October 29, 1904, a serious shooting incident shocked the state. Unknown parties fired shots into a group standing in front of Stratton's resort, hitting Lulu "Red Top" Johnson, a female employee, and two male civilians. Johnson died the next day. Soldiers were immediately blamed when witnesses claimed two men with rifles had been seen heading to the fort just after the shooting and a number of fired military cartridges were found where the shots seemed to have originated. The governor of Nebraska quickly offered a two hundred dollar reward for information, but a conspiracy of silence—foreshadowing future events—seems to have ruled among the soldiers. Although a political leader claimed that "numbers of the enlisted men might have full knowledge of men and motive," no guilty parties were ever identified.[49]

The wide-open lifestyle readily available to Fort Niobrara soldiers led to calls for reform. Early in the spring of 1904 the Valentine city council ordered the saloons in Valentine to remove all gambling machines and devices. By 1905 the council ordered the local saloons, which had an income of sixty thousand dollars a year, to close at midnight every night and stay closed all day Sunday. Naturally, this drove business to the resorts.[50] In the same year the town cracked down on prostitution. Deliah Cole was arrested and charged with renting rooms for lewd purposes and harboring prostitutes. After subsequent raids on her place a local paper carefully pointed out, "such places will be prosecuted regardless of color." Its editor urged more action: "Our town has too long been run a 'happy go easy way' to the detriment of every citizen of good intent."[51]

In the winter of 1905–6, Colonel Hoyt and county officials (strongly supported by Chaplain Steward) confronted the river resorts. Prostitution trials in town divulged that when gambling in town shut down, Valentine saloon owners sent their machines and paraphernalia to the resorts. W. P. Westover, the district judge from Rushville, quickly ordered the sheriff to raid the river resorts and seize all gambling devices. According to the *Valentine Republican*, "The blow almost took the breath away from interested parties in town."[52]

The raids were generally successful, but apparently Charlie Price had advance warning; nothing related to gambling activity was found at his place. (Price of course claimed nothing was found because no gambling went on.) Shortly afterward, Stratton's place mysteriously burned to the ground. County officials had instructed the county attorney to "prosecute these keepers until houses of such character are closed up and done away with." Illegal liquor sales also drew prosecutions. In March 1906 the three principal resort operators were each fined five hundred dollars and costs for selling liquor without license.[53] Steward noted the favorable effects of prosecuting the resorts, citing an increase in church attendance by the enlisted men and also "a change on the part of the wives of the soldiers."[54]

Resort business slowed but did not stop. In the spring of 1906, soldier rows continued at Charlie Price's, and in mid-May two soldiers were seriously wounded in a dispute at an unidentified resort south of town. One benefit of the crackdown on the resorts and local whorehouses was noted by the post surgeon, however, who reported "a diminution of venereal disease."[55]

Maneuvers

As usual the soldiers participated in the large maneuvers held in October 1903 at Fort Riley. The Fort Niobrara battalions marched overland to Norfolk, Nebraska, then took the train south to Fort Riley. All along the march, they played baseball games prearranged with local teams. For several weeks, the Twenty-fifth joined some ten thousand regular soldiers, guardsmen, and militia for training. Of the maneuvers, one soldier later recalled:

> we went through a month of strenuous field maneuvering, marching, and counter marching—covering a wide area—sometimes the attacking forces, sometimes the defending forces, but I was never able to determine when we had won or lost, and I don't believe that many of the enlisted men ever were any wiser than me.[56]

The crowning achievement of Fort Niobrara baseball came during an inter-departmental baseball championship series at the close of the maneuvers. The Tenth Cavalry team from Fort Robinson was the favorite, but the Niobrara soldiers played their way to the finals, even defeating the Second Battalion team from Fort Reno. In the championship game, the Niobrara team battled the Robinson cavalrymen for ten innings before winning 3–2.[57]

A Nasty Incident

The maneuvers, however, also brought an ominous harbinger of things to come. The Twenty-fifth Infantry was camped next to a regiment of Texas militia. The Texans first started some trouble with the Tenth Cavalrymen then directed their animosity toward the black infantrymen, hissing, jeering, and openly insulting soldiers and officers of the Twenty-fifth. The constant barrage of racial epithets from the southerners led to several altercations between the two regiment's enlisted ranks. To the Texans, coming from a southern state, "a colored man in uniform represents authority, and this idea suggests superiority, which is bitterly resented."[58] The encampment broke up, and the units returned home, but the incidents with the

Texas soldiers were the beginnings of a legacy of racial problems with Texans for the Fort Niobrara soldiers.

Although the War Department had announced in 1904 that Fort Niobrara was to be abandoned, the post remained in use for a few more years. Valentine residents faced the loss of a large source of revenue, but not all mourned their loss. The *Valentine Democrat* stated, "There may be some consolation for those who derive no benefit from the soldiers . . . and looked on the prevalence of soldiers as a menace to the peace and quietude of the home."[59]

Going To Texas

Formal orders closing Fort Niobrara came in May 1906. By this time many soldiers were ready for a new station; some were jubilant over the news. With deteriorating living quarters, an isolated location, and crackdowns on their off-duty social outlets, the black soldiers were ready to leave Nebraska, regardless of the fair treatment they had received from nearby whites. One soldier recalled, "I was glad to get away from Fort Niobrara, we had been staying there so long, I was glad to get to any old place."[60]

The Twenty-fifth was not unaware that there were potential problems with their transfer to forts in Texas, however. A Nebraskan advised one soldier, "Well, you are glad to leave us now, but you won't be treated so well in Texas as we do here." Another soldier heard, "They will give you a warm reception down there." Many brushed off or ignored any fears. When questioned by a white associate, one soldier replied, "Well, we can give them as good as they send." Recalling the 1903 incidents, Chaplain Steward openly stated in one Sunday service that the people in Texas did not want black soldiers stationed there.[61] Such talk continued until the troops departed.

New stations for the Fort Niobrara garrison placed the First Battalion at Fort Brown, at Brownsville, and the Third Battalion at

Fort McIntosh; regimental headquarters staff and the band were assigned to Fort Bliss. Both battalions were to stop at Camp Mabry, near Houston, to participate in maneuvers with Texas state troops before moving to their new stations.

Rumors quickly broke out that the Texans intended to use live cartridges against the black soldiers during the maneuvers. As a result, Colonel Hoyt strongly protested sending his soldiers to Camp Mabry, and many of his officers predicted that violence would break out between the soldiers and Texas militia. Chaplain Steward feared that Texas would be a quasi-battleground for the Twenty-fifth. Plans to deploy the men to Camp Mabry were dropped, but one company commander warned that, "In my opinion the sentiment in Texas is so hostile against colored troops that there is always danger of serious trouble between the citizens and soldiers whenever they are brought in contact."[62]

Although the maneuver idea was scrapped, the army remained firm in its decision to move the regiment to Texas. At 7:30 p.m. on July 23, 1906, the troops marched out of Fort Niobrara for the last time. At the Valentine depot, the soldiers had to wait for several hours for the train south while hundreds of Valentine citizens gathered to see them off. At midnight the Twenty-fifth Infantry boarded several special trains and left Nebraska. Exactly three weeks later came the infamous Brownsville shooting.

The peaceful coexistence of black soldiers and local Valentine whites sharply contrasts with the racial atmosphere faced by the soldiers in Texas. The racial climate differed for several reasons, including the close proximity of a large Indian population. But the most likely reason for the harmony was economic. The money generated by Fort Niobrara was vitally important to Valentine. As a consequence, the soldiers were treated with respect—even if that respect had to be purchased—and their presence was largely appreciated by the local white population. For a brief period, the Twenty-fifth Infantry was an accepted, valued segment of the community. Here was one case of cooperation and harmony rarely found in a deteriorating racial climate for African American civilians and soldiers.

Notes

1. For more on the Brownsville raid, see Marvin Fletcher, *The Black Soldier and Officer in the U.S. Army 1891–1917* (Columbia: University of Missouri Press, 1974), Ann J. Lane, *The Brownsville Affair-National Crisis and Black Reaction* (Port Washington NY: Kennikat Press, 1971), and John D. Weaver, *The Brownsville Raid* (New York: Norton & Co., 1970).

2. *Summary Discharge or Mustering out of Regiments or Companies*, Senate Document 402, part 1, 60th Congress, 1st Session, 1907–8, p. 238; John M. Carroll, ed., *The Black Military Experience in the American West* (New York: Liveright, 1971), p. 480.

3. *The Brownsville Affray—Orders and Messages of the President, Etc.*, Senate Document 389, 60th Congress, 1st Session, 1907–8, p. 33.

4. All information on the organization and service of the Twenty-fifth Infantry is from Arlen L. Fowler, *The Black Infantry in the West 1869–1891* (Westport CT: Greenwood, 1971), and John Nankivell, *History of the Twenty-fifth Regiment, U.S. Infantry* (1927; rpt. Fort Collins: Old Army Press, 1972).

5. For more on Fort Niobrara, see Thomas R. Buecker, "Fort Niobrara, 1880–1906: Guardian of the Rosebud Sioux," *Nebraska History* 65 (Fall 1984): 301–25.

6. *Crawford Tribune*, June 28, 1901.

7. Fletcher, *The Black Soldier*, pp. 28; *Valentine Democrat*, September 5, 1901.

8. Richard Johnson, "My Life in the U.S. Army, 1899–1922," typescript, U. S. Army Military History Institute, Carlisle Barracks, Pennsylvania, pp. 67–68, 73; Theophilus Steward, *Fifty Years in the Gospel Ministry* (Philadelphia: A.M.E. Book Concern, 1921), p. 354.

9. *Valentine Republican*, August 29, 1902. All information on 25th Infantry troop movements and assignments at Fort Niobrara is compiled from "Post Returns, Fort Niobrara, September 1902–September 1906," RG 393, Records of U.S. Army Continental Commands, National Archives.

10. Steward, *Fifty Years*, p. 354

11. "Post Returns," Fort Niobrara, September 1902.

12. Fletcher, *The Black Soldier*, p. 109.

13. Frank N. Schubert, "Black Soldiers on the White Frontier: Some Factors Influencing Race Relations," *Phylon* 32 (Winter 1971): 410, 415.

14. "Monthly Reports of Chaplains, Fort Niobrara, September 1902–June 1906," January 1903, RG 393 National Archives.

15. *Valentine Republican*, September 19, 1902.

16. William Seraile, "Saving Souls on the Frontier, A Chaplain's Labor," *Montana* 42 (Winter 1992): 41; Steward, *Fifty Years*, p. 356.

17. George Schuyler, *Black and Conservative: The Autobiography of George Schuyler* (New Rochelle NY: Arlington House, 1966), p. 118.

18. *Valentine Republican*, September 19, 1902.

19. Fletcher, *The Black Soldier*, p. 25; *Valentine Democrat*, September 22, 1904.

20. Schubert, "Black Soldiers," pp. 414–15.

21. *Summary Discharge*, pp. 209–10.

22. *Proceedings of a General Court-Martial Convened at Headquarters, Department of Texas, San Antonio, February 4, 1907, in the Case of Maj. Charles W. Penrose, Twenty-fifth United States Infantry*. Senate Document 402, part 2, 60th Congress, 1st Session, 1907–8, p. 795.

23. *Report of the Proceedings of the Court of Inquiry Relative to the Shooting Affray at Brownsville, Texas, August 13–14, 1906 by Soldiers of Companies B, C, and D, Twenty-fifth United States Infantry*. Senate Document 701, 61st Congress, 3rd Session, 1910–11, pp. 1345–46.

24. *Valentine Democrat*, December 4, 1902; "Monthly Reports of Chaplains," March 1905.

25. "Post Returns, Fort Niobrara, September 1902–June 1906," Record Group 393, Records of Continental Commands, National Archives.

26. "Monthly Reports of Chaplains," June 1905.

27. Johnson, "My Life in the U.S. Army," p. 71.

28. *Orders and Messages*, p. 32.

29. *Hearings Before the Committee on Military Affairs Concerning the Affray at Brownsville, Texas, on the Night of August 13 and 14, 1906*. Senate Document 402, 60th Congress, 1st Session, 1907–8, p. 3191; *Report of Proceedings*, p. 751.

30. Fletcher, *The Black Soldier*, p. 84.

31. *Hearings Before Committee*, p. 3190.

32. *Valentine Democrat*, November 26, 1903.

33. *Valentine Republican*, December 11, 1903. Information on Twelfth Cavalry violence is found in the "Newspaper Articles 1910–1918" file at Fort Robinson Museum.

34. *Valentine Democrat*, September 11, 1902.

35. Nankivell, *History of the Twenty-fifth Regiment*, p. 168.

36. *Valentine Republican*, January 22, February 19, 1904.

37. Steward, *Fifty Years*, p. 358; *Valentine Democrat*, December 4, 1904; June 11, 1903.

38. *Valentine Democrat*, January 1, March 5, 1903.

39. *Valentine Democrat*, March 26, 1903, November 23, 1905; "Monthly Reports of Chaplains," May 1903; *Valentine Democrat*, February 9, 1905.

40. "Monthly Reports of Chaplains," November 1905; December 1902; November 1904.

41. "Monthly Reports of Chaplains," November 1904; October 1902; July 1903.

42. *Proceedings of a General Court-Martial Convened at Headquarters*, pp. 723, 858; *Report of Proceedings*, p. 473.

43. Nankivell, *History of the Twenty-fifth Regiment*, p. 115.

44. Johnson, "My Life in the U.S. Army," pp. 68, 73; *Valentine Democrat*, November 30, 1905.

45. All information on violent incidents is compiled from articles in the *Valentine Democrat* and *Republican* between 1902 and 1906; *Valentine Republican*, January 12, 1906.

46. "Medical History of Fort Niobrara, August 1902–July 1906," October, November 1905, RG 94, Records of the Adjutant General's Office, National Archives.

47. Lane, *The Brownsville Affair*, pp. 60; *Report of Proceedings*, pp. 406–7.

48. "Monthly Reports of Chaplains," December 1902, June 1904.

49. *Summary Discharge*, pp. 361–65; *Valentine Democrat*, November 3, 1904; C. H. Cornell, Chairman Republican Congressional Committee, Sixth District, cited in *Summary Discharge*, p. 363.

50. *Valentine Democrat*, April 28, 1904, December 14, 1905.

51. *Valentine Democrat*, March 23, 1905.

52. "Monthly Reports of Chaplains," January 1906; *Valentine Democrat*, November 30, December 7; *Valentine Republican*, December 1, 1905.

53. *Valentine Democrat*, January 11 (quoted), March 15, 1906; *Valentine Republican*, March 9, 1906.

54. "Monthly Reports of Chaplains," January 1906.

55. "Medical History of Fort Niobrara," January 1906.

56. Johnson, "My Life in the U. S. Army," p. 76.

57. Nankivell, *History of the Twenty-fifth Regiment*, pp. 167–68.

58. *Report of Proceedings*, pp. 1665–68; Carroll, *The Black Military Experience*, p. 525 (quoted).

59. *Valentine Democrat*, February 18, 1904; "Medical History of Fort Niobrara," June 1904; *Hearings Before Committee*, p. 1107; *Valentine Democrat*, April 5, 1906.

60. *Report of Proceedings*, p. 884.

61. *Report of Proceedings*, p. 387; Weaver, *The Brownsville Raid*, p. 236; Steward cited in *Report of Proceedings*, p. 767.

62. *Report of Proceedings*, pp. 1390–91; protests from 25th Officers found on pp. 1665–68; objection of Chaplain Steward, p. 1475; Lane, *The Brownsville Affair*, p. 13.

CHAPTER 5 | Black Enclaves of Violence:
            | Race and Homicide in Great
            | Plains Cities, 1890–1920

CLARE V. MCKANNA JR.

Badly Shot in a Drunken Row.
White Man and Colored Man "Mix" at Coffeyville.
Three Shots Struck Home.

   —*Montgomery Daily Reporter*, January 14, 1904

Killed by a Negro: Another Murder in Coffeyville's Tenderloin

   —*Montgomery Daily Reporter*, February 5, 1907

These killings, occurring three years apart in Coffeyville, Kansas, offer bookend images of interracial homicides in the Great Plains. In the first shooting, Charles Vann, a black man and the victim, had been drinking at Walnut and Eleventh Streets in the "tenderloin" district, a black neighborhood in Coffeyville. This region, near the railroad yards, provided entertainment for black customers and occasionally whites in saloons, brothels, and gambling parlors. William Rodecker, a white male horse trader, had just arrived from Missouri and started drinking heavily in this area. About 8 p.m. Rodecker accosted Vann at the corner of Twelfth and Walnut Streets and began to "rag" him. Apparently, Vann took offense and allegedly put his hand on his hip pocket. Rodecker quickly pulled a .38 revolver and fired four shots in quick succession, mortally wounding Vann.[1] In the second example, on February 5, 1907, Rodecker, just released from prison, became involved in an argument in the exact same area. Al Jesse (one of Vann's friends) pulled a revolver and shot Rodecker three times.[2] Not surprisingly, the killing of Rodecker occurred less than one block from the previous shooting.

These shootings typified violent behavior in Coffeyville at the beginning of the twentieth century. Since many men carried handguns, it is not surprising that violent confrontations often ended in death. Both homicides are especially significant because of the interracial factor. In the first case Rodecker, the white defendant, appeared before a justice of the peace and was quickly released on a $500 bond, and at a preliminary hearing the Montgomery County district attorney charged Rodecker with murder. Months later a jury found him guilty of manslaughter and a judge sentenced Rodecker from one to five years in prison.[3] In the second killing, despite the defendant pleading self-defense (both men had drawn their handguns), an all-white jury found Al Jesse guilty of second-degree murder; he received a twenty-year sentence.[4] These dramatic shootings provide historians with a window of opportunity to ask the question: how common were black homicides in Coffeyville, Topeka, and other eastern Kansas cities?

Measuring Black Violence Levels

There is considerable literature on the black experience in Kansas. For example, Nell Painter and others have examined the black migration of the "Exodusters" who arrived to make a new life in rural Kansas after the Civil War. However, most of these studies deal with rural agricultural communities such as Nicodemus, Hodgeman, Morton City, and Parsons, which developed when blacks fled the South to escape mob violence, lynching, and discrimination.[5] Arriving in large numbers, blacks soon discovered that discrimination also existed in Kansas and Nebraska. Thomas C. Cox and others have graphically described the black experience in cities such as Topeka, Wichita, and Parsons.[6] Nevertheless, there is a dearth of information on violent crime involving blacks in Kansas.

In the past few decades, social scientists and historians have collected data on violence among blacks in Miami, Philadelphia, Houston, and other urban centers.[7] Data reveal black homicide rates in 1980 reached 55 per 100,000 in Dallas, 77 in Cleveland, and 98 in Miami and were ten times higher than white rates.[8] The disparity between these two ethnic groups is remarkable. It is the thesis of this essay that such high rates for blacks is not of recent origin; the data will demonstrate that black homicide rates have been high for more than a century and can be traced to "enclaves of violence" that developed in Coffeyville and Topeka, Kansas, and Omaha, Nebraska.[9]

A variety of factors illuminate the development of black violence in Kansas and Nebraska cities. For example, the railroads that developed in these cities attracted hundreds of young blacks searching for steady employment. While Coffeyville and Topeka may have seemed to be tranquil to some observers, certain regions became "killing zones" for blacks who lived and worked in these cities. Alcohol also played an important role in violence levels. Railroad workers, meatpackers, and common laborers often spent their leisure hours in saloons, gambling parlors, and restaurants located near the railroad yards. Guns offer another part of the violence equation: cheap handguns, selling for less than $3, made their appearance during the 1880s and continued to flood the market well into the twentieth century. Finally, place provided the nexus where a variety of factors, such as the rapid, critical convergence of young men, guns, alcohol, and minor grievances, came together to create deadly "enclaves of violence."

This study focuses mainly on black homicides in four eastern Kansas counties during the period 1890 to 1920 but includes a comparison with Omaha, Nebraska. Labette, Leavenworth, Montgomery, and Shawnee Counties were selected because of the presence of a significant black population. Leavenworth and Shawnee Counties, in northeastern Kansas, provide urban areas that offer a natural comparison with two rural counties. Although not large cities, Leavenworth and Topeka, Kansas (population between 20,000 and 50,000), offer an opportunity to examine the treatment of black defendants accused of homicide in an urban setting. These cities displayed a stable black population during the study period. Leavenworth County, with 4,465 blacks in 1890, declined to 3,780 by 1920 (10 percent of the total population), while Shawnee County's black population averaged 5,700 over the three decades (9.7 percent of the population).

Labette and Montgomery Counties, located in southeastern Kansas (bordering Oklahoma), provide a rural setting in which to assess the impact of black migration. Although the black population is smaller than in the urban counties, Montgomery Country experienced significant growth, with the black population jumping from 947 in 1890 to 2,954 by 1920. This included in-migration of blacks who worked on three railroads that passed through Coffeyville. Neighboring Labette County's black population was 2,045 in 1890 and declined slightly over three decades to 1,980, suggesting a more stable environment in towns like Oswego and Parsons than in Coffeyville.

Black Population Migration

A series of push-pull factors explain the black in-migration to Kansas cities. Many blacks viewed southern police power as repressive and unjust and left to escape oppression. Police brutality was common in Richmond, Atlanta, and other cities, and this created unrest among southern urban blacks. Sometimes blacks resisted this form of violence, especially in Atlanta.[10] Lynching also served as a push factor. For example, two historians discovered "a very striking relationship between migration and lynching in Georgia and South Carolina."[11] Pull factors such as job opportunities, better living conditions, and the absence of blatant racial persecution contributed to the black migration to Kansas and Nebraska. Railroads especially offered job opportunities for blacks moving into Great Plains cities.

Coffeyville experienced social change that created problems during the early part of the twentieth century. Blacks began to migrate into Coffeyville slowly, numbering 803 in 1900, or about 16 percent of the total population. By 1910 the black population had jumped to 1,309 (10 percent) and finally to 1,480 by 1920 (9 percent). The 1900 census reveals that 84 percent of the black males in the black district that developed along the railroad yards had migrated from the South, with an additional 12 percent from western states. By 1910, 75 percent of the black males claimed the South as their birthplace.[12] The black neighborhood in Coffeyville became concentrated near the Missouri Pacific Railroad yards that extended along a corridor north to south for several blocks, paralleling Walnut Street. The pool halls, gambling parlors, saloons, and houses of prostitution were frequented not only by black patrons but also by whites.

Topeka also proved to be a popular destination for blacks, with 77 percent migrating from the South. The black population peaked in Topeka in 1890 with 5,037 persons (16 percent) and then declined to a low of 4,272 (8.5 percent) by 1920. By 1895, 42 percent of the blacks migrating into Topeka lived in the second ward, near the Missouri Pacific and Atchison, Topeka and Santa Fe Railroad yards.[13] Historian Thomas Cox noted that blacks employed by the Topeka Railway Company "were relegated to the most menial tasks"; however, black workers were more successful in finding jobs with the Kansas Pacific Railroad.[14] Despite discrimination in Topeka, blacks found employment in service-related businesses or operated their own barbershops, restaurants, and saloons. Cox found that "service businesses were most numerous, with barbers and caterers heading the list." Blacks usually had to settle for jobs as common laborers and they experienced blatant racism, such as signs stating "Negroes Need Not Apply" in Topeka factories.[15]

During their leisure hours some black workers leaving the railroad yards visited the saloons, gambling parlors, houses of prostitution, and pool halls nearby. Alcohol abuse created problems, and newspaper editors criticized excesses that brought crime to Topeka, especially prostitution. One editor suggested that such "women should be driven to the suburbs" and regulated "by a competent physician."[16] This enticing region, just west of the railroad yards, became a prominent gathering place for young blacks.

Omaha experienced similar pull factors. The Union Pacific Railroad, Union Stock Yards, and Cudahy, Armour, and Swift meatpacking companies offered job opportunities in Omaha. Blacks moved into the region west of the Union Pacific Railroad yards and some became involved in service-related businesses such as saloons, gambling parlors, pool halls, and brothels. By 1910 Omaha's red-light district became concentrated in a core of city blocks that extended from Davenport Street south three blocks to Douglas, and from Ninth Street west three blocks to Twelfth. Many saloons served as social gathering places for railroad and stockyard workers in this highly concentrated district. Local officials attributed any crime that occurred in this region to blacks who lived in and around it. Black newspaper editor H. J. Pinkett protested that disreputable saloons created problems for neighboring black residents. He ran several editorials calling for cleaning up of the "bootlegging and gambling joints" that seemed to be everywhere.[17]

Enclaves of Violence

Coffeyville's "enclave of violence" developed in the Tenderloin district that ran north to south for four blocks along Walnut Street and extended eastward from the railroad yards four blocks. The Missouri-Kansas-Texas Railroad crossed Walnut Street at about the 1300 block and continued northeast on a parallel course. Virtually all of the homicides that were committed by blacks and that could be identified with a specific street location (eight cases) occurred along Walnut Street from the 1000 to 1300 blocks. This black neighborhood proved to be a killing zone for blacks in Coffeyville.[18]

For example, around 4 a.m. on October 28, 1902, Jess Brown and Frank Lee were sitting and playing poker in a gambling house at 1014 South Walnut Street. Apparently, Lee accused Brown of cheating, jumped up from the table, and threw the cards in Brown's face. Brown pulled a .44 Colt revolver and shot Lee through the heart. Police found a cocked .41 Colt revolver lying next to Lee; apparently he was too slow on the draw. Jess Brown was a well-respected black; Lee, however, appeared to be an unsavory character who had recently assaulted a police officer. A jury found Jess Brown not guilty.[19] In a similar case, on June 7, 1907, Thomas Clark and Frank Emerson became involved in a dispute about an obscene note that had been sent to Emerson's wife. Known locally as "Society Red," Emerson confronted Clark at about midnight at Maple and Thirteenth Streets near the railroad yards. After a heated argument, Emerson pulled a revolver and fired one fatal shot into his victim.[20]

White males sometimes became the victims of black assailants. In January 1917 Ed Brown, a white male, had been living with Lucille Jones, a black woman, at 1208 Beech Street. Brown became jealous of Simon Raines, Jones's seventeen-year-old nephew who also lived in the house. Apparently Brown had been abusing Lucille and threatened Raines with a butcher knife. Raines pulled a revolver and fired four shots, with three hitting their mark. Raines claimed self-defense; a jury agreed and found him not guilty.[21] Recent homicide studies reveal that assailants usually kill their victims in their own neighborhoods. Virtually all of the killings involving blacks in Coffeyville occurred in this black neighborhood along Walnut Street.

Topeka's "enclave of violence," commonly called "Smoky Row," was located in the second ward, south of the Kansas River and west of the railroad yards. Most of the killings took place within a zone stretching from Crane Street south three blocks to Second Street and extending east from Van Buren four blocks to Monroe. Twelve homicides occurred within this small area, two others east of the railroad yard, and six more a few blocks south in Tennesseetown, in the third ward.[22] Women rarely committed homicides, but there were exceptions. On November 5, 1899, Joanna Dupree became involved in an argument with Thomas "Red" Erwin on Smoky Row. Erwin, a tough talker, challenged Dupree: "If you can shoot any faster than I can, get your gun."[23] Dupree went back into her house, picked up a .41 Colt revolver, returned to the street, and shot Erwin dead on the spot. Although she was indicted for murder, a jury found her not guilty.[24]

Young black males carried concealed weapons that proved to be an invitation to violence. For example, on March 21, 1900, Robert Smith, age eighteen, became involved in a dispute over a baseball that a group of boys had been playing with. William Richardson, age sixteen, took the ball and tried to leave. Smith pulled a revolver and shot Richardson in the face, killing him instantly.[25] Arguments over such trivial issues as a baseball or some other item of property and small bets often became deadly. In August 1904 Harvey Enochs stabbed Shadrack Simms to death in a crap game dispute in "Will Guy's Dive" on First Avenue and Monroe.[26] Nine years later James McCoy shot Clarence Sydnor in an argument in Sydnor's Pool Hall at 404 Kansas Street.[27] In 1915, in a fight over personal honor in an alley behind 218 Kansas Street, James Williamson shot Harry White three times because "he insulted my sister." A jury found Williamson guilty of second-degree murder and sentenced him to six to ten years in prison.[28] Finally, in 1915 Ada DuPree killed John Bronsema in a dispute over twenty-five cents on the corner of Monroe and Crane Streets. DuPree plea-bargained guilty to manslaughter.[29] Petty disputes, personal honor, concealed weapons, and alcohol proved to be deadly.

Omaha's "enclave of violence" developed in the region west of the Union Pacific Railroad center where most of the shootings involving blacks occurred. Omaha's unsegregated black neighborhood was the focal point of various racial groups; this accounts for the high interracial killings, with whites accounting for 32 percent of the victims of black assailants.[30] With killers and victims alike under the influence of liquor and well armed, minor disagreements often ended in violence.

Interracial homicides involving black assailants usually occurred in or around pool halls, gambling parlors, or saloons. Two interracial killings involving women suggest prostitution-related issues or the possibility of an insult. On the night of July 27, 1905, William Miles, a black male, stood talking to Florence Flick, a white woman, who had been living with him for two years. Recently, Harry McGechin, a white man, had taken up with Flick. Miles and McGechin met in front of the Cambridge Hotel on the corner of Thirteenth and Capitol Streets and began to argue. Miles pulled a knife and quickly cut McGechin's throat; he died within minutes.[31] In a similar case, a black male known as Lucky Brown took offense to remarks made by three inebriated white men at Twenty-sixth and N Streets about a woman he was escorting. Brown pulled a pistol and fired several rounds that left one man dead. Police were unable to apprehend the killer.[32] These two cases display aspects of southern culture such as a heightened degree of personal honor. A careless comment, an unintended jostle on the street, or a gesture could bring a quick and deadly response from blacks conditioned by living in the South. Many black southerners had a strong sense of honor that dared not be sullied.

Sometime in 1908, Henry Brown, a black dining-car waiter for the Union Pacific Railroad, fought with Carrie Carter, a black woman who lived with him. After a bitter quarrel, she left him and moved into separate living quarters. Henry discovered her new residence and tried to convince her to return and live with him. She refused. On February 8, 1909, exasperated by her refusal, Brown visited a neighborhood pawnshop where he hocked his overcoat in exchange for a cheap handgun and a box of shells. He loaded the weapon and walked to Carrie's new residence at 1223 Capitol Avenue. After a brief argument in front of her house, Henry fired two shots, one of which struck her under the right arm, proving fatal. This scenario displays the ease with which individuals could obtain handguns in Omaha. It also indicates the single-mindedness and the premeditation of this killer; he pawned his overcoat in the dead of winter in exchange for a handgun.[33]

Discussion of Data

Research uncovered 381 homicide indictments within the four Kansas counties. Despite population differences, rural Montgomery County had virtually the same number of homicide indictments as Shawnee County, which is dominated by urban Topeka. This suggests that rural county homicide indictment rates sometimes mirror those of urban counties. Since indictment data were unavailable, the 162 cases in Leavenworth County reflect actual homicides taken from coroner's records.[34]

Coffeyville, with a modest black population, had a higher black homicide indictment rate than Topeka; however, both exhibited higher rates for blacks compared to whites. Coffeyville and Topeka proved to be the most dangerous homicide hot spots in these four Kansas counties. Coffeyville, with a population of 13,452 in 1920, recorded forty-four homicide indictments (sixteen blacks and twenty-eight whites). Topeka, with 50,022, had fifty-six homicide indictments (thirty-one blacks and twenty-five whites). In Coffeyville and Topeka, with just 13 and 11 percent of the population, respectively, blacks contributed 36 and 55 percent of all homicide indictments. In Omaha, blacks received 37.5 percent of the homicide indictments but represented 7.6 percent of the total population. The transient nature of Coffeyville's black population and three railroads that enticed black workers into the region help to explain high violence levels. Coffeyville, Topeka, and Omaha had railroads, rapid population growth, and racial discrimination.[35] Equally important, high indictment rates for blacks may indicate a bias in the criminal justice systems. This was probably caused by a skewed accused/indicted ratio, meaning that blacks would more likely be indicted if accused of a crime, especially if they killed white victims. The accused/indicted ratio is the percentage of those individuals actually indicted selected from those who were identified and accused of murder.[36] Finally, lower black homicide indictment rates within Topeka may suggest a more stable society.

Black homicide indictment rates for 1900–1909 were 69 per 100,000 population for Coffeyville, 13 per 100,000 for Topeka, and 56 per 100,000 for Omaha. The rates for 1910–19 remain high, with 54, 42, and 54 per 100,000, respectively, for Coffeyville, Topeka, and Omaha. White homicide indictment rates during this period averaged 4 per 100,000 in all three cities. Black homicide indictment rates exceeded white rates by a factor of ten or more. These Great Plains cities, however, were not the only ones that displayed such disparate figures; Roger Lane discovered similar high rates among blacks in Philadelphia.[37]

The black homicide indictment rates for Coffeyville, Topeka, and Omaha have seldom been equaled except in some modern cities during the 1980s and 1990s.[38] Critics might complain that Coffeyville, with sixteen cases, is too small a sample to be reliable compared with the much larger population in Omaha, with sixty-five cases. However, statistics reveal that if you were a black male living in Coffeyville, your chances of being killed would be higher than if you lived in Omaha. Sixteen of 1,309 blacks were killed in Coffeyville compared to thirty-one out of 4,538 in Topeka, and sixty-five victims out of 5,143 blacks in Omaha. Blacks were also at risk in Leavenworth and Independence.

Following trends discovered in earlier studies, handguns played an important role; blacks selected handguns to commit their homicides 65 percent of the time, while whites chose them 53 percent of the time. Blacks usually selected handguns patterned on the Webley British Bulldog double-action revolver (patented in 1883), probably because they were cheap. This model, with a two- or three-inch barrel, allowed for easy concealment in a coat pocket. American arms manufacturers copied this design and produced large quantities of the five-shot revolvers in several sizes, including .38 and .32 calibers. In the 1880s, the Iver Johnson Arms Company named its versions the American Bull Dog and Boston Bull Dog. The Harrington and Richardson Company, noted for making "Suicide Specials," switched to a similar design. Forehand and Wadsworth, Remington, Stevens, and other American gun manufacturers also produced similar guns. These cheap handguns sold for less than three dollars.[39]

The combined population of the four Kansas counties reached 191,253 in 1920, compared to a population of 204,524 in Douglas County, Nebraska. Three of these Kansas counties had a combined total of 219 homicide indictments, and Leavenworth County had 162 homicides, compared to 237 indictments and 391 actual homicides in Douglas County, Nebraska between 1880–1920. Previous research suggests that if coroners' inquest records had been available, the actual homicides would have been approximately 25 percent higher, or about 436 homicides for the four counties.

Convictions rates in the four Kansas counties offer a similar pattern to those discovered earlier in Omaha, where 84 percent of black defendants were found guilty. Black defendant conviction rates reached 86 percent in Shawnee County and averaged 77 percent in Labette and Montgomery Counties.[40] White defendant conviction rates were 52 percent in Labette and Shawnee Counties and 43 percent in Montgomery County, compared to 37 percent in Omaha. Black defendant plea bargain rates were 41, 31, and 12 percent, respectively, in Shawnee, Labette, and Montgomery Counties, while Omaha had a plea bargain rate of 32 percent. Whites rarely plea bargained in either state.[41] The data reveal that blacks were especially at risk in these Great Plains cities.

Final Observations

In his discussion of a "regional culture of violence," Raymond Gastil used the term "southernness" to help identify the persistence of southern culture in transplanted members of black society who moved to other regions such as the Great Plains cities of Coffeyville, Topeka, and Omaha. They carried with them their cultural tradition that included a propensity to settle problems, especially those involving "honor," with force that often could be lethal. Gastil established high correlations of southernness with blacks and high homicide rates.[42] This supports an earlier study on black crime in Philadelphia by W. E. B. Du Bois.[43] Many years later, Roger Lane, in his discussion of blacks in Philadelphia, suggested that "a different social psychology resulting from blacks' exclusion from the dominant experience with factory, bureaucracy, and schooling; a heritage of economic and other insecurities; and a long and complex experience with criminal activity" best explain black crime.[44] One is left with the conclusion that blacks brought their proclivity for violence with them when they left the South and moved into Kansas and Nebraska.

As noted earlier, in 1904 William Rodecker killed Charles Vann, a black patron in front of a saloon in Coffeyville. Three years later, just released from prison, Rodecker returned to Coffeyville's black neighborhood and was shot by Al Jesse, one of Vann's friends. Not surprisingly, both shootings occurred within this "enclave of violence." Authorities had sentenced Rodecker, a white man with a history of violence, to five years in prison, while Jesse received a harsher sentence. Black defendants paid a higher price in the criminal justice system, especially if they killed white victims.[45] These killings reveal the problems that many blacks faced in late-nineteenth- and early-twentieth-century Kansas and Nebraska. Whether in Montgomery, Labette, Shawnee, Leavenworth, or Douglas County, young black males were at risk.

There are a series of factors that tie the homicides of Vann and Rodecker and many of the other killings together: gender, race, alcohol, guns, and place. First, most of the victims were men: 86 percent of all homicide victims in Kansas and 90 percent in Nebraska. These killings usually involved two young males arguing over a grievance such as a fifty-cent pool hall bet, an affront of honor, or a woman. These affairs often escalated into deadly violence. Although ranging in age from eighteen to sixty, the majority were men in their twenties and thirties.

People usually kill within their own ethnic group, but there were exceptions; race played an important role in interracial killings such as the Walker, Vann, Rodecker, and Jesse cases. In fact, 32 percent of the black killings in Omaha involved white victims. In the Kansas counties, blacks killed white victims 19 percent of the time. Kansas and Nebraska were the recipients of an ethnically diverse population that included blacks, Hispanics, and other whites. And, of course, ethnic minorities were treated differently by a criminal justice system that favored the white majority who controlled it; sheriffs, jury members, attorneys, and judges came mainly from white society.

Alcohol provides another strong connection among these homicide cases, as many of the young men, both victims and killers, had been drinking. Railroad workers, merchants, and common laborers gathered in saloons, gambling parlors, and brothels in Coffeyville, Topeka, and Omaha for entertainment, especially at night and on weekends. In Omaha, 75 percent of the killers had been drinking, while in the four Kansas counties an average of 71 percent had been.[46] Consequently, alcohol became a catalyst for violence. Although not a causal factor, alcohol consumption tended to reduce inhibitions and sometimes made young men reckless.

Guns bind these murders together as well, with most killers selecting cheap handguns to commit their crimes. Kansas and Nebraska, like much of the American West, developed a strong gun culture. Anyone could carry a small revolver, enter a saloon, have a few drinks, and if challenged, draw and use it to settle any real or imagined grievance. Black assailants in these Kansas counties used handguns 65 percent of the time to kill their victims, while 75 percent of the black killers in Omaha used them. The carrying of handguns ensured that physical confrontations would often be deadly. Victims of assaults with knives, blunt instruments, and fists had a better chance of surviving than those shot with firearms. By their very nature, guns were more lethal. If the victim survived the initial shock of being shot, infection remained a great danger due to the nature of the wound. Doctors were ill equipped to deal with the effects of shock and trauma associated with gunshot wounds, especially the massive trauma caused by abdominal gunshot wounds, which often led to peritonitis. Consequently, most shootings were fatal.[47]

Place also played an important role. Because of labor shortages, railroad companies enticed black workers to move to Coffeyville, Topeka, and Omaha. This new, fluid, transient black population was essential to the economic success of railroads and other industries in these cities. Blacks migrating from the South established their own neighborhoods, including saloons, pool halls, and gambling houses near the railroad yards and factories. Virtually all of the black homicides occurred within these enclaves where young male patrons, black and white, intermingled.

Finally, in evaluating the data, one can distinguish a well-defined pattern of interaction among minor disputes, alcohol, and heavily armed men. This modus operandi, coupled with the critical convergence of a young, ethnically diverse, and transient male population into these cities, explains high homicide levels. It is also possible that other Kansas counties would reveal similar violent patterns to those shown in this study.⁴⁸ Unfortunately, the factors of gender, race, alcohol, guns, and place assured that these cities would develop "enclaves of violence" that would be deadly for young blacks who were, ironically, fleeing the South to escape injustice in the courts and white violence.⁴⁹

Notes

The author wishes to thank the College of Arts and Letters, San Diego State University, for awarding a CSU Mini-Grant (1997) to support this research. A special thanks goes to the Kansas State Historical Society Center for Historical Research.

1. *Montgomery Daily Reporter*, January 14, 1904.

2. *Montgomery Daily Reporter*, February 5, 1907.

3. *People v. William Rodecker*, January 30, 1904, *Criminal Appearance Dockets*, Montgomery County KS, County Clerk, Independence KS.

4. *People v. Al Jesse*, May 22, 1907, *Criminal Appearance Dockets*, Montgomery County.

5. Nell Irvin Painter, *Exodusters: Black Migration to Kansas after Reconstruction* (New York: Knopf, 1977); Anne P. W. Hawkins, "Hoeing Their Own Row: Black Agriculture and the Agrarian Ideal in Kansas," *Kansas History* 22 (autumn 1999): 200–13; Judith R. Johnson and Craig L. Torbenson, "Stories from the Heartland: African American Experiences in Wichita, Kansas," *Kansas History* 21 (winter 1998–99): 220–33; Nudie E. Williams, "Black Newspapers and the Exodusters of 1879," *Kansas History* 8 (winter 1985–86): 217–25; and Kenneth M. Hamilton, "The Origins and Early Promotion of Nicodemus: A Pre-Exodus, All-Black," *Kansas History* 5 (winter 1982): 220–42.

6. Thomas C. Cox, *Blacks in Topeka, Kansas, 1865–1915: A Social History* (Baton Rouge: Louisiana State University Press, 1982); Jean Van Delinder, "Early Civil Rights Activism in Topeka, Kansas, Prior to the 1954 Brown Case," *Great Plains Quarterly* 21 (winter 2001): 45–61; Arnold Cooper, "'Protection to all Discrimination to None': The *Parsons Weekly Blade*, 1892–1900," *Kansas History* 9 (summer 1986): 58–71; Timothy Miller, "Charles M. Sheldon and the Uplift of Tennesseetown," *Kansas History* 9 (fall 1986): 125–37; Randall Bennett Woods, *A Black Odyssey: John Lewis Waller and the Promise of American Life, 1878–1900* (Lawrence: Regents Press of Kansas, 1981); and James C. Carper, "The Popular Ideology of Segregated Schooling: Attitudes toward the Education of Blacks in Kansas, 1854–1900," *Kansas History* 1 (winter 1978): 254–65.

7. See Harold M. Rose and Paula D. McClain, *Race, Place, and Risk: Black Homicide in Urban America* (Albany: State University of New York Press, 1990); Margaret A. Zahn,

"Homicide in the Twentieth Century United States," in *History and Crime: Implications for Criminal Justice Policy*, ed. James A. Inciardi and Charles E. Faupel (Beverly Hills CA: Sage Publications, 1980), pp. 111–32; William Wilbanks, *Murder in Miami: An Analysis of Homicide Patterns and Trends in Dade County (Miami) Florida, 1917–1988* (New York: University Press of America, 1984); Darnell F. Hawkins, *Homicide among Black Americans* (Washington DC: University Press of America, 1986); Marvin E. Wolfgang, *Patterns in Criminal Homicide* (Philadelphia: University of Pennsylvania, 1958); Lawrence E. Gary, "Drinking, Homicide, and the Black Male," *Journal of Black Studies* 17 (September 1986): 15–31; and Anthony E. O. King, "Understanding Violence among Young African Males: An Afrocentric Perspective," *Journal of Black Studies* 28 (September 1997): 79–96.

8. Rose and McClain, *Race, Place, and Risk*, p. 26; and Wilbanks, *Murder in Miami*, p. 142.

9. H. C. Brearley, *Homicide in the United States* (Montclair NJ: Patterson Smith, 1932), pp. 218–19. During the period 1920–1925, Brearley discovered that black homicide rates had reached 87, 99, and 101 per 100,000, respectively, for Kansas City (KS), Dallas, and Cleveland. Also see Clare V. McKanna Jr., "Seeds of Destruction: Homicide, Race, and Justice in Omaha, 1880–1920," *Journal of American Ethnic History* 14 (fall 1994): 65–90.

10. See Howard N. Rabinowitz, "The Conflict between Blacks and the Police in the Urban South, 1865–1900," *The Historian* 39 (November 1976): 62–76. Rabinowitz found examples of "the effective use of intimidation by blacks against white policemen."

11. Stewart E. Tolnay and E. M. Beck, "Black Flight: Lethal Violence and the Great Migration, 1900–1930," *Social Science History* 14 (fall 1990): 360–61.

12. A 20 percent random sample of heads of black household was collected for this study. See U.S. Bureau of Census, 1900 and 1910, *Twelfth Census: Population, Thirteenth Census: Population* (Washington DC, 1901, 1911). Kansas, Montgomery County, Coffeyville.

13. Cox, *Blacks in Topeka*, pp. 203–8.

14. Cox, *Blacks in Topeka*, pp. 115–16.

15. Cox, *Blacks in Topeka*, pp. 87 and 90–93.

16. *Daily Capital* undated, as quoted in Cox, *Blacks in Topeka*, p. 107.

17. *Omaha Monitor*, April 19 and August 17, 1919.

18. *Criminal Appearance Dockets*, 1890–1920, Montgomery County, County Clerk, Independence KS.

19. *Coffeyville Daily Journal*, October 29, 1902, and *People v. Brown*, November 21, 1902, *Criminal Appearance Dockets*, Montgomery County.

20. *Coffeyville Daily Journal*, June 11, 1907. A jury found Emerson guilty of manslaughter, see *People v. Emerson*, October 24, 1907, *Criminal Appearance Dockets*, Montgomery County.

21. *Coffeyville Daily Journal*, January 12, 1917, and *People v. Raines*, February 13, 1917, *Criminal Appearance Dockets*, Mongomery County.

22. The location of an additional eleven homicides remains undetermined. See *Criminal Appearance Dockets*, 1890–1920, Shawnee County, County Clerk, Topeka KS.

23. *Topeka Daily Capital*, November 9, 1899.

24. *People v. DuPree*, November 25, 1899, *Criminal Appearance Dockets*, Shawnee County.

25. *Topeka Daily Capital*, March 22, 1900, and *People v. Smith*, April 4, 1900, *Criminal Appearance Dockets*, Shawnee County. Smith plea bargained guilty to second-degree murder.

26. *People v. Enochs*, September 20, 1904, *Criminal Appearance Dockets*, Shawnee County. Enochs plea bargained to manslaughter and received a sentence of five years in prison.

27. *People v. McCoy*, May 5, 1913, *Criminal Appearance Dockets*, Shawnee County. McCoy plea bargained to second-degree murder and received a ten-year sentence.

28. *People v. Williamson*, February 19, 1916, *Criminal Appearance Dockets*, Shawnee County.

29. *People v. DuPree*, September 29, 1915, *Criminal Appearance Dockets*, Shawnee County.

30. McKanna, "Seeds of Destruction," pp. 71.

31. *Omaha World-Herald*, July 28, 1905, and *People v. Miles*, August 2, 1905, *Criminal Appearance Dockets*, Douglas County, County Clerk, Omaha NE. Convicted of manslaughter, Miles received a five- to ten-year sentence.

32. *Omaha World-Herald*, August 16, 1913.

33. *Omaha World Herald*, February 9, 1909. *People v. Brown*, April 26, 1909, *Criminal Appearance Dockets*, Douglas County NE. Convicted of first-degree murder, Brown received a life sentence and was paroled in 1929.

34. Coroner's records were unavailable for Shawnee, Montgomery, and Labette Counties.

35. Cox, *Blacks in Topeka*), pp. 92–93; and McKanna, "Seeds of Destruction," pp. 68–69.

36. The accused/indicted ratio could not be calculated because of the unavailability of coroner's records in Labette, Montgomery, and Shawnee Counties and indictment records in Leavenworth County. Similar research in California has revealed a significant disparity, with authorities indicting accused Indians 82 percent compared to whites with 46 percent. See Clare V. McKanna Jr., *Race and Homicide in Nineteenth-Century California* (Reno: University of Nevada Press, 2002), p. 100.

37. Roger Lane, *Roots of Violence in Black Philadelphia, 1860–1900* (Cambridge: Harvard

University Press, 1986), pp. 142–43. Another earlier study indicates that homicide rates for blacks in urban areas continued to be high during the 1920s, with Nebraska's urban black homicide rates (mainly Omaha) reaching 69 in 1920 and 1925, while Kansas black rates in Kansas City and Leavenworth, respectively, were 87 and 31 per 100,000. See H. C. Brearley, *Homicide in the United States* (1932; reprint, Montclair NJ: Patterson Smith, 1969), pp. 99 and 218. Brearley used actual homicides, rather than indictments, collected from federal government statistics.

38. For other comparisons see Rose and McClain, *Race, Place, and Risk*; Zahn, "Homicide," pp. 111–32; Wilbanks, *Murder in Miami*; and Wolfgang, *Patterns in Criminal Homicide*, pp. 361–83.

39. A. W. F. Taylerson, *Revolving Arms* (New York: Walker and Company, 1967), pp. 32–44; Geoffrey Boothroyd, *The Handgun* (London: Cassell, 1970), pp. 221–24, 345–57. One could purchase handguns through Sears, Roebuck for less than two dollars. See *The Sears, Roebuck Catalog* (Chicago: Sears, Roebuck and Company, 1902), pp. 316–21.

40. Without indictment data conviction rates in Leavenworth were unavailable.

41. See McKanna, "Seeds of Destruction," pp. 77–78; and *Criminal Appearance Dockets*, 1890–1920, Montgomery, Labette, and Shawnee Counties, County Clerk, Oswego KS.

42. Raymond D. Gastil, "Homicide and the Regional Culture of Violence," *American Sociological Review* 36 (June 1971): 421.

43. W. E. B. Du Bois, *The Philadelphia Negro: A Social Study* (Philadelphia: University of Pennsylvania Press, 1899), pp. 238–68.

44. Lane, *Roots of Violence*, p. 173. For an earlier study on homicide and aggressive behavior, see Martin Gold, "Suicide, Homicide, and the Socialization of Aggression," *American Journal of Sociology* 58 (May 1958): 651–61.

45. *People v. William Rodecker*, January 30, 1904, and *People v. Al Jesse*, May 22, 1907, *Criminal Appearance Dockets*, Montgomery County KS.

46. Clare V. McKanna Jr., *Homicide, Race, and Justice in the American West, 1880–1920* (Tucson: University of Arizona Press, 1997), p. 27; "Coroner's Inquest, 1890–1920," Leavenworth County KS. Topeka: Kansas State Historical Society Center for Historical Research; *Criminal Appearance Dockets, 1890–1920*, Labette, Montgomery, and Shawnee Counties; and *Coffeyville Daily Journal, Montgomery Daily Reporter, Topeka Daily Capital, Leavenworth Advocate, Leavenworth Herald, Labette County Times*, and *Oswego Independent*.

47. David McDowall, "Firearm Availability and Homicide Rates in Detroit, 1951–1986," *Social Forces* 69 (June 1991): 1085–1101; and Gary Kleck and Karen McElrath, "The Effects of Weaponry on Human Violence," *Social Forces* 69 (March 1991): 669–92.

48. During my 1997 research trip to Kansas, I collected partial data in Cherokee County

that revealed 94 homicide indictments; 27 percent were black defendants. Conviction rates for blacks reached 95 percent and 21 percent plea bargained. See also Wyandotte (Kansas City), Atchison (Atchison), Douglas (Lawrence), Sedgwick (Wichita), and Crawford (Pittsburg) Counties; they also had significant pockets of black population.

49. Tolnay and Beck, "Black Flight," p. 354.

CHAPTER 6 | A Socioeconomic Portrait of Prince Hall Masonry in Nebraska, 1900–1920

DENNIS N. MIHELICH

On March 6, 1775, a British military lodge of Freemasons initiated Prince Hall (his name, not a title) and fourteen other African Americans after the white colonial lodge at Boston had rejected their petition. Independence did not alter the attitude of white American Masons; thus, a separate black Masons organization evolved. Hall secured a charter from the "mother" grand lodge in England and reconstituted his group as the African Grand Lodge of North America. Following his death in 1807 the fraternal order renamed itself in his honor.

Prior to the abolition of slavery, Prince Hall Masonry spread slowly among the free black population in the northern and border states. The fraternity established a confederation structure in which each state could create a sovereign grand lodge. After the Civil War, membership mushroomed and migrating African Americans carried the institution to the trans-Missouri West. Prince Hall Masons affiliated with the Missouri Grand Lodge organized the first blue (subordinate) lodge in Nebraska at Omaha in 1875. By the end of the century blue lodges also existed in Lincoln, Hastings, Grand Island, Alliance, and Scottsbluff. The Great Migration of World War I increased the membership significantly, making it feasible for four Omaha lodges to join with those in the other five towns to form the independent Prince Hall Mason Grand Lodge of Nebraska in 1919.

Existing scholarship argues that Masonry among blacks was a middle-class phenomenon that produced class strife in the African American community. Until recently in the post civil rights era, the delineation of classes within the segregated black caste in the United States has produced conflicting hierarchical schemes and controversy. Nonetheless, the titles of William A. Muraskin's *Middle-class Blacks in a White Society: Prince Hall Freemasonry in America* and Loretta J. Williams's *Black Freemasonry and Middle-Class Realities* announce their socio-economic interpretation.[1] The charter members of the Prince Hall Grand Lodge of Nebraska, however, exhibited a wide range of wealth, incomes, and occupations. The Nebraska story demonstrates the impact and the persistence of regional diversity in American history in general and in African American history in particular. The desire for a sovereign grand lodge and the relatively small African American population precluded elitist class-based exclusion. Prince Hall Masonry in Nebraska was not the overwhelmingly middle-class institution described by previous scholars; it was a multi-class fraternity consisting of individuals who accepted a Christian code of values (allegorically cast in reference to the craft of stone masons), who demanded moral and ethical conduct, and who promoted "self-help" and "racial uplift" for the entire black community.

An analysis of the few rosters in the Nebraska materials for the pre-Grand Lodge years supports the multi-class interpretation and highlights the nineteenth-century origins of the characteristic. For the pre–World War I years, however, anecdotal evidence, such as stories in the black press, suggested that Prince Hall Masonry in Nebraska at the turn to the twentieth century took on an elitist aura. Obviously, news coverage stressed the entertainments of the "leading lights" of the community, meaning its professionals, politicians, and entrepreneurs.

In comparison, the rosters reveal the wide variety of unskilled, skilled, and service-area jobs held by the majority of Prince Hall

Masons. They also reveal how specific jobs changed labor categories as the Nebraska economy evolved and the Great Migration altered the circumstances of the black community. For example, barbering for a white clientele offered some blacks an opportunity at skilled service or entrepreneurship that largely disappeared after World War I. On the other hand, unskilled and semi-skilled industrial employment in the rapidly expanding meat-packing companies mushroomed during and after the First World War.

Prince Hall Masons before 1900

The oldest roster in the Nebraska files lists the membership of only one Omaha lodge, Rescue No. 25 (Iowa Jurisdiction) in 1899. It portrays a multi-class group, although the end-of-the-century date means it cannot necessarily be read backward to an earlier era. The occupations of seventeen of twenty-three members who could be traced included four barbers, four porters, three retired, two laborers, a postal clerk, a fireman, a waiter, and a janitor.[2] These were among the survivors of the depressed 1890s that had witnessed the diminution of the black population of Omaha from 4,566 in 1890 to 3,443 in 1900.

Perchance the earliest lodges during the 1870s and 1880s differed in occupational composition. The depression of the 1890s may have drastically altered the economic opportunities for blacks in Nebraska, thus affecting the membership in Prince Hall Masonry. Perhaps a dwindling number of persons in middle-class occupations were forced to accept stable blue-collar workers in order to maintain the viability of the lodge. Alternatively, Prince Hall Masonry may have followed the route of the United Order of True Reformers, which began as a middle-class dominated benevolent society but rapidly evolved into a multi-class organization.[3] Moreover, as Roger Lane has pointed out, the 1880s had witnessed a notable upsurge in the education of black professionals; thus, they may have played a more prominent role in Prince Hall Masonry in Nebraska prior to the depression of

1893.[4] On the other hand, the depressed nineties had sounded the death knell for Marvin Lodge No. 127 (Missouri Jurisdiction) located at Hastings, Nebraska, and most of the adult African Americans living in that community had worked as domestic servants.[5] Moreover, Rescue Lodge rosters mirror the situation found in the black communities of Cleveland, Detroit, and the cities of the Pacific Northwest.[6] Therefore, it is likely that the multi-class nature of Prince Hall Masonry in Nebraska dated from its origins in the state and that the membership of Rescue Lodge in 1899 reflected an established tradition of occupational diversity.

Early Twentieth Century

At any rate, the early twentieth-century rosters document the occupationally diverse, multi-class nature of Prince Hall Masonry in Nebraska. At the turn to the twentieth century it included the professional and entrepreneurial elite as well as the skilled service and industrial middle class, and the unskilled laborer. To lump these distinct groups into one category or to generalize the membership as middle-class based on the officer corps or a percentage of the membership camouflages the manner in which Prince Hall Masonry, at least in Nebraska, bridged the class lines of the compressed social scale that existed in the black communities. Because the application of white middle-class wealth, income, and occupational standards result in a lower-class placement for almost all blacks during the late nineteenth and early twentieth centuries, several scholars have introduced non-economic traits such as education, personal values, and social behavior to categorize class among African Americans. Important as these characteristics are to understanding the divisions within black society, they are virtually impossible to apply. Such information is not available for the hundreds of charter members of the Prince Hall Mason Grand Lodge of Nebraska. Moreover, to imply that a Prince Hall Mason had the "correct" values and thus was middle class is a tautology that relies on stereotypes and denigrates unskilled and semi-skilled workers. Class and values interact but are not the same. Belief in hard work, thrift, temperance, etc., is neither exclusive to the middle class nor held by all middle class individuals. Class models based on qualitative characteristics that cannot be measured using sources such as census data are not useful in my study. I am, therefore, arguing that a substantial class difference existed between a physician, an electrician, and a porter in a pool hall, even though they socialized together and although they may have held the same values.[7]

By 1908, Rescue's membership had jumped to thirty-nine, revealing renewed African American migration to the area prior to World War I and the Great Migration. Between 1900 and 1910 the black population in Nebraska increased by 1,420 (22 percent) to a total of 7,689. Omaha absorbed 983 of the total, average for a Midwestern or Western city prior to the Great Migration. Only seven cities outside the old Confederacy had a black population of ten thousand or more in 1910. Thus, while Omaha's black community was much smaller than Chicago's, it was comparable to communities in Cleveland, Minneapolis, Denver, and Los Angeles.[8]

During the first decade of the twentieth century twenty individuals joined Rescue lodge; the occupations for eight of them could be identified: three laborers (two of them worked for a meat-packing firm, possibly survivors from the black strikebreakers used in 1904[9]), two janitors, two entrepreneurs, and a porter. Finally, as of 1913, twenty-two more men were initiated, although total membership only climbed to forty-one. The high proportion of initiates to total membership demonstrates, on the one hand, the mobility of transient opportunistic men searching for success and, on the other hand, the economic insecurity that led to frequent suspension of members for non-payment of dues—although some individuals probably ceased payment and were suspended because they no longer wanted to be members.

The final twenty-two initiates maintain the variety of occupations of the thirteen fraters who could be identified, there were eight waiters, three porters (two Pullman porters, the first time anyone made that specific designation), a fireman at a meat-packing house, and the city inspector of weights and measures, for decades a black patronage position.[10] Rescue Lodge illustrated the variety of vocations, from professional to unskilled, at which black Masons labored and demonstrated the significance of service-sector employment, including the pervasive category of porter. The 1920 census, which not only asked for a person's job but also the nature of his or her employer, revealed that men listing themselves as porters worked at a wide array of establishments, including barber shops, saloons, retail stores, banks, railroad stations, clubs, restaurants, and pool halls.

The only pre–Great Migration Nebraska roster from the Missouri Jurisdiction discloses the same occupational composition for eastern Nebraska, except that two of the small-town lodges included farmers. In Omaha in 1912, Rough Ashler had fifty-six members (twenty-nine identified) and Excelsior had twenty-seven members (nineteen identified). Within that group were two professionals, three skilled laborers, six entrepreneurs, eight unskilled workers, and twenty-nine service-area employees. Lebanon lodge in Lincoln had sixty-nine members (forty-seven identified) including one physician, two entrepreneurs, thirteen unskilled laborers, and twenty-six service-area workers. Two members were retired and one listed himself as a student.

In comparison, the central and western Nebraska lodges of the Missouri jurisdiction demonstrated a slightly different occupational configuration. In 1912 St. John's in Grand Island had fifteen members and Shelton No. 87 in Alliance had nineteen members, but only seven and five members, respectively, could be identified, even after line-by-line scrolling the 1910 census for the entire county of each lodge. Possibly members in these less populated areas of Nebraska lived in other counties or had migrated within the two-year interval between the census and the roster, but the low identification rate may indicate that the alleged undercounting of blacks by the census bureau is neither recent nor solely urban. With few exceptions, black professionals and entrepreneurs did not reside in western or central Nebraska; the small African-American populations could not support lawyers, physicians, or dentists, and even the clergy were itinerants. George A. Flippin, MD, of Stromsburg was a rare exception, as were extraordinary entrepreneurs supported by the white community, such as J. S. Craig of Hastings and Sam Shelton of Alliance. Most of the Masons in central and western Nebraska lodges found unskilled and service-area jobs, many associated with the railroad or allied establishments such as hotels.[11]

The Grand Lodge of Nebraska

The rosters of the charter members of the Grand Lodge of Nebraska show that Prince Hall Masonry retained its multi-class character after the Great Migration, which both increased the membership of extant lodges and sparked the formation of new ones. Of the 513 men, however, 137 (27 percent of the membership) could not be identified in the 1920 census or in the city directories. Most city directories in Nebraska ceased using the (c) to designate "colored" in 1918, although M-H Directory Service of Brush, Colorado not only applied the (c) but also an (m) for Mexican in its 1939 publication for Alliance. This odious identification was functional for researchers so it is significantly more difficult to trace individuals during the years of rapid expansion immediately prior to the creation of the Nebraska Grand Lodge than for earlier years.

Unfortunately, Masonic record keeping exacerbated the problem. The rosters contain frequent misspellings (obvious references to the same person spelled differently), or give the last name only, or initial(s) plus last name. The absence of addresses, except on occasion for officers, eliminates the most obvious way to distinguish among people with common names—e.g., the 1920 Omaha City Directory listed nine men named Robert Johnson; the census revealed that three of them were black; which one was the Prince Hall Mason?

The census presented several problems. The soundex, a finder system that converts names to numbers in order to minimize spelling errors or problems with homophonous names, keys on heads of households, making it difficult to track lodgers. Many blacks simply did not get listed on the soundex. I found scores of unrecorded Prince Hall Masons in the manuscript census by scanning heavily black populated enumeration districts line by line.

Many factors contributed to the 1920 census undercount. Enumerators were poorly paid and often incompetent, and they were instructed to obtain information about families not at home from just about anyone living nearby. Many people avoided being counted because they feared data would go to the recently created Internal Revenue Service or Selective Service boards.[12] The Red Scare with its Palmer Raids restrained immigrant and African American participation. Omaha's last lynching, followed by a race riot, had preceded the count by only three months and probably intimidated both the white enumerators and the black residents. Thus, Rough Ashler No. 1 had 129 members listed on its charter roster; forty-five could not be found on the census rolls, yet sixteen of those forty-five had listed themselves in the City Directory of 1918, the last with the (c) designation. A total of fifty-five charter members from the rosters of eight different lodges not listed in the 1920 census (10 percent of the membership), were found in city directories. These men were not transients, although many of the others probably had come to Omaha during the Great Migration, may have been single, and had not established themselves as a head of a household. The absence of men in the city directory from the census is evidence of the under counting of African Americans.

Housing Patterns of Prince Hall Masons

The 1920 census asked for information related to family, residence, personal characteristics, education, nativity, and occupation. By 1920 Prince Hall Masons were becoming ghettoized in Omaha. Twenty years earlier only seven of the seventeen identified members of Rescue Lodge lived in the area that became the Near Northside, one of the eventual de facto segregated residential areas for blacks in Omaha. (A second one developed adjacent to the stockyard-meatpacking area in the former suburb of South Omaha, annexed in 1915.) Thirteen of the sixteen identified new initiates from 1913 resided on the Near Northside. Despite their "respectability" and relative economic security, Prince Hall Masons did not escape the trend in housing discrimination. While blacks found themselves increasingly confined, these areas actually remained significantly integrated until after the second Great Migration of World War II because of the relatively small number of African Americans in the total population.[13]

Researching mobility in pre–World War I Omaha, Howard Chudacoff traced the residential patterns of a "few" blacks during the 1890s who "occupied the lower occupational strata" and found that they "moved in directions and frequencies similar to those of their white counterparts." By 1902, however, housing notices "for colored families" began to appear in the local press, and "the segregation index for blacks increased from 36.2 in 1910 to 47.9 in 1920."[14] The absence of nineteenth-century rosters for the other lodges precludes longitudinal analysis of residential configurations in the other Nebraska cities.

The Great Migration solidified the segregated pattern in Omaha. Of the 249 (of 349) identifiable Prince Hall Mason heads of household residing in the city in 1920, 83 percent lived in the areas subsequently described as the ghettos. Only four of the sixteen Prince Hall householders in the formerly independent area of South Omaha resided beyond the stockyards vicinity and a mere forty of 233 heads of households in historic Omaha lived outside the Near Northside. Fourteen non-ghetto residents were identified in the City Directory, which did not distinguish between a homeowner and a renter, but eighteen of the forty-two identified owned their residences, while one was a medical student in a dormitory, two lived in an all-black hotel operated for Union Pacific Rail Road employees in an otherwise all-white neighborhood, and another five were live-in janitors at white-occupied apartment buildings. In some cases employment, not equal access, determined a person's non-ghetto residence. The two most significant areas of non-ghetto residence for Prince Hall Masons consisted of a smattering of homeowners on contiguous streets north and west of the contemporary Near Northside and a group of owners and renters in an area stretching a few blocks south of Dodge Street from 11th to 30th.

Despite the increased concentration, or possibly because ghettoization enabled African Americans to purchase dwellings in older neighborhoods with depressed values, Prince Hall Masons displayed a high percentage of home ownership. Of 306 Masons identified by type of residence, 128 or 42 percent owned their home (forty-three freeholders and eighty-five with a mortgage). The 207 missing cases probably distort the rate of home ownership upward, as property owners were most likely to list themselves in a city directory or to get counted in a census. Yet, even assuming that all 207 were non-homeowners, possibly distorting in the opposite direction, the homeowners represented 25 percent of the 513 total Prince Hall Masons, a figure still above the national average for black home ownership in 1920 (22.3 percent).[15]

Obviously, the rate of home ownership increased with age. Lodgers were predominantly young, while renters spread about evenly across the age spectrum. Well over 90 percent of the homeowners were married, although one half of the married Prince Hall Mason couples rented their living space. Less evident was the geographic dispersal of home ownership: 58 percent of the lodge members in Grand Island, 49 percent in Lincoln, and 43 percent in Omaha owned their homes, while fewer than a quarter of the Prince Hall Masons in Alliance, Hastings, and Scottsbluff did so. The three smaller towns had only a few black residents, mostly associated with the railroad. Short stays and lack of available housing may also have influenced the ownership rates.

Generally occupation level did not determine home ownership. A similar percentage of unskilled laborers (thirty-nine of 114, 34 percent) owned a home as did professionals (six of seventeen, 35 percent). The percentage of unskilled laborers who purchased homes matched the percentage for the entire Grand Lodge of Nebraska and speaks well for the usually ignored social mobility of that class. Scholars have documented property acquisition among blue-collar European migrants, but not among African Americans. Home ownership figures for the Prince Hall Masons of Nebraska compare favorably with those of immigrants in Northern cities.[16] Prince Hall Masons employed in the service sector acquired property at a slightly higher rate (forty-one of ninety-eight, 42 percent), while 62 percent of entrepreneurs (nineteen of twenty-nine) were homeowners.

Skin Color and Class Issues

Skin tone also frequently denotes class division among African Americans. According to William Muraskin, Prince Hall Masonry's "selectivity and elite character in the nineteenth century" gave it "a strong 'mulatto' caste." He claimed that "intraracial 'blackballing' by light-skinned blacks against darker ones was probably fairly widespread in the Order," and continued "well into the twentieth century. The relative 'democratization' of the fraternity, by the admission of middle-class, non-elite, darker blacks appears to have come after the turn of the century when thousands of new members entered." Muraskin admitted that "hard evidence for the color factors in black Masonry are hard to come by," but he cited photographs of Masonic leaders and an interview with a "prominent California Mason."[17] Historical and geographic factors, however, may have been more significant than intraracial color prejudice. As of 1850, "the proportion of mulattoes in the free colored population greatly exceeded the proportion in the slave population," and a man had to be free to join Prince Hall Masonry. Furthermore, during the second half of the nineteenth century the West contained the highest percentage of mulattoes within its black population.[18] The evidence from Nebraska, at any rate, does not support a powerfully selective racial bias.

The few extant photographs of nineteenth-century Prince Hall Masons in Nebraska do not necessarily show mulatto predominance and their evidence, like that of contemporary newspapers, distorts the image. Using the handful of leaders to characterize the entire order is problematic. Local circumstances probably produced a wide variety of demographics. For example, an 1897 photograph of Prince Hall Masons from Mississippi and another turn-of-the-century picture of a military lodge that had recently served at Ft. Robinson, Nebraska, reveal a rich diversity of skin tones with no apparent numerical or "political" superiority by light-skinned individuals.[19] Mulattoes certainly played a significant role but, in the numerically small black communities in Nebraska, they could not establish a light-skinned restriction. Moreover, dark-skinned, Negro-featured individuals such as M. O. Ricketts, a physician, a Nebraska state legislator during the 1890s, worshipful master in Omaha, and subsequent Grand Master of the Missouri jurisdiction, demonstrated that non-mulattoes not only gained entrance but rose to the very top of the fraternity and the community.

The 1920 census revealed that 33 percent of the 318 identified Prince Hall Masons claimed mulatto as their "race or color." Ultimate racial designation, however, relied upon "the personal impression of the enumerator.... The delineation between black and mulatto [the two choices specified, Negro was not used] was also at the discretion of the enumerator; black being defined as 'Negroes of full blood' and mulatto as 'all Negroes having some portion of white blood.'"[20] The Census Bureau's loose definition renders its figure suspect for calculating the actual size of a light-skinned elite. Nonetheless, Prince Hall Masons took pride in the mulatto classification in 1920. In all eleven cases where a black person had married a mulatto and the couple listed children, they designated their offspring as mulatto (and the enumerator agreed). How many of the adult mulattoes also fit that imprecise definition? Only two interracial marriages existed in the fraternity; both were black men with white wives, despite the state anti-miscegenation law. As the census did not list the location of marriages or the length of residence in a state, one cannot ascertain when or where those unions commenced or what they mean in terms of the Nebraska miscegenation statute.

Although the enforcement of the bans on interracial marriages probably differed according to place and time, the rapid spread of bans during the post–Civil War era indicated widespread official opposition to such marriages, and miscegenation was "extremely uncommon" (less than .2 percent) in the United States before World War II.[21] A sizeable percentage of Prince Hall Masons of all ages, but particularly those between thirty-one and sixty years old, designated themselves as mulatto. It is not possible, however, to calculate the actual number of mulattos as opposed to those who were only a quarter or an eighth or less in descent from one race or the other. While it is probable that blacks in Nebraska manifested some sort of the widely reported color status system, none of the evidence suggests that a restrictive light-skinned elite dominated Prince Hall Masonry.

Occupational Status of Prince Hall Masons

Neither did an economic elite dominate the fraternity in Nebraska. Prince Hall Masons worked at an array of specific jobs that reflected the general distribution of blacks in the Omaha and Nebraska economies. The fraternity presented a cross section of the employed African American community, not a distorted elite segment. More than one-third of the members held unskilled jobs while another 32 percent worked in the service sector. Service sector jobs on the railroads were more prestigious and paid better than those in small local establishments. Only 26.9 percent of the members occupied the traditional middle class and elite occupations such as skilled laborer, white collar worker, civil servant, professional, or entrepreneur, but railroad cooks, porters, and so on claimed middle class status. Prince Hall Masonry in Nebraska united all respectable classes in the black population that could afford and that desired membership. Surprisingly, although three-fourths of the members toiled at non-middle-class jobs, only one-fourth (sixty-five of 254) of the wives of Prince Hall Masons worked. The percentage of wage-earning wives shrinks further when one considers that five wives assisted their husbands in family businesses and another eleven provided services from their homes. The proportion of Prince Hall Mason working wives was almost half the average for blacks in Northern cities with limited industrial employment for black males.[22] Moreover, despite the oft repeated claim that entrepreneurs joined fraternities to establish business contacts, the Prince Hall Masons of Nebraska attracted only a few of the limited number of black entrepreneurs in the state. Increasing segregation and discrimination provided opportunity to blacks elsewhere, but the black population in Nebraska cities was too small to support black-owned businesses serving black-only clienteles.

A Multi-Class Fraternity

While I differ from him on job categorization and socioeconomic interpretation, Muraskin's occupational list for Good Hope Lodge of Oakland, California, for 1923 reads very much like my Nebraska statistics. I did not separate "public employees" and "railroad men" as categories, classifying jobs by socioeconomic and skill levels (i.e., a janitor at a post office and a laborer at a railroad yard are unskilled). Both our lists reveal a significantly high percentage of unskilled workers fraternizing with professionals.[23] Those multi-class bodies contrast sharply with the white Masons of Oakland. Lynn Dumenil constructed an employment chart for three white Mason lodges in 1919. The figures revealed few blue-collar workers of any type. Less than 1 percent of the membership of each lodge was unskilled labor and only one of the three lodges nudged above 6 percent of its members in the semi-skilled category.[24] In comparison to the distinctly middle-class white Masons of Oakland, the Prince Hall Masons of Nebraska were multi-class.

Each of the various Nebraska lodges included members from the full range of occupational categories. While at least 30 percent of the members of each lodge worked as unskilled laborers, for geographic-economic reasons the three western Nebraska lodges had significantly higher rates—Alliance No. 7, 43.8 percent; True American No. 6 in Grand Island, 58.8 percent; and Marvin No. 5 in Hastings, 61 percent. None of the lodges had an elite membership based on class distinctions. All were multi-class groups of neighbors and co-workers. The differences among lodges were based on location and history, but the social and economic variations were minor and the non-elite pattern held for the grand lodge as a whole. Because of Nebraska's small membership pool and restricted economic opportunities—the Prince Hall Grand Lodge of Nebraska was a multi-class fraternity, an exemplary American institution of young geographic and socially (within the constricted scale of the segregated community) mobile African Americans.

Notes

I would like to thank Lynn Dumenil, David Fahey, and Charles L. Harper for commenting on drafts of this article.

1. William A. Muraskin, *Middle-class Blacks in a White Society: Prince Hall Freemasonry in America* (Berkeley: University of California Press, 1975); Loretta J. Williams, *Black Freemasonry and Middle-Class Realities* (Columbia: University of Missouri Press, 1980).

2. Roster in the Proceedings of the Twelfth Annual Communication, Prince Hall Grand Lodge of Iowa, 1899, pp. 42–43. Author's possession. Individual's occupations were derived from *Omaha City Directory*, 1899.

3. James D. Watkinson, "William Washington Browne and the True Reformers of Richmond, Virginia," *The Virginia Magazine of History and Biography* 97 (July 1989): 379–80.

4. Roger Lane, "Black Philadelphia Then and Now: The 'Underclass' of the Late 20th Century Compared with Poorer African-Americans of the Late 19th Century," *Drugs, Crime, and Social Isolation: Barriers to Urban Opportunity* (Washington DC: Urban Institute Press, 1992), pp. 30–31.

5. Dorothy Weyer Creigh, *Adams County: The Story* (Hastings NE: Adams County–Hastings Centennial Commission, 1972), pp. 330–31.

6. All of the following indicated that Prince Hall Masonry in their locale was a multi-class institution: Kenneth Kusmer, *A Ghetto Takes Shape: Black Cleveland, 1870–1930* (Urbana: University of Illinois Press, 1976), p. 97; David M. Katzman, *Before the Ghetto: Black Detroit in the Nineteenth Century* (Urbana: University of Illinois Press, 1973), p. 148; and Quintard Taylor, "The Emergence of Black Communities in the Pacific Northwest: 1865–1910," *Journal of Negro History* 64 (1979): 343–44. Kusmer and Katzman analyzed Prince Hall Masonry directly, while I derive Prince Hall masonry membership in the Pacific Northwest from Taylor's discussion of employment patterns of the small black population in the area.

7. For analysis of the African American class structure prior to World War II see W. E. B. Du Bois, *The Philadelphia Negro* (1899; rpt. New York: Benjamin Bloom, 1967); St. Clair Drake and Horace Cayton, *Black Metropolis*, rev. ed. (New York: Harper and Row, 1962); and Gunnar Myrdal, *An American Dilemma* (1944; rpt. New York: McGraw-Hill, 1964).

8. Bureau of the Census, *Negro Population, 1790–1915* (Washington DC: Government Printing Office, 1918), pp. 92–93, 100.

9. William C. Pratt, "Divided Workers, Divided Communities: The 1921–22 Packinghouse Strike in Omaha and Nebraska City," *Labor's Heritage* 5 (Winter 1994): 56.

10. Proceedings of the annual communications of the Prince Hall Grand Lodge of Iowa for the years 1900–1913. Author's possession. Occupations from *Omaha City Directory*, 1900–1913 and from Manuscript Census of the United States, 1900 and 1910.

11. Rosters in the Proceedings of the Forty-sixth Annual Communication, Prince

Hall Grand Lodge of Missouri, 1912, pp. 117–35. Author's possession. Occupations from *Alliance City Directory, 1939; Grand Island City Directory, 1912; Hastings City Directory, 1912; Lincoln City Directory, 1912; Omaha City Directory, 1912;* and Manuscript Census of the United States, 1910 and 1920.

12. Kellee Green, "The Fourteenth Numbering of the People: The 1920 Federal Census," *Prologue* 23 (Summer 1991): 133–35.

13. The boundaries for the Near Northside are described in Dennis N. Mihelich, "World War II and the Transformation of the Omaha Urban League," *Nebraska History* 60 (Fall 1979): 402, 405; I culled the information from John P. Zipay, "The Changing Population of the Omaha SMSA, 1860–1967" (Omaha Urban Research Project, University of Omaha, 1967), pp. 11–15; James R. Mead, "An Ecological Study of the Second Ward of Omaha" (Master's thesis, University of Omaha, 1953), pp. 10–34; Murphy Cleophus Williams, "An Ecological Study of the Negro in Ward Seven" (Master's thesis, University of Omaha, 1947), pp. 6–7.

14. Howard Chudacoff, *Mobile Americans: Residential and Social Mobility in Omaha, 1880–1920* (New York: Oxford University Press, 1972), pp. 127, 155.

15. Each characteristic in the analysis of the economic attributes of the Prince Hall Masons is based on available data. The absolute number in each group analyzed varies because census enumerators on occasion failed to record information for a question or because an individual was identified through a city directory that provided limited information on residence and occupation. Bureau of the Census, *Negroes in the United States, 1920–32* (Washington DC: Government Printing Office, 1935), p. 260.

16. Stanley Lieberson, *Ethnic Patterns in American Cities* (Glencoe IL: The Free Press, 1963), pp. 206–18. Lieberson's figures are for 1930, following a prosperous decade of home buying that saw the percentage of black homeowners in Nebraska climb to 33.9 percent (*Negroes in the United States*, p. 260). I do not have home ownership data for the Prince Hall Masons for 1930, but their rates from 1920 already compare favorably with the immigrant data from 1930.

17. Muraskin, *Middle-class Blacks*, pp. 41n119–21.

18. Bureau of the Census, *Negro Population*, p. 209.

19. The Mississippi photograph is included in the article "Fraternal Societies" in the *Encyclopedia of Black America*, ed. W. Augustus Low (New York: McGraw-Hill, 1981), p. 394, and the Nebraska photograph is in Joseph A. Walkes, Jr., *Black Square and Compass: 200 Years of Prince Hall Freemasonry* (Richmond VA: Macoy Publishing and Masonic Supply Co., 1979), p. 73.

20. Green, "Fourteenth Numbering," p. 136.

21. Deborah Lynn Kitchen, "Interracial Marriage in the United States, 1900–1980" (PhD dissertation, University of Minnesota, 1993), p. 100.

22. Jacqueline Jones, *Labor of Love, Labor of Sorrow: Women, Work, and the Family from Slavery to the Present* (New York: Basic Books, 1985), p. 162.

23. Muraskin, *Middle-class Blacks*, pp. 93; for an interpretation of Prince Hall Masonry that asserts its middle-class nature, see Williams, *Black Freemasonry*, pp. 92–93, 105.

24. Lynn Dumenil, *Freemasonry and American Culture, 1880–1930* (Princeton: Princeton University Press, 1984), pp. 227, 229.

CHAPTER 7

Diplomatic Racism:
Canadian Government and Black Migration from Oklahoma, 1905–1912

R. BRUCE SHEPARD

From the turn of the century until World War I, hundreds of thousands of American farmers migrated to western Canada.¹ Not all of them were welcomed. Between 1905 and 1912, more than one thousand black men, women, and children joined the trek.² They came mainly from Oklahoma, and they settled in Saskatchewan and Alberta. While their numbers were small in comparison to the total American migration, the appearance of these black settlers aroused bitter race prejudice among western Canadians, many of whom demanded that the Canadian government stop more blacks from coming. How the government went about this task is the subject of this article.

Who were these black immigrants? They were ex-slaves and the descendants of former slaves who had moved westward from the older Southern states following Reconstruction.³ These people settled in what were then the Oklahoma and Indian Territories, and began leaving for western Canada at the time these "Twin Territories" began preparing for statehood in 1907.

The immediate cause of the migration was racist legislation that Oklahoma aimed at blacks living in the state. Immediately after statehood was achieved in 1907, segregation legislation was passed that confined blacks to separate schools, railroad cars, and seating on street cars. The very first bill introduced in the new state House of Representatives was a "Jim Crow" measure, while in the state Senate it was only the fourth. In 1910, the blacks' rights were again cut back when their right to vote was taken away. Black Oklahomans reacted immediately to these laws by challenging them in the courts and organizing protests. Some even turned to violence.[4] Nothing worked, however, and many began looking for a way out of Oklahoma.

Segregation and disfranchisement were the key factors that sent the blacks toward Canada. Jeff Edwards of Amber Valley, Alberta, claimed that he first became interested in western Canada when Oklahoma began its segregation policies. The blacks who went north to eastern Canada were fleeing slavery, he said; "We in Amber Valley are here because we fled something almost as hard to bear—'Jim Crowism.'" One black emigrant group reached St. Paul, Minnesota, in March 1911 and said they had been driven from Oklahoma by the theft of their property and the denial of their right to vote. They also said that there were five thousand more blacks ready to follow them. These sentiments were echoed by one member of a group of black Oklahomans who tried to enter Canada in British Columbia. Only two were admitted, and one was reported in Vancouver as stating, "The people of Oklahoma treat us like dogs. We are not allowed to vote and we are not admitted to any of the theatres or public places. They won't even let us ride the street cars in some of the towns." When asked why they chose Canada, he answered, "We heard about the free lands here and also that everyone had the right to vote and was a free man."[5]

The black migrants learned about Canada by reading their local newspapers. Before World War I the government of Canada advertised extensively in American newspapers, attempting to lure farmers to the Canadian plains. Even though the Canadian government did not issue special promotional material for blacks, as it did for other

American ethnocultural groups, advertisements for Canadian land filled black Oklahoma newspapers. The Canadian government appears to have contracted through a press service and may not have checked the end products too closely in its haste to attract settlers.[6]

These advertisements cast doubt on the argument that black farmers had no way of becoming informed about Canada because they were poorly educated and often illiterate and that, therefore, Canada was never especially attractive to them.[7] In fact, the opposite was true—Canada was very attractive to the blacks, and they could easily learn about it.

Extensive advertising about Canadian settlement appeared in the black Oklahoma press. While it is true that African Americans had a high illiteracy rate, that rate had fallen from 1865, when only one in twenty could read and write, to one out of every two by 1900.[8] In any case, it takes only one literate person to read a paper to a group of illiterates, and once word of a movement starts, it spreads easily. Furthermore, to take one example, the black *Boley Progress*, in which Canadian advertisements appeared, was distributed throughout the South in an effort to attract blacks to that town. Therefore, blacks in other states could have known of Canada's desire for settlers.[9] The question then is not why only several hundred blacks trekked to western Canada, but what stopped several thousand from following them? The answer lies in the actions of the government of Canada.

In 1910 the Democratic party of Oklahoma began a campaign to disfranchise the state's black citizens. This sent many more blacks toward the Canadian border. Frank Oliver, the Canadian minister of the interior, and thus the man responsible for immigration, became so concerned with the developing black exodus that he sent his inspector of United States agencies on a five-day trip to Oklahoma. The minister received a letter on the issue in September 1910.[10]

Following this visit, the Canadian government took steps to try to halt the migration. It contacted its agent in Kansas City, who was closest to the scene, and suggested that he contact the postmasters of the towns stamped on inquiries, asking whether the person writing was black or white. The idea was that if the agent could find out which writers were black, he would not send immigration literature to them. Some of the postmasters' replies show the state of race relations in Oklahoma at the time; one from Keystone used the term "Nigger," while another from Hominy read, "black as hell." The border points of Emerson, Manitoba, and Portal, Saskatchewan, were also alerted, and the agents told to examine any blacks carefully, since the American agents were no longer issuing settlers' certificates to them.

When several black families appeared in Edmonton late in December 1910, Frank Oliver wanted to know who had let them in and whether they had been medically examined. On January 5, 1911, the minister got his answer. This group had gone from Oklahoma to Vancouver, on Canada's West Coast, and then up to Edmonton. The government immigration officers in Vancouver were then given the same instructions as those at the other border crossings. The Edmonton agent also got a telegram on January 5, telling him to take action if he could discover any reason for deporting any of the immigrants and suggesting that he call in the city health officer if he suspected any would not meet the physical qualifications.[11]

Clearly, the Canadian immigration authorities believed they could stop the influx by depriving the blacks of information. This proved to be haphazard at best, so they tried to use vigorous medical examinations at the border as a deterrent. They even went so far as to try to bribe the medical authorities. In the spring of 1911 the American consul-general in Winnipeg, John E. Jones, had to help a group of his black countrymen enter Canada. Jones later determined that the commissioner of immigration for western Canada had offered the medical inspector a fee for every potential black immigrant he turned away.[12] To his credit, the doctor does not appear to have taken the money. In any case, tough medical inspections were rendered ineffective when obviously healthy black men, women, and children presented themselves. In March 1911 a large group led by one Henry Sneed, bound for northern Alberta, shattered the medical examination idea because of their good physical condition. This fact, plus their numbers, attracted considerable publicity.[13] The publicity, in turn, provoked comment and revealed western Canadians' deep feelings on the subject of black immigration.

White western Canadians reacted overwhelmingly against the black settlers. Sneed's group aroused negative comments from newspapers across the prairies. The Edmonton chapter of the Independent Order Daughters of the Empire, a women's patriotic group, petitioned the minister of the interior in Ottawa to keep the blacks out. The Edmonton Board of Trade launched a vigorous and successful petition campaign in that city. They also contacted other similar agencies, and by the end of May 1911, boards of trade across western Canada had all joined the Edmontonians in denouncing the black immigration. Several chapters of the United Farmers of Alberta also went on record as favoring an end to the migration.[14] This widespread public response was echoed in the House of Commons in Ottawa. On April 3, 1911, William Thoburn, the Conservative member for the Ontario riding of Lanark North, asked the minister of the interior whether the government was prepared to stop the developing black influx and whether it would not be preferable "to preserve for the sons of Canada, the lands they propose to give to niggers?"[15]

While Ottawa tried to find a solution to its dilemma, events in Oklahoma were forcing more blacks to try to escape. In 1911, their condition was only too clear, especially after an ugly lynching in May of that year. A black mother and son, arrested for murdering a deputy sheriff, were taken from the Okemah jail, dragged to a railway bridge south of the town, and hanged. Blacks were predictably horror-struck by the event. According to one black journal, pictures of the crime were being openly sold. It did not attempt to conceal its anguish when it cried:

> Oh! where is that christian spirit we hear so much about
> -What will the good citizens do to apprehend these mobs
> -Wait, we shall see-Comment is unnecessary. Such a crime is simply Hell on Earth. No excuse can be set forth to justify the act.[16]

Western Canada was still an escape from these horrors, for despite their concern with black immigration, the Canadian government had not removed its advertisements from black Oklahoma newspapers. Throughout 1911, the qualities of the northern prairies continued to be described in glowing terms. The Canadian authorities were well aware of the continued interest of black Oklahomans. On March 14, 1911, the secretary of the Department of the Interior, L. M. Fortier, wrote to W. W. Cory, deputy minister of the department, arguing that, "if we are to prevent a large influx of these people during the next six months, some steps will have to be taken at once."[17]

Another measure of the continued black interest in moving to Canada was the commentary this issue stirred in the black Oklahoma press. Little of it was favorable, however, since black editors felt that their people should stay where they were and face their problems. The *Clearview Patriarch*, for example, understood that it had cost more than five thousand dollars to transport one large party north, and argued that such a sum, if added to another, could operate a huge business that would be a "credit to the race." It also did not believe that the best results could be obtained by moving so often. Another black journal was even more emphatic. After noting that many blacks had come to Oklahoma in its early days, overcome crises, built themselves homes and farms, and now had a place where they could raise their heads, it argued that these same people were now selling everything they had without due consideration. Conditions in Oklahoma were improving, it urged.[18]

Reports on the agitation against the black immigration into western Canada obviously buttressed the black editors' arguments, and they were noted and commented upon. In a front-page editorial in its April 13, 1911 issue, the *Clearview Patriarch* reprinted an entire editorial from the *Edmonton* journal of March 27 that recognized the existence of anti-black prejudice in western Canada. The black newspaper then argued that the Canadian item proved that, wherever he went, the black man had to face a problem. Not quite a month later, the black *Oklahoma Guide* of Guthrie carried a front-page item from an unidentified New York newspaper headlined, "Protest against Immigration-Race Prejudice Caused by Colored People in Canada." This piece noted the increase in antiblack feeling in Alberta and Saskatchewan due to the rise in black immigration from Oklahoma, and observed that, for the first time since they began moving north, a class of American citizens was being deemed undesirable by Canada. The resolutions of the boards of trade in Edmonton and other western Canadian communities were noted, as was the argument that blacks could not adapt to the climate. This, the article suggested, was only a polite way of saying that the blacks were not welcome. The Canadian government was obviously feeling the pressure of public opinion, and it could be forced to pass restrictive immigration regulations. The journal's argument concluded by noting that the American federal authorities were also in a delicate position, "in view of the fact that although the federal government does not protect the Negro from disfranchisement at the hands of the Southerns, it does hold him entitled to the same rights as the white man under foreign treaties and conventions."[19]

Black Oklahomans continued to be informed of Canada's reception of their brethren. The Muskogee *Baptist Informer* carried an item on June 8, 1911 about a resolution of the Calgary Board of Trade against black immigration.[20] But there was a more personal source of information, albeit somewhat biased, for blacks interested in going to Canada or for those who were headed north. Sometime in April or May 1911, the Canadian government sent the first of its agents to Oklahoma to report on the black situation and take action against their migrating to Canada. The government had finally found a way to stop, and not merely frustrate, the black trek.[21]

Sending an agent to Oklahoma was part of a Canadian government plan to stop the black immigration. The strategy was revealed to John Jones, the United States consul in Winnipeg, by Bruce Walker, the Canadian commissioner of immigration in that city, in a confidential meeting held on May 22, 1911. During the meeting Walker stated that an order-in-council would be passed shortly that would bar blacks from entering Canada.[22] In the meantime, the Canadian government was doing all that it could to persuade blacks not to go to western Canada. The agent in Oklahoma, Walker stated, was pointing out to blacks the trouble they would have with the Canadian climate and the prejudice that was emerging in western Canada against their entry. Walker also told Jones that his agent was suggesting to black Oklahomans that they were the innocent victims of a scheme, engineered by a major railroad company operating in Oklahoma, to get their land for less than it was worth by telling them to go to Canada.

Walker also revealed to Jones that he had hired a black physician from the United States and had sent him to investigate the existing black settlements in western Canada. Once the black doctor had completed his report, it would be sent to Ottawa. In the meantime, the usual medical inspection of immigrants would be dropped for blacks, Walker indicated, since it was his intention to bar them completely.[23]

The agent sent to Oklahoma was C. W. Speers. He contacted W. J. White, the inspector of United States agencies in Ottawa, on May 8 and again on May 17 to describe his visits to Muskogee, Tulsa, Oklahoma City, and Wellston, Oklahoma. He described the blacks' poor housing and generally inferior conditions, and argued that "Jim Crow" segregation and disfranchisement were the "great source" of their problems. He had been able to discuss the emigration issue with several black preachers and believed that this was the area with the best potential for stopping the flow. Dr. S. S. Jones, president of the Oklahoma Conference of Black Baptists and editor of the *Baptist Informer*, had readily agreed with Speers's assessment of the situation and had promised to use his influence to stop the blacks from leaving. Several of his colleagues had joined him in this vow. Jones was as good as his word, for he publicized his meeting with Speers and the other black ministers in his newspaper. Speers was correct, the preacher argued; black people should stay in Oklahoma and fight for their rights. Jones also wrote to W. D. Scott to inform him that he felt the blacks should not enter Canada because of the harsh climate, and he gave the Canadian official permission to use his letter in any way he saw fit.[24]

The Immigration Branch became aware of Speers's success on May 15 when it received a letter from the Reverend H. H. Edmond of Oklahoma City. Edmond contacted the superintendent of immigration to get information about Canada before advising his congregation on whether to leave. He was having second thoughts since Speers contacted him and told him not to leave, but he wanted to know for certain what the weather and the country were like. The superintendent replied to Edmond's queries with a letter arguing that for climatic reasons he and his black followers should not come.[25]

Speers was in Chicago during the last week in May, but his interest still lay further south. On May 24 he addressed virtually identical letters to Jones in Muskogee and to a Reverend Hernagin in Oklahoma City, obviously following up his earlier contacts. In his letters, Speers referred to Booker T. Washington's teachings and stated,

Surely with a degree of confidence they [black Oklahomans] can let their buckets down and draw from their own resources in the midst of their own congenial surroundings.

Why should your people be driven hither and thither, through oppressive and despotic measures to climates and conditions wholly unsuitable? Why cannot they dwell in peace enjoying every privilege of full citizenship in the country and under conditions best suited to themselves?

I feel assured that your advice to the colored people will not only benefit them, but reflect credit upon yourself.[26]

On May 31 Speers, now in Ottawa, wrote to W. D. Scott regarding other matters relating to black immigration. Speers said he had observed the agents of American railroads operating in Oklahoma, trying to increase traffic by encouraging blacks to go to Canada. He had spoken to railroad officials when he was in Kansas City, and they had promised to stop the soliciting. He had also spoken to D. B. Hanna, third vice-president of the Canadian Northern Railway, when he was in Toronto, and Hanna had promised to use his influence on the southern companies. Speers then suggested that William Whyte, second vice-president of the Canadian Pacific Railway, should also be asked to use his influences, "as there is a strong international courtesy between the railway companies. I feel assured that this would have a very good effect," he said.

Speers's apparent success with the black clergymen and his continual reference to Booker T. Washington's ideas may have been the basis for a suggestion by W. H. Rogers, now the Canadian agent in Kansas City. In a letter to an unnamed superior in Ottawa, Rogers argued that the only way to stop the blacks was by striking the fear of death into them. He proposed that evidence of blacks dying in cold climates be collected and sent to Booker T. Washington, who believed that blacks should stay in the South. "I feel sure his influence would be material advantage to us in this matter," Rogers said. While there is no evidence that this proposal was ever acted upon, it did reflect a fertile mind for schemes to stop the black movement, and this was not Rogers's only proposal. In an earlier letter to W. D. Scott, the Kansas City agent had said that he was *very* pleased with Speers's work and recommended that he continue it. Rogers said he felt that Speers's approach was the most effective way of dealing with the problem, but if that agent were unable to return to Oklahoma, a Reverend J. B. Puckett could be used. "This man," Rogers said, "would not cost the Department nearly as much as that colored man from Chicago."[27]

"That colored man from Chicago" was Dr. G. W. Miller, the American black medical doctor who had been hired to tour the black settlements in western Canada. Apparently satisfied with his report, the Canadian government employed Miller as its second agent to be sent to Oklahoma to try to stop the black migration. Miller was clearly the more effective agent because he was black and was thus more readily accepted. In addition, he had professional medical qualifications and could therefore buttress the idea that blacks would be affected by Canada's climate.

Exactly when the doctor arrived in Oklahoma is as obscure as how much he was being paid, but beginning on June 24, 1911, he sent daily reports to Chicago. In his first report, sent from Muskogee, Miller said he had interviewed a Reverend Perkins of the Second Baptist Church and had convinced him to keep his congregation in Oklahoma. In the next day's report, he said he had spoken to large audiences at the First and Second Baptist churches and thought that he had managed to change a number of minds. He also said he had arranged to have his address printed in Reverend Jones's Muskogee *Baptist Informer*, but that the clergyman-publisher wanted to be paid for the service.

Miller's first two reports were a blueprint for his activities over the next month. He would enter a town or city, contact the black clergymen and anyone he heard was interested in going to Canada, arrange to speak in the churches or at some large gathering, and have his speech reprinted in the local black newspaper, if there was one. He did not waste any time, either, for he crisscrossed eastern Oklahoma rather quickly. On June 26 he reported from Okmulgee that he had spoken to several black clergymen who promised to help stop the flow. On June 27 he was reporting from Weleetka, having stopped at Bryant and Henryetta "en route." He had not found any blacks in either of the latter places, but many in Weleetka seemed interested in going north, and he called a meeting for the next night. "It is quite an easy matter to get the people here," he said, "as they are all anxious to hear about Canada."

On June 28 Miller described the meeting at Weleetka and once again claimed to have convinced many not to head north. He began his talk by "describing minutely" what happened to him when he entered Canada, a snow storm he had witnessed, and the early and late frosts he had encountered. He found that these descriptions were new to the people. His aim, he said, was not only to discourage the northward migration, but to get the blacks to see how thankful they should be to live in Oklahoma, with its bountiful soil and good climate.[28]

Miller was modest in describing his talks. An article he wrote for the Guthrie *Oklahoma Guide* has survived, and it is possible to gain an insight into his discussions. Miller began with a running commentary on what blacks could expect when reaching Canada and then singled out specific areas that they would be interested in. He said he felt it was his solemn duty to his race to make them aware of the conditions he found when he traveled in western Canada and of the plight of those who had already headed north without question or investigation. He could not understand why people would sacrifice what they had spent their lives acquiring, to go to a country "that is desolate, frigid, unsettled, unknown and to which they are climatically unfamiliar and financially unfit."

The blacks' problems began at the international boundary. A government inspector would meet them, Miller said, and examine their luggage. Then the entire family would be subject to a thorough medical examination, "where your wife and daughter are stripped of their clothes before your very eyes and examined by a board of men. What man of you would desire his family undressed and humiliated in such a manner," he asked. Their livestock was also examined, but since this commonly took thirty days, the extra expense was a real burden. And all of this took place, he said, even before they were allowed to enter the "so-called promised land."

Nor should the blacks think they had escaped racial prejudice by entering Canada, for wherever there were two distinct races, hostility appeared. Yet there were those who would disregard his warnings, who would rush off and waste their life's savings in one season, reduce their families to poverty, and do it all in a land where the winters were long and cold, and the summer, "but a dim memory of morning." They should stay where they were, Miller argued, where they had friends, happiness, and bountiful harvests. Besides, their children had to go to school, and there were none in the Canadian woods. If they wanted to go to a city or to church, they would have to travel great distances.

They would also have to go at least seventy-five miles to find a doctor, whereas they had medical help at their door where they were. Above all, there was the intense Canadian cold—snow fell waist deep, and the ground froze to a depth of from six to ten feet. They had all been born and raised in the South: "it will cost your life to live one winter in Canada," Miller argued.

Miller then turned his attention to specific areas such as food, clothing, the soil, crops, the seasons, water, and shelter, but his overwhelmingly negative tone did not change. They would find that food would cost twice as much in Canada as it did in Oklahoma, he said, and because of the climate, they would find they ate more. Their farms would not keep up with their demands, and they would end up buying food imported from the United States. They could not get many of the foods they would want, and if it was true that man lived to eat, then many of them would surely die. If they did not starve, then they would freeze to death or die of consumption or pneumonia because they lacked the proper clothing. After spending all of their money to be transported to their new homes, they would find that they did not have funds for the necessary warm clothing and furs.

The soil in western Canada was not what they had been led to believe, Miller continued. It was a sand-based light sod, and anyone with farming experience would know that nothing profitable would grow in it. Their homesteads would be covered with timber and bush, which was hard to clear, and in every open area grew a vegetable called muskeg. They would need to know scientific farming to raise crops in Canada, for they would have to deal with a killing frost in June and another one in August. Furthermore, there were only two seasons in Canada: winter and summer, and the winters were so long that they would start to think summer would never come. The only houses to guard against the climate were log cabins, which they would have to build themselves. They would have to fill the cracks with mud, but when it rained the mud would fall out and the cold wind would blow in. As if all this were not bad enough, the only water they could get was a mixture of alkali that would injure their stomachs and make them ill.[29]

Miller carried his message from Weleetka to Clearview, Oklahoma, and on June 29 he reported from the latter town that many blacks there were planning to leave for Canada. He spoke to a large gathering and arranged to have his address published in a local black newspaper. On June 30 he was in Boley speaking to a number of prominent blacks and was informed that a local movement was under way to try to stop the movement northward. Guthrie was his next stop, and in that town he spoke to several black ministers. They arranged for him to speak to a large audience by announcing the meeting in all of the town's black churches.

At the gathering Miller's statements were challenged by relatives of settlers already in Canada who had written that they were doing well. Miller left, however, "satisfied that they were convinced that such is not the case." From July 4 until July 8 he was in Oklahoma City, speaking with families who had expressed an interest in moving to Canada. He again displayed confidence in having dissuaded them, but he was not having quite the same success with black newspapers. Apparently some editors were reluctant to print his article, perhaps because Miller did not wish to pay for the publicity.

From July 9 until July 11 he was in Watonga, speaking at churches and interviewing families who were thinking of leaving. He reported his usual success but found that some families were so poor that they did not have the means to leave in any case. Back in Oklahoma City on July 12, he spoke to a few more potential migrants. There he found that some had already heard unfavorable reports, as a former black settler had returned from Canada spreading "cold winter" stories. From Oklahoma City he proceeded to Bristow, spending two days there convincing nine families not to leave. From July 15 to 17 he was in Sapulpa and again found that a returning settler with an unfavorable report had preceded him. In his last report, dated Sapulpa, Oklahoma, July 17, Miller said, "The Canadian Boom is rapidly dying out, as the unfavourable reports relative to Canada seem to have spread over the entire state. Everywhere I go, people say they have heard of me and the unfavourable report of Canada."[30] Miller was substantially correct, and for all intents and purposes the black migration from Oklahoma to western Canada faded as 1911 progressed. Miller had done his work well.

Miller's success at dissuading the black Oklahomans from migrating was not immediately apparent. Even as he traveled through the state, his employers looked for other ways of stopping the trek. One solution was simply to bar the blacks from entering the country. The *Calgary Herald* had earlier suggested this method. Its Ottawa correspondent had noted that a section of the Immigration Act of 1910 gave the Canadian government the power, with an order-in-council, to exclude for a period, or permanently, any race thought unsuitable to Canada's climate. The problem with this approach, however, was that it could discourage white Americans from heading north. Indeed, an official of the Canadian Pacific Railway Colonization Department in Chicago had written to Frank Oliver on April 28 to complain that newspaper reports citing this argument had already prevented some whites from migrating. This did not stop the minister of the interior, and on May 31, 1911, he sent a recommendation to the cabinet for an order-in-council barring blacks from entering Canada for a period of one year.[31]

The federal cabinet did not pass the order-in-council immediately. There were several arguments against such a drastic move. It could cause stormy diplomatic relations with the United States when the reciprocity question was still in the air; and every vote was needed for the upcoming Canadian election, so why alienate the black voters of Nova Scotia and southern Ontario? In addition, the fear of scaring off white American immigrants was undoubtedly a powerful argument against the move.

On August 12, 1911, the cabinet in fact passed an order-in-council barring blacks from entering Canada. It stated,

> For a period of one year from and after the date hereof the landing in Canada shall be and the same is prohibited of any immigrants belonging to the Negro race, which race is deemed unsuitable to the climate and requirements of Canada.[32]

This order-in-council was never acted upon, however. It was repealed on October 5 of the same year on the pretext that the minister of the interior had not been present at the August meeting.[33] The fact that it was passed indicates how serious Canada was about keeping the northern plains white.

The chronology of events involving the order-in-council also suggests that it was a "pocket" order, to be used if Dr. Miller failed in his mission to Oklahoma. The idea was originally suggested in May, when the physician was touring black settlements in western Canada. It was passed in August when he was in Oklahoma, and it was repealed in October when his success in stopping the migration was becoming clear.

Several months later, in February 1912, Canadian immigration officials again became concerned with the black immigration issue. Word spread that the blacks were still restless and again looking to Canada as a possible home. Government officials recommended that an agent be stationed in Oklahoma City or Muskogee to handle the problem, and once more it was argued that legislation barring the blacks be passed. W. J. White, the inspector of United States agencies, was in Ottawa on February 22, 1912, writing letters to American railroads (the Soo, the Rock Island, the Missouri, Kansas, and Texas, the Frisco, and the Union Pacific lines), asking them not to encourage blacks to emigrate from the southern United States to Canada. He told these railroads that he was also contacting the Great Northern, Northern Pacific, and Santa Fe lines on the matter, although no record of this correspondence is in the files of the immigration Branch. The fears of a renewed black migration never materialized, however, and the only concern that Canada had regarding blacks in 1912 was a number of friends and relatives who were trying to visit settlers already in the country. The Canadian officials' apprehension about these people was expressed in a reply to a query from John Foster, United States consul in Ottawa, regarding one visiting black who had been turned back at the border. Foster was told that Canada was concerned that these people were, in fact, trying to settle in Canada, but were entering "under the guise of tourists or visitors."[34]

The unfavorable press reports, the critical commentary of black editors and preachers, and the activities of C. W. Speers and especially Dr. G. W. Miller stopped black Oklahomans from moving to western Canada. It was clear that they were not wanted and would encounter trouble if they tried to enter, and given the expense and other difficulties of the journey, they put the thought out of their minds.

In the decades following the American Civil War, many black Americans headed westward hoping to find peace and land of their own. One destination was the future state of Oklahoma, and before it reached statehood, thousands of blacks had migrated to it. White Americans had also been attracted, and they brought their racism with them. White Oklahomans succeeded in segregating their black neighbors shortly after statehood was achieved. In 1910, they also took away the blacks' right to vote. Canada was advertising homestead lands in its western provinces in black and white Oklahoma newspapers at this time, and a number of black Oklahomans took advantage of the opportunity. While hundreds headed north, thousands watched with anticipation.

The Canadians' reaction to the black migration indicated that they believed many of the same stereotypes and myths about blacks as did the white Americans. While western Canadians did not resort to violence to halt the black migration, they did urge their government to develop policies to stop the blacks. Although covert and deceptive, this effort was in itself a form of violence, for it condemned other black Oklahomans to continue to face racist violence in that state. The Canadian government reacted to a sea of petitions, resolutions, and editorials, all aimed at keeping western Canada white. The government began a campaign of diplomatic racism. Discriminating against blacks through medical examinations and depriving potential black settlers of immigration material were haphazard methods, however, and Canada eventually sent two agents to Oklahoma to dissuade blacks from migrating. Their work was highly successful, and by the fall of 1911, the black migration from Oklahoma to western Canada was coming to an end.

Notes

1. Estimates vary greatly, some citing figures of more than one million American settlers. See Marcus Hansen and John B. Brebner, *The Mingling of the Canadian and American Peoples* (Toronto: Ryerson Press; New Haven CT: Yale University Press, 1940), p. 220; Paul Sharp, "The American Farmer and the 'Last Best West,'" *Agricultural History* 21 (April 1947): 65–75; Paul Sharp, *The Agrarian Revolt in Western Canada: A Survey Showing American Parallels* (St. Paul: University of Minnesota Press, 1948; reprint, New York: Octagon Books, 1971), p. 1; Paul Sharp, "When Our West Moved North," *American Historical Review* 55 (January 1950): 286–300; Karel Denis Bicha, "The American Farmer and the Canadian West, 1896–1914: A Revised View," *Agricultural History* 38 (January 1964): 43–46; idem, *The American Farmer and the Canadian West, 1896–1914* (Lawrence KS: Coronado Press, 1968), pp. 114 and 140.

2. The exact number of black immigrants is not known. The 1921 Census of Canada, however, showed 1,444 blacks in Alberta and Saskatchewan in that year. Canada, *Census of Canada, 1921, vol. 1, Population*, p. 355.

3. There is a debate among certain Canadian historians regarding the possible Indian ancestry of some of the black migrants to Canada. This debate is too involved for recapitulation here, and the bibliography too extensive for citation. My own view is that substantial, convincing documentary evidence does not exist to support the view that the migrants were partly of Indian ancestry. In fact, the surviving homestead applications that the black immigrants filed with the government of Canada point to their being ex-slaves and the descendants of former slaves who had moved westward after Reconstruction.

4. R. B. Shepard, "Black Migration As A Response to Repression: The Background Factors and Migration of Oklahoma Blacks to Western Canada, 1905–1912, As A Case Study" (MA thesis, University of Saskatchewan, Saskatoon, 1976), pp. 48, 50, and 77.

5. Stewart Grow, "The Blacks of Amber Valley: Negro Pioneering in Northern Alberta," *Canadian Ethnic Studies* 6 (1974): 17–38; Ina Bruns, "Kind Hearts and Gentle people, *Montreal Family Herald*, June 25, 1959; *Okemah (OK) Ledger*, March 23, 1911; *Calgary Herald*, April 22, 1911.

6. Harold Troper, *Only Farmers Need Apply: Official Canadian Government Encourage- I meat of Immigration from the United States, 1896–1911* (Toronto: Griffin House, 1972), p. 124. Troper has argued that the Canadian government did not advertise for black

settlers. Technically, this is true: however, such advertisements did appear in the black Oklahoma press, including the *Boley Beacon*, February 20, 1908, and March 19, 1908; *Clearview Patriarch*, March 2, 1911, and May 18, 1911; *Muskogee Cimeter*, January 8, 1909, February 4, 1910, and December 2, 1911; *Boley Progress*, March 16, 1905, October 12, 1905, January 18, 1906, March 11, 1909, and January 13, 1910.

    7. Troper, *Only Farmers Need Apply*, p. 123.

    8. Lerone Bennett, Jr., *Before the Mayflower: A History of the Negro in America, 1619–1964*, rev. ed. (Baltimore: Penguin, 1964), p. 240; United States, *Fourteenth Census of the United States, 1920*, vol. 3, Population, p. 814.

    9. *Boley* (Oklahoma) *Progress*, August 24, 1905.

    10. W. J. White to Frank Oliver, September 13, 1910, *Immigration Files*, RG 76, vols. 192–93, file 72552, part 1 (microfilm), Public Archives of Canada.

    11. L. M. Fortier to J. S. Crawford, November 8, 1910; Keystone, Oklahoma, to Ottawa, Ontario, November 11, 1910, and Hominy, Oklahoma, to Ottawa, Ontario, December 20, 1910; J. L. Doupe to J. S. Crawford, December 30, 1910; telegram from W. J. White to J. Bruce Walker, December 30, 1910; telegram from W. J. Webster to W. J. White, January 5, 1911; telegram from W. J. White to J. L. Doupe, January 5, 1911; telegram from W. D. Scott to W. J. Webster, January 5, 1911, *Immigration Files*, RG 76, vols. 192–93, file 72552, part 2 (microfilm), Public Archives of Canada.

    12. Robin Winks, *The Blacks in Canada* (New Haven CT: Yale University Press, 1971), pp. 310–11.

    13. Shepard, "Black Migration as a Response to Repression," pp. 97–102.

    14. Shepard, "Black Mountain as a Response to Repression," pp. 102–3, and 110.

    15. Canada, House of Commons, *Parliamentary Debates*, April 3, 1911, 6523–28; Ernest J. Chambers, ed., *The Canadian Parliamentary Guide, 1910* (Ottawa: Mortimer, 1910), p. 168. Also see Winks, *Blacks in Canada*, pp. 306–7.

    16. William E. Bittle and Gilbert Geis, *The Longest Way Home: Chief Alfred C. Sam's Back-To-Africa Movement* (Detroit: Wayne State University Press, 1964), pp. 55–56; *Okemah OK Ledger*, May 25, 1911, June 1, 1911, and June 8, 1911; *Clearview OK Patriarch*, June 1, 1911.

    17. For examples of the Canadian advertisements, see the *Boley OK Progress*, March 2, 1911, and the *Clearview OK Patriarch*, April 13, 1911. Both of these journals carried such material until well into 1912. L. M. Fortier to W. W. Cory, March 14, 1911, *Immigration Files*, RG 76, vols. 192–93, file 72552, part 4 (microfilm), Public Archives of Canada.

    18. *Clearview OK Patriarch*, March 23, 1911; *Oklahoma Guide* (Guthrie), May 11, 1911.

    19. *Clearview OK Patriarch*, April 13, 1911; *Oklahoma Guide* (Guthrie), May 11, 1911.

    20. *Baptist Informer* (Muskogee, OK), June 8, 1911, *Immigration Files*, RG 76, vols. 192–93, file 72552, part 4 (microfilm), Public Archives of Canada.

    21. Winks, *Blacks in Canada*, p. 306. Winks argues that the Canadian government

successfully frustrated attempts by black immigrant groups to reinforce their numbers. By sending agents to Oklahoma to try to stop the flow, the government was actively trying to check, not just frustrate, the black migration.

22. An order-in-council is a regulation passed by a federal or a provincial cabinet under the authority of the governor-general or a provincial lieutenant governor.

23. John E. Jones, consul-general, Winnipeg, Manitoba, to the secretary of state, May 22, 1911, *Department of State Decimal Files, 1910–1929*, RG 59, Box 8868, no. 842.511/7, National Archives, Washington DC.

24. C. W. Speers to W. J. White, May 8, 1911, and May 17, 1911; newspaper clipping, *Baptist Informer* (Muskogee, OK), no date; Reverend S. S. Jones to W. D. Scott, May 20, 1911, *Immigration Files*, RG 76, vols. 192–93, file 72552, part 4 (microfilm), Public Archives of Canada.

25. Reverend H. H. Edmond to W. D. Scott. May 15, 1911; W. D. Scott to Reverend H. H. Edmond, May 19, 1911, *Immigration Files*, RG 76, vols. 192–93, file 72552, part 4 (microfilm), Public Archives of Canada.

26. C. W. Speers to Reverend S. S. Jones, May 24, 1911; C. W. Speers to Reverend Hernagin, May 24, 1911, *Immigration Files*, RG 76, vols. 192–93, file 72552, part 4 (microfilm), Public Archives of Canada.

27. C. W. Speers to W. D. Scott, May 21, 1911; W. H. Rogers to an unidentified party, June 4, 1911; W. H. Rogers to W. D. Scott, May 25, 1911, *Immigration Files*, RG 76, vols. 192–93, file 72552, part 4 (microfilm), Public Archives of Canada. There is a certain irony in Rogers's proposal, since blacks have lived in Canada since 1628; Winks, *Blacks in Canada*, pp. ix.

28. Dr. G. W. Miller to an unidentified party in Chicago, June 24–28, 1911, *Immigration Files*, RG 76, vols. 192–93, file 72552, part 4 (microfilm), Public Archives of Canada. An exhaustive search of the budgets of the Department of the interior and the auditor-general's reports in the Canadian Sessional Papers for 1911 and 1912 failed to reveal Miller's salary.

29. *Oklahoma Guide* (Guthrie), July 6, 1911.

30. Daily letters, Dr. G. W. Miller to an unidentified party, June 29–July 17, 1911, *Immigration Files*, RG 76, vols. 192–93, file 72552, part 4 (microfilm), Public Archives of Canada.

31. *Calgary Herald*, April 17, 1911; Canada, *Statutes of Canada*, 9–10, Edward VII, chap. 27, An Act Respecting Immigration, May 4, 1910, sec. 38, sub. sec. "c"; Poynter Standly to Frank Oliver, April 28, 1911, and an order-in-council recommendation from Frank Oliver to the governor-general, May 31, 1911, *Immigration Files*, RG 76, vols. 192–93, file 72552, part 3 (microfilm), Public Archives of Canada.

32. Order-in-Council no. 1324, August 12, 1911, *Orders-in-Council*, RG 2/1, vol. 269, Public Archives of Canada.

33. Order-in-Council no. 2378, October 5, 1911, *Orders-in-Council*, RG 2/1, vol. 772, Public Archives of Canada.

34. W. H. Rogers to W. D. Scott, February 15, 1912; W. J. White to W. W. Cory, February 16, 1911; W. J. White to the Soo, the Rock Island, the Missouri, Kansas and Texas, the Frisco and Union Pacific lines, February 22, 1912; James Veal, Junkins, Alberta, to W. D. Scott, April 13, 1912; J. C. Johnson, Wewoka, Oklahoma, to the secretary of state, Washington DC, June 25, 1912, received by Canadian officials July 9, 1912; John Foster to W. D. Scott, July 8, 1912; W. D. Scott to John Foster, July 11, 1912, *Immigration Files*, RG 76, vols. 192–93, file 72552, part 4 (microfilm), Public Archives of Canada.

CHAPTER 8 | "This Strange White World":
*Race and Place in Era Bell
Thompson's* American Daughter

MICHAEL K. JOHNSON

Aboard a train heading out of Minneapolis toward frontier North Dakota, Era Bell Thompson in her autobiography *American Daughter* (1946) describes a landscape that grows steadily bleaker with each mile farther west: "Suddenly there was snow-miles and miles of dull, white snow, stretching out to meet the heavy, gray sky; deep banks of snow drifted against wooden snow fences.... All day long we rode through the silent fields of snow, a cold depression spreading over us." Thompson's realistic winter landscape descriptions also allegorically represent the social situation of herself and her family. The phrase "this strange white world," which she uses to describe the view from the train window, refers to both natural and social environments. "Aren't there any colored people here?" her mother asks. "Lord, no!" responds her father, who has preceded the family to North Dakota. As the only black child in her school, Thompson soon discovers the difficulty of her situation in this strange white world: "When they . . . called me 'black' and 'nigger' . . . I was alone in my exile, differentiated by the color of my skin, and I longed to be home with the comfort of my family; but even with them I would not share my hurt. I was ashamed that others should find me distasteful."[1]

In *American Daughter*, the changed appearance of the physical world signals the crossing of the border from such settled and urban areas as Minneapolis to a frontier space recently opened for homesteading, and from a sense of belonging to an African American community to a sense of "exile" in a predominately white western settlement. Richard Slotkin argues that frontier narratives emphasize an opposition between "the frontier" and "civilization," or the "wilderness" and the "metropolis," that often falls along a geographical divide between the wild, unsettled American West and the urban East.[2] Thompson revises this traditional opposition of frontier literature-the essential difference between the wilderness and the metropolis—to symbolize what W. E. B. Du Bois describes as "double-consciousness," the psychological tension and turmoil the African American individual experiences as he or she attempts to maintain a sense of belonging to two worlds, one black, one white.[3] Gerald Early comments that Du Bois "saw blacks as being caught, Hamlet-like, between" the choice of living as "an assimilated American" or as "an unassimilated Negro."[4] In *American Daughter*, the metropolis represents the black world, the place of African American community and culture. Moving west to the frontier means assimilating into mainstream society, separating from the black community, and becoming part of a strange white world.

Although the role of black Americans in settling the West has not always been adequately acknowledged, contemporary historians are rapidly filling in the details of African American contributions to westward expansion—from the work of black soldiers and cowboys to the community-building efforts of groups of black settlers. According to Quintard Taylor, census data reveal that black cowboys had a widespread presence in the American West. In the late nineteenth century, the Exodusters became part of a wave of black migration that helped settle Kansas. When the Oklahoma Territory opened to settlement in 1889, "an estimated 10,000 blacks" were among the "Sooners" who raced to stake claims.[5]

Several African American writers who experienced frontier life firsthand have set down those experiences in autobiographies or fictionalized accounts of their own stories. As does Thompson's autobiography, these accounts primarily tell the stories of African American individuals or of single black families living as part of predominately white frontier communities. Nat Love's autobiography, *The Life and Adventures of Nat Love, Better Known in the Cattle Country as "Deadwood Dick"* (1907), recounts highlights of his career as a black cowboy in what he calls the "Wild and Woolly West." Oscar Micheaux (better known as the pioneering black filmmaker who began his career making all-black-cast silent movies) wrote several novels, including *The Conquest* (1913) and *The Homesteader* (1917), based on his own experiences as a farmer and homesteader in South Dakota. We also might note Montana-born Taylor Gordon, whose entertaining autobiography *Born to Be* (1929) begins in his hometown of White Sulphur Springs (where, he writes, "If God ever did spend any time here on earth, that must have been His hang-out, for every little thing that's natural and beautiful to live with is around White Sulphur") and follows his adventures as he travels around the country by train as the private porter for circus impresario John Ringling.[6]

As do the narratives of Micheaux and Gordon, *American Daughter* describes a sense of restless movement, with Thompson sometimes shuttling back and forth between her frontier home and urban black communities as her race-based and place-based senses of self repeatedly diverge, conflict, and intersect. Although Thompson shares with Micheaux and Gordon an understanding that descriptions of place can serve an allegorical purpose (as indicated by her use of the wilderness/metropolis opposition as a metaphor for double-consciousness), she balances that allegorical approach with naturalistic and poetic descriptions of a prairie landscape that she observes closely and comes to appreciate for its variety and beauty.

Describing the Prairie

Era Bell Thompson ends up in North Dakota when her father, concerned about his sons' futures, observes, "[W]e'd better take the boys to Dakota. . . . They need to grow and develop, live where there's less prejudice and more opportunity" (21). The Dakota frontier represents for Tony Thompson an opportunity unavailable in the civilized East with its system of legal and social segregation. "Nothin' for colored boys to get in this town," Tony states, "but porter work, washin' spittoons" (21). Inspired by his half-brother John, who writes to him praising "the boundless prairies" as a "new land of plenty where a man's fortune was measured by the number of his sons, and a farm could be had even without money," Tony strikes out "for far-off North Dakota to find a new home in the wide open spaces, where there was freedom and equal opportunity for a man with three sons. Three sons and a daughter" (18, 22). As "a daughter," Thompson is barely an afterthought in her father's plans of freedom and equal opportunity—and is certainly inadequate as a measure of his success. For the first third of the story, Thompson almost seems an afterthought in her own narrative as she downplays her own actions in favor of reporting the successes and failures of her father and brothers Tom, Dick, and Harry. Her witness-participant persona, however, enables an objective and often ironic commentary on the men's wilderness-taming efforts.

The Thompsons eventually sign a tenant lease on the "old Hansmeyer place," a homestead that comes with a house, barn, land, and a pair of horses, let loose on the prairie. Those horses immediately capture her father's imagination: "Them's the wildest tame horses I ever see. But ain't no horse livin' I can't handle. No, sirree. Ain't no horse livin'" (39–40). As Tony is seduced by the sight of the wild horses, he is also taken in by Hansmeyer's sales pitch about the "hidden possibilities of the soil (hidden two feet under the snow)" (39).

When the snow melts, the family discovers beneath the snow not possibilities but "rocks, millions of rocks pimpling the drab prairie: large blue-gray boulders . . . long, narrow slits of rocks surfacing the soil like huge cetacean monsters" (41). The horses prove as troublesome as the rocky ground. After the spring thaw, the men (with much effort) succeed in luring the horses into the barn. While Tom follows them inside, the no longer boastful Tony takes "a safe position outside the barn window—club in hand" (42). From inside the barn "came a high shrill whinny, the thudding sound of bodies, splintering stalls. The old barn moved ominously" (43). Eventually, with the help of a neighbor (Gus, a Norwegian immigrant bachelor with a fondness for whiskey), Tom gets the horses hitched to a wagon. Leaping forward from the barn, "the horses made a new gate through the yard fence and tore down the muddy road on a dead gallop, as Gus sat waving his bottle and yelling in Norwegian" (43). Two hours later, Tom guides the exhausted horses home: "The buggy was a shambles, Gus was stone sober, but we had a team" (43). Tom tames the horses, but only temporarily, as Tony continues to have trouble with them. Although he drives the team into town one day without mishap, the horses return an hour later "on a dead run, heads up, heels flying, a picture of rhythmic beauty. Turning in the gate on two wheels, they stopped only when the buggy lodged in the barn door. Pop and one seat were missing" (44).

As her brothers take to the tasks of taming the horses, plowing the fields, and "dodging the rocks," the nine-year-old Thompson enviously watches "the shining shares slide along beneath the stubborn sod, turning over long rows of damp, blackish earth like unending dusky curls" (46–47). Excluded by age and gender from plowing, Thompson begins to develop a different relationship with the prairie than her father and brothers do. Once the initial shock of the North Dakota winter passes, Thompson indicates a growing sense of appreciation for the natural world around her:

> As fall drew near, the intense heat subsided. There were quiet, silent days when the grainfields were hills of whispering gold, undulating ever so softly in the bated breeze. So warm, so tranquil was the spell that one stretched out on the brown, dry earth, whose dead, tufted prairie grasses made the lying hard, but put even the breeze above you. The sun alone stood between you and the blue sky of God. (58)

If bleak winter landscape descriptions reflect Thompson's sense of "exile, differentiated by the color of my skin," she nonetheless establishes a sense of belonging to this world. She does not make the land into home by trying to transform it (as do her father and brothers) but rather by reshaping her vision of her self in relation to the world. She does not dominate the land so much as place herself within it, "stretched out on the brown, dry earth." According to Joanne Braxton, Thompson achieves a sense of "perceptual unity with nature."[7] In Thompson's landscapes, prairie, sun, sky, and individual each exist in close relation to the other.

We might compare Thompson's perspective on landscape to that of Oscar Micheaux, who similarly tells of an early twentieth-century African American pioneer trying to establish a prairie farm. In his novel *The Homesteader*, Micheaux writes that his protagonist, Jean Baptiste, came to South Dakota "because he felt it was the place for young manhood," and because "here with the unbroken prairie all about him; with its virgin soil and undeveloped resources . . . here could a young man work out his own destiny." Writing in the social context of early twentieth-century prejudice, Micheaux uses Baptiste's transformation of a wild place into a profitable enterprise to symbolize what African Americans in general can accomplish in a world of equal opportunity. His landscape descriptions are shaped by that purpose, so much so that he shows little interest in the prairie's natural beauty. Rather, he emphasizes storms, fires, droughts—natural obstacles to success that Baptiste overcomes through the quality of his character and his admirable work ethic. Whereas Thompson comes to appreciate the prairie in and of itself, Micheaux's Jean Baptiste most appreciates a prairie transformed: "[H]e gazed out over a stretch of land which two years before, had been a mass of unbroken prairie, but was now a world of shocked grain." In Baptiste's eyes, "no crops are like the crop on new land," and the land itself "seemed to appreciate the change, and the countless shocks before him were evidence to the fact." Baptiste does not stretch "out on the brown, dry earth," but rather he "gaze[s] over" it, establishing himself in a position of visual dominance rather than perceptual unity.[8]

Thompson's descriptions often take the form of a catalogue of the flora and fauna of the prairie that emphasizes a naturalist's eye for detail and a poet's sensibility. "The tumbling tumbleweeds," writes Thompson, "heralded the coming of winter. Huge Russian thistles, ugly and brittle now, free of their moorings, rolled across the prairie like silent, gray ghosts, catching in fence corners, piling up in low places, herded and driven mercilessly by the cold wind that whistled down from the far North" (66). As does Micheaux, Thompson is attentive to planted fields as well as undisturbed prairie, but her descriptions emphasize beauty over bounty. If "a world of shocked grain" represents financial success for Micheaux, Thompson finds that there is "something clean and sweet about the harvest," discovers that there is "an art in shocking grain" (58–59). Even her descriptions of crop failure recognize the beauty in a natural process that begins with the transformation of a "stubbornly" green "twenty-acre strip of flax" into a "whole field burst into delicate blue flowers, miniature stars against the yellow mustard blooms" and ends when "the blue flowers disappeared as quickly as they had come, and tiny bulbs of seed began to form in their place, to brown and ripen too quickly in the searing wind" (50).

As Annette Kolodny suggests, male writers who describe the American landscape often use the figure of "virgin" terrain that "apparently invites sexual assertion and awaits impregnation."[9] Through references to the prairie's "virgin soil and undeveloped resources" and to the "virgin soil [that] had been opened to the settler" (to name just two examples), Micheaux follows this pattern by implicitly sexualizing the landscape.[10] Other male writers indulge in a more explicitly sexual relationship through descriptions of physically merging with or penetrating the land. Although sensual, Thompson's landscape descriptions are not allegorical representations of the earth as a female body to be taken, opened, possessed, penetrated, or dominated. Although she may animate her landscapes (they "whisper" and "undulate"), she does not overtly sexualize them, nor does she penetrate or physically merge with the environment. Though "stretched out on the brown, dry earth," she observes that the "prairie grasses made the lying hard," a description that emphasizes both close proximity and distinct physical separation of the individual and the environment (58). Returning from delivering a load of grain, she observes, "[S]ometimes I sat silently on the high seat or stood down in the bottom of the deep wagon . . . watching gold-streaked heavens turn blue with approaching night" (101). Thompson's landscape descriptions pointedly include her presence as part of the depicted scene. Although she does not establish a dominating gaze that inscribes a hierarchical relationship between observer and observed, she nonetheless maintains a distinct sense of boundaries between self and other. By describing her position within the scene as the observer "on the high seat" or "in the bottom" of the wagon, she implies both perceptual unity with and physical separation from the scene under observation.

Although her landscapes do not connote the female body, she does connect the prairie to her mother. That connection is emotional rather than physical, for she increasingly turns to the prairie for the sort of comfort—especially in terms of salving the consciousness wounded by prejudice—and restored sense of wholeness that her mother provides earlier in the autobiography. During her first day at the Driscoll school, she is subjected to the intrusive curiosity of the other children: "One of Sue's friends put her arm around me and felt of my hair; Tillie stared at the white palms of my hands, and I closed my fists tight until they hurt. For the first time I began to wonder about that and about the soles of my feet" (33). When she returns home, she discovers her mother waiting. She "clasped me in her arms, hugging me as though she had never expected to see me again, and I soon forgot about the soles of my feet and the palms of my hands" (33). Later in the narrative, she turns for such forgetfulness to the natural world, or she loses herself in the rhythm of farm chores: "With my dog and my pony I was happy beyond the realm of people, for I had found a friendship among animals that wavered not, that asked so little and gave so much of loyalty and trust, irrespective of color" (84). "The coming-home on a load of hay in the warm silence of twilight," Thompson writes, "had a sacredness about it that filled us with the inner happiness that comes of a day's work well done" (52). The prairie becomes a place of peace and healing that supplements or substitutes for her family.[11]

Repeated throughout her landscape descriptions are references to beauty, tranquility, silence, and peace, but also to solitude and loneliness. Alone with a horse and wagon, Thompson describes the experience of hauling grain to the elevator: "I loved the long, solitary ride through the golden autumn sunshine . . . when the days stood still and the warm silence was unbearable in its poignant beauty" (100). Although the prairie represents healing, her moments of experiencing a sense of wholeness are most often achieved at the cost of separation from the social world. "Of all the family, I alone was happy on our land, content to call it home," Thompson writes, but that happiness in solitude mirrors the sense of social isolation she often feels in her predominately white community (111). Thompson's landscape descriptions encode a seemingly contradictory sense of both isolation from and unity with her surroundings that points to the central question of the narrative: how does one establish a sense of natural wholeness and unity as part of a social world divided by race?

Double-Consciousness and the
Wilderness/Metropolis Opposition

For W. E. B. Du Bois, the question of how to achieve a sense of whole self in an America divided by the color line is the central dilemma of African American experience.[12]

Thompson's unique contribution both to the literature of the frontier and to African American literature is her clever joining of the central oppositions of each body of literature, using frontier literature's wilderness/metropolis opposition as a metaphor for double-consciousness. The metropolis for Thompson represents African American culture and identity, and the wilderness (prairie) represents assimilation into the predominately white world of the American mainstream. Although Thompson ultimately tries to overcome these oppositions, others in the book try to resolve their sense of double-consciousness by severing their connection to the black East. In response to her mother's curiosity about other black people in the area, Thompson's uncle John states, "What'd you want with colored folks, Mary? Didn't you come up here to get away from 'em? Me, I could do without 'em for the rest of my days" (27–28). In the mythology of the frontier, life on the frontier is always better than in "civilization," and for Thompson's uncle John, assimilation in the frontier community is preferable to an unassimilated life among black people in the metropolis.

Others indicate less certainty than John does. As Early observes, for Du Bois, "To be an assimilated American and to be an unassimilated Negro were both real and, more importantly, equally or near equally appealing choices," and many of the characters we meet in *American Daughter* address the difficulty of that choice.[13] Ed Smith, an African American man whom Tony Thompson rooms with while he is working in Bismarck, exemplifies this dilemma. In Bismarck, he operates a successful pawnshop, but he acknowledges his wife's loneliness: "[S]he hasn't got anybody to associate with but white folks. Oh, they're nice enough, treat us fine and all that, but they're not colored, see" (80). The African American, writes Du Bois, "ever feels his two-ness,—an American, a Negro; two souls, two thoughts, two unreconciled strivings."[14] With the birth of their son, the Smiths find themselves similarly divided. They "don't want to bring the kid up ignorant about his own people," but at the same time they "don't want him to learn how to run from white folks" (80). As Ed states, "I was bred and born in the South, lived there most of my life, but I don't want my son to be brought up there either" (80).

Thompson's brother Dick, who abandons the farming enterprise early in the story, makes a different choice and migrates eastward to the city as soon as he's old enough to leave the family. In a letter, he asks, "How . . . can you folks stay out there in that Godforsaken country away from civilization and our people?" (113) Dick also sends a copy of the *Chicago Defender*, "the first Negro newspaper I had ever seen" (113). While the newspaper represents part of Thompson's education in African American culture, it also reminds her of the problems blacks face back in "civilization"—through a story on lynching and a photograph of a hanging. "The lifeless body dangling from the tree," writes Thompson, "became a symbol of the South" and of "Dick's civilization," a place where "black and white Americans fought each other and died" (113). Through the stories of individual family members and neighbors, Thompson describes the different responses and psychological adjustments of these pioneers who have left behind black communities to become part of a strange white frontier world—a world that offers greater opportunity for landownership, less (but not a complete lack of) racism, a degree of safety from the antiblack violence erupting throughout much of early twentieth-century America, and escape from the corrupt Jim Crow culture of segregation and second-class citizenship. That escape, however, comes at the cost of separation from African American culture and community. Forced to make a choice, which is preferable? Remaining isolated from "our people" in the relative safety of the frontier, or risking the dangers of antiblack violence in the civilized metropolis?

Just before Christmas, the family experiences their first blizzard, and Thompson describes the storm closing in and "forming a blurry whiteness" (69). Even within the whiteness of the storm, the family recreates a sense of belonging to the black world left behind when several African American families get together to celebrate Christmas:

> Now there were fifteen of us, four percent of the state's entire Negro population. Out there in the middle of nowhere, laughing and talking and thanking God for this new world of freedom and opportunity, there was a feeling of brotherhood, of race consciousness, and of family solidarity. For the last time in my life, I was part of a whole family, and my family was a large part of a little colored world, and for a while no one else existed. (74)

The physical distance between the urban black world and the predominately white frontier community exaggerates the dilemma of double-consciousness, but the Thompson family is able to find "a little colored world" within the surrounding blurry whiteness and maintain a feeling of "race consciousness" and a sense of solidarity with black friends and family that contributes to their ability to transform this new world into "home." Although many frontier narratives maintain an essential difference between civilization and wilderness, *American Daughter* undermines that distinction by recreating a sense of the urban black community on the Dakota frontier.

Transforming North Dakota from a strange white world into home involves not only adjusting to the new natural environment but also connecting with other families—white and black—in order to create an integrated community. At the Christmas celebration, "two white families stopped by to extend their greetings. The spell of color was broken, but not the spirit of Christmas, for the way Mack greeted them and their own warm response erased any feeling we may have had of intrusion" (74). Thompson complicates her initial image of the "white world" by acknowledging that her frontier community is multiethnic if not multiracial. The establishment of an integrated community involves friendships established between the Thompsons and other neighbors—primarily European and Scandinavian immigrants. A German neighbor, seeing that the Thompsons are in desperate straits, buys them sacks of food: "Nein, nein! I no vant money. Ven you git it you pay me, if you vant. I got money, I your neighbor, I help you. Dot iss all" (55). Integration for Thompson does not mean assimilation—losing one's black identity by merging completely with the surrounding white world—but involves rather a mixing of cultural elements, as symbolized in one example by her brothers developing their own patois, which they dub "Negrowegian" (82). Although Driscoll, North Dakota, is no utopian space free from racial prejudice, Thompson consistently (if temporarily) locates here and elsewhere the possibility of integrated communities that represent her vision of what America should be.

Feelings of "at-home-ness" are fleeting, however, and the wholeness of the "little colored world" enjoyed at Christmas fragments with the untimely death of Thompson's mother the following February. The family begins to break apart as one by one her brothers abandon the farm, leaving only Thompson and her father, who walked around "in a halo of grief, whistling or humming the old hymns" (97). Braxton observes that Mary Thompson symbolizes Era Bell's "connection with the primary source of [her] black and female identity."[15] Her mother's death begins a process whereby Thompson becomes more and more alienated from the black world which she feels so much a part of at Christmas. Although the prairie landscape she turns to for comfort may substitute as a source of maternal and female identity, the land does not provide that same sense of connection to black identity. The loss of her mother—and the connection to black identity she symbolizes—initiates a search both for self and for a lost home, a physical and psychological space representative of wholeness rather than two-ness. The prairie that Thompson loves, with its "white clouds of peace and clean, blue heavens," cannot overcome the pull she feels to learn more about the black world of the East (113).

After his wife's death, and after his sons leave, Tony abandons farming to move farther west to Mandan, North Dakota, where the mountain time zone and "the real West" begin (145). At this midpoint in her autobiography, Thompson's story becomes a narrative of education and of discovery of a voice—as symbolized by her developing career as a writer. As her father moves west, she travels in the opposite direction seeking the "land of my people," where she secures a summer job with the Smiths in St. Paul and begins to explore "the world of colored girls and boys . . . of colored stores and churches" (159). Her people, resentful that an outsider has taken one of the few available white-collar jobs for African Americans, do not accept her with open arms, and by summer's end, "I was glad to leave . . . glad to get away from grocery stores and restaurants and rows of colored houses and colored people's gates—gates where I was still a stranger—and colored boys and girls who did not want me" (164). Thompson's effort to resolve her sense of double-consciousness is reflected after her mother's death by the narrative's restless movements back and forth. "I wondered what it was I had sought to escape," Thompson writes, "running back and forth from prairie to city" (198). In each move, she finds herself located either in white or black worlds—or uneasily negotiating the space between the two. At the same time that she loves the silence of the prairie, she also loves the voice that she discovers in her journeys to the city. To be on the prairie is to be comforted and healed, but it is also to be silent and alone.

Rejected by the black community of St. Paul, she turns her attention to another strange white world—as one of the few African American students at the University of North Dakota. Thompson inherits the ability to survive in this and other environments from her father, who emerges as someone who flourishes when asked to bring together black and white social worlds. After taking over a furniture store in Mandan, he and Era Bell set up in a new house that is separated from their neighbors, the Harmons, by "a high fence" through which "four little boys fretted" and "tried to make friends through the cracks. Mrs. Harmon didn't approve of Negroes for neighbors" and spends her day "watching from behind her starched curtains" (137). Thompson writes:

> Pop was irked by the constant watching, and he felt sorry for the little boys jailed in behind the fence, so gradually he began to break the lady down. Every morning he'd come outside by the kitchen window and bow politely to the starched curtains and say good morning to the kids. His whistling about the yard and garden drew them to the fence like a magnet. He talked to them as he worked, apparently unmindful of the woman's watching eyes. Little by little the curtains began to part, slowly Mrs. Harmon began to nod, then smile. It wasn't long before she came out on her back porch to sit and listen to what Pop said to her boys, before the little boys were slipping over the fence and into our yard. (138)

Not all walls that separate black and white are so easily breached, and we have plenty of examples in the book of people whose prejudice is able to withstand even the considerable Thompson charm. Nonetheless, Thompson's father provides her with strategies for surviving in the white world that she must negotiate to earn her college degree. His talent for creating friendships across ethnic and racial boundaries is one that Thompson will develop as well.

Following her mother's death, Thompson establishes a series of relationships with girls and young women of different ethnic groups, and it is from these friendships that she begins to reestablish a sense of female identity and community. After her father abandons the farm, the two live in several North Dakota towns where Thompson finds a wider sampling of ethnicities than in the farming community of Driscoll. Her new community includes Russian German friends who live in neighborhoods where "English was seldom spoken," as well as her Sioux friend Priscilla Running Horse whose non-English-speaking mother, Thompson observes, was likewise "Old Country," except that "it wasn't Old Country: it was this country" (145–47). In Bismarck, she befriends the Jewish Sarah Cohn, and the two "became inseparable" (127). Together, they wander "into enemy territory, neighborhoods where the kids called us names; but if they called me a coon, they called her a kike, and when I was with her there was none of the embarrassment I felt when I was with my other friends" (128). As a student at the University of North Dakota, she takes up residence with the adventurous Opal Block in the Jewish section of Grand Rapids, where she adds Yiddish to her "strange vocabulary" of Norwegian, German, and English, and where she develops "a taste for lokshen and kosher fleish" (174). Through female friendships, Thompson creates a multiethnic social community whose members transgress the official and physical boundaries that segregate groups of people within distinct areas of space—the German neighborhood, the Jewish section, the Indian school.

She begins to experience through these social relations a sense of unity and comfort similar to that found earlier in her solitary sojourns on the prairie, but her task remains to find a way to bring together her experiences of the social and natural worlds—and to connect both to an African American community that seems increasingly distant. Although Thompson enjoys a degree of social mobility as an individual, that mobility does not exist for the majority of African Americans who remain confined by the physical patterns of segregation. Her task is made more difficult with the death of her father, which also symbolizes the severing of the final familial connection to the western landscape: "Between two deaths I stood at prairie eventide; the last symbol of family lay lifeless at my feet. Gone, too, were the bonds and obligations, and in their stead a bereftness, a desolate freedom. My life was my own choosing, and there could be no more coming home" (201). After her father's death, her explorations take her farther east, and the narrative emphasis turns to a search for a place in the world of the metropolis.

Thompson eventually finds a place in the home of a white family, the Rileys, who help sponsor her attendance at Morningside College in Iowa. Although she is happy and comfortable within both the Riley family and the Morningside College community, after graduation Thompson moves to Chicago "seeking work and a home among my people" (249). Although her "new home was ideal," her African American landlord and landlady "didn't like white people," and when she brings her white friend Silver to visit, "we were met with a cold, hostile silence" (267). Individual efforts to create an integrated society of close friends are made difficult by the larger divisions of the social world, and her Chicago experience—rather than resolving her sense of double-consciousness—leaves her "feeling that I was fighting the world alone, standing in a broad chasm between the two races, belonging to neither one" (268). In segregated Chicago, she also finds herself under tighter economic and social restrictions than she had experienced while under the protective care of white friends in North Dakota and Iowa. When the Rileys come to visit, "for a while I was back in the boundless white world, where all gates were open, all the fences down. . . . It was a temptation to go home with the Rileys, but I chose to stay in my new black world, feeling that somewhere I would find a happy side, that between the white and the black there must be a common ground" (255).

That wished-for common ground is sometimes found. When visited by her white friend Gwyn, Thompson takes her to a "shady knoll in Washington Park, where we could sit on the cool grass and talk, where, under the pure blue sky and the whispering trees, no shadow of race would come between us" (268). Natural space operates as both the figurative opposite of the urban metropolis and as a possible point of mediation between the black and white social worlds that split Thompson's allegiance. Thompson occasionally finds in such natural spaces as the park momentary integrated "homes" that exist in contrast to the segregated social spaces we see in the book. As Braxton observes, "Chicago's 'pure blue sky' brings back Era Bell's childhood sense of wholeness symbolized by her perceptual unity with nature and the blue skies of her North Dakota girlhood."[16] In contrast to those earlier moments of unity with nature, Thompson shares this moment with another. If Thompson figures double-consciousness through her twin desires to find a sense of unity in both the natural world of the prairie and the social world of the metropolis, the park, which exists within urban Chicago, represents the interrelationship of both those worlds. The "whispering trees" recall the whispering grain fields of the prairie. That the same "pure blue sky" exists above both Chicago and North Dakota posits the two not as opposing terms but rather as part of the same continuum of experience. Thompson realizes that she must rethink the separation of natural space from social space, must overturn the frontier narrative's metropolis/wilderness opposition in order to be able to create for herself places of healing, comfort, and integration—in order to create "home" in other environments.

In the final chapter, Thompson narrates a trip by bus across America. Through her travels, she claims a place in all parts of America.

Thompson herself becomes a figure who links different regions (North, South, East, West) and seemingly opposed social worlds. Thompson resists seeing the city and the frontier as essential markers of difference, as inferior and superior places; neither does she lift one social world, black or white, over the other—for she calls both regions and both communities home. Still, she realizes that she alone cannot close the social gap, that the resolution to two-ness ultimately involves social forces larger than the self. She concludes with the comment, "The chasm is growing narrower. When it closes, my feet will rest on a united America" (296). Although *American Daughter* registers a pattern of location and dislocation, of finding home, of being in exile, Thompson never abandons her effort to resolve double-consciousness by establishing, even if tenuously, a sense of home and of belonging in both the city and the prairie, in both the black and the white worlds.

Notes

1. Era Bell Thompson, *American Daughter* (1946; St. Paul: Minnesota Historical Society Press, 1986), 26–27, 83–84. Subsequent references to this work will be given parenthetically in the text.

2. Richard Slotkin, *The Fatal Environment: The Myth of the Frontier in the Age of Industrialization* (1985; New York: HarperPerennial, 1994).

3. William Edward Burghardt Du Bois, *The Souls of Black Folk* (1903; New York: Penguin, 1989), 5.

4. Gerald Early, introduction to *Lure and Loathing: Essays on Race, Identity, and the Ambivalence of Assimilation*, ed. Gerald Early (New York: Penguin, 1993), xx.

5. Quintard Taylor, *In Search of the Racial Frontier: African Americans in the American West, 1528–1990* (New York: Norton, 1998), 158; Nell Irvin Painter, *Exodusters: Black Migration to Kansas after Reconstruction* (1976; New York: Norton, 1986); William Loren Katz, *The Black West* (1987; New York: Touchstone, 1996), 248.

6. Nat Love, *The Life and Adventures of Nat Love* (1907; Lincoln: University of Nebraska Press, 1995); Oscar Micheaux, *The Conquest* (1913; Lincoln: University of Nebraska Press, 1994); Oscar Micheaux, *The Homesteader* (1917; Lincoln: University of Nebraska Press, 1994); Taylor Gordon, *Born to Be* (1929; Lincoln: University of Nebraska Press, 1995), 4.

7. Joanne M. Braxton, *Black Women Writing Autobiography: A Tradition within a Tradition* (Philadelphia: Temple University Press, 1989), 162.

8. Micheaux, *The Homesteader*, 24, 131.

9. Annette Kolodny, *The Lay of the Land: Metaphor as Experience and History in American Life and Letters* (Chapel Hill: University of North Carolina Press, 1975), 67.

10. Micheaux, *The Homesteader*, 24, 109.

11. Kevin L. Cole and Leah Weins usefully place *American Daughter* in the context of the genre of the spiritual autobiography, and they observe that while criticism on the book has recognized the thematic centrality of displacement, overlooked has been "the problem of religious displacement, perhaps the most complex aspect of Thompson's coming-of-age autobiography" (226). Cole and Weins point out that Thompson's use of religious language in her landscape descriptions can be interpreted as a "rhetorical strategy" that figures "the absence of a black religious community" in North Dakota (223). Viewed from the perspective established by Cole and Weins, Thompson's application of religious language ("sacredness") to her descriptions of experiences in nature might suggest that the prairie supplements or substitutes for not only her family but also that absent black religious community. Kevin L. Cole and Leah Weins, "Religion, Idealism, and African American Autobiography in the Northern Plains: Era Bell Thompson's *American Daughter*," *Great Plains Quarterly* 23 (Fall 2003): 219–29.

12. "Herein lie buried many things which if read with patience may show the strange meaning of being black here in the dawning of the Twentieth Century," writes Du Bois, who continues, "This meaning is not without interest to you, Gentle Reader; for the problem of the Twentieth-Century is the problem of the color-line." Du Bois, *Souls*, 1.

13. Early, *Lure and Loathing*, 20.

14. Du Bois, *Souls*, 5.

15. Braxton, *Black Women Writing Autobiography*, 146.

16. Braxton, *Black Women Writing Autobiography*, 174.

CHAPTER 9 | The New Negro Arts and Letters Movement among Black University Students in the Midwest, 1914–1940

RICHARD M. BREAUX

The 1920s, 1930s, and 1940s were an exciting time for black artists and writers in the United States. Much of the historical literature highlights the so-called Harlem Renaissance or its successor, the Black Chicago Renaissance. Few studies, however, document the influence of these artistic movements outside major urban cities such as New York, Chicago, or Washington DC. In his 1988 essay on black education, historian Ronald Butchart argued that the educational effects of black social movements such as the Harlem Renaissance on black schooling are unclear and underexplored.[1] This article explores the influence of the New Negro arts and letters movement on black students at four midwestern state universities from 1914 to 1940.

Black students on white midwestern campuses like the University of Kansas (KU), University of Iowa (UI), University of Nebraska (UNL), and University of Minnesota (UMN) aligned themselves with various New Negro philosophies that marked the onset of the New Negro arts and letters movement, or the Harlem Renaissance. The New Negro arts and letters movement had a profound influence on black college students. Black students expressed a New Negro consciousness in at least two ways: (1) they indirectly engaged in the discourses that surrounded the New Negro movement through black scholarly and popular publications, and (2) they engaged in racial vindication through classroom assignments, research, and other intellectual products that challenged prevailing myths of blacks' intellectual and cultural inferiority to whites. Interestingly, black students at KU, UI, UNL, and UMN seemed less interested in who financed the arts movement than in casting their creative works into the growing sea of black literature and art. Newspapers such as the *Topeka Plaindealer*, the *Iowa Bystander*, and the *Omaha Monitor*, along with *Opportunity* and *Crisis* magazines, artistically and politically inspired black students at KU, UMN, UI, and UNL to behave, dress, and research issues relevant to black people like never before. National black fraternity and sorority publications such as Alpha Kappa Alpha's *Ivy Leaf* provided young people the opportunity to publish their creative works. Literary scholars and historians largely ignore such publications, yet these sources offer a different view of the work produced by those associated with various New Negro arts and letters movements outside Harlem. In fact, black students and alumni did not simply follow the lead of black performing and visual artists in Harlem. These students created their own movement replete with its own poetry, music, and means of expression. Black students from all four universities left their distinct mark on the New Negro arts and letters movement.

As scores of black men returned from World War I, they and many other blacks began to articulate a new militancy. If whites in the United States thought that they would continue to ignore blacks' political, social, cultural, and economic concerns and contributions, they were wrong. An editorial in the *Messenger*, a black socialist magazine, said it best when it announced, "As among other peoples, the New Crowd [Negro] must be composed of young men who are educated, radical, and fearless. . . . The New Crowd would have no armistice with lynch law; no truce with Jim-Crowism, and disfranchisement; no peace until the Negro receives his complete social, economic, and political justice."[2] This and other New Negro philosophies permeated the minds of black students at UI, UMN, KU, UNL, and other universities. To a small degree, the very presence of these black students on predominantly white college and university campuses signaled their endorsement of one of the basic tenets of New Negroism—to demonstrate, consciously or unconsciously, that they were whites' intellectual equals.

When Alain Locke's anthology, *The New Negro: An Interpretation*, appeared in 1925, those blacks who subscribed to the black intelligentsia's New Negro philosophies finally had their printed manifesto. Of course, in earlier decades Booker T. Washington, William Pickens, and a growing number of Black Nationalist and black socialist magazines had used the term "New Negro," but this term took on new meaning for blacks during and after World War I. "In the last decade," opened Locke's essay in the first section, "something beyond the watch and guard of statistics has happened in the life of the American Negro."[3] Locke asserted that the "Old Negro" and the so-called Negro problem had largely been a charge of the "sociologist, philanthropist, and race leader." Indeed, the Old Negro was a myth, "a creature of moral debate, historical controversy" and a perpetuation of historical fiction.[4] "The day of 'aunties,' 'uncles,' and 'mammies'" was gone, and now many blacks demanded self-respect, self-dependence, self-expression, and self-determination.[5] The major point stressed by this collection of essays was that black contributions to fiction, poetry, history, philosophy, and the dramatic, performing, and visual arts had existed for centuries. The migration of southern blacks to the urban North just made such contributions more evident.

Despite numerous literary and historical studies on the Harlem Renaissance, scholars continue to disagree about the precise beginning and end of this historical period. The period that spanned from World War I to the Great Depression marks the Harlem Renaissance for Nathan I. Huggins. Historians David Levering Lewis and Bruce Kellner, on the other hand, mark the return of the 369th Infantry

Regiment in 1919 as the beginning of the Harlem Renaissance and the year 1934 as the year when the New Negro arts and letters movement came to a "sputtering end." Still others, such as Cheryl Wall, argue for a more generously broad periodization, especially if historians take into account the works of Harlem Renaissance women.[6] A recent addition to the literature, an examination of the NAACP in the 1920s, seeks to completely reconceptualize the New Negro movement as the civil rights movement of the Jazz Age, ranging roughly from 1919 to 1930. While such a classification is a bit of a stretch, it does capture the idea that blacks have continually sought to live on their own social, political, religious, economic, and artistic terms. Harlem may have very well been the "Cultural Capital" for a number of black ethnic groups, but historian Mark R. Schneider reminds us that "to understand African Americans in the 1920s, we must get off the A train to Harlem and head out of Manhattan to points west and south."[7]

For historians who conceptualize the New Negro arts and letters movement by the creative arts and literature produced at the time, or the move of many black intellectuals or working people to the political left, the Chicago arts and letters movement deserves as much attention as Harlem's literary and political explosion. By 1935 Chicago emerged as a black cultural hub in its own right. Although Harlem receives, and has received, the majority of historians' attention, some scholars have also suggested that Chicago became just as important in producing black writers, artists, sociologists, dancers, and Marxists.[8] While these scholars may agree to disagree about the extent to which the Chicago black arts and letters movement was a continuation of the arts and letters movement in Harlem, at least two points are not debatable: (1) the Chicago arts and letters movement, of which a few UI alumni were a part, lasted at least into the 1940s; and (2) most of Chicago's black artists engaged in dialog with those black artists associated with Harlem.

The history of the New Negro arts and letters movement, like the history of black education in the United States, presses scholars to think about white philanthropy and the black arts. While scholars like Nathan I. Huggins and Harold Cruse believed the New Negro movement was a showpiece for white bohemians thirsty for a taste of the nativistic and exotic, others like David Levering Lewis, Ann Douglas, and Thomas Bender see the New Negro arts and letters movement as a constant struggle between two groups of cultural power brokers—white philanthropists and black artists.[9] In higher education, similar struggles emerged as to what disciplines black students would study, especially in advanced degree programs. Rising accreditation standards in white and black colleges alike precipitated the need for faculty with more specialized, intensive, and advanced training. With the absence of graduate programs on most predominantly black college campuses, and the color line drawn at predominantly white southern colleges, some black college faculty, with assistance from the General Education Board, the Rockefeller Foundation, and the Rosenwald Fund, took courses and graduate degrees at northern white colleges.[10] Just as northern white philanthropists sought to control the direction of southern black education, a smaller number of white philanthropists developed a similar interest in having some say in the direction of intellectual discourses among an emerging black intelligentsia on northern college campuses.

White philanthropic interest in black intellectual discourse did not begin in the 1920s; this interest went back, at least, to the early Jim Crow era. Indeed, Louis Harlan's two-volume biography of Booker T. Washington demonstrates that in the early twentieth century, a number of white and black power brokers fought for control over black newspapers and political organizations. Blacks who challenged Washington's philosophies found themselves targets of the infamous "Tuskegee Machine." Washington forced some black newspapers that criticized him to shut down, and he arranged for several black critics of Tuskegee to lose their jobs.¹¹ White philanthropic interest in black political opinions and scholarship continued after Washington's death in 1915. Historians August Meier and Elliott Rudwick contend that although white philanthropists showed moderate interest in Carter G. Woodson's *Journal of Negro History* few philanthropists gave generous contributions to studies of black life or black intellectual institutions that were primarily administered or controlled by black scholars and artists before 1922.¹²

Despite their early philanthropic work among black schools and black teachers, white philanthropists did not establish formal scholarship programs for advanced study among blacks until the 1920s. The two most powerful and wealthy philanthropic groups that campaigned to develop black teachers, black intellectuals, and leadership were the General Education Board (GEB) Fellowship and the Rosenwald Fellowship Fund in 1924 and 1928, respectively.¹³ Both funds gave money for promising black instructors at southern black schools and resources for their instructors to earn credentials and maintain their jobs. They were also inspired by the intellectual and creative direction of the New Negro arts and letters movement, and gave money to a number of creative artists. Between 1922 and 1933 the GEB Fellowship focused almost exclusively on the black teacher shortage, and the Rockefeller Foundation endorsed black students in the medical and health industries. By 1940 GEB Fellowship funds went exclusively to whites and blacks who planned to teach in southern schools. The Rosenwald Fund supported black students in at least four major areas: (1) medicine and nursing; (2) library science and teacher education; (3) unusually promising blacks who would study at northern white or European colleges; and (4) vocational and industrial teachers.¹⁴ All had to send informal requests to the Rosenwald Fund Committee and those who would teach in southern black schools and colleges were particularly encouraged. Despite the undeniable influence of the GEB Fellowship and Rosenwald Fund on black education, only a handful of black students at KU, UI, UNL, and UMN received funds from these organizations. According to the Rosenwald Fund database at Fisk University, a total of eight students who received Rosenwald Fellowships for advanced study between 1928 and 1936 earned master of science, master of arts, or master of music degrees from UMN (3), UI (3), KU (1), or UNL (1).¹⁵ Some students obviously had changes in their plans because a total of twelve black students chose UMN (9) or UI (3) to complete their advanced study with Rosenwald Fellowship funds. No students requested funds to attend KU or UNL with Rosenwald money.¹⁶ Between 1936 and 1941 only two Rosenwald fellows attended UMN, although not one of these students intended to enroll at UMN, UI, UNL, or KU.

Those who received Rosenwald and Rockefeller fellowships were an assorted lot. For example, KU alumnus Sterling V. Owens used a Rosenwald Fellowship to study social work in New York, but ended up taking a job as executive secretary of the St. Paul Urban League.¹⁷ Owens also lectured at UMN in the 1930s. Similarly, two Georgia State College teachers, Annie Dixon and Clarence Ross, used Rosenwald Fellowship money to study at UMN in the 1930s, but neither earned a degree. Maurice Thomasson used a Rosenwald Fellowship to earn a master's degree in education at UMN so he could become an instructor at Johnson C. Smith College. Ollie Lee Brown turned her money from the Rosenwald Fellowship into a bachelor's degree in library science from UI in 1931. Others, like Elmer E. Collins, received both GEB and Rosenwald Fellowship funds; Collins successfully earned a doctor of medicine degree from UI in 1933 and later taught at Howard University. Vernon A. Wilkerson, who earned a BA at KU, an MD at UI, and a PhD at UMN, completed his studies with GEB funds, as did one of black America's first women history PhDs, Lulu Merle Johnson, at UI. Johnson later taught at several black colleges including Cheney State University.¹⁸ Charles W. Buggs, who earned his MS and PhD from UMN, found a job at Dillard University and later Wayne State

University.¹⁹ Finally, UNL graduate Aaron Douglas and UI graduate Margaret Walker used Rosenwald Fellowship funds to further their creative works well after they graduated from these institutions. Walker taught at Jackson State University and Douglas taught art at Fisk University. Despite the achievements of these dozen or so recipients, the GEB and the Rosenwald Fellowship Fund's staff had its greatest influence on southern black colleges and blacks who conducted advanced study at the University of Chicago, Columbia University, Hampton Institute, and the larger, more heftily endowed black and white universities.²⁰

The Harmon Foundation, like most white philanthropic organizations that gave money to blacks, was not without its critics. While some scholars praise the Harmon Foundation for its role in disseminating black art, others, like Mary Ann Calo, criticize it for divorcing black art from its political context, making black art "sociological, rather than aesthetic" and "constricting the critical frame" in which audiences viewed black art. Much of the foundation's writing about black art, argues Calo, "was simply Harmon Foundation publicity posing as art criticism."²¹

A New Negro consciousness swept across midwestern college campuses just as it took Harlem by storm. Black students, black alumni, and politically active blacks in Iowa City, the Twin Cities, Lawrence, and Lincoln launched a number of antidiscrimination campaigns in their respective cities. They simultaneously challenged institutional racism in a number of academic disciplines on midwestern college campuses and created an extensive set of intellectual opportunities for themselves.

Outside the classroom, most black students, and a small group of left-thinking white students, embraced the writings of New Negro arts giants such as Countee Cullen, Claude McKay, and Langston Hughes. Members of the *Dove*, a socialist newspaper at KU, seemed particularly interested in poems such as Countee Cullen's "Yet Do I

Marvel" because it symbolized black people's seemingly futile struggle for equality.[22] Such poems drew upon the tragic Greek stories of both Tantalus and Sisyphus, mythic trickster figures who suffered in Hades for varying reasons and could never quite escape their predicament.

Black students at KU found the works of Langston Hughes and Claude McKay engaging. Blacks at KU, UI, and UMN not only immersed themselves in Langston Hughes's verses, but in 1932 invited the New Negro movement's poet laureate back home to the Midwest to speak to college students, black and white. At UI, Hughes played to a packed house in the liberal arts auditorium. He read from *Weary Blues*, his first published book of poetry, and read selections such as "When Sue Wears Red" and "Negro Dancers." He also read his poem "Dressed Up" and reportedly interspersed his poems with reflections of his life experiences. Hughes had graciously accepted the invitation sent under the auspices of the Graduate College to come to UI. Professor Frank L. Mott, a journalism professor who had previously organized a night of black poetry readings, introduced Hughes to the crowd. After Hughes's program he was off to the Alpha Phi Alpha fraternity house where he rested after his lecture.[23] According to one report, Hughes chatted, joked, and played a few hands of cards with students.[24] One week after his appearance at UI, Hughes returned to his childhood home in Lawrence. Hughes's mother, Carrie Langston, attended KU in the late nineteenth century, and Langston Hughes lived with his grandmother in Lawrence through the early 1910s. Hughes's lecture in Lawrence was sponsored by Alpha Kappa Alpha Sorority, which delighted in its ability to bring the Midwest kid turned Harlemite to campus in the midst of a depression.[25] The visit marked the first of three times Hughes returned to Lawrence to speak at KU after he left the city in 1915.[26] In 1935 Hughes made a trip to the upper Midwest and spoke to a crowd of 4,000 students at UMN's Northrop Auditorium. According to historian and Hughes biographer Arnold Rampersad,

Hughes spoke on the topic of interracial socialism. Hughes argued that "the basic economic problem of the Negro is the same as that of his white compatriots, and it is through the labor movements that some sort of solution must be reached." Hughes made complimentary visits to several classes and a meeting of UMN students.[27] He also made a special visit to an off-campus site where at least five students formed a committee to petition UMN officials to defy Tulane University's request to withdraw a black UMN football player from their upcoming match.[28]

During their respective visits to the Twin Cities and UMN, Langston Hughes, Roland Hayes, Paul Robeson, Charles S. Johnson, James Weldon Johnson, and a host of other blacks associated with Locke's *New Negro* anthology made their way to the UMN and Minneapolis's black Phyllis Wheatley Settlement House in the late 1920s and early 1930s.[29] Often these visitors attended special parties and gave talks or performances for people who used the settlement house's services. The black tenor Roland Hayes played to a packed group on UMN's campus in 1926 and 1929. In his first concert Hayes reportedly "scored his usual triumph" and in his second visit to UMN, students filled the newly completed Northrop Memorial Auditorium to hear Hayes give his performance of European classics and black spirituals.[30] When Paul Robeson performed in Kansas City, Missouri, in 1927, students traveled from KU to hear the performance. Robeson also performed for white and black students at UMN in 1930.[31] The following year, black women students at UMN invited Fisk University's Charles S. Johnson to campus to speak on the "Contribution of Negroes to American Civilization." Closer to the end of the decade, and just three years before the infamous Constitution Hall incident, contralto Marian Anderson performed at UMN much to the delight of the Eta chapter of Alpha Kappa Alpha. Anderson also performed at KU's Hoch Auditorium in January 1938.[32]

While the songs of New Negro musicians and the poetry of

Harlem's literati became a point of pride among black college students, these students threw their own hats into the literary ring. Some UNL, UI, UMN, and KU students and alumni began to plant the seeds of the New Negro arts and letters movement as early as 1911. William N. Johnson, a former student and football player at UNL, wrote several poems and short stories for the *Crisis* including a story titled "The Coward," which relayed the tale of Horton, a black plowman who reflects on his family's history as slaves and tenant farmers, and yet refuses to strike back at an abusive landlord:

> Back in the dark night of his memory there was only the somber race of plowmen. He seemed to see them, all prototypes of himself, in a single file, plowing the same furrow. The end—the wearying end of the long curving row—was a black chasm. This was his race, the Hortons. They had borne chains with no whining; their great broad backs had been lacerated there at the whipping post by the biting lash, yet they never struck back!
>
> "Damn you, nigger."
>
> It was the landlord's rasping voice that startled the dreaming plowman. A frail blue-white fist stung his twitching black face. There was pause, and in that pause, the thrush still chanted its anthems to Heaven; Horton the plowman, shrank away from the face of his master. The sweet breeze cooled his hot brow.[33]

Although Johnson's main character did not express characteristics of a New Negro consciousness, Johnson's venture into poetry and short-story writing did.

While a number of historians note that black men often dominate discussions and examinations of a New Negro consciousness expressed through the arts, black women students, particularly at UMN and UNL, turned out a number of poems, songs, short stories, and plays of their own. In the 1920s UMN graduate student Ruth Pearson studied black folklore while she taught in the sociology department.[34]

Zanzye H. Hill received her bachelor's degree from UNL and became the school's first black woman law school graduate in 1929. One year before she earned her law degree, Hill wrote a coming of age poem in AKA's *Ivy Leaf*, titled "My Nantie":

> My Nantie she's the funniest thing
> She looks real hard when I help her sing
> When company comes, and I run out,
> To see what they're all laughing 'bout.
> She just says, you go right back
> And don't be peeping through the crack
> Company they say, Oh that's all right
> She's only just a little might
> And some day when she grows up tall
> Then you'll be wishing she small
> Then company says Nantie, listen dear
> Why does Mollie act so queer?
> Nantie looks around to see if I'm listening
> And if I'm not she began hissing
> And says, what else could she be
> The way Mrs. Jones acted at her tea
> Why I think it was terrible, don't you
> The way she whispered, just those two
> And company asks Nantie what was it
> And Nantie said why it was the rite
> Her curtains once were white as snow
> But she decided to make a show
> And when she went down to the ten-cent store
> 'Cause she couldn't afford any more
> And bought herself some dye of red
> To match she said her bedroom spread
> I listened hard but couldn't hear any more

> 'Cause just then my Nantie she shut the door
> When I get old and have little girls
> And company comes to my house
> I'll never tell them to go and sit
> And be quite as a little mouse.[35]

Zanzye Hill also published another poem in the same *Ivy Leaf*, titled "At Dawning."[36] Ruth Shores Hill, also a student at UNL, wrote a poem that blended her creative spirit with a solicitation to get more literary contributions to AKA's *Ivy Leaf*.[37]

Amateur music impresario Florence Webster at KU wrote a poem that many would not classify as representative of the New Negro arts and letters movement; yet a few scholars like Houston Baker and Jon Michael Spencer might argue that Webster evoked one of the era's most misunderstood tropes—the "mastery of form":

> A Symphony in note was mine
> With cellos, flutes and violins
> Tuned in accord to suit the tastes
> Of critics and without amends
> The concord must be rarely bent
> To please the ears of thousands
> The Melodies are subtle strains
> For moments soothing hungry souls
> Appeasing crowds, frustrated mind
> But unremembered in a time.
> A symphony in words was yours
> Played on the strings of hearts—just two
> Tuned in accord to mark the time
> Of lovers just for me for you
> The harmonies are heaven-sent
> Oblivious to the thousands
> The melody is your dear voice

>Accompanied by tender sighs
>Crescendos are but raptures taut
>To never, never be forgot
>Oh! Years will pass as must they do
>But this has been my happiness
>Your symphony, I think, is best
>But God has heard my song for you.[38]

Although these students' poems may not have reflected the more sophisticated style of those poets historians typically associate with the New Negro arts and letters movement, the poems by black women students share some of the themes and styles adopted by New Negro arts and letters movement women writers. Historian Cheryl Wall argues that the cultural milieu of the time forced black women to suppress their gender and privilege their race; nevertheless, black women poets were not only less race conscious, but also less innovative in form when compared to black male writers of the time. This meant the black women poets rarely experimented with black vernacular, or cultural expressions such as jazz, blues, or spirituals.[39] This was certainly the case for black student writers at KU and UNL. By 1940, however, Margaret Walker, whom Langston Hughes advised to attend a northern college, used literary forms and themes not typically associated with women in the New Negro arts and letters movement to write her poetry. Inspired by Langston Hughes, Robert Hayden, Arna Bontemps, and the emerging young writer Richard Wright, Walker drew on the political environment of the 1930s (the depression, labor struggles, and a literary left) to transform black women's poetry. Two verses from one of the poems that comprised her UI master's thesis spoke to the irony that many blacks felt when they experienced institutional racism despite their education.[40] The poems in Walker's master's thesis speak to a folk tradition that only a few black students at UI, UMN, KU, and UNL had an opportunity to study formally.

While a student at UI, Walker recalled that she skipped an entire week of classes to read, and reread, the brand new novel that some scholars argue represented the last rites for the New Negro arts and letters movement—Richard Wright's *Native Son*. Walker recalled that she was in Iowa when she saw a copy of *Native Son* early in February 1940. Walker remembered that the shock of the book "rocked me on my heels." Walker had developed at least an intellectually passionate friendship with Wright. Before she came to UI, Walker had sent Wright clippings from the Rob Nixon case, which Wright used as a prototype for Bigger Thomas's trial in the novel.[41]

In addition to creative writing and poetry, black students developed an interest in the dramatic arts and play writing. Although most of the plays that students performed were those written by white Negrotarians whose names became attached with Harlem or the New Negro arts and letters movement, a few black students wrote and directed small productions of their own. Eugene O'Neil's *The Emperor Jones*, Marc Connelly's *Green Pastures*, and DuBose and Dorothy Heyward's *Porgy* became favorites among black students on white campuses. In 1929 a member of AKA's Ivy Leaf Club at UNL appeared with other black members of the University Players in a staged production of *The Emperor Jones*. One year later, an all-black cast of students at KU presented Octavius Roy Cohen's *Come Seven*. In October 1939 several black students and some white students at KU opened the Speech and Dramatic Arts Department's season double feature with *The Emperor Jones*. Actor and political activist Paul Robeson had made *The Emperor Jones* a hit in the screen adaptation of the play. At KU, the reporter for the *Daily Kansan* appeared much more impressed with black students' acting ability than with the total production: "Last night's reenactment revealed that there is lots of dramatic talent among the negro students of the Campus," wrote the reviewer, "that their peculiar gifts are adaptable to such a theatrical carriage.... But, 'My Heart's in the Highlands' was the high spot of the evening's entertainment. It seemed to achieve fully what 'The Emperor Jones' attempted—a strikingly new method of dramatic expression."⁴² KU historian Robert Taft immortalized the cast of *The Emperor Jones* in his book *Across the Years on Mount Oread*.⁴³ Many of these students maintained the Paul Robeson Dramatic Club at KU, which twenty-three black students established in 1931.⁴⁴

If local blacks and black and white students in Lincoln and Lawrence applauded the student production of *The Emperor Jones*, blacks in Lincoln and the Twin Cities launched full-scale campaigns to shut down proposed productions of *Porgy* at the universities of UNL and UMN. First published as a novel in 1925, and later developed as a play and musical, which attracted scores of whites and some blacks to the theater, *Porgy* is the story of a crippled black beggar who witnesses a murder during a dice game and becomes enamored with the murderer's woman friend. When Crown, the murderer, returns to claim Bess, Porgy kills Bess's ex-lover and escapes conviction because no one can believe a man in Porgy's condition could kill the brutish Crown. Porgy returns to Catfish Row only to discover that Bess becomes strung out on "happy dust" and gets "turned out" into a life as a New York City prostitute.

For some blacks, particularly those outside the arts and among the black middle class, *Porgy* glorified the worst in black folk and urban street culture. Langston Hughes, a champion of creative license and artistic freedom, praised the theater adaptation of *Porgy*, but some black actors and celebrities later lambasted the play. In Lincoln, local black ministers organized against the production sponsored by the University Dramatic Club. Ministers claimed, "The play was a deliberate attempt to feature the race at its worst."⁴⁵ If the play continued on as scheduled, they charged, it would intimidate blacks in Lincoln and at UNL, and it would damage the growing spirit of interracial cooperation in the city. Representatives of the drama department refuted the ministers' claims. They maintained that the play was "art with no thought of reflecting on the group," the cast was almost entirely made up of black students, and the suppression of the play would represent an attempt to squash students' artistic expression.[46]

Debates surrounding the production of *Porgy* became much more heated at UMN. The university's theater department argued in favor of the all-black student production of life in South Carolina's "Catfish Row," but the UMN's Council of Negro Students opposed the production. Caught in the middle, and leaning heavily toward the argument for creative license and free artistic expression, the thirty or so black students hoped the production would proceed. Anne Fenalson, a white associate professor of sociology and advisor to the Council of Negro Students, assured the fifty members who objected to the play that Dr. C. Lowell Lee of the theater department would concede to council demands to replace *Porgy* with a more suitable production. However, divisions emerged within the council. A second vote of forty-six against the play, six for the play, and twelve who abstained, later gave way to an eighteen-to-sixteen vote to get rid of the play. When theater department officials found no suitable replacement and continued to prepare for the play's opening, the St. Paul and Minneapolis branches of the NAACP and Urban League stepped in to support the Council of Negro Students' slim majority. Spearheaded by the St. Paul NAACP, the group issued a statement that argued that because black students had opposed the production after three votes, "the members of the St. Paul Branch of the NAACP strongly oppose the presentation of this play."[47] This joint committee also threatened to take the matter up before the UMN president Guy S. Ford and the Board of Regents if the theater department ignored its request.

In addition to staging performances of popular plays with their assortment of black characters, black students, particularly black women, at UNL and KU wrote and directed their own mini-dramas. Ruth Shores Hill wrote *The Glorious Adventure*, a four-scene romantic comedy about black college students who fall in love after discovering their mutual interest in an assigned course reading.[48] Ruth Gillum at KU wrote a musical aptly named *Heading for Harlem*, performed before "an enthusiastic and appreciative audience."[49] The production and performance of these and other plays demonstrate the degree to which the cultural movement so often associated with Harlem, and on occasion Chicago, spread even farther west.

In the truest spirit of black creativity, white philanthropy, and the New Negro arts and letters movement, several black students won awards and wide recognition for their creative academic work. Clifton Lamb, the director of the Prairie View State College drama department, who studied at UI in the summers to receive a master's degree and maintain his job, won a $100 first prize and a publishing contract with the Dramatic Publishing Company for his play *God's Great Acres*. One contest judge remarked that the play, a story of the influence of industrialization on sharecroppers in western Texas, was "a powerful and sympathetic treatment of a phase of the sharecropper problem that has not yet been fully exploited."[50] Beulah Wheeler at UI, Earl Wilkins at UMN, and Charles Stokes at KU won first place in speech contests on their respective campuses in 1921, 1925, and 1927. Wheeler's speech was titled "Uniform Marriage and Divorce Law," Wilkins's topic was "John Doe, Colored Student," and Stokes spoke on "The New Negro."[51] When artist Elizabeth Catlett created the statue *Mother and Child* for her UI master's project, she walked away with UI's first MFA and a first prize at the American Negro Exhibition in Chicago. Catlett recalled that it was UI professor Grant Wood, not New Negro patriarch Alain Locke, who encouraged her to take on black women as an artistic subject.[52] Budding writer Margaret Walker, who incidentally was Catlett's UI roommate, earned a master of arts in writing from UI. Her master's thesis, a collection of folk ballads titled *For My People*, earned her the coveted Yale University Series of Younger Poets award. This published thesis became one of the first books of poetry published by a black woman since New Negro arts poet Georgia Douglas Johnson published her work nearly a decade earlier. Nick Aaron Ford, who came to UI to study for a master of arts in literature while on leave from his teaching post, published his recently completed master's thesis as *The Contemporary Negro Novel: A Study in Race Relations*. Zatella Turner, who received bachelor's and master's degrees from KU, published *My Wonderful Year*, a memoir of her time at the University of London, where she studied drama with the assistance of an AKA fellowship.[53] The New Negro arts movement's signature artist, Aaron Douglas, emerged as an outstanding student while enrolled at UNL from 1917 to 1922. The "fairhaired boy" of the arts department took his BFA and won first prize in a student show.[54] In 1936, fourteen years after Aaron Douglas graduated from UNL with a degree in fine art, the Nebraska Fine Arts Council honored the artist through the acquisition of his painting *Window Cleaning*, which remains a part of UNL's permanent art collection.[55]

Various black intellectuals who were proponents of the New Negro philosophies significantly influenced visual artists such as Aaron Douglass and Elizabeth Catlett and literary artist Margaret Walker. Douglas and Catlett gained recognition beyond their wildest dreams, and KU and UI also gave birth to other black visual artists influenced by the New Negro arts and letters movement. Tony Hill, K. Roderick O'Neal, and Bernard Goss represent only three examples of those who never became as prominent as Douglas and Catlett and yet received the attention of people like Alain Locke. They helped to develop several more widely known black visual artists. Tony Hill, who graduated with a sociology degree from KU in 1928 and a master's in social work from the University of Chicago, became an internationally known sculptor and ceramics artist. After he honed his skills at the University of Southern California, he enjoyed a celebrated career.[56] K. Roderick O'Neal received his bachelor of arts degree in graphic arts in 1931 and another degree from UI in 1933. As a student, he had exhibitions in the Iowa Memorial Union, and he later developed into one of Illinois's most celebrated architects.[57] Bernard Goss, who came to UI from Sedalia, Missouri, also exhibited work during his time as a student. Goss's star rose quickly, and *Opportunity* printed a story about Goss, his work, and other newly arrived black Chicago artists, just five years after his 1935 graduation from UI. While in Chicago, Goss enrolled in the Art Institute, married another aspiring artist, Margaret Taylor, and, with her, developed the South Side Community Arts Center and later founded the DuSable Museum of Black History. Goss's 1939 painting *Musicians*, appeared in Alain Locke's *The Negro in Art*.[58]

Some historians often admittedly overlook music's influence on the New Negro arts and letters movement. Historian Arnold Rampersad writes in a foreword to a new edition of Alain Locke's influential work, *The New Negro: Voices of the Harlem Renaissance*, that if he were writing the book again, he would have paid much more attention to the role of music, especially blues and jazz, in the New Negro arts and letters movement. New Negro arts patriarch Alain Locke, Rampersad argues, wholly excluded any mention of the blues, and the editor treated jazz like a wayward stepchild.[59] Locke and West-Indian-born popular historian Joel A. Rogers certainly believed that black spirituals, as they related to black folk traditions, as well as jazz, symbolized the spirit of New Negroism.[60] Students and community people usually did not formally engage in jazz, blues, or folk discourses in the classroom, but at dancehalls and house parties one would be hard pressed to hear anything but jazz coming from the phonograph. KU alumnus Nicholas Gerran recalled that although he and other black students did not study jazz formally in the classroom or music departments, this certainly does not mean that black students did not listen to or play jazz outside the classroom. Among many middle-class blacks, "a jazz musician," recalled KU alumnus Nicholas

Gerran, "wasn't recognized as an honorable profession." Gerran later joined black KU classmate Florence Webster at the Moscow Conservatory of Music in the Soviet Union.[61]

The connection between classically trained black musicians and the Soviet Union has largely been ignored in Harlem Renaissance and black music history. While several scholars note that Roland Hayes and Paul Robeson performed in Moscow, and Alain Locke praised the Soviet Union for its policy toward ethnic minority artistic development, few have explored the depth to which Russian and black folk music, or Soviet classical and black classical music traditions, influenced each other. All these artists, including the young student Nicholas Gerran, took note of the lack of prejudice they experienced in the Soviet Union, but the question that remains, although outside the scope of this study, is how did these experiences influence black musicians' view of Communism? Did the Stalinist-Hitler pact alter their view of Communism? Outside of Paul Robeson, we know very little about how the Soviet Union, Communism, or the Moscow Conservatory shaped black musicians' political philosophies.[62]

The sheer number of black students, particularly black women, who seemed to have some classical music training may seem phenomenal now, but such was a typical gender-appropriate undertaking during the first decades of the twentieth century. As early as 1908, several black women and men who were enrolled in KU's music department performed vocal, violin, and piano solos at musicals held at St. Luke AME church. KU students like Doris R. Novel, Etta G. Moten, Ruth Gillum, Maxine Bruce, and Lillian Webster continued this tradition well into the 1930s.[63] Cleopatra Ross, a fine arts student at UNL, played the piano, the pipe organ, and sang at a number of recitals and black student programs held at Quinn Chapel AME and First Christian churches.[64] Three years later, members of APHIA at UNL, with help from AKA, sponsored a similar recital at Quinn Chapel.[65] KU graduate Etta G. Moten took her guitar, piano, and singing talents to the national concert stage, screen, radio, and equally shared it with chapters of AKA throughout the country.⁶⁶

For many scholars today, classically trained black musicians who perfected European musical traditions do not merit a place among those who embraced any form of New Negroism. Black intellectuals young and old debated the issue of what types of plays, poetry, literature, and music should represent black people. Literati writers Claude McKay and Langston Hughes appreciated black performances of more mainstream and classical troupes affiliated with the white middle class as long as they rightfully shared a place with black spirituals, jazz, and blues. Still, few historians of the New Negro arts and letters movement share McKay's and Hughes's opinion. Music historians Jon Michael Spencer and Paul Allen Anderson argue that black classical musicians and jazz and blues musicians engaged in what literary scholar Houston Baker calls the "mastery of form" and the "deformation of mastery."⁶⁷ Baker and Spencer, building on Baker's thesis, suggest that both the "mastery of form" and the "deformation of mastery" were attempts to usurp racism. The "mastery of form" required that blacks, particularly black students, perfect Anglo-Saxon, upper-class white American and European "high culture" in an effort to force white people to see black people's humanity and respect blacks as equals. Within the area of education, "mastery of form" translated into mastering the "form of 'standard' educational process in the West."⁶⁸ Yet some blacks, even college students, engaged in a "deformation of mastery," a conscious effort to deconstruct mainstream culture, literature, and music through a black rural folk and black urban cultural lens. To be sure, Baker maintains that deformation is "a go(uer)rilla action in the face of acknowledged adversaries." Moreover, deformation "distinguishes rather than conceals. It secures territorial advantage and heightens a group's survival possibilities."⁶⁹ On rare occasions, students like George O. Caldwell managed to incorporate black folk music into his thesis at UI when he compared traditional black folk songs to Russian composer Igor Stravinsky's 1910 ballet *Firebird*.[70]

A small number of sources offer a view of black student life that demonstrates that all students were not trying to put up a middle-class front. In their leisure time, students demonstrated an affinity for the blues and blues musicians, who were constantly in the act of deforming mainstream culture. To be sure, black students at UNL, who were by many accounts more working class than their contemporaries at KU, UI, and UMN, listened to and performed songs like the "St. James Infirmary Blues," "Just a Gigolo," "Baby Won't You Please Come Home," and "He May Be Your Man But He Comes to See Me Sometimes."[71]

The spirit and sociopolitical consciousness that surrounded the New Negro arts and letters movement in Harlem and the black arts and letters movement in Chicago emerged as an enormous influence in the intellectual lives of black KU, UMN, UNL, and UI students and alumni. The examples of students' creative work, however, demonstrate that students also produced their own poetry, fiction, and visual arts, and by extension their own arts movement. Despite historical debates about who should and should not be termed New Negroes, sources from the 1910s, 1920s, and 1930s reveal that blacks with a variety of talents and political views deserved the title New Negroes.

Notes

1. Ronald Butchart, "Outthinking and Outflanking the Owners of the World: A Historiography of the African American Struggle for Education," *History of Education Quarterly* 28, no. 3 (Autumn 1988): 361. The standard work about the New Negro movement at historically black colleges and universities remains Raymond Wolters, *The New Negro on Campus: Black College Rebellions of the 1920s* (Princeton NJ: Princeton University Press, 1975).

2. A. Philip Randolph, "A New Crowd—A New Negro," *Messenger*, May–June 1919, 27.

3. Alain Locke, "The New Negro," in *The New Negro: An Interpretation*, ed. Alain Locke (New York: Albert and Charles Boni, 1925), 3.

4. Locke, "The New Negro," 3.

5. Cheryl Wall, *Women of the Harlem Renaissance* (Bloomington: Indiana University Press, 1995), 2; Alain Locke, foreword to *New Negro*, ix; Locke "New Negro," 4, 5.

6. Nathan I. Huggins, *Harlem Renaissance* (New York: Oxford University Press, 1971), 3012; David Levering Lewis, *When Harlem Was in Vogue* (1997; New York: Penguin Books, 1981), xxviii; Wall, *Women of the Harlem Renaissance*, 10.

7. Mark Robert Schneider, *"We Return Fighting": The Civil Rights Movement in the Jazz Age* (Boston: Northeastern University Press, 2002), 4.

8. James Edward Smethurst, *The New Red Negro: The Literary Left and African American Poetry, 1930–1946* (New York: Oxford University Press, 1999), 5; Robert Bone, "Richard Wright and the Chicago Renaissance," *Callaloo* 28 (Summer 1986): 446–68; Joyce Russell-Robinson, "Renaissance Manqué: Black WPA Artists in Chicago," *Western Journal of Black Studies* 18, no. 1 (1994): 36–43; Craig Werner, "Leon Forrest, the AACM and the Legacy of the Chicago Renaissance," *Black Scholar* 23, nos. 3–4 (1993): 10–23.

9. Lewis, *When Harlem Was in Vogue*, xxiii; Ann Douglas, *Terrible Honesty: Mongrel Manhattan in the 1920s* (New York: Noonday, 1996); Thomas Bender, *New York Intellect: History of Intellectual Life in New York from 1750 to the Beginning of Our Time* (New York: Knopf, 1987).

10. Jayne R. Beilke, "To Render Better Service: The Role of the Julius Rosenwald Fund Fellowship Program for the Development of Graduate and Professional Educational Opportunities for African Americans" (PhD diss., Indiana University, 1994); Horace Mann Bond, *The Education of the Negro in the American Social Order* (1934; New York: Octagon Books, 1966), 364; James D. Anderson, *The Education of Blacks in the South, 1860–1935* (Chapel Hill: University of North Carolina Press, 1988), 275–77.

11. For more on the power and influence of the "Tuskegee Machine," see Louis Harlan, *Booker T. Washington: The Making of a Black Leader, 1856–1901* (New York: Oxford University Press, 1972), 254–71; Louis Harlan, *Booker T. Washington: The Wizard of Tuskegee, 1901–1915* (New York: Oxford University Press, 1983), 84–106.

12. August Meier and Elliott Rudwick, *Black History and the Historical Profession, 1915–1980* (Urbana: University of Illinois Press, 1986). For more on the roller-coaster ride to finance the *JNH* in the early years, and the role of Rosenwald, Carnegie, and the Laura Spelman Rockefeller Memorial Fund, see Darlene Clark Hine, "Carter G. Woodson: White Philanthropy and Negro Historiography," in *Hine Sight: Black Women and the Re-Construction of American History*, by Darlene Clark Hine (Brooklyn NY: Carlson, 1994), 203–22.

13. Beilke, "To Render Better Service," 50.

14. Beilke, "To Render Better Service," 51–52, 61–63.

15. Beilke, "To Render Better Service," 157–59.

16. Beilke, "To Render Better Service," 159–60.

17. Earl Spangler, *The Negro in Minnesota* (Minneapolis: T.S. Denison and Co., 1961), 126.

18. Harry Washington Greene, *Holders of Doctorates among American Negroes* (Boston: Meador, 1946), 63, 136.

19. Beilke, "To Render Better Service," 68.

20. A much smaller, yet equally important white philanthropic fund to the New Negro arts and letter movement's proliferation was the William E. Harmon Foundation. The white Negrotarian and New York real estate magnate William E. Harmon acquired the resources, after several successful business ventures, to leave Iowa for New York. From his post in New York, William E. Harmon developed the Harmon Foundation, which, among other things, sponsored traveling exhibits of black art and bestowed the Distinguished Award for Achievement Among Negroes prize. Archie Alexander, black UI alumnus and architect, received the Harmon Prize in 1927. "Archie Alexander Given the Harmon Award," *Omaha Monitor*, March 11, 1927.

21. Mary Ann Calo, "African American Art and the Critical Discourse between World Wars," *American Quarterly* 51, no. 3 (1999): 587. For opposing views of the Harmon Foundation's work, see Calo, "African American Art," and William S. Doan, "Iowa and the Artist of African Descent," in *Outside In: African Americans in Iowa, 1838–2000*, ed. Bill Silag, Susan Koch-Bridgford, and Hal Chase (Des Moines: State Historical Society of Iowa, 2001), 497–99.

22. Countee Cullen, "Yet Do I Marvel," reprinted in the *Dove*, February 15, 1926.

23. "Mott Talks to Group on 'Negro Poetry,'" *Daily Iowan*, February 27, 1932; "Negro Poet to Give Lecture," *Daily Iowan*, March 1, 1932; Margaret Schlundt, "Hughes Paints Vivid Portrait of Negro Life," *Daily Iowan*, March 4, 1932.

24. "Alpha Phi Alpha," *Daily Iowan*, March 5, 1932.

25. "Delta Doin's," *Ivy Leaf*, March 1932, 6.

26. Alison Watkins, "Celebrating Langston Hughes," in *Lawrence: The Art of a City* (Lawrence: Convention and Visitor's Bureau, 2001–2), 46–47.

27. Arnold Rampersad, *The Life of Langston Hughes: I, Too, Sing America, vol. 1, 1902–1941* (New York: Oxford University Press, 1986), 313. Rampersad also mentions the campus visits to UI and KU in 1932; see Rampersad, *Life of Langston Hughes*, 1:234.

28. "Tulane's Attitude on Reed Sought," *Minnesota Daily*, October 15, 1935.

29. Michiko Hase, "W. Gertrude Brown's Struggle for Racial Justice: Female Leadership and Community in Black Minneapolis, 1920–1940" (PhD diss., University of Minnesota, 1994), 31.

30. "The Concert Courses," *Gopher* (1927), 205; "The University Concert Courses," *Gopher* (1930), 208.

31. "Paul Robeson," *Topeka Plaindealer*, January 14, 1927; "The University Artists Course," *Gopher* (1931), 174, 176; "Record Audience to Pack Northrop to Hear Robeson," *Minnesota Daily*, February 11, 1931. Both Hayes and Robeson are noted in Alain Locke, "The Negro Spirituals," in *New Negro*, 208.

32. "Negro Sociologist to Be Guest at Tea," *Daily Minnesotan*, January 30, 1931; "Visiting Artists," *Gopher* (1936), 218; "University Concert Course," *University Daily Kansan*, January 13, 1939. In 1939 the Daughters of the American Revolution prohibited Anderson from performing at Constitution Hall. First Lady Eleanor Roosevelt responded by resigning from the Daughters of the American Revolution and arranged for Anderson to sing at the Lincoln Memorial.

33. Will N. Johnson, "The Coward," *Crisis*, October 1911, 252. Also see "The Call," *Crisis*, November 1916, 15.

34. "Who's Who," *Opportunity*, November 1925, 341.

35. "Deaths," *The Nebraska Alumnus*, May 1935, 28; J. Clay Smith, *Emancipation: The Making of the Black Lawyer, 1844–1944* (Philadelphia: University of Pennsylvania Press, 1993), 328, 465, 471.

36. Zanzye H. Hill, "My Nantie," *Ivy Leaf*, November 1928, 46; Zanzye H. Hill, "At Dawning," *Ivy Leaf*, November 1929, 16.

37. Ruth Shores Hill, "A Reporter's Query," *Ivy Leaf*, June 1931, 31.

38. Florence M. Webster, "Symphony," *Ivy Leaf*, June 1931, 30. Also see poem by UNL student Ellen Roy, "To Alpha Kappa Alpha," *Ivy Leaf*, June 1931, 29.

39. Wall, *Women of the Harlem Renaissance*, 6, 12–13.

40. Margaret Walker, *For My People* (New Haven: Yale University Press, 1942), 13.

41. Margaret Walker, *Richard Wright, Demonic Genius: A Portrait of the Man, A Critical Look at His Work* (New York: Amistad Press, 1988), 146, 122–25.

42. "Alpha Theta," *Ivy Leaf*, March 1929; "Delta Doin's," *Ivy Leaf*, September 1930, 5; Ken Postlethwaite, "Double Feature Opens Dramatic Season," *University Daily Kansan*, October 31, 1939.

43. Robert Taft, *Across the Years on Mount Oread* (Lawrence: University of Kansas Press, 1955), 155.

44. "Robeson Club to Give Play," *University Daily Kansan*, March 17, 1932; *Jayhawk* (1936), 364, 369; *Jayhawk* (1937), 375, 381.

45. J. Harvey Kerns, "Social and Economic Status of the Negro in Lincoln, Nebraska" (Race Relations Committee in Lincoln, 1933), 28, Nebraska Historical Society, Lincoln, NE.

46. Kerns, "Social and Economic Status of the Negro in Lincoln," 28.

47. "N.A.A.C.P. Branches To Seek Ban on 'U' Production of Disputed Play 'Porgy,'" *St. Paul Recorder*, November 17, 1939. Article includes the resolution printed in its entirety.

48. Ruth Shores Hill, "The Glorious Adventure," *Ivy Leaf*, June 1931, 35.

49. "Delta," *Ivy Leaf*, March 1934, 21.

50. "Drama of Negro Life Ties for First Prize in Iowa Contest," *Opportunity*, September 1939, 279.

51. "Beulah Wheeler Wins Contest By Default," *Daily Iowan*, January 12, 1921; "Women to Speak Tonight at 7:30," *Daily Iowan*, January 18, 1921; "Non-Literary Woman Given First Place in Extempore," *Daily Iowan*, January 20, 1921; "Women's Extempore Contest," *Hawkeye* (1922), 325; "Freshman-Sophomore Oratorical Contest," *Gopher* (1927), 236; "Kansas Student Wins Cup With 'New Negro' Oration," *Omaha Monitor*, December 30, 1927.

52. Elizabeth Catlett, letter to the author, January 16, 1999; Samella Lewis, *The Art of Elizabeth Catlett* (Claremont CA: Hancraft Studios, 1984), 23; Michael Brenson and Lowery Stokes Sims, *Elizabeth Catlett Sculpture: A Fifty-Year Retrospective* (Purchase NY: Neuberger Museum of Art, SUNY, 1998), 12–13; Melanie Herzog, *Elizabeth Catlett: An Artist in Mexico* (Seattle: University of Washington Press, 2000), 17–23.

53. "Former Negro Graduate's Book to Be Published," *University Daily Kansan*, November 2, 1939.

54. Amy Helene Kirschke, *Aaron Douglas: Art, Race, and the Harlem Renaissance* (Jackson: University Press of Mississippi, 1995), 6–7. Douglas also enrolled at UMN for a short time after he was removed from the Student Army Training Corps. For a study of the philosophical foundations of Douglas's work, see Audrey Thompson, "Great Plains Pragmatist: Aaron Douglas and the Art of Social Protest," *Great Plains Quarterly* 20, no. 4 (Fall 2000): 311–22.

55. Margaret Walker, *For My People*; "Painting," clipping, and "1922," clipping, "Douglas, Graduate of School of Fine Arts, Lauded for Drawings," MS#159, folder 1, box MS #158–161, Aaron Douglas File, University of Nebraska at Lincoln Archives, Lincoln, NE.

56. "Ceramics by Tony Hill," *Ebony*, November 1946, 31–34; "Tony Hill," in *A Biographical History of African American Artists, A-Z*, Anderson Delano Macklin, (Lewiston NY: Edwin Mellen Press, 2001), 128.

57. Theresa Dickason Cederholm, "Kenneth Roderick O'Neal," *Afro-American Artists: A Bio-Bibliographical Directory* (Boston: Trustees of the Boston Public Library, 1973), 58; "Roderick O'Neil—Leader among Negro Architects," *Iowa Alumni Review*, October 1954, 10–11.

58. Willard F. Motley, "Negro Art in Chicago," *Opportunity*, January 1940, 20–21; Macklin, "Bernard Goss," in *Biographical History of African American Artists*, 107; Alain

Locke, *The Negro in Art* (Washington DC: Association in Negro Folk Education, 1940), 117, 132; see Goss illustrations in a book of unpublished poems celebrating his life, Evangeline Zehmer, "Form of a Woman" (unpublished booklet, 1976), Margaret Taylor Goss Burroughs Papers, Chicago IL. Copy in author's possession.

59. Arnold Rampersad, introduction to *The New Negro: Voices of the Harlem Renaissance*, by Alain Locke (1925; New York: Atheneum, 1992), xx.

60. Alain Locke, "The Negro Spirituals," in *New Negro: An Interpretation*, 199–213; J. A. Rogers, "Jazz at Home," in *New Negro: An Interpretation*, 216–24.

61. Nichols Gerran interview, reprinted in *Narratives of African Americans in Kansas, 1870–1992* (Lewistown NY: Edwin Mellen Press, 1993), 68, 69–70; "Florence Webster," *Ivy Leaf*, September 1936, 13. For more on blacks and their interest and trips to Russia during this period, see John L. Garder, "African Americans in the Soviet Union in the 1920s and 1930s: The Development of Transcontinental Protest," *Western Journal of Black Studies* 23, no. 3 (1999): 190–200.

62. Paul Allen Anderson, *Deep River: Music and Memory in Harlem Renaissance Thought* (Durham NC: Duke University Press, 2001), 160–62.

63. "Lawrence, Kansas," *Topeka Plaindealer*, March 6, 1908; "Soror Doris Reita Novel," *Ivy Leaf*, November 1928, 72; "Delta Doin's," *Ivy Leaf*, December 1930, 9; "Delta," *Ivy Leaf*, June 1929; "Delta Doin's," *Ivy Leaf*, September 1930, 5; "More Graduating Sorors," *Ivy Leaf*, September 1936, 17; Walter Belk, "The Lawrence Black Community and Its Relationship to Black Students on Mount Oread, 1870–1930," Sociology 165 paper, University of Kansas, Unpublished Paper, Watkins Community Museum, Lawrence, Kansas, May 10, 1971, 17–18.

64. "Lincoln, Neb.," *Omaha Monitor*, April 13, 1928; "Lincoln, Nebraska," *Omaha Monitor*, May 25, 1928; "Soror Cleopatra Elaine Ross," *Ivy Leaf*, November 1928, 65.

65. "Negro Musicians Will Give Recital Tonight," *Daily Nebraskan*, January 16, 1931.

66. "Soror Moten," *Ivy Leaf*, March 1935, 3. Moten met with AKA members at UMN before a concert in a Minneapolis theater.

67. Claude McKay, *The Negroes in America*, trans. Robert J. Winter (1921; Port Washington NY: Kennikat Press, 1979), 60–61; Langston Hughes, "The Negro Artist and the Racial Mountain," *Nation* 122 (June 28, 1926): 692–94; Jon Michael Spencer, *The New Negroes and Their Music: The Success of the Harlem Renaissance* (Knoxville: University of Tennessee Press, 1997), xxii; Anderson, *Deep River*, 7, 9, 10.

68. Houston Baker, *Modernism and the Harlem Renaissance* (Chicago: University of Chicago Press, 1987), xv.

69. Baker, *Modernism and the Harlem Renaissance*, 50, 51.

70. George O. Caldwell, "A Comparison of Selected Material of Stravinsky's *Firebird* with Traditional Negro Folk Music," (master's thesis, University of Iowa, 1932).

71. Ruth Shores Hill, "Alpha Theta Chapter," *Ivy Leaf*, June 1931, 37–38. David Levering Lewis notes that black women dressed as men performed "St. James Infirmary Blues"; see Lewis, *When Harlem Was in Vogue*, 242. Louis Armstrong recorded the "St. James Infirmary Blues" in 1929 and Cab Calloway recorded the same tune in 1930. Blues singer Bessie Smith recorded "Baby Won't You Please Come Home" in 1923.

CHAPTER 10 | Great Plains Pragmatist:
*Aaron Douglas and the Art
of Social Protest*

AUDREY THOMPSON

Like most of the luminaries of the Harlem Renaissance, its leading visual artist, Aaron Douglas, was not himself a product of Harlem.¹ Although Winold Reiss and Alain Locke were to guide Douglas in the development of his artistic vision once he arrived in Harlem, his early years in Kansas, Missouri, and Nebraska gave rise to both the communal values and the artistic sense of isolation that were to lead him to Harlem. It was in the black church and in Topeka's "cohesive and politically active" African American community that Douglas first experienced black solidarity and embraced "the values of education and social uplift."² Many years later, meeting William Dawson, a like-minded black musician, in Kansas City proved to be a "first step" out of artistic and racial isolation.³

Growing up in Kansas, pursuing a bachelor of fine arts degree at the University of Nebraska, and teaching in Missouri, Aaron Douglas developed the commitment to pressing against the limits of the known that was to shape his artistic vision as a "pioneering Africanist."⁴ His vision partook simultaneously of a sense of political urgency and artistic expansiveness, both referenced to the situation and possibilities of blacks in America. Among the influences on that vision were the writings of W. E. B. Du Bois, debates in Topeka's progressive black press, and Douglas's own experiences as a soldier and a laborer.⁵

Together with the "optimism and self-help philosophy" imbibed from the black community in Topeka, Douglas's experiences of racism, racial solidarity, and adventure infused him with an eagerness to play a role in promoting social change.[6] Under the influence of Winold Reiss and Alain Locke, Douglas was to forge that desire for social change into a bold and liberating artistic vision.

This essay examines the tension between art and politics in Aaron Douglas's art of social protest by framing his project in the terms set by the African American pragmatism of the era. As George Hutchinson argues, "a large proportion" of those "fighting for black liberation . . . in the first three decades of the twentieth century had been molded by pragmatism and considered themselves pragmatists," although not necessarily "in the strict philosophical sense."[7] As a general phenomenon, pragmatism represented a rejection of fixed cultural assumptions about the way things had to be; instead, pragmatists sought multiple, new ways of framing meaning. Whereas conventional approaches to knowledge solidified existing assumptions about the nature of reality into a foundation upon which all further knowledge would be built, pragmatists set aside prevailing assumptions about truth. Rather than taking their cue from supposedly universal truths, pragmatists attempted to construct new, emergent knowledge based on both actual conditions and as-yet-to-be-imagined possibilities.

Because they saw all existing forms of knowledge as problematic, African American pragmatists sought to create the conditions for constructing *new* knowledge from social experience. Simply trying to persuade whites—or blacks—that the racist stereotypes of blacks were untrue would not lead to significant change, for any new racial knowledge explicitly tied to the old "knowledge" would have to "build upon" falsehoods. The solution, therefore, was to shift away from existing frameworks of knowledge by appealing to an altogether different framework. Inducing shifts in perception and experience afforded the opportunity to reorganize social relationships and therefore social possibility. Whether ideational (as in the case of art and literature) or material (as in the case of economic relations), such shifts were to be guided not by reference to timeless standards or absolute truth but by instrumental considerations: by projections as to whether they might promote socially useful change.

African American pragmatism thus stood for progress *tied to* experiential and interpretive pluralism. It also stood for possibility: under the terms of pragmatist instrumentalism, meaning depended not on the innate character of things but on the uses to which things were put. Insofar as Aaron Douglas, Alain Locke, W. E. B. Du Bois, and other contributors to the Harlem Renaissance sought to gain leverage on blacks' shared experience by devising new intellectual and cultural tools, and insofar as they saw planned cultural activism as helping to guide social progress, they formed part of the newly emerging tradition in African American pragmatism.[8] Aaron Douglas figured among the African American pragmatists of the twenties and thirties whose work was to shape a new understanding of black experience and black possibility.

Alain Locke and African-American Pragmatism

Rejecting fixed categories and absolute truths as the reference for knowledge, pragmatism regards experience as the ground of knowledge; for that experience to be meaningful, however, it must be *mediated* by the tools of intelligence. While Aaron Douglas brought considerable cultural and political experience with him to Harlem, he did not yet have the artistic tools he would use to interpret and frame that experience. Winold Reiss was the German artist who introduced Aaron Douglas to a new way of painting African Americans; Alain Locke, a philosopher and a leading spokesman for the Harlem Renaissance, provided Douglas with the pragmatist framework that identified art as playing a crucial role in social protest and racial education.

Overcoming the Effects of Mis-Education

While most white pragmatists of the time did not understand experience in racial terms, African American pragmatists such as Alain Locke, W. E. B. Du Bois, and Carter G. Woodson pointed out that, in the context of American culture in the early part of the twentieth century, race was a defining aspect of black experience. Because of the stigma attached to blackness, African Americans could not choose to ignore race; insofar as African Americans were beginning to realize and celebrate the distinctiveness of black culture, however, they could choose to emphasize race as a positive factor in experience.

Before African Americans could address black cultural experience in all its diversity and complexity, they had to be in a position to acknowledge and understand that experience on its own terms. Having learned to think like whites, educated African Americans were among those least likely to understand their experience outside the deficit terms set by the dominant social order.[9] So successfully had whites framed blackness as a problem, Locke said, that "the thinking Negro" had been led to neglect his own experiential standpoint as a basis for knowledge.[10] Confirming Locke's emphasis on the need to overcome the effects of mis-education, Aaron Douglas commented enthusiastically on Winold Reiss's portrayal of African Americans in his drawings for *The New Negro*.

> Many colored people don't like Reiss's drawings. We are possessed, you know, with the idea that it is necessary to be white, to be beautiful.... It takes lots of training or a tremendous effort to down the idea that thin lips and straight nose is the apogee of beauty. But once free you can look back with a sigh of relief and wonder how anyone could be so deluded.[11]

The new artistic tools of racial representation that Douglas encountered in New York allowed him to return to his youthful experiences of blackness with a fresh eye. Church, work, education, and community were to figure in Douglas's art not as provincial, Great Plains imitations of the high culture of New York but as the authentic folk culture at the heart of a new racial vision.

Art as Social Protest

With John Dewey, Alain Locke believed that "the moral function of art . . . is to remove prejudice, do away with the scales that keep the eye from seeing, tear away the veils due to wont and custom, perfect the power to perceive."[12] If art was to tap the African American experience, artists had to learn to see that experience afresh, setting aside the racist conventions that prevented the perception of beauty in blackness.[13] From a pragmatist perspective, posing a rational challenge to deficit conceptions of blackness was unlikely to make a significant difference in how either blacks or whites perceived the "race problem." Because appeals to reason can only engage us in terms of what already makes sense to us—thereby appealing to the very assumptions that challenges to old ways of thinking are meant to unsettle—they cannot induce shifts in our overall system of beliefs but can only effect adjustments between existing beliefs. African American art grounded in an authentic folk culture, however, offered the possibility of reorienting both white and black thinking.

In order for African American artists to achieve freshness and spontaneity of perception, Locke advocated that they return to sources largely untouched by white influence: the ancestral legacy of Africa and the contemporary riches of black American folk culture.[14] Because Africa represented a pre-contact past, it served to move the perception of blackness outside the context of the American Negro "problem." Africa pointed to a history before 1619, when the first black slaves were brought to the American colonies. Insofar as New World slavery and racial oppression had prevented assimilation, they could be said to have provided the conditions that had helped keep the African legacy pure and uncontaminated. Drawing upon the African legacy also allowed Harlem Renaissance artists to capitalize on the European interest in Africa that was leading to a new appreciation of black artistry. "To American Negroes, long deprived of the importance of a past, save that which meant humiliation and despair, this renaissance of knowledge" regarding Africa brought a "new and growing enthusiasm for self-expression."[15]

African American folk culture, meanwhile, provided the historically American experience upon which black artists could draw in developing an art form that would be distinctively new, distinctively American, and distinctively black. Because it had arisen under conditions of cultural segregation, black folk culture represented an organically African-American framing of experience that could be seen as independent of white culture. Like some of the white patrons of the Harlem Renaissance, Locke saw black folk culture as a source of vitality, purity, and spirituality not available to the dominant, materialist strain in American culture *except* through the intermediary of the black artist, who would transform "primitive" feelings and insights into high culture.[16]

Modernism and Primitivism in the Work of Aaron Douglas

Primitivism

Primitivism for Aaron Douglas, as for Alain Locke, referred both to the ancestral legacy of Africa and to the folk culture of African Americans—folk culture meaning, above all, the blues, jazz, spirituals, and dance. The appeal to primitivism was in part a celebration of the spirit and culture that had been strong enough to survive slavery, in part a recognition of working-class African Americans (as opposed to the black aristocracy or the Talented Tenth that the older generation of race propagandists preferred to feature), and in part a bow to the contemporary fad of exoticism connected to the urban dance halls. Although to some extent the themes in Douglas's illustrations and murals reflect "decadent" primitive themes stressing night life in the cabarets, much more of his work invokes African masks, fetishes, and plant life, African forms of dance and music, and Egyptian imagery such as pyramids. Folk imagery also plays an important rote, bespeaking a close familiarity with black religious beliefs and symbolism. Douglas's painting was in fact intended to be a visual counterpart to black music, based especially on the iconography of the spirituals.[17] Romare Bearden and Harry Henderson quote Douglas as saying, with respect to his illustrations for *God's Trombones*,

> I tried to keep my forms very stark and geometric with my main emphasis on the human body. I tried to portray everything not in a realistic but [an] abstract way—simplified and abstract as . . . in the spirituals. In fact I used the starkness of the old spirituals as my model—and at the same time I tried to make my painting modern.[18]

Among the themes in Douglas's work are the struggle, work, and suffering involved in the African American experience. *The Crucifixion*, for example, depicts a monumental black figure carrying the cross for Jesus, the soldiers' spears pressing behind him. Jesus himself, a much smaller figure, is painted as a figure of light surrounded by circles of light.[19] The central and dominant figure in the painting is "the legendary Simon, a Black man who took upon himself the yoke of Jesus' cross"; upon his face we see imprinted the "strain and agony of his travail," for he carries the "weight of the world" on his shoulders. "He is the worker among men, the builder of cities that circumscribe his access."[20] But while our attention is drawn to Simon's suffering, we do not lose sight of his faith. Even in works wherein struggle and pain are foregrounded, strength, hope, and spirituality maintain a powerful presence.

The illustrations and paintings that celebrate black folk creativity, on the other hand, in some cases include violent counterpoints to the black cultural experience. *Charleston*, for example, depicts a relaxed nightclub scene framed by a noose hanging from overhead and clutching hands reaching in from the foreground.[21] In other works, Douglas included portrayals of chattel slavery, industrial enslavement, and lynching. Yet while Douglas never lost sight of the threat posed by racism, perhaps the most important effect of his concentration on African and African American folk themes is the rendering of an all-black world in which whiteness is not a point of reference. Racism, oppression, and violence are all factors in black experience—represented in the paintings and illustrations by chains, nooses, clawlike hands, and spears, for example. But although racism and its consequences impinge upon black experience, they do not define it. Still less does whiteness define blackness in Douglas's work: racism is acknowledged as a historical and sociological fact, but it is not allowed to give whiteness center stage. Indeed, whiteness appears only by implication.[22]

The centrality given to black experience in Douglas's work reflects the foregrounding of racialized experience characteristic of African American pragmatism. Like both Carter G. Woodson and Alain Locke, Douglas avoids letting white frameworks set the terms for understanding black experience; the world he portrays is a black world. To the extent that Douglas emphasizes work and struggle, he shares Woodson's political, often oppositional, pragmatist orientation. To the extent that Douglas emphasizes the artistic and expressive achievement represented by the spirituals, he participates in Locke's cultural pragmatist tradition, which ties the distinctive experience of African Americans to universal forms of experience.

In calling artists' attention to African and African American folk themes, Locke urged a specifically instrumental and emergent use of primitivism—a way of framing black experience outside the terms set by the prevailing discourse of race. By contrast, most critics have assumed that primitivism refers to a fixed, racist set of meanings. In reifying primitivism as a sentimental, white view in which "the Negro" was exoticized and treated as a spectacle, such critics have ignored the actual uses to which primitivism was put in the art of the Harlem Renaissance. Nathan Huggins, for example, takes a foundationalist rather than instrumental view of the imagery of primitivism, arguing that it "rested on very superficial imagery of African life," with correspondingly superficial realizations in the art produced.[23] Yet Huggins acknowledges that the African influence had different effects in the visual arts, particularly in the work of Aaron Douglas, than it did in the poetry and fiction of the Renaissance: "Aaron Douglas borrowed two things from the Africans. He thought that art should be design more than subject. And his personal predilections for mysticism encouraged him to find racial unity and racial source in Africa." Because Douglas's emphasis was on design, the appeal to African primitivism as symbol was more successful than in work intended as representational; nevertheless, Huggins sees him as subordinating art to the idea of the primitive and argues that Douglas was "abstract for philosophical not for painterly reasons." In Douglas's work, Huggins argues, the legacy of Africa was "necessarily abstract: mere design through which he wanted to see a soul-self."[24]

Certainly Douglas saw African Americans as sharing a unique racial gift and believed that there was a universal dimension to the black experience.[25] His notes from a meeting of the editors of *Fire!!* proclaim, "We believe that the Negro is fundamentally, essentially different from their Nordic neighbors. . . . We believe these differences to be greater spiritual endowment, greater sensitivity, greater power for artistic expression and appreciation."[26] But while Douglas was not unaffected by the romantic conception of primitivism, he cannot be said to have accepted a fixed or static account of the African American spirit. His notes also stress that the young black artists involved, while "group conscious," were not unified by any specific message or cause: "We have no axes to grind."[27] What unified the group was the spirit of the artistic community itself. As Douglas was to explain in a 1971 interview, the "togetherness" of the black artistic community "was the thing that created the Renaissance."[28]

Calling upon the African heritage, while a way of symbolizing and celebrating a shared community and a shared history, also offered a way to gain perspective on the present by looking at the black American experience from another angle. In effect, primitivism became a tool of modernism. As Amy Kirschke notes, Douglas followed the basic Egyptian "rule of stylizing the body by painting the figure as if it were being observed from several different viewpoints."[29] In his early work in analytical cubism, Picasso took the same approach, but whereas Picasso's work "suggested three-dimensional form through faceted-angular shapes with more depth," Douglas favored a flat, hard-edged, silhouette style.[30] In both cases, the viewer sees a scene from several perspectives at once. Such an effect is impossible in naturalistic approaches, but in cubism and so-called primitive folk painting traditional (academic) perspective is absent. The refusal of "correct" perspective represents a refusal of the conventions of realism and thus a refusal of the description of reality that those in power take to be obvious or natural or neutral.

Metaphorically, the juxtaposition of perspectives in Douglas's work suggests a pragmatist and modernist endorsement of pluralism: of multiple, simultaneous perspectives as the measure of truth, rather than a single, unifying God's eye view. Douglas's own observation supports this metaphorical reading. Africanism, he said, could not simply be transplanted into the life of black Americans. Instead, he suggested, "we can go to African life and get a certain amount of understanding, form and color and use this knowledge in development of an expression which interprets our life."³¹ The primitive legacy thus affords both leverage on the present and a "classic" library of images that serve as a resource for interpolating and reinterpreting present experience. By using "primitivism" as a means of representing the distinctive group experience of blacks, Douglas avoided framing that experience in the terms set by racism; by including modernist motifs, he emphasized that that experience was not to be conceived in static or sentimental terms but was to be understood as an emergent experience, a journey into possibility.

Modernism

Much of the art of the Harlem Renaissance, argue the authors of *Rhapsodies in Black: Art of the Harlem Renaissance*, was the very prototype of modernist art.³² Not only did Renaissance artists draw on explicitly modern themes such as migration to the cities, urban life, and alienation in the modern industrial workplace, but primitivism itself represented a modernist theme. The admittedly problematic and sentimental "modern cult of the primitive" was only one dimension of this modernism.³³ Just as integral to modernism was the "celebration of the primordial in art: truth, beauty and power residing in basic elemental forms, rather than in overwrought ones."³⁴ The return to basic forms organizes such modern art forms as Art Deco, cubism, and orphism, among others.

Because the combination of primitivism and futurism is one of the hallmarks of Art Deco, I wish to focus particularly on Douglas's affinities with Art Deco, which features simplicity and boldness of outline, formalism in the concentration on geometric shapes, and abstract, idealized, stylized depictions of the human body. Associated both with fine art and with art for the masses, Art Deco bridges the usual high/low culture divide—an important consideration for any art of social protest. To the extent that it is a popular style, Art Deco speaks in a language more directly accessible than that associated with high culture. In much of its expression, moreover, Art Deco has been more visible to a mass audience than paintings or sculptures confined in private collections or museums. Most of Aaron Douglas's work was either in the form of murals, such as those in the 135th Street branch of the New York Public Library (now the Schomburg Center for Research in Black Culture), or in the form of illustrations in books and magazines—more often than not on the covers of magazines like *The Crisis* and *Opportunity*—and thus was particularly accessible to broad audiences.

As with Art Deco more generally, Douglas's work finds in stylized abstraction the possibility of a universal art form. The modernism of his figures consists in their abstraction: while identifiably black, the figures represent, above all, human beings. Symbolic and idealized, Douglas's abstract, elegant human figures are devoid of any superficial characteristics that might lend themselves to caricature. Human beings in their simplest form—objects reduced "to their basic shapes"[35]—are portrayed as creatures of dignity, who work, suffer, dance, and pray. Abstraction thus helps to clear away some of the debris of stereotypic detail and racial caricature attached to depictions of blackness. Yet the simplicity in Douglas's work also lends itself to an emotional starkness that is at once unsentimental and dramatically evocative. His murals and illustrations have an undecorated, bold directness that differentiates his work from the formalism of Art Deco, which is usually associated with decorativeness and a kind of leisure, even luxury. The illustrations for *God's Trombones*, for example, are concerned not with the body as object but with the body as objectified: the black body under the institution of slavery. In contrast to much other work in the Deco style, Douglas's figures are emotionally expressive, stark in their depiction of human suffering.

Far more than is typical of Art Deco, Douglas's work has a specifically historical and narrative orientation to the past; many of his illustrations and murals depict periods in African or African American history. The narrative focus speaks to his interest in experience, above and beyond style or form. Whereas most artists in the Deco style treat "primitive" art as a storehouse to be mined for its patterns and motifs, Douglas takes up the historical and political themes, as well as the decorative elements, of the collective African American past.[36] Because they are engaged in action that has narrative meaning, his figures are not simply elements of decoration but symbolic figures: mythic, idealized figures that speak for both the past and the future.

While the primitive motifs in Douglas's work serve to foreground blackness and celebrate the historical dimensions of the African American experience, Douglas's modern themes and modernist style speak to his belief in progress and a possible future to be shaped by present action. In the words of Bearden and Henderson, Douglas believed that "art can be the deepest communicative channel between the races" and across national divides.[37] In-deed, the symbolism of the concentric circles in much of Douglas's work speaks specifically to this theme. *Song of the Towers*, the final panel of the mural *Aspects of Negro Life*, depicts a jazz saxophonist, a desperately scurrying worker with a briefcase, and an exhausted figure in the corner, all framed by a giant cog, skyscrapers, industrial chimneys, and ribbons of smoke; grasping, threatening hands intrude in the foreground. In the distant background—central, but so small as almost to escape notice—is the Statue of Liberty.[38] Despite the dominant impression of despair conveyed by the painting, the circles of sound that surround the musician offer some degree of hope. The pattern of expanding circles invokes the possibilities of mass communication represented by radio sound waves.[39] And communication, of course, carried a promise not only of the spread of information but of organization for social change.

Most of Douglas's work suggests a forward-looking stance, whether through the use of modern symbols such as skyscrapers or the smoking chimneys of modern industry, the aspiration signified by upward turned faces, or the play of light and angles of vision indicative of a modern outlook. Yet his masks, pyramids, skyscrapers, and industrial cogs cannot be read literally, as a straightforward celebration (or, alternatively, condemnation) of primitivism and modernism. For Douglas, African symbolism serves primarily to *frame* perception—to provide a formal, classical reference point for perceptions of blackness, thereby offering a perspective that de-centers such perceptions from the framings imposed by American racism. Just as African tropes are not meant to represent a literal, known past, the modernist imagery is not meant to offer a simple endorsement or celebration of "progress." Rather than using skyscrapers, for example, in the way that many Art Deco painters did, as a wholesale celebration of *form* as progress, Douglas included his skyscrapers to remind viewers of the contribution that black labor was making to the building of the future.[40] That Douglas shared much of the cultural pragmatists' optimism regarding the future seems clear; that his outlook was unromantic must also be acknowledged. Neither social progress nor skyscrapers were inevitable: both were produced by work. The future could not be predicted or controlled in absolute terms but it could be redirected from its existing racist course and guided by an emergent understanding of alternative possibilities.

The progressive orientation of Douglas's work is a matter both of theme and of treatment. His narrative framework speaks of progress for the race and for civilization as a whole. The style and technique of the murals and illustrations also express the sensibility of "Art Moderne," particularly in the use of light, which suggests the kind of spotlighting that came to be associated with the movies. There is the same alternation between large picture and close-up, except that the two coexist in a single image. The fragmentation and multiplication of the circles and rays of light, while challenging conventions of realism in light and shadow, also suggest the multiplicity of perspectives, of focal points or centers. The multiple rays of light work to focus our attention, giving narrative structure to the viewer's gaze and creating an impression of movement and relationship beyond the flat juxtapositions of the figures.[41] Suggestive of hope, the light also may be seen as religious; in most cases, the central figures seem to look up both to God and the future. In other cases, the light may be that of the future on the past, probing an obscure past for knowledge to be used in creating a new future.

The treatment of both primitive and modern themes in Douglas's work, then, is far more political and historical than that of Art Deco painters in general. Douglas shares the modern faith in progress, but he also pays attention to having come, as the spiritual says, "a mighty long way." Looking back on the legacy of the Harlem Renaissance, Locke was to comment, "By stages, it seems, we are achieving greater democracy in art,—and let us hope through art."[42] Locke's view of art was that it afforded Americans the opportunity to really *see* blackness for the first time: to see blackness not as the shadow of whiteness but as a distinctive culture to be understood on its own terms. By putting into practice Locke's philosophy of racial art, Douglas "effected the crucial move toward affirming the validity of the Black experience and thereby made one of America's most worthy contributions to art," argues David Driskell. "Had Douglas not led the way in using African-oriented imagery," Alain Locke's vision of "'return[ing] to the ancestral arts of Africa for inspiration'" might have been delayed much longer in its realization.[43]

The "Universal" Art of Aaron Douglas

Among the more politically minded of the artists and writers associated with the Harlem Renaissance, Aaron Douglas participated enthusiastically in the Renaissance project as Alain Locke framed it: as an artistic attempt to set the United States on the path toward full political inclusiveness and cultural understanding.[44] A measure of the resistance of racism to "cultural" reconstruction, unfortunately, is the virtual invisibility of Aaron Douglas's work and of African American themes in most contemporary discussions of Art Deco. In *American Art Deco*, for example, Alastair Duncan opens his chapter on painting and graphics with the words, "One has to search hard to find an Art Deco influence in American paintings of the 1920s and 1930s"—and although Duncan then discusses the Works Progress Administration projects sponsored under the New Deal (in which Douglas participated), Aaron Douglas goes unmentioned.[45]

The lag in the art world's recognition of Aaron Douglas as an artist of "universal" caliber suggests the inadequacy of analyses claiming that Douglas's rendering of the African American experience traded upon stereotypes. So radical was Douglas's challenge to Eurocentric conceptions of art, in fact, that his work has been dismissed as failing to meet the "neutral" and "individual" terms upon which blackness can safely be acknowledged. It is ironic, therefore, that Douglas was accused by some of his contemporaries of playing into racist assumptions regarding black primitivism. James A. Porter, for example, called Douglas's paintings "tasteless" and reminiscent of black minstrel stereotypes.[46] As Bearden and Henderson were later to read this reaction, it represents that of "many academic artists to painting that did not present black people as well-dressed citizens, charmingly preoccupied in comfortable surroundings. The same attitude was expressed by members of the black middle class who were ashamed of jazz."[47]

As Douglas commented, the decision to represent black experience in particular ways is always a response to a certain historical situation: "What the Negro artist should paint and how he should paint it can't accurately be determined without reference to specific social conditions."[48] Such a view of art is pragmatist insofar as it suggests setting aside any appeal to ultimate truths, instead taking an instrumental approach to the making of meaning. Douglas's own explicit view was that black art could not be understood or appreciated apart from a recognition of the role played in experience by the politics of race. In contrast to colonizing approaches to universalism that assimilate all human experience to that of the specifically individual experience of the white, middle- and upper-class art connoisseur, Douglas's form of universalism stressed the shared historical and cultural experience of African Americans as a group. Not only did he challenge the notion of universalism predicated on parallels between individual forms of experience, but he challenged the equation of universalism with colorblindness. Instead, he sought universalism in the historical particularity of black experience. His "universal man" was black—and sometimes a woman.

In conjuring a black modernist vision of possible worlds, Aaron Douglas and his fellow Renaissance artists and writers looked toward a New Negro and a New Nordic not confined to Manhattan life. Drawing on their localized experiences of blackness in California, Kansas, Utah, Jamaica, Illinois, Florida, Nebraska, and elsewhere, and on their shared dream of Africa, the Renaissance artists and writers projected rediscovered "folk" and "primitive" values into a future articulated to a black, modernist perspective. The effects of their visionary and revisionary insight into possibility continue to resonate today. In setting aside the white-centered frameworks of meaning attached to race, urban life, and history, and reinventing modernity in black-centered terms, the artists of the Renaissance instigated a form of social protest that helped to shift racialized understandings.

Almost three quarters of a century after the Harlem Renaissance, the generative themes found in the work of Aaron Douglas and other Renaissance artists are again being taken up by black artists, activists, and others both in the United States and in the diaspora; indeed, the Harlem Renaissance itself is being reconceived as a movement confined neither to Harlem nor to the 1920s. Artists and writers connected with the movement, including Aaron Douglas, Jacob

Lawrence, and Langston Hughes, produced important work many decades after the Renaissance was said to be over. Today, other artists on both sides of the Atlantic continue to explore the themes and insights of the Harlem Renaissance.[49] The original Renaissance artists came from almost everywhere but Harlem: from the West and the Midwest, from the Great Plains, from the South, from the East, and from outside the United States. Their successors are found not only in the Americas but in Europe, Africa, and everywhere else in the diaspora.[50]

Notes

1. During the period between the mid-twenties and the mid-thirties, the term "Negro Renaissance" was used to refer to the flourishing of African American arts and letters that later came to be known as the "Harlem Renaissance." Calling it a "Negro Renaissance" rather than the "Harlem Renaissance" signaled the integral character of the renaissance. As Jeffrey Stewart points out, "after 1925, cities such as Chicago, Philadelphia, Cleveland, and Washington DC, experienced their own 'renaissances.'" Jeffrey C. Stewart, "Introduction," in *The Critical Temper of Alain Locke: A Selection of His Essays on Art and Culture*, ed. Jeffrey C. Stewart (New York: Garland Publishing, 1983), pp. xviii. Some recent commentaries also refer to this period as the "First Black Renaissance" to distinguish it from the "Second Black Renaissance," which stretched from the early fifties through the seventies. In addition to Aaron Douglas, other Harlem Renaissance emigrants included Zora Neale Hurston (Florida), Alain Locke (Philadelphia), Wallace Thurman (Salt Lake City and Los Angeles), Claude McKay (Jamaica), Jessie Fauset (Washington DC), Langston Hughes (Missouri, Topeka, Chicago, Cleveland, and Mexico), Louis Armstrong (New Orleans), Alberta Hunter (Chicago), and Augusta Savage (Florida).

2. Amy Helene Kirschke, *Aaron Douglas: Art, Race, and the Harlem Renaissance* (Jackson: University Press of Mississippi, 1995), pp. 2, 3. Douglas was born in Topeka, Kansas, in 1899; he graduated from the University of Nebraska in 1922.

3. Quoted in Kirschke, *Aaron Douglas*, pp. 9.

4. This description of Aaron Douglas is attributed to Alain Locke in Steven Watson, *The Harlem Renaissance: Hub of African-American Culture, 1920–1930* (New York: Pantheon, 1995), pp. 89.

5. Although middle-class, Aaron Douglas "experienced some of the hardships of the

new black proletariat . . . taking shape in the cities of the North," and "sympathized with" the common worker. Kirschke, *Aaron Douglas*, pp. 5, 8.

6. Kirschke, *Aaron Douglas*, p. 4; see also p. 2.

7. George Hutchinson, *The Harlem Renaissance in Black and White* (Cambridge: Belknap/Harvard University Press, 1995), p. 38. Hutchinson sees pragmatism in the first decades of the twentieth century as a pervasive philosophy to which American intellectuals and artists in general responded, whether or not they were directly informed by it. At the same time, pragmatism was itself influenced by other movements; Hutchinson makes an argument for a mutually informing relation between pragmatism and the aesthetics of the Harlem Renaissance. For example, he sees Dewey's *Art as Experience* as "at least partly indebted to African and African American aesthetics as filtered through Barnes" (p. 46).

8. In *The American Evasion of Philosophy: A Genealogy of Pragmatism* (Madison: University of Wisconsin Press, 1989), Cornel West makes a case for Du Bois as a pragmatist, but because he took a variety of theoretical and political positions over the course of his long and active career, it is difficult to categorize Du Bois with any finality. As I concentrate here on the Harlem Renaissance years, when Du Bois's position was in some ways more conservative than Locke's but still identifiably pragmatist, I have simply identified Du Bois as a pragmatist. It should be noted, however, that Du Bois embraced a number of political positions, including socialism and pan-Africanism.

9. Pragmatists are concerned specifically with the uses and misuses to which tools of thought are put, and the degree to which the intellectual tools accepted by a society promote or preclude new ways of understanding experience. Carter G. Woodson's *The Mis-Education of the Negro* (1933; Washington DC: The Associated Publishers, 1972) gives the classic analysis of the inadequacy of white intellectual tools for understanding or shaping black experience. Because of its emphasis on structural conflict as well as cultural difference, Woodson's analysis might be characterized as an instance of political or radical pragmatism.

10. Alain Locke, "The New Negro," in *The New Negro*, ed. Alain Locke (1925; New York: Atheneum, 1992), pp. 3–4.

11. Quoted in Kirschke, *Aaron Douglas*, pp. 61. (Quote dates from 1925.)

12. John Dewey, *Art as Experience*, in *John Dewey: The Later Works, 1925–1953*, set. ed. Jo Ann Boydston, vol. 10 (1934), ed. Harriet Furst Simon (Carbondale: Southern Illinois University Press, 1987), p. 328.

13. See Alain Locke, "Harlem Types-Portraits by Winold Reiss," in *Critical Temper*, p. 18. (Originally published in 1925.)

14. Stewart argues that most African American Renaissance artists had no real interest in Africa or in being race representatives, and that Locke's own sense of Africa

was too vague to allow for any insights into distinctively African artistic motifs or techniques. Nevertheless, Stewart credits Locke with helping to legitimate Africa in African Americans' eyes and with helping to pave the way for the Second Black Renaissance in the 1960s. Jeffrey C. Stewart, "A Biography of Alain Locke: Philosopher of the Harlem Renaissance, 1886–1930" (PhD diss., University of Michigan–Ann Arbor, 1979), pp. 68–70, 193, and 335–36. Also see Alain Locke, "The Legacy of the Ancestral Arts," in *New Negro*, pp. 254–67.

15. W. E. B. Du Bois, "A Negro Art Renaissance," in *W. E. B. Du Bois: A Reader*, ed. David Levering Lewis (New York: Henry Holt, 1995), p. 507. (Originally published in 1925.)

16. Many commentators—including Aaron Douglas and the other young artists and writers connected with the *Fire!!* Project—have been troubled by the influence that the white patrons of the Harlem Renaissance exerted on black art. Some critics have even gone so far as to dismiss the entire Renaissance as a failure, arguing that writers and artists were compromised by the need to placate white patrons and consumers. (For a provocative discussion of these arguments, see Hutchinson, *Harlem Renaissance* [note 7 above].) To the extent that the Harlem Renaissance appeal to "primitivism" did partake of the sentimentalization of African Americans as untouched by modern decadence, it is of course problematic; it is a simplification of "primitivism," however, to see it as a strictly white, strictly patronizing trope. As I discuss in the next section, primitivism also had other meanings, particularly as interpreted in Aaron Douglas's work. See, too, the extended discussion of this issue in Kirschke's *Aaron Douglas*. As Kirschke points out, the patrons of black art were by no means exclusively white—most of Douglas's illustrations, for example, appeared in black periodicals.

17. David Driskell, "Aaron Douglas: Singing a New Song of Heritage" (paper presented at the African Americans and the Great Plains Conference in Lincoln NE, February, 1997).

18. Romare Bearden and Harry Henderson, *A History of African-American Artists: From 1792 to the Present* (New York: Pantheon, 1993), p. 130.

19. Reproduced in The Studio Museum of Harlem, *Harlem Renaissance Art of Black America* (New York: Harry N. Abrams, 1987), p. 121 (plate 32).

20. David Driskell, "The Flowering of the Harlem Renaissance: The Art of Aaron Douglas, Meta Warrick Fuller, Palmer Hayden, and William H. Johnson," in *Harlem Renaissance Art of Black America*, p. 112.

21. *Charleston*, an illustration from *Black Magic* (1929), by Paul Marand, is reproduced in Kirschke, *Aaron Douglas*, fig. 62.

22. For example, David Driskell identifies the "Roman sentinel" in *The Crucifixion* as "representing the white guardianship of Black affairs in America and Africa." Driskell,

"Flowering," p. 112. Interestingly, there is nothing in the actual portrayal of this figure to suggest whiteness; his coloring and the distinctive Aaron Douglas eyes resemble those of black Simon. Even the grasping hands that appear in images like *Charleston* and *Song of the Towers* are not explicitly identified with whiteness, for although in one instance they are white, in the other they are black.

23. Nathan Irvin Huggins, *The Harlem Renaissance* (New York: Oxford University Press, 1971), p. 188. Huggins criticizes Countee Cullen's "Heritage" in this regard, for example (pp. 164–65).

24. Huggins, *The Harlem Renaissance*, pp. 169, 171, 172.

25. In the first part of the twentieth century, many African Americans accepted the view that the white and black races were fundamentally and naturally different, not only by virtue of their different histories but by virtue of "race" itself as a quasi-biological category. Liberal and leftist African Americans, however, repudiated the Social Darwinist characterization of those differences in deficit terms, instead emphasizing parallelism and the distinctiveness of the race spirit, "gift," or racial identity that set African Americans apart from white Americans. Among the prominent African Americans subscribing to the idea of an inherited racial identity were Marcus Garvey, Carter G. Woodson, Alain Locke, and Aaron Douglas.

26. Quoted in Kirschke, *Aaron Douglas*, p. 87. (Quote presumably dates from 1926.)

27. Quoted in Kirschke, *Aaron Douglas*, p. 87.

28. Quoted in Kirschke, *Aaron Douglas*, p. 51. Kirschke's discussion makes a strong argument for the centrality of group consciousness in Aaron Douglas's work.

29. Kirschke, *Aaron Douglas*, p. 77.

30. Kirschke, *Aaron Douglas*, p. 79.

31. Douglas, quoted in Kirschke, *Aaron Douglas*, p. 47.

32. Richard J. Powell et al., *Rhapsodies in Black: Art of the Harlem Renaissance* (Berkeley: University of California Press with the Hayward Gallery and the Institute of International Visual Arts, 1997).

33. Richard J. Powell, "Re/Birth of a Nation," in *Rhapsodies in Black*, p. 25.

34. Powell et al., *Rhapsodies in Black*, p. 26. Powell draws here upon Robert Goldwater's 1938 book, *Primitivism in Modern Painting*, reprinted as *Primitivism in Modern Art* (Cambridge: Belknap Press/Harvard University Press, 1986).

35. Bearden and Henderson, *History*, p. 128.

36. Art Deco during the years between the wars took a particular interest in folk and Native American art, African art (particularly sculpture and carving), Egyptian art (after Tutankhamen's tomb was opened in 1922), and pre-Columbian art.

37. Bearden and Henderson, *History*, p. 134.

38. The original mural (painted in 1934) is at the Schomburg Center; a reproduction can be found in *Harlem Renaissance Art of Black America*, p. 24 (plate 10).

39. Aaron Douglas, who worked with David Driskell at Fisk University for many years, described this connection between radio sound waves and the concentric circles in some of his paintings, in a conversation reported in Driskell, "Aaron Douglas."

40. Driskell, "Aaron Douglas."

41. By contrast, the majority of other work in the Art Deco tradition seems to resist narrative or dynamic composition. In most examples of the style, it is the thing itself that is dynamic, forward-looking, not the thing in relation to other things. Hence the fascination with the contours of objects (including persons as objects) as symbolic of movement—for example, the stepped silhouettes of futuristic skyscrapers, which of course do not actually move.

42. Alain Locke, "Up Till Now," in *Critical Temper*, p. 194. (Originally 1945.)

43. Driskell, "Flowering," p. 131.

44. By no means did all those associated with the Harlem Renaissance see its project in political terms. Aaron Douglas was among the more self-consciously political of the artists and writers of the time. Like the other contributors to *Fire!!*, an artistically successful but short-lived magazine, he took an economically as well as artistically Africentric stance; for a time, he also studied Marxism.

45. Alastair Duncan, *American Art Deco* (New York: Harry N. Abrams, 1986), p. 234. In the many books on American Art Deco that I have examined, only one mentions Aaron Douglas at all, and even that book does not offer any illustrations of his work. The author does, however, provide some brief discussion of Aaron Douglas and of African-American issues in the '20s and '30s. See Eva Weber, *Art Deco in America* (New York: Exeter Books, 1985), also published in an identical version but with a different cover in Greenwich CT, by Dorset Press (1985). Given that books on Art Deco published by prestigious art houses like Abrams, Rizzoli, and Abbeville mention neither the Harlem Renaissance in general nor particular African Americans such as Aaron Douglas, it may be a comment on the politics of art that both versions of Weber's book are published by bargain presses.

46. Quoted in Mary Schmidt Campbell, "Introduction," in *Harlem Renaissance Art*, p. 50.

47. Bearden and Henderson, *History*, pp. 133–34. A painting by Palmer Hayden from around 1937, *The Janitor Who Paints* is testament to the artistic tensions between demeaning racial stereotypes and the politics of "correct" racial representation. When the painting was x-rayed a few years ago, it was discovered that the underpainting was almost grotesquely unflattering to blacks. The painting, says Regenia Perry, "was undoubtedly altered by Hayden in response to widespread criticism of his works by his peers

who felt that Hayden was caricaturing blacks for the amusement of whites." Regenia A. Perry, *Free within Ourselves: African-American Artists in the Collection of the National Museum of American Art* (Washington DC: National Museum of American Art and San Francisco: Pomegranate Artbooks, 1992), p. 89. The gorgeous silver print photographs of James Van Der Zee from the Harlem Renaissance, of elegant, middle-class blacks, are representative of the preoccupation of Harlem Renaissance artists with presenting best-foot-forward images of black Americans to the rest of the world.

48. Quoted in Bearden and Henderson, *History*, p. 132.

49. Powell et al., *Rhapsodies*.

50. An earlier version of this essay was presented at the *African Americans and the Great Plains Conference* in Lincoln, Nebraska (February, 1997). I would like to thank Wilfred Samuels for his very helpful comments on an earlier draft of the paper.

CHAPTER 11 | Frompin' in the Great Plains: Listening and Dancing to the Jazz Orchestras of Alphonso Trent, 1925–1944

MARC RICE

During the 1920s and 1930s, dozens of African American dance bands of various sizes crisscrossed the Midwest and Southwest United States. These organizations are called "territory bands" by jazz historians because they typically maintained a city such as Oklahoma City, Kansas City, Omaha, or Tulsa as a home base, from which they mounted tours of the surrounding towns. The territory bands had their best years just prior to the Great Depression, but most were devastated by the 1930s and disbanded. Most of these bands included jazz in their repertoire and were vital to its development, creating a style of music distinct from that of New York, New Orleans, or Chicago. This midwest jazz style did not die with the demise of the early bands, for the careers of the Count Basie Orchestra and Charlie Parker were their legacy.

This paper focuses on one of the most popular and influential of the territory band leaders, Alphonso Trent. From 1925 to the mid 1940s, his groups were acknowledged by listeners and by other musicians as among the very best of the jazz bands performing in the Southwest and Great Plains. In the cities and towns that they visited, their performances were always a special event, particularly in the African American communities. Trent's orchestras played an important role as musicians and entertainers of African Americans in the Great Plains states in the 1920s and 1930s.

Although Trent did lead his first orchestra through the Midwest and Northeast, most of his career was set in and around the Great Plains, specifically in three cities, Dallas, Texas; Kansas City, Missouri; and Deadwood, South Dakota. In Dallas Trent met with his first triumph, securing well-paying jobs that had previously been off-limits to African American orchestras. Kansas City saw him during a period of hard times, when tragedy and the Depression had taken its toll on his group. In Deadwood, at the end of his music career, Trent again found financial success and stability.

Alphonso Trent

Alphonso Trent was born in Fort Smith, Arkansas, in 1902. He came from a solidly middle class African American family that emphasized greatly the importance of education. According to Henry Rinne, his father was the principal of the black high school in Fort Smith, and was one of the first black graduates of Ohio State University.[1] In addition to formal classroom education, Alphonso was given piano lessons at an early age. By his early teens, he was playing professionally with local bands.[2]

In 1925 Trent joined a group of musicians in Little Rock, Arkansas. The personnel included Edwin Swayzee, trumpet; Eugene Crooke, banjo; James Jeter, alto saxophone; John Fielding, vocals; Leo "Snub" Mosely, trombone; and Trent on piano.[3] In the spring of 1925 the band, now called the Alphonso Trent Orchestra, traveled through Texas and eventually arrived in Dallas.

In most cities the Trent orchestra played their primary engagements at extravagant, exclusively white hotels. These hotels, catering to the economic elite, could offer the band steady long-term employment. During their off nights, however, in whatever city they were in, the Trent orchestra booked themselves into African American establishments. The orchestra did not make much money on these nights, but as their reputation grew, these dances became important events in the black communities.

Dallas

The orchestra first established this method of operation in Dallas. In 1925 the city had three arenas for an African American orchestra to play and for a black audience to dance and listen. There was an outdoor pavilion in a section of Dallas called "Oak Cliff." There was the Pythian Temple, a large building downtown for the use of black businesses and organizations. And there were two nightclubs in the area, the L. B. Mose Theater and the Hummingbird.[4]

The Oak Cliff pavilion was the scene of the Trent Orchestra's first engagements in Dallas. According to Essie Mae Trent, Alphonso's widow, who first met her husband shortly after he moved to Dallas, the pavilion at Oak Cliff was at a ballpark in a predominantly African American neighborhood. The audience was generally ninety percent black as well. In Mrs. Trent's words, the facility was

> a large area and plenty of parking space. I wouldn't say that it was cultivated like they have now. It wasn't like the modern parks and things are now. But you had your space. Plenty of parking space. Oh it took up, say, two blocks.
>
> It wasn't anything modern. You had your bandstand. It was large. Huge, you could say. You could accommodate 1,000 people easily. During those times it was outstanding. I wouldn't be wrong in using those words.[5]

In the beginning of their stay in Dallas, the Trent Orchestra struggled with small crowds and little recognition, but their biggest break came a few weeks after their arrival. A bellman from the luxurious, white Adolphus Hotel convinced the hotel secretary to attend one of the band's Oak Cliff performances. She persuaded her boss to offer the orchestra a two-week engagement.[6] The two weeks became an eighteen-month stay, during which the orchestra established itself as the best band in the Southwest.

In the segregated Adolphus Hotel, the dances that the Trent Orchestra played were off-limits to African Americans. The bandsmen and their families, including Trent's future wife Essie Mae, endured the Jim Crow policies at the hotel, but these dances were broadcast over a 50,000 watt radio station, WFAA. It was heard throughout much of the country and served to disseminate the music of the band to people across the land, particularly the African Americans of Dallas.[7]

In this manner the Trent Orchestra became an important element in the multi-faceted musical culture of Dallas. During the 1920s, jazz and blues-based music thrived in the African American communities of the city. The Central Track section of the town in particular was host to many blues singers, boogie-woogie pianists, and small combos, who worked in various types of small clubs.

Buster Smith, a saxophonist who grew up in Dallas during the twenties, was a witness to the musical activities in the African American communities. As Smith recalled, "there were many, many good bands and musicians around [Dallas] then, and you'd see them everywhere you went . . ." Smith remembered hearing African American orchestras such as those led by Jap Allen, George E. Lee, and T. Holder. There were also "any number of little four- and five-piece bands playing around the roadhouses and after hours spots." Smith was quite familiar with the Trent Orchestra; it and the Troy Floyd Orchestra from San Antonio, "were the big bands."[8]

Their radio broadcasts quickly spread the popularity of the Trent Orchestra in the African American communities of Dallas and across the Midwest and Southwest. When they were not playing at the Adolphus Hotel, the band frequently played in either the L.B. Mose Theater downtown or the Hummingbird on Hall street in the Central Track district. According to Buddy Tate, then a young Dallas musician who eventually became a member of the Count Basie Orchestra:

> [The Trent Orchestra] would come uptown [to black dance halls] and play from 9 to 12 every Sunday after they finished their date at the Adolphus . . . and man, you couldn't get in when they played. They used to make as much as $75 a night a man, they were so popular. They had all that airtime over WFAA in Dallas, and they were heard all the way to Canada.[9]

In addition to the Oak Cliff pavilion and the two nightclubs, African Americans could also hear the Trent Orchestra at the Pythian Temple, a downtown, black-owned building used by various businesses. In the words of Mrs. Trent, the building was

> all brick. And there was a ballroom in there. And of course on the first floor there was a drug store. On the second floor you had your different doctors. And then you had your schools like your commercial schools. This is owned by Blacks. A five story building. And you could rent the auditorium out, if one wanted to rent it. Bands and things would come in, they would book them in there. Oh it was a lovely place. It was first class.[10]

The Pythian Temple's dance hall could be rented out for various occasions. As Mrs. Trent recalled

> the dance floor was just for anybody who wanted to rent it. For organizations. Lodges. Dances. Church affairs. If they wanted to have school affairs or plays. Sometimes the different clubs they'd say, "Well now what are we going to do? Let's have a play." So we know what we have in our club, and we know what they can offer. Well, we'll have a play.[11]

Often the Temple was rented out for public dances. In fact, when the Trent orchestra had a night off, they themselves sometimes rented it out. Their tuba player, Brent Sparks, was in charge of advertising, and anyone who could afford the admission price could come. The dance hall could also be rented for private affairs, and the Trent Orchestra were frequently hired to provide the entertainment. Most important were the dances given by the two society clubs to which Mrs. Trent belonged, the Idlewild and the Dunbar clubs, which presented the African American debutantes. Mrs. Trent's sister was in charge of selecting the girls who would have their coming out at the Pythian Temple dances.[12]

These private clubs played an important role in the culture of Dallas's mid- and upper-class African Americans. They were a meaningful part of Mrs. Trent's life, and she met her husband at one of their meetings. She still has vivid memories of society dances at the Pythian Temple, for which the Trent Orchestra often played. When asked what one would see upon entering such a dance, she recalled with much laughter,

> the band playing and people dancing. And women getting cool drinks or punch or whatever. No setups and tables like they have now. You would go to this fountain and they'd serve you punch. But they had chairs around and people'd sit and visit with their friends that way. Then they'd get up and dance. And some of the dances would have programs. And fellows was coming, wanting to see my program and fill in You're there! Everybody's frompin'! Everybody's doing their own thing! Everybody's got their own flask and bottle of whatever.[13]

The Respectability of Jazz

The popularity of the Trent Orchestra spread like wildfire among both black and white audiences. Dancing to jazz was a vital mode of social expression. There were those people, both African American and white, however, who saw jazz such as that played by the Trent Orchestra as dangerously decadent. Historian Paula Fass described this phenomenon among whites:

> By accepting the sensuous and exciting rhythms of modern jazz and its well-known association with the least savory parts of the cities, the young accepted as respectable what their elders logically could not, the excitement and those very qualities of indecency that they formally disdained.[14]

There were also African American parents who found dancing to this music to be less than respectable. For example, a 1927 editorial, "The Dance Craze!" in the black-owned *Kansas City Call* states:

> After all has been said that can be said in favor of the dance, it remains true that it is demoralizing. It rests on a purely carnal basis. It is absolutely and exclusively of the flesh. But for its sex complex it never would have been known. Take this out of it and it would perish for lack of motive. It is a pleasure, no doubt, but it is the pleasure of sin. It excites and thrills—and kills . . . police courts and morgue records testify to the debasing influences of the dance . . . [15]

This attitude was also found in the Great Plains states. Ralph Ellison, an African American writer and social commentator who grew up in Oklahoma City in the 1920s described the social status of jazz in his home town:

> Jazz was regarded by most of the respectable Negroes of the town as a backward, low-class form of expression and there was a marked difference between those who accepted it and lived close to their folk experience and those whose status stirrings led them to reject and deny it.[16]

Thus, when dancing to jazz became popular in the twenties, some adults, both African American and white, had a certain fear for the souls of their children. Even if their music was seen by some as decadent, however, the members of the Trent Orchestra, contrary to the image of the jazz musician as a shifty social degenerate, were well-educated young men of middle- and upper-middle class backgrounds. In addition, when they arrived in Dallas, the band associated primarily with the residents of the city who had similar backgrounds. In the words of Mrs. Trent, the band members

> were all high school graduates. And they were not like regular musicians at all. They had culture. These young men had been reared, you know, had had training at home. And you could tell from the churches [that they attended] on down. See, they got with the people that they'd been used to being around at home, and they'd go to church and the people there just fell in love with them.[17]

According to Mrs. Trent, the culture of the upper-class African Americans in Dallas, the culture to which the Trent Orchestra attached themselves, was quite vibrant. Perhaps she is a bit biased, but she feels that neighboring towns such as Fort Worth were "cowtowns" in comparison. As Mrs. Trent recalled, "When you get that society in Dallas, you're hitting something heavy. With carriage, culture, everything. That's the way people acted and carried themselves. These folks went from the top and entertained from the top."[18]

Young people danced two main types of dances to the music of the Trent Orchestra. Historians cite the Charleston and the Black Bottom as the two most important dances in the 1920s. Both were introduced in black vaudeville shows in the mid-1920s and were quickly appropriated by the young. Mrs. Trent remembers both white and African American dancers performing these steps to the music of the Trent Orchestra.[19]

On Tour

After eighteen months, the Trent Orchestra concluded their engagement at the Adolphus Hotel in the spring of 1926. In 1927 the orchestra worked the major cities of Texas and toured Louisiana, Arkansas, and Mississippi. They then headed east, playing St. Louis,

Louisville, Lexington, Cincinnati, Cleveland, and Buffalo in 1928 and 1929.[20] In each city they would play the major white hotel for two weeks to three months and on the side play dances for African Americans at various venues. As the engagement ended, tuba player Brent Sparks would secure them a job at another white hotel and accommodations in the new city.

These were prosperous times for the band. Their radio broadcasts at the Adolphus gave them a great deal of recognition. Dancing was more popular than ever, and they had no trouble finding places to play. In early 1930, however, tragedy struck. The club in Cleveland in which they were booked caught fire, and their instruments, uniforms, and sheet music were all destroyed. The disaster and the deepening of the Great Depression reversed their fortunes.

Hard Times

Trent's father paid for new instruments and uniforms, but jobs were difficult to come by. In early 1931 the band played its last job in the East and returned to the Southwest to re-group. Hayes Pillars, a saxophonist in the band, recalled that through most of 1931 and into 1932 the band based themselves in Trent's hometown of Fort Smith, Arkansas, while playing jobs in Oklahoma, Texas, Louisiana, and Missouri, but they also required financial help from their families.[21]

Their first jobs upon returning to the Southwest in 1931 were in Tulsa, Oklahoma City, and smaller towns in the same vicinity. Then they returned to Arkansas, where their financial situation deteriorated rapidly. For some jobs they were paid only three or four dollars a person. According to Hayes Pillars, "things just never got better... everybody kept thinking it would be better next week or next month or the next few months, but it just kept getting worse and worse, so we finally realized that we were in the grip of a deep depression and that was it."[22]

The bright spot during this dark period was a two-week booking at the end of October and beginning of November 1931, in El Torreon, a white dance hall in Kansas City, Missouri, that also allowed them to play one night at the African American Paseo Dance Hall. Perhaps this engagement rejuvenated the band, for jazz and dancing were vital aspects of Kansas City life, and indeed, this city is of crucial importance in the history of jazz.

Kansas City Jazz

From the mid-1920s through the 1930s, Kansas City was the scene of the most vibrant jazz community in the western United States. It had several large dance halls, and, especially in the African American communities, many smaller cabarets where enthusiasts could hear and dance to jazz throughout the night. Most large cities were host to one territory band, but no less than three, and at times as many as eight, bands called Kansas City home.[23]

Kansas City nightlife was the beneficiary of Thomas Pendergast's control of city government. According to Theodore Brown and Ross Russell, alcohol was, for all practical purposes, legal in most Kansas City establishments during Prohibition. Pendergast controlled the police department, and for a price, would keep the law away from any nightclub.[24]

The abundance of alcohol and music established dancing and listening to jazz as important pastimes for both Kansas City residents and visitors. An advertisement in a July 1931 *Kansas City Call* announces excursion trains for Kansas City from Dallas, Tulsa, and Oklahoma City, to bring African Americans to the Paseo Dance Hall for two nights of celebration. The music would be provided by the George E. Lee Orchestra, that, like other bands based in Kansas City, had traveled throughout the Southwest and was quite famous in that part of the country.[25]

During these years the entertainment section of the *Kansas City Call* was filled with advertisements describing dances in the African American halls and nightclubs. Some of the most vivid ads depict the spectacular battles of the bands, in which a hometown band, such as the Bennie Moten Orchestra, would perform with a visiting band, such as the Fletcher Henderson Orchestra from New York City.[26] Also advertised were the dances held by the African American musicians' union, Local No. 627, at which eight or more large orchestras would perform.[27]

One advertisement for the Trent Orchestra's performance at the Paseo Hall appeared in the October 30, 1931, *Kansas City Call*.[28] Most notable is the statement "Victor Recording Band." In fact, the Trent Orchestra never had the opportunity to record for the famous Victor label. Eight recordings, made for the smaller Gennet label, represent the only extant music of any of Trent's orchestras. It is quite possible that the advertisement used the Victor name to attract a larger audience. Victor was highly recognizable to Kansas City dancers because the favorite local band, the Bennie Moten Orchestra, recorded for it.[29]

One week after the advertisement appeared, the *Call* carried a review of the band in a column titled "Dance Gossip." Since the Trent Orchestra's eight Gennet recordings vary in quality, the review provides insight into the sound of the band:

> With a might tooting of trumpets, a flock of "horsing around" by the men in the band, a great deal of "oompah-oompah" on the tuba and a new variety of low down stomps, Alphonso Trent and his band moved into Paseo Hall last Tuesday night to receive a positive ovation . . . the band played a lot of fast hot numbers, but they stayed the dancers with their rendition of the blues tunes . . .[30]

The reviewer described violinist Anderson Lacy as a "bundle of vertical motion," while Trent "handled the instrument in the most approved fashion." And "good-looking Chester Clarke (a Kansas City native) did some special tricks on his trumpet for the home folks." The bandsmen were not only good looking but, as Mrs. Trent had said, well-reared. Eppie Jackson, a tuba player originally from Kansas City who had joined the orchestra in 1929, told the reviewer "nearly all of the men are college men, and they all act like gentlemen. I consider it rare good fortune to be associated with them."[31]

The article describes three types of tunes performed by the Trent Orchestra: fast hot numbers, blues tunes, and low down stomps. In fact, the band was exceptionally versatile and could play music not only for jazz dances but also "sweet music" for dances attended by older, white audiences. As saxophonist Hayes Pillars recalled,

> They played everything you could think of: dinner music; they played hot music . . . they had a glee club in the band. I joined that band, and I found out that all of our arrangements were head arrangements. They would take a tune and start rehearsing it, and everybody'd put their idea in it and sometimes they would be a week rehearsing one tune. But they rehearsed every day.
>
> And in the brass section they had a trio singing, and in the reed section we had a trio singing. Then we all sang together as a choral group. We had novelties. We could clown. We did everything . . . Back in those days you'd play a dance, and the people just wouldn't dance. They'd just stand around the band, watch the band.
>
> Everybody had big tones in this band. They could play waltzes. They could play that pretty music, and could play hot music too.[32]

When the job at the El Torreon Ballroom ended, the band went to Texas, but they were no longer the top band in the state. As trombonist Snub Mosely recalled, the musicians' union excluded them from playing the white ballrooms and hotels and they were relegated to the less profitable African American dances.[33] The band had a few more profitable times, including an engagement at the

Ritz Ballroom in Oklahoma City and a tour of Indiana with jobs at Indiana University. During a tour of New England in the spring of 1933, however, the work finally stopped coming. The band staggered back to Albany, New York, and disbanded.

Several of the musicians reorganized in Cleveland, but Alphonso Trent, who had actually left the band in late 1932 to return to Fort Smith, was not among them. By 1934 he had organized another orchestra, and at some point before 1935 he and his wife had taken this group to a far more profitable place, Deadwood, South Dakota.

Deadwood

According to Mrs. Trent, Alphonso's new orchestra spent most of the next eight years playing for the largest nightclub in Deadwood. Occasionally they would go on tour through the Dakotas and Wyoming. The band was so successful that Trent was soon asked to organize another orchestra for a club in a nearby city, perhaps Rapid City. For most of these eight years Trent directed both bands concurrently.[34]

Moving to Deadwood, the Trents literally discovered a gold mine. The city is adjacent to Lead, South Dakota, the location of one of the largest gold mines in the country. During a gold rush in the 1870s, Deadwood had become legendary for its brothels, bars, and other forms of nightlife, patronized by miners who had made their fortunes at Lead. By the early 1930s, however, Deadwood was in economic decline. The gold at Lead was not attracting miners, and the population of Deadwood had declined from 4,200 to 2,400, but through the 1930s the population rose dramatically, reaching 4,100 in 1937. The increase came in response to the 1934 Federal Gold Reserve Act, which prohibited the use of gold as legal tender and made the federal government the sole buyer of Lead's gold—at higher prices. As the price of gold rose, miners flocked to Deadwood.[35]

Alphonso Trent and his two orchestras returned to economic success in the middle of the Depression. As Mrs. Trent recalled, money was pouring into Deadwood. According to her,

> those people didn't care about money. They made money. That's where your money was. They didn't care nothing about money, only to spend. You take the kids that were going to school. They'd get out of school, and do you know how much money they would make in the bowling alley? The children, just the kids, would make $3.50 an hour, just the little bit they'd be doing around the bowling alley. See those folks made money, they didn't care anything about it, they drank, they had a good time.[36]

Not only were the residents of Deadwood prosperous during the Depression, but Alphonso Trent's new orchestra was one of the few entertainments in town. According to Mrs. Trent,

> the nightclub in Deadwood was the largest nightclub, and of course that just drew people from all around, you know, and those small places . . . And you see, those people hadn't really been, I don't mean to say used to music, they hadn't had the opportunity. And they were just wild about musicians. And they enjoyed themselves, enjoyed the music. Because, you see, there wasn't a lot of activities . . .[37]

The Trent orchestras drew listeners from as far away as Minneapolis and Sioux City. According to Mrs. Trent, many people would come just to listen or to watch the tap dancer who performed with the band. Others would dance, but by the late 1930s the Charleston and BlackBottom had been replaced by the Jitterbug and the Lindy Hop.[38]

Aside from a woman married to a white man and their two children and a doctor who owned a downtown building, the Trent players and their families were the only African Americans in Deadwood. Perhaps this fact, the band's status as the city's best-known entertainers, and the presence of a much larger "minority" population—the Lakota people of the nearby Pine Ridge and Rosebud reservations—accounted for a perceived lack of racism toward the orchestra. According to Mrs. Trent, the treatment that the band received in Deadwood was a far cry from the days when they could not stay or even eat at the white hotels where they played.

> It reminded me in a measure sometimes when I think about it of when I was in Europe. It seemed like you just went out of the United States, because it's different, and the people were different. They acted different, they talked different, they treated you different.
>
> The people there were happy to know you. They were happy you were there cause you brought happiness to them. They appreciated the music, and we were known by everybody. You were just like a baby in the arms of Jesus.[39]

Conclusion

By the end of World War II Alphonso Trent's prosperous days in South Dakota had come to an end. For many different reasons he was never able to achieve national recognition and financial security. He was also vulnerable to losing his best musicians to more famous and wealthier orchestras, as when the great guitarist Charlie Christian joined Benny Goodman.

At some point in the mid 1940s, Alphonso and Essie Mae Trent returned to Fort Smith. During the last years of his life, Mr. Trent still played music professionally on occasion, and the couple managed a large housing project. Alphonso Trent died in 1959, and every musician that ever played with him has also passed. In the autumn of 1994, however, Mrs. Trent was alive and well, and extremely gracious in the telling of her story.

Notes

1. Henry Q. Rinne, "A Short History of the Alphonso Trent Orchestra," *Arkansas Historical Quarterly* 3 (March 1986): 213.

2. Uncited biographical information was compiled and corroborated from these sources: Rinne, "A Short History"; interviews with musicians Hayes Pillars and Snub Mosely, conducted as part of the Jazz Oral History Project, Institute of Jazz Studies, Rutgers University, cited hereafter as JOHP, IJS; and personal interviews with Essie Mae Trent.

3. Rinne, "A Short History," p. 232.

4. Personal interview with Essie Mae Trent, October 1994, and Don Gazzaway, "Conversations with Buster Smith," *Jazz Review* 2 (December 1959): 20.

5. Essie Mae Trent interview.

6. Rinne, "A Short History," p. 233.

7. In 1926 a listener with good equipment could hear a radio station the size of WFAA from hundreds of miles away. For more information concerning the distance of radio broadcasts, see Susan Smulyan, *Selling Radio: The Commercialization of American Broadcasting 1920–1934* (Washington DC: Smithsonian Institution Press, 1994), pp. 13–36.

8. Gazzaway, "Conversations with Buster Smith," p. 20.

9. Buddy Tate, "My Story," *Jazz Review* 2 (February 1958): 18.

10. Essie Mae Trent interview, October 1994. Tate, "My Story," 11.

12. Essie Mae Trent interview, October 1994.

13. Personal interview with Essie Mae Trent, November 1994.

14. Paula Fass, *The Damned and the Beautiful: American Youth in the 1920s* (New York: Oxford University Press, 1977), p. 301.

15. S. M. Brown, "The Dance Craze!" *Kansas City Call*, January 27, 1927, p. 6.

16. Ralph Ellison, *Shadow and Act* (New York: Random House, 1974), p. 238.

17. Essie Mae Trent interview, October 1994.

18. Essie Mae Trent interview, November 1994.

19. Essie Mae Trent interview, November 1994. For more information concerning African Americans and jazz dance see Lynne Fauley Emery, *Black Dance: From 1619 to Today* (Princeton: Princeton Book Company, 1988); Russel B. Nye, "Saturday Night at the Paradise Ballroom: or, Dance Halls in the Twenties," *Journal of Popular Culture* 7 (July 1973): 14–21; and Marshall and Jean Stearns, *Jazz Dance: The Story of American Vernacular Dance* (New York: Schirmer Books, 1968).

20. Rinne, "A Short History," pp. 238–43.

21. Pillars interview, JOHP, IJS.

22. Pillars interview, JOHP, IJS.

23. For more information on jazz in 1920s Kansas City, see Ross Russell, *Jazz Style*

in *Kansas City and the Southwest* (Berkeley: University of California Press, 1971), and Gunther Schuller, *Early Jazz: Its Roots and Musical Development* (New York: Oxford University Press, 1968).

24. Russell, *Jazz Style*, p. 8, and Theodore A. Brown, *The Politics of Reform: Kansas City's Municipal Government 1925–1950* (Kansas City: March 1958), p. 54.

25. "Dances Monday and Tuesday," *Kansas City Call*, July 31, 1931, p. 10.

26. For example, "Mighty Monarch of Melody," *Kansas City Call*, February 11, 1927, p. 8.

27. "Musicians Ball," *Kansas City Call*, September 4, 1931, p. 10. The bands featured in this advertisement are Andy Kirk and his 12 Clouds of Joy, George Lee's Great Novelty Band, Elmer Payne's Music Masters, Bill Little and his Little Bills, the Bennie Moten Orchestra, Alvin Wall's Rhythm Band, the Jap Allen Orchestra, and Paul Banks Rythm [sic] Aces. These are just a few of the dozens of musical ensembles active in the Kansas City area in the late 1920s and 1930s.

28. "Alphonso Trent Orchestra," *Kansas City Call*, October 30, 1931, p. 10.

29. In their many appearances in the *Kansas City Call*, the Bennie Moten Orchestra is always described as being "Victor Recording Artists." Indeed, with approximately thirty-five recordings for this label by 1935, the Moten band was by far the most recorded, and probably most nationally known, of the territory bands.

30. "Dance Gossip," *Kansas City Call*, November 6, 1931, p. 10.

31. "Dance Gossip," *Kansas City Call*, November 6, 1931.

32. Pillars interview, JOHP, IJS.

33. Mosely interview, JOHP, IJS.

34. Essie Mae Trent interview, October 1994.

35. John Milton, *South Dakota: A Bicentennial History* (New York: W. W. Norton, 1977), p. 118.

36. Essie Mae Trent interview, October 1994.

37. Essie Mae Trent interview, November 1994.

38. Essie Mae Trent interview, November 1994.

39. Essie Mae Trent interview, October 1994.

CHAPTER 12 | Early Civil Rights Activism in Topeka, Kansas, Prior to the 1954 *Brown* Case

JEAN VAN DELINDER

On an early spring day in the city of Topeka, Kansas, a father walked his child to their neighborhood school. His child was refused admission and was instructed to attend one reserved for "colored children." The parent filed a lawsuit and sued the Topeka Board of Education, demanding that his child be received and instructed at that school, regardless of race. The case went to the Kansas State Supreme Court where it became a precedent for maintaining school segregation in Topeka and other cities in Kansas. The year was 1902. Despite its outcome, this lawsuit illustrates the local-level issues and distinctive color-line practices that characterized challenges to segregation in Topeka before the civil rights movement. Like the famous *Brown v. Board of Education of Topeka* some fifty years later, the issues in the 1902 *Reynolds v. Board of Education* grew out of efforts by the local board of education to maintain school segregation against challenges from African Americans dissatisfied with the status quo. The ongoing legal battles in Topeka revolved around segregation contingencies not addressed in the Kansas state constitution written in 1861. Confrontations over maintaining the color line erupted as public schools began to develop junior high schools separate from elementary schools (which were covered under segregation statutes) and high schools (which were exempt).[1] Challenges to the color line also occurred as the city limits of Topeka expanded to incorporate rural communities in outlying areas that had already established their own informal, yet distinctive, patterns of integration and segregation. Each annexation created new fault lines along the color line as its practices were renegotiated as part of the confrontations between real estate developers, city government officials, the board of education, and parents of school-age children.

The important role that the community of Topeka played in the events that eventually led up to the famous 1954 Supreme Court case has been underemphasized. This lack of interest might be related to the fact that Topeka, Kansas, was not located in the deep South and did not have the same history of violence in race relations as, for instance, a place like Birmingham, Alabama. There were no spectacular events such as bombings, race riots, mass marches, or boycotts that characterized the mass mobilizations in the South. Little acknowledgment has been given to Topeka's own unique history of race relations and the fact that its subsequent type of resistance to segregation is related to that history.

Historical Legacy of Race Relations

Kansas's distinctive color-line practices regarding public education are illustrated by the shift back and forth between integration and segregation in school legislation. Instead of mandating a uniform system of segregated schools, the original constitution left that determination up to local school districts and local custom. This allowed a small window of opportunity for African Americans to establish some legal basis from which to challenge the constitutionality of segregated schools in their own communities. It also gave them the right to appeal to the local board of education to review its policy of segregation if the policy did not conform to state statutes. The National Association for the Advancement of Colored People (NAACP) in Topeka did this in 1948, before pursuing the actions that resulted in the *Brown* case. Challenges to school segregation resulted in modifications to the school segregation laws in 1867 and 1879.[2] The paradoxical role Kansas would come to play in outlawing national school segregation is illustrated by events in 1867; it ratified the Fourteenth Amendment the same year it passed a law that empowered its larger cities to segregate their schools.[3] The equal protection clause of the Fourteenth Amendment was the basis upon which the "separate but equal" was later found to be unconstitutional in *Brown*.[4] The 1867 statute that permitted school segregation did not specify separate schools; it simply denied African Americans admission to its public schools. Later that same year, this exclusionary action was tempered by an inclusive policy that fined school boards and threatened them with imprisonment if they denied eligible children to enroll, regardless of race.[5] If a school district wanted to segregate its schools, it would have to be able to afford the cost. It could not simply deny children an education because of their race. The ambiguous pattern of inclusion and exclusion had begun.

The reaction to the requirement that school districts integrate their schools if they had no separate facilities for African Americans was similar to the actions in the post-*Brown* era in the South nearly a century later: they closed their public schools and opened private ones for whites only.[6] This practice to circumvent integration was noted in the 1867 annual report of the Kansas state superintendent:

> It is a notorious fact that in many districts of the State, the public schools have been broken up and discontinued the moment that an attempt was made to force colored children into such schools with white children, and that in such districts the schools have been discontinued entirely, or replaced by subscription schools.[7]

Three years later, in 1870, a bill was defeated that would have "*required* racially separate schools."[8] The bill's sponsors rationalized their actions by arguing that "equality of opportunity for African

American students could be assured only in separate African American schools subject to the same standards and supervision as other schools. It was contended that in mixed schools discrimination was inevitable."[9] Once again, the rationalization for segregation was similar to the arguments used in the twentieth century against desegregation: the fear that integration meant African Americans would not be treated fairly.

Although after 1867 segregated schools were lawful in any community whose school district could afford them, the implementation of a uniform system of segregated schools remained unresolved. There was another effort toward integration in 1874 when the Kansas legislature passed a civil rights act prohibiting discrimination "on account of race, color or previous condition of servitude" that applied to "schools and public institutions on all levels, to common carriers, and to places of public accommodation and entertainment licensed by municipalities."[10] Several factors could be related to this legislation, both regional and national, but one significant demographic change was that in the first part of the 1870s, the African American population decreased in Kansas, while its white population increased.[11] This suggests that a decrease in the African American population contributed to an increase in toleration toward racial integration, as indicated by the civil rights act of 1874. Consistent with this interpretation, a significant increase in the African American population after 1877 was followed by a significant reversal regarding segregated schooling—the 1879 law that made it constitutional for some cities to segregate their schools.

Kansas School Segregation after 1879

The end of Reconstruction, the Compromise of 1877, and the subsequent withdrawal of federal troops out of the South accelerated the migration of African Americans to the north and west. This mass "exodus" was directed toward Kansas in particular, and those former slaves or freedmen who rode the wave of this migration were called "Exodusters." The Exodust migration was the first significant African American migration after the Civil War.[12] This migration had such a dramatic impact that the U.S. Senate formed a special committee to investigate "the causes of the removal of the Negroes from the Southern States to the Northern States."[13] A consequential and direct response to the Exodust movement was the modification made to the color line in 1879 law *permitting* segregation in elementary schools in cities of the first class, or those with a population over 15,000.[14]

In 1879 only three cities were large enough to legally segregate: Leavenworth, Atchison, and Topeka.[15] This did not prevent smaller cities from trying to implement segregation. The local school boards in Ottawa and Independence were both sued for establishing illegal segregated schools. The Ottawa (1881) and Independence (1891) cases involved plaintiffs who had experienced some difficulty in traveling to a segregated school. Since neither Ottawa nor Independence were cities of the first class, segregation was not legal according to the 1879 law. In a statement dated May 19, 1880, the Ottawa Board of Education's Committee on Building and Grounds announced that because of overcrowding in Ottawa's schools, "colored children of school age" would be assigned to a smaller wood building across the street from the main school. Elijah Tinnon objected to his son being assigned to a segregated school and sued the local school board to admit his son. In a decision reported in the 1881 July term of the Kansas Supreme Court, William Wheeler, principal of public schools in Ottawa, was ordered to admit Leslie Tinnon "to the white school house, second grade."

In Independence, the parents of Bertha and Lilly Knox objected to their children being required by the Board of Education to pass by a white school to attend a segregated school. They filed a lawsuit against the board in 1890, and since Independence was a city of the second class, it was ordered to integrate. Meanwhile, in Topeka, attorney

James Guy initiated activism resulting in a strategic "accommodation" to the color line. Guy demanded that Topeka begin employing African American teachers in Topeka's segregated schools. The practice of hiring white teachers to teach in its segregated schools began in 1876 when two of the three teachers hired were white.[16] This practice was continued until Guy challenged it in the early 1890s.[17] Pressure from Guy and other African Americans in the community resulted in the exclusive hiring of African American teachers for the segregated schools after 1894.

Guy's actions could be interpreted as accommodation and submission to the color line. In an article in the *Times-Observer* on May 28, 1892, Guy stated, "We should not attempt to be in places that we are not wanted. We should recognize our differences and need to establish race pride and confidence." Given the historical social situation and opportunity for success, this action could also be evaluated as a challenge to the boundaries of segregation. Though it was not a direct challenge, Guy's actions were not exclusively an accommodation to the color line. African Americans had gained an important element of control over the quality of instruction in their schools by hiring teachers of their own race, though they still had to contend with the stigma of attending separate schools. Thomas C. Cox interprets this as "reinforced segregation" and a detriment to the African American community, but not all African Americans favored integrated schools.[18] This ambivalence toward inclusion and exclusion was felt on both sides of the color line.

The Reynolds Case, 1902–1903

The *Reynolds* case was the first significant confrontation over the configuration of the color line in Topeka's neighborhood schools between real estate developers, city government officials, the Topeka Board of Education, and African American parents. Reynolds objected to his son being forced to attend a segregated school several blocks away when Lowman Hill Elementary was close by. The plaintiff's brief described the segregated school, Buchanan Elementary, as "unsanitary, inconvenient, and, undesirable . . . a veritable cesspool."[19] Overlooking the physical condition of the school and its location several blocks away from Reynolds's neighborhood, the school board defended its segregation policy on the basis that African American children and white children had "somewhat different intellectual requirements."[20]

William Reynolds and his son lived in an area of Topeka called Lowman Hill. Originally designated as an "outlying area" under the jurisdiction of the county school district, it was annexed by the city in 1890. Lowman Hill had "been a mixed school for both races, and was continued as such by the Board of Education until the year 1900. The reason for this was that the Board of Education was financially unable to provide separate schools." After Lowman Hill was incorporated into the Topeka school district, segregation was not implemented until after the old Lowman Hill School burned down on July 20, 1900, six weeks before classes were scheduled to begin. This forced the school board to find temporary school facilities for the 175 white and 35 African American children affected by this catastrophe. Although a building called Campbell Court was found to serve as a temporary school, it could not accommodate all the students. The decision was made that it was easier to transfer the 35 African American students to Buchanan School, which was eight blocks away, than to transfer the 175 white students to Clay Elementary School, which was thirteen blocks away. Meanwhile, construction was planned to build a new Lowman Hill School.[21]

William Reynolds was outraged that his son, who had previously attended an integrated neighborhood school, was now being forced to travel several blocks to a segregated school. In the lawsuit pursued by Reynolds, he claimed that the school board had promised that the new Lowman School would continue to be integrated. Reynolds objected to the implementation of segregation of his son and other children sent to Buchanan School on a permanent basis. The school board denied they had promised that the new school would be integrated, arguing that the two schools were equal, in compliance with *Plessy v. Ferguson* (1896).

Rather than file a lawsuit, other African Americans living in the Lowman Hill area petitioned the superintendent to provide a neighborhood segregated school in the Lowman Hill area for their children. These parents did not petition for integration: they just requested their children attend a school that was closer. Their stated objection to attending Buchanan was its distance, not that it was segregated. As the brief for the defendants in the *Reynolds* case relates: "After this decision, a committee waited upon the Superintendent asking him to provide a building in the Lowman Hill locality and the committee was told that the Board would he glad to provide such a building if one could be found." The reason for this request by the African American parents is described by the brief for the board of education as follows: "All these committees of colored people which called upon the Superintendent during this time expressed themselves in favor of separate schools. It was school accommodations in their immediate vicinity they desired, and not the mixing of schools."[22] The school superintendent found a building at Tenth and Spruce Streets that served as a temporary school building for the African American children in time for the 1902 fall term. Though Reynolds and the rest of the African American community lost this important challenge to segregation, it would not be the last time that an African American would challenge the status quo of race relations in Topeka, Kansas.

Three Challenges to Segregated Schools in Topeka

The *Rich* (1928), *Wright* (1929), and *Foster* (1929) cases were almost concurrent challenges to the color line in Topeka in the late 1920s.

They involved plaintiffs who had lived in outlying areas that were now incorporated into the city of Topeka. These three cases were all instigated during a time when the school board was acting in ways that increased segregation. The historical sources used in this study (newspapers, documents, letters, etc.) were supplemented with oral history interviews I gathered as a principal researcher for the *Brown v. Board of Education* of Topeka Oral History Project on the history of school desegregation in Topeka, Kansas. This study was funded by the Hallmark Cards Foundation and was commissioned by the Brown Foundation and the Kansas State Historical Society in 1991.

The three sampling techniques used to identify informants were snowball, stratified, and purposive.[23] Personal recommendation or snowball sampling was initially used to draft a list of possible informants involved in school desegregation. One important criterion for selection was longevity in the community, which led me to former segregated school teachers, school board employees, and ordinary citizens who were living in Topeka during segregation.

The informant list was then expanded through stratified sampling to obtain as many different perspectives as possible. In New York I interviewed three former national NAACP Legal Defense Fund attorneys who were involved in researching and preparing the briefs for national desegregation cases. In Topeka I interviewed surviving rank and file members of the Topeka NAACP branch. The three former Legal Defense Fund attorneys I interviewed were Constance Baker Motley (who later represented James Meredith in his attempt to enroll at the University of Mississippi in 1962), Robert Carter, and Jack Greenberg. Carter and Greenberg both traveled to Topeka in 1951 when the *Brown* case was first argued in Federal District Court. Robert Carter would later argue the *Brown* case before the U.S. Supreme Court. Currently, Motley and Carter are both Federal District judges in Lower Manhattan. Greenberg was Dean of Columbia College in New York at the time of the interview and is now a law professor at Columbia Law School.

Informants were also identified through the use of purposive sampling. This sampling technique was used to find those persons who opposed desegregation or might have been employed as teachers and administrators in the segregated schools and lost their jobs when desegregation was implemented. Purposive sampling was also used to identify informants from white Topeka, such as Summer Elementary School principal, Frank Wilson, who turned away Oliver Brown when he tried to enroll his daughter, Linda, on that fateful day in September 1950.

Through these interviews I learned of a system of informal integration operating during the 1920s at the discretion of individual principals and tolerated by the school superintendent and local school board. Former teacher and long-time Topeka resident, El Dorothy Scott, remembered that as a child in the late 1920s, she

> could have gone to Highland Park, and that was all white. . . . They would have had to accept me. . . . Oh now there was a time in Topeka where African American children went to white schools. . . . They went to Sumner. They didn't go to . . . [segregated] Buchanan School. They do tell this story that some of the African American principals wanted the African American schools so that some of the African American women and men could get jobs. Now you could go to the white schools but they didn't hire the African American teachers. That's where the rub came. . . . And then as they began to plead for some schools where they might hire some African American teachers, we got our African American schools. They said that the African American principals tried to hold onto that. But before that time, I could have gone down to a [white] school called Parkdale, where I later taught.[24]

The *Rich* (1928) and the *Wright* (1929) cases both involved African American plaintiffs petitioning to attend Randolph Elementary School. In September 1928, Mrs. Maude Rich tried to enroll her three children in Randolph School, which was five blocks from her home. School

Superintendent A. J. Stout ordered Blanche, age 12, Richard, age 8, and Yvette, age 5, to attend the segregated Buchanan School that was twenty blocks away from their home. Mrs. Rich stated "as her cause of action that she lived within five blocks of Randolph . . . and that some colored students were permitted to enter Randolph. . . . Mrs. Rich declared the board's ruling arbitrary."[25] The Topeka Board of Education did not deny Mrs. Rich's claim that African Americans had been attending Randolph School prior to 1928. Superintendent Stout admitted that two African American families were attending classes at Randolph in the present term. His reason for this, however, was that both of the families had lived in the area before it had been annexed by Topeka. When the rural school was closed, all pupils were placed into Randolph School, including the children in the two African American families who had been attending the white school. About letting the few African Americans who were permitted to attend Randolph, Stout said, "Perhaps we have been wrong in doing that but those children grew up with the school. I understand that the Rich family has just moved into the neighborhood. If this case goes to court and it becomes a matter of throwing all the schools open or excluding these older pupils from Randolph, I suppose we will have to take them out of the school." Superintendent Stout was willing to modify the color line on a case-by-case basis, but he would not go so far as to "throw all the schools open."

The limited flexibility of Superintendent Stout was what William Reynolds wanted for his son in the annexed Lowman Hill area, which when annexed resulted in his son being moved from an integrated to a segregated school. The willingness of Superintendent Stout and the school board to negotiate outside the legal boundaries of segregation stopped far short of changing the general effects of the segregation policy. In the 1920s and 1930s, there was an apparent tightening of policies that excluded African Americans from white schools, as indicated by these cases. The growth in Topeka's population, partially due to its annexation of outlying areas populated by African Americans, caused an increase in the number of African Americans living nearer white schools. The school board handled this on a case-by-case basis, as indicated by the court cases examined. However, by the late 1920s the number of instances of African Americans being allowed to attend white schools outside the legal boundaries of segregation had increased enough to capture the attention of both African Americans and whites. When there were only a few African Americans in a white school, they were tolerated, but when that number threatened to substantially increase, the status quo was little challenged. On the other side of the color line, African Americans wanted to be able to attend their neighborhood schools rather than being transported several blocks away. Preference toward attending neighborhood schools contained a hidden economic threat fewer pupils meant less demand for African American teachers. The enforcement of segregation protected the continued employment of African American teachers in the segregated schools. This fear was realized in 1940 with the *Graham* case, as will be discussed later.

After 1929 segregation began to be uniformly enforced. Wilhemina Wright was transferred to a segregated school (Buchanan) after having attended Randolph School. Although a court case was filed to prevent her transfer to Buchanan School in 1929, she lost the case and subsequent appeal to the Kansas State Supreme Court. Even though she lived within a few blocks of Randolph School, the court ordered her to attend Buchanan, as "[n]o contention is made that the Buchanan school is not as good as a school and as well equipped in every way as is the Randolph school." Furthermore, the school district provided "transportation to and from the Buchanan school without expense to her or to her parents . . . (and] . . . [t]here is no contention that this transportation is not adequate, appropriate or sufficient."[26]

That same year, Howard K. Foster tried to enroll his children into the new Gage School, which had opened that September. His children had also previously attended an integrated school, in this case the old Gage School. Foster was told in 1929 that because of their race, his children would have to ride a bus to the segregated Buchanan Elementary School. Foster filed a lawsuit against the Topeka Board of Education and superintendent A. J. Stout.[27] In a decision written by Judge Whitcomb, Second Division, District Court, it was determined that the school board had no authority to hire buses in order to segregate children living in outlying districts. Since the Fosters lived in Mission Township, an outlying district from Topeka, they were allowed to attend the new Gage School at Eighth and Prospect Avenues. The new situations created with the expansion of Topeka are illustrated in this case. As long as the Fosters remained outside the boundary of the city, they could attend the Gage School. Once their area was annexed by the city, the Foster children were subject to segregation. According to the *Topeka Kansas Capital*, dated October 14, 1929, a mass meeting attended by over three hundred people was held at Calvary Baptist Church to discuss the Foster lawsuit and the recent actions of the school board toward segregation.

The Graham Case, 1940–1941

The case that desegregated the junior high schools in Topeka was again filed on behalf of one named plaintiff, Oaland Graham, although newspaper accounts about the story state that a group of citizens were involved in supporting the case.[28] Oaland Graham was twelve years old at the time of the court case, and his uncle U. A. Graham appeared as his "next friend" on the complaint. The plaintiff, Oaland Graham, lived with his mother, Beatrice Graham, at 1418 Munson Avenue in Topeka. Before trying to enroll in Boswell Junior High School, Oaland Graham had attended Buchanan Elementary School. Prior to this lawsuit, all African American children in Topeka attended seventh and eighth grades at one of the four segregated elementary schools or attended segregated Roosevelt Junior High.

On January 26, 1940, Oaland Graham Jr., accompanied by his uncle, Ulysses Graham, tried to enroll in seventh grade classes at Boswell Junior High in Topeka, Kansas. He was refused admittance on the basis of his race. Graham had just graduated from the sixth grade at Buchanan Elementary School and desired to start junior high in January rather than waiting until September. The "normal" sequence of schooling for African Americans was that they went to Buchanan Elementary School through the eighth grade and either went to Boswell for ninth grade or to Roosevelt Junior High for one year. Roosevelt was farther away than Boswell, and it was also segregated. After the ninth grade, all students, regardless of race, went to Topeka High School for the tenth through twelfth grades.

Graham's challenge to the color line in Topeka arose from the change in educational segregation in Topeka. On March 20, 1925, the junior high system was adopted in Topeka through the Laws of 1925, chapter 240. Though the school district could lawfully segregate elementary grades but not its high school, Kansas's law did not specifically say whether junior highs were elementary schools. One way to determine the line between elementary and high school grades would be to challenge it in court. Prior to Graham, the practice followed by African American children in Topeka was to remain in segregated schools through the eighth grade, choosing either to enter an integrated ninth grade at Boswell or to remain in a segregated class by electing to attend Roosevelt Junior High.

Graham's lawsuit also challenged the assumption that the course of instruction at Buchanan Elementary was equal to that at Boswell Junior High. Boswell was built for the express purpose of being a junior high, and it contained many more classrooms than the elementary schools, allowing for specialized teaching. In the segregated schools, one instructor taught most of the subjects. At Buchanan School, Miss Mamie L. Williams, an outstanding African American teacher, taught a wide variety of math and English courses. At Boswell Junior High, different instructors taught all these subjects. In the testimony provided by witnesses in the Graham case, the home economics teacher at Buchanan, Miss Ruth Ridley, reported that although her students were well prepared when they graduated from the eighth grade, they did not have the modern sewing and cooking rooms that Boswell did. But it was her opinion that there was no real difference between the two schools. Mr. J. B. Holland, principal of Buchanan, reported that the quality of instruction and the well preparedness of his students going on to high school were equal to those of the students attending the integrated school.

The only witness to express dissatisfaction with the course of instruction at the segregated school was Daniel S. Sawyer, a serviceman for the city water department. He testified that the schools were the same as far as he could tell, but he also remarked that Buchanan seldom failed students. If students did not "pass" a grade they were obliged to go to summer school, where they did remedial work that sometimes did and sometimes did not bring them up to par with the other students. Regardless of their "actual" improvements, at the end of the summer students were promoted to the next higher grade.

After the *Graham* case, eight African American teachers lost their jobs due to the integration of the junior highs. Mamie Williams, Ruth Ridley, and J. B. Holland all kept their jobs for several more years. J. B. Holland was one of the first African Americans to he hired in an integrated school after the *Brown* case.[29] Daniel Sawyer, who had expressed some dissatisfaction with the quality of instruction in the segregated schools, had a sister who had taught in the Topeka school district for twenty years prior to the *Graham* case. She lost her job in 1941 after the junior high was integrated.[30]

The Brown Case, 1946–1955

The eventual desegregation of Topeka's schools developed out of civil rights actions that began by challenging segregation in public accommodations during the 1940s. These challenges were initiated by individuals addressing singular grievances and were joined by others who were affiliated with various types of organizations, including the civil-rights-oriented NAACP as well as the community-based American Veterans Committee (AVC) and Parent-Teacher Association (PTA). Challenges to segregated schools were orchestrated through the NAACP but included an ad hoc Citizens Committee, as well as individual efforts from attorneys Charles and John Scott, along with their law partner, Charles Bledsoe.[31] School desegregation was furthered by challenges undertaken by white elites opposed to Superintendent McFarland's administration, including a campaign to remove unsympathetic school board members. Other efforts to eliminate school segregation were directed through the white PTA, and were opposed by the black PTA and African American teachers. Diverse actions, separately controlled, loosely combined into what became the 1954 *Brown* case.

Challenges to Segregated Public Accommodations, 1944–1948

Topeka's color-line practices limited the movements of African Americans in the 1940s:[32]

> There was one colored hotel, the Dunbar, and all the rest were for whites. Almost no restaurants downtown served colored customers. Before the Second World War, a number of . . . [restaurants] had a sign in the window reading: 'Negroes and Mexicans served in sacks only,' meaning they could take out food in bags but not eat on the premises. One movie theater in town admitted colored people to its balcony. Another, called the Apex, was for colored only. The other five movie houses were for whites only. The swimming pool at Gage

Park was off-limits to colored, except one day a year when they were allowed in for a gala picnic.

This limited access to public accommodations in Topeka resulted in a challenge to the color line in 1944. It came about when the local NAACP protested the proposed repeal of a municipal licensure requirement that "prohibited state universities, colleges, public schools, inns, hotels, or vehicles of public transportation" from discriminating on the "basis of race, color, or previous condition of servitude."[33] The president of Topeka's local chapter of the NAACP, R. J. Reynolds, stated that by repealing this law "Topeka will he showing the rest of the cities in Kansas how to find a loophole in the law to deny Negroes of their rights."

Reynolds's action stalled the tightening of the color line for three more years, another instance of ambivalence toward segregation. This ambivalence soon shifted toward exclusion when an African American patron named Phillip Burton sued a local movie theater after he was denied admission because of his race. The theater managers were found guilty of violating the local municipal ordinance prohibiting discrimination on the basis of race, color, or previous condition of servitude. They were both fined ten dollars.[34] This successful challenge to segregation resulted in a backlash against integration when a few weeks later, on October 1, 1947, the Topeka city commission repealed its permissive licensing requirement for local theaters.[35]

Three days later, on October 4, 1947, Ava and Arthur Lee Stovall were refused admission to the same Dickinson Theater that Burton had sued a month earlier.[36] Though once again the local NAACP protested, as it had done in 1944 to prevent reinforcement of the color line, this time their efforts were unsuccessful: the legal grounds to sue local businesses over limited access to public facilities had been removed."[37] Movie theaters, as well as any other public facility in Topeka operating under a municipal license, could segregate as they wished.[38] This setback caused the NAACP to shift attention from public accommodations to public schools: another phase of civil rights activism was initiated in 1948.[39]

Another organization seeking to redress race issues was the American Veterans Committee. It attracted newly hired staff members employed at the Menninger Foundation, many of whom were Jewish and from the East Coast. They had a reputation for "leftist" activities, which included campaigning for Henry Wallace's Progressive Party in 1948.

> The AVC nucleus included a number of Jewish staff members at the Menninger Foundation, who were seen as menacing "pinkos" from the East Coast. . . . [The AVC] helped the Scotts raise money to cover the costs of their action to de-Jim Crow the public pool in Gage Park and other legal measures.[40]

Years later, Marita Burnett Davis, daughter of then-president McKinley Burnett of the Topeka NAACP, argued that school desegregation in Topeka was secretly funded by some Jewish physicians who worked at the Menninger Clinic.[41] Although there is no hard evidence of their involvement, the AVC was involved in efforts to desegregate public facilities in Topeka during the 1940s.

Challenges to Elementary School Segregation in Topeka, 1948–1950

After losing ground to segregation in late 1941, the NAACP decided on a low-key approach to school integration. The Legal Redress Committee of the local NAACP studied the options available to legally challenge Topeka's segregated schools and decided to draw attention away from the recent failure of the NAACP by using an intermediary group called the "Citizens Committee."[42] The Legal Redress Committee included two brothers, Charles and John Scott, who were both serving on the committee while attending Topeka's Washburn University Law School.

They were following in the footsteps of their father, Elisha Scott, a noted civil rights attorney. They also became the attorneys for the 1954 *Brown* case. Charles Scott later recalled that in 1948 he and his brother John began to "research for a sound legal theory on which to proceed" to challenge elementary school segregation after the attempts to desegregate the local movie theaters.[43] The first action selected was to simply ask the local school board to end segregation.[44]

The 1940 *Graham* case was the last time the NAACP had involved itself in school desegregation, it almost self-destructed. On one side were the African American teachers and administrators who sought to protect their jobs and found themselves aligned with white community leaders also hostile to integration but for different reasons: whites wanted to preserve the racial status quo. On the other side were those people in the community—black and white—who were sympathetic to desegregation and anxious to redress the injustice of segregation. It was this faction, oriented toward civil rights and desegregation, that had gained control of the local NAACP after 1940 and remained in power throughout the desegregation era.

Soon after the *Graham* case, Topeka School Superintendent Stout, a moderate on segregation, had been fired and replaced by Dr. Kenneth McFarland, who took a hard-line approach toward maintaining segregation. McFarland immediately tightened the boundaries of the color line by announcing that "separate schools are here to stay."[45] Under his leadership, the school board solidified school segregation begun during Topeka's urban expansion and population growth in the 1920s and early 1930s. McFarland "held back the tide" of desegregation that was gathering momentum in Topeka according to local resident Samuel Jackson.[46] McFarland later defended his segregation policy as consistent with the status quo in Topeka's schools:

> [W]e were operating the schools under essentially the same structure that we took them over in 1942.... We have no objective evidence that there is any substantial desire for a change among the people that the

board represents. . . . [T]here is nothing in the record historically, that it's the place of the public school system to dictate the social customs of the people who support the public school system.[47]

That there was still some ambivalence toward segregation is illustrated by the willingness of the school board to negotiate and compromise. Jackson continued, "The school board might have gone along with desegregation . . . if McFarland had not resisted."[48] Charles Scott's law partner, Charles Bledsoe, also observed that the school board was divided over the issue of continuing segregation. He wrote Robert Carter at the NAACP in New York that

one of our good friends of the white race has polled every member of the Board of Education; two of them were bitterly against integration, and four of them would welcome a law suit, in order to take the load off their shoulders. . . . We interpret this as meaning that the Board will not wage an all-out defense; but this is opinion only.[49]

Despite the ambivalence of some members of the school board toward rigid color-line boundaries, McFarland was adamant that school segregation be continued in the primary grades. All departments and divisions of the school system were unified under him, and he alone was responsible to the board for the execution of its policies. He had managed to consolidate his power by eliminating the autonomy of the school board committees, which allowed him to override the authority of the elected school board.[50] McFarland's actions raised concern on both sides of the color line. He played on the economic fears of the African American teachers by hiring Harrison Caldwell as the director of Negro School Education to administer the segregated schools.[51] Caldwell continuously reminded the teachers that they would all lose their jobs if the schools were integrated.[52] Caldwell conducted yearly performance reviews of the teachers that included weighing their teaching in the classroom against their attitude toward the administration.⁵³ Mamie Williams, who taught at Buchanan School and later was principal at Washington School, recalled that her fellow teachers did not protest this practice for fear of losing their jobs: "Since nobody had tenure then and most of the teachers were unmarried women dependent on their salaries for their livelihood, you went along."⁵⁴

Divisions in the African American community toward integration also erupted through school organizations, such as the Negro PTA. According to Speer and Adler, the African American teachers in turn put pressure on Topeka's Negro PTA to further oppose challenges to segregation by influencing the parents of the children they taught.⁵⁵ This resulted in African Americans acting in support of a white supremacist segregationist policy in order to preserve community and economic stability. NAACP President Burnett stated that

> the Negro PTA ... [had] sent a letter to the Board of Education expressing their official support of the *Board* position. Public ... [segregated] schoolteachers hesitated even to comment on the case as it was being prepared for court (emphasis in original).⁵⁶

The local NAACP tried to overcome the teachers' reluctance and win their support for school integration. President Burnett stated,

> At one point we called a meeting of the team. First, we had a man from the National Office (NAACP), a lawyer, who was going to speak to us. ... We invited the teachers to come. They didn't come, not a one.⁵⁷

Objections to McFarland arose on the other side of the color line by white elites who quickly grew tired of his autocratic policies. This white resistance had emerged by the late 1940s, about the time the NAACP began to target school segregation.⁵⁸ Efforts to remove McFarland focused on his overbearing management style. Frank Wilson, principal of Sumner Elementary School, indicated that during McFarland's era one was either a "company man" and went along with his policies, or one sought employment elsewhere as it was too uncomfortable to remain."[59]

The actions to eliminate school segregation and remove McFarland from office coalesced by early 1951. While the *Brown* brief was being prepared in April 1951, half of the school board responsible for hiring McFarland in 1942 was up for reelection.[60] On April 3, 1951, they were voted out of office.[61] A few days after the election, on April 5, 1951, Superintendent Kenneth McFarland turned in his resignation effective August 1951.[62]

The election of new school board members and the resignation of Superintendent McFarland changed the commitment of the board of education to segregation. In September 1953, two-and-a-half months before the State of Kansas was to reappear before the U.S. Supreme Court in defense of its permissive segregation statute, the Board of Education of Topeka, Kansas, voted to abolish segregation in its elementary schools.[63]

The types of civil rights actions utilized to end segregation in Topeka were shaped by the ambiguity of color-line practices in Kansas and were organized around local-level issues. As the city limits of Topeka expanded to incorporate rural communities, it unknowingly created new fault lines along the color line as its practices were renegotiated as part of the confrontations between real estate developers, city government officials, the board of education, and parents of school-age children. The civil rights actions used to help eliminate segregation were shaped by Kansas's mixture of segregationist and integrationist cultural patterns. The state's permissive segregation statute prohibited publicly funded school segregation except for elementary schools in its "first class" cities with a population over 15,000.[64] The expansion of Topeka's city limits through annexation during the first part of the twentieth century resulted in some African Americans being moved from integrated rural county schools to segregated city grade schools. This shift in the boundaries of the city also shifted color-line practices in the newly annexed areas.

Those African Americans who were caught between pressures to preserve segregation within Topeka's city limits brought the resulting challenges to the color line to maintain the informal tradition of integration to which they were accustomed outside the city limits. The period between 1944, following the 1940 *Graham* case which desegregated the junior high schools), and the 1954 *Brown* decision (which desegregated the elementary schools), can be characterized as a curious mix of accommodation and exclusion.

The civil rights actions undertook between 1944 and 1954, the year of the *Brown* case, can be further divided into three phases, the first two of which were discussed in this essay. First, up to 1947 African Americans challenged Topeka's segregated public facilities—the municipal swimming pool and movie theaters. Next, local initiatives were shifted toward challenging elementary school segregation in a second phase beginning in 1948. These actions were undertaken by breakaway groups from the local NAACP who approached the Board of Education and whose efforts culminated in legal petition through the courts. Finally, in 1950 the third phase began when the lawyers of the national NAACP Legal Defense Fund carried the *Brown* case forward. The legal basis and significance of the case changed in this phase from addressing local grievances to national public interests as it was incorporated into the NAACP Legal Defense Fund's desegregation agenda, which resulted in the landmark school desegregation case, the 1954 *Brown v. Board of Education of Topeka*.

Notes

A previous version of this paper was presented at African Americans and Their Great Plains Experience Conference, Lincoln, Nebraska, February 20–22, 1997.

1. The only legally segregated high school in Kansas was Sumner High School in Kansas City, Kansas. It was established in 1905 after a special act of the legislature changed the 1879 statute allowing segregation of a secondary school in this one instance. According

to historian William Worley, the African American population in Kansas City, Kansas, was concentrated north of the downtown area along Minnesota and State Avenues. Sumner High School was located in that general vicinity. See William Worley, "An Overview of the Ethnic Geography of the Kansas City, Region," unpublished report, June 14, 1994, Johnson County Museum, Shawnee, Kansas.

2. Paul E. Wilson, *A Time to Lose: Representing Kansas in Brown v. Board of Education* (Lawrence: University Press of Kansas, 1995), p. 29.

3. Wilson, *A Time to Lose*, p. 37.

4. Attorneys are still debating the validity of this argument forty years after Brown. In a recent article in *Southern Illinois University Law Journal*, Michael J. Berry argues that the school desegregation cases were incorrectly decided on the Fourteenth Amendment (due process), but rather were in violation of the Fifth Amendment (individual rights) (20 [fall 1995]: 53–73). One of the cases was decided on the basis of the Fifth Amendment, *Bolling v. Sharpe*, the Washington DC, case. Since Washington DC is not a state, it never ratified the Fourteenth Amendment. Indeed, according to the oral arguments before the Supreme Court in the *Brown* case, the Thirty-ninth Congress in 1866 enacted laws "to implement and expedite the administration of the segregated system of public schools" in Washington DC (791).

5. Wilson, *A Time to Lose*, p. 37.

6. See Bob Smith, *They Closed Their Schools: Prince Edward County, Virginia, 1951–1964* (Chapel Hill: University of North Carolina Press, 1965).

7. State Superintendent of Public Instruction, *Annual Report* (Topeka KS: Kansas State Historical Society, 1867), p. 72.

8. Emphasis my own. House Bill 219 (1870), cited in Wilson, *A Time to Lose*, pp. 37, 234.

9. Wilson, *A Time to Lose*, p. 37.

10. Wilson, *A Time to Lose*, p. 39.

11. Nell Painter, *The Exodusters: Black Migration to Kansas after Reconstruction* (New York: W. W. Norton, 1986), p. 146.

12. See Painter, *The Exodusters*, and Robert G. Athearn, *In Search of Canaan: Black Migration to Kansas, 1879–1880* (Lawrence: Regents Press of Kansas, 1978).

13. See U.S. Senate, "Report and Testimony of the Select Committee of the United States Senate to Investigate the Causes of the Removal of the Negroes from the Southern States to the Northern States," 46th Cong., 2d sess., 1880, S. Rept. 693, part 2.

14. Wilson, *A Time to Lose*, p. 39.

15. By 1952, after the Brown litigation had begun, there were twelve cities of the first class, but only half were still practicing segregation (Coffeeville, Fort Scott, Kansas City, Leavenworth, Parsons, and Salina). Of the remaining six, one never exercised its option

to segregate (Hutchinson), one had partial segregation (Lawrence), two had already terminated segregation (Pittsburg and Wichita), and two had begun to implement desegregation (Atchison and Topeka). See Wilson, *A Time to Lose*, pp. 29–39.

16. The three teachers were Deacon Farnsworth, an African American, and a white couple from Ohio, Mr. and Mrs. James Abbot. See "Kukendall's Memoirs of Early Topeka," *Topeka Plaindealer*, December 19, 1902.

17. Thomas C. Cox, *Blacks in Topeka, Kansas, 1865–1915: A Social History* (Baton Rouge: Louisiana State University Press, 1982).

18. Cox, *Blacks in Topeka, Kansas, 1865–1915*. In South Carolina, for example, teacher and activist Septima Clark worked hard to get African American teachers hired in the public schools. Since the public schools were limited for African Americans, many African Americans, including Clark herself, attended private high schools. However, in 1919 she and some other African American teachers tried to get that policy changed. She felt that African American students in the public schools "were just at the mercy of the white teachers, who often didn't care anything about them" (see Eliot Wigginton, ed., *Refuse to Stand Silently By: An Oral History of Grass Roots Activism In America, 1921–1964* [New York: Doubleday, 1992], p. 18). Clark and her friends gathered 22,000 signatures from African Americans stating that they did want African American teachers in the public schools. In 1920 a few African American teachers were hired in the city of Charleston. Because of segregation laws, there was not any legal way that teachers of different races could teach in the same school, just as there was no legal way for children of different races to attend the same schools. Any policy that stipulated that only African American teachers could be hired in African American schools would mean that the local school board would have to fire whites in order to maintain segregation. The introduction of African American teachers in the segregated schools was gradual and came twenty-five years later than in Kansas.

19. *William Reynolds, Plaintiff, v. The Board of Education of Topeka*, 66 Kan. 672 (1903).

20. *William Reynolds, Plaintiff, v. The Board of Education of Topeka*. Also see Cox, *Blacks in Topeka, Kansas, 1865–1915*, p. 113.

21. "Brief for the Plaintiff," *Reynolds v. Board of Education of Topeka*, 66 Kans. 672–37 (1903).

22. "Brief for the Plaintiff," pp. 3–4.

23. Valerie Yow, *Recording Oral History: A Practical Guide for Social Scientists* (Thousand Oaks CA: Sage Publications, 1994).

24. El Dorothy Scott interview by Jean Van Delinder, January 27, 1992, transcript *Brown v. Board of Education Oral History Project*, Kansas State Historical Society, Topeka, Kansas.

25. "A.J. Stout, Supt. of Topeka City School Creates Race Prejudice: Ku Klux Klan Sentiment Entering Public Schools." *Topeka Plaindealer*, September 28, 1928, 1.

26. *Wright v. Topeka Board of Education*, 129 Kansas Supreme Court Reports 853 (1930).

27. One of the attorneys working on the Foster case was William Bradshaw, who would be involved in the Graham case as counsel for the plaintiff in 1940.

28. See *Topeka Plaindealer*, January 26, 1940, 1.

29. Stan Stalter, interview by author, Topeka, Kansas, July 17, 1994, transcript *Brown v. Board of Education Oral History Project*, Kansas State Historical Society. Stalter was principal of Lowman Hills School, where Holland integrated the teaching staff in 1955.

30. Connie Sawyer (niece of Daniel Sawyer) interview by author, Topeka, Kansas, March 5, 1992, transcript *Brown v. Board of Education Oral History Project*, Kansas State Historical Society. Daniel Sawyer's brother, Nathaniel, was involved with the NAACP faction that favored the lawsuit and remained active up until the Brown case, when his health forced him out of activism.

31. During the *Graham* case, the Topeka NAACP split into two rival factions. Civil rights attorney Elisha Scott, who did not support desegregation of the junior high schools in Topeka in 1941, led one faction. This faction represented the interests of African American teachers, including a relative of Scott, who taught in the segregated schools. As indicated above, some African American teachers did lose their positions after desegregation of the junior high schools. After *Graham*, Scott's group gave way to the faction in favor of desegregation, one which included Scott's two sons, Charles and John.

32. Richard Kluger, *Simple Justice* (New York: Vintage, 1975), p. 375.

33. *Kansas General Statutes*, sec. 21–2424 (1935).

34. *Kansas General Statutes*; *Kansas City Call*, September 26, 1947 and November 24, 1947.

35. *Kansas City Call*, October 17, 1947.

36. *Kansas City Call*, October, 17, 1947.

37. *Kansas City Call*, October 10, 1947.

38. Why Topeka revoked its permissive municipal ordinance at this time cannot be fully explained as simply a reaction to the indirect actions of the NAACP and other individuals involved in civil rights litigation. First, the NAACP was not the only organization involved in challenging segregation. Another biracial organization seeking to redress race issues was the local American Veterans Committee (AVC). The AVC was founded in 1946 by returning World War II veterans as an alternative to the American Legion, which was segregated. Also see Kluger, *Simple Justice*, p. 391.

39. Among those individuals who belonged to both organizations were two recently returned veterans named Charles and John Scott. The Scott brothers were both sons of

local civil rights attorney Elisha Scott and would later argue the *Brown* case in Kansas federal district court (Charles S. Scott Papers, [RH:MS:494:1] Box 1, Kansas Collection, University of Kansas Libraries).

40. Kluger, *Simple Justice*, p. 391.

41. Marita Burnett Davis, interview by author, Kansas City, Kansas, August 11, 1994, transcript *Brown v. Board of Education Oral History Project*, Kansas State Historical Society.

42. "The NAACP meetings that McKinley Burnett chaired rarely drew more than a dozen or so people and usually degenerated into gripe sessions" (Kluger, *Simple Justice*, p. 393). The Citizens Committee did not present itself as an NAACP delegation, since "mention of the NAACP, it was presumed, would have earned the back of the school board's hand," Kluger, *Simple Justice*.

43. Charles S. Scott Papers, RH:MS:494:1 Box 1, folder 1, Kansas Collection, University of Kansas Libraries.

44. The petition read: "Our main complaint is against Dr. McFarland . . . [who] says separate schools are here to stay and separate secondary schools are in the plans . . . [r]egardless of added expense, the extra drain on a short supply of teachers, . . . [r]egardless of the national trend toward integration; regardless of the fact that separation in our schools prevent[s] the educational process from acting positively in the field of race relations (Kluger, *Simple Justice*, p. 393).

45. McFarland denied his or the school board's involvement in expanding an informal system of segregation in Topeka High School (see *Brown v. Board of Education*, 98 F. Supp. 797 [1951]), transcript of record in lower court, pp. 235–36. NAACP President McKinley Burnett later described the color line in the high school as: "Up there at the high school while they called it integrated, it was integrated only from the outside. When you got inside, it was just as Jim Crow as Alabama." See McKinley Burnett interview by Dr. Hugh Speer, April 1967, reported in Hugh Speer, "The Case of the Century: A Historical and Social Perspective on Brown v. Board of Education," unpublished (1968), p. 22. Written with the aid of a federal grant, the manuscript is available (as a photocopy) from Document Reproduction Service, Bethesda MD. See also Kluger, *Simple Justice*, p. 393.

46. Kluger, *Simple Justice*, p. 404.

47. *Brown v. Board of Education*, 98 F. Supp. 797 (1951), transcript of record in lower court, p. 234.

48. *Brown v. Board of Education*.

49. Correspondence from Charles Bledsoe to Robert Carter, Topeka NAACP Branch Files, Kansas State Historical Society, Topeka, Kansas.

50. Kluger, *Simple Justice*, p. 380.

51. Caldwell had worked under McFarland in Coffeyville, Kansas (Kluger, *Simple Justice*, p. 381). For a personal account of Caldwell, see Merrill Ross's interview by author, Topeka, Kansas, October 9, 1991, transcript, *Brown v. Board of Education Oral History Project*, Kansas State Historical Society. Ross was a coach and teacher under Caldwell during the 1940s.

52. Caldwell was described by the Citizens Committee as "stumbling block to our progress and had . . . reduced the morale of the colored teachers 'to an all time low'" (Kluger, *Simple Justice*, p. 393).

53. Kluger, *Simple Justice*, p. 381.

54. During the *Graham* case, Mamie Williams taught sixth and seventh grades at the Buchanan School. See Brief for the Defendants, *Graham v. Board of Education of Topeka*, 153 Kan. 840 (1941). During the time of the *Brown* case, Miss Williams was principal at Washington School. Also see Kluger, *Simple Justice*, p. 381.

55. Speer, "The Case of the Century," p. 27; Frank Adler, *Roots in a Moving Stream*, (Kansas City: Spangler Printing, 1972), p. 253n103.

56. Speer, "The Case of the Century," p. 27.

57. McKinley Burnett interview with Dr. Hugh Speer, "The Case of the Century," p. 27.

58. Stan Stalter interview by author, Topeka, Kansas, July 17, 1994, transcript *Brown v. Board of Education Oral History Project*, Kansas State Historical Society. Mr. Stalter, a former Randolph School principal, recalled that faculty at Washburn University who had children in Topeka's public schools were particularly opposed to Superintendent McFarland's policies. Stalter felt that the "movement" to remove McFarland began in the schools located in the vicinity of Washburn University.

59. Frank Wilson interview by author, Topeka, Kansas, October 9, 1994, transcript *Brown v. Board of Education Oral History Project*, Kansas State Historical Society. Mr. Wilson was principal of Sumner Elementary when Oliver Brown tried enroll his daughter Linda in 1950.

60. Wilson, *A Time to Lose*, p. 25; Stalter interview, "The Case of the Century."

61. Two years later, on April 7, 1953, the remaining half of the members of the Board of Education were voted out of office. All who had been on the board when the *Brown* lawsuit was filed were off the board by August 1953. The *Brown* case went to the U.S. Supreme Court on December 7, 1952 (Memorandum on Brown compiled by the University of Kansas Law Library, Reference Desk, August 1995. Copy in the private collection of the author).

62. *Topeka Capital*, April 4, 5, 1951.

63. There was only one negative vote, by Mr. Oberhelman, who stated "he was no [sic] opposed to the policy, but felt that an orderly program should be worked out before the resolution was passed" (Segregation Policy, Topeka Board of Education, Charles S. Scott Papers).

64. Wilson, A *Time to Lose*, p. 39.

CHAPTER 13 | The Great Plains Sit-In Movement, 1958–1960

RONALD WALTERS

In 1960 black youths conducted a "sit-in" in Greensboro, North Carolina, to obtain the right to eat at a segregated lunch counter. Others quickly replicated sit-ins throughout the South and, just as quickly, the press labeled Greensboro the "first" sit-in. Historian David Levering Lewis, for instance, said: "There were not a few white southerners, and probably a majority of white northerners, who would have wished to say to *the first sit-in students*, as did the woman in the Greensboro Woolworth's, 'you should have done this ten years ago.'" Even data-oriented social scientists such as Doug McAdams portray the sit-ins as "beginning in early February of 1960."[1] Some studies of the NAACP during the civil rights movement mention Oklahoma sit-ins but do not mention Wichita, Kansas, at all.[2] And yet the first modern sit-in may have been in Wichita.

These accounts are inaccurate and incomplete but they also symbolize the extent to which the civil rights movement in general has been written about almost exclusively from the perspective of what occurred in the South. Considering that journalists wrote the first accounts, it may have been their initial perspective that was responsible for the subsequent lapse by serious scholars.

For example, in the throes of the Montgomery Bus Boycott in 1956, the editor of the *Montgomery Advertiser*, Grover Hall, Jr., challenged northern journalists to report on northern race friction. Hall wrote *U.S. News and World Report* describing how northern papers such as the *Minneapolis Morning Tribune* and the *Chicago Daily News* put the Montgomery story on the front page and news about their own race friction on the back pages. Obviously, to the northern editors, the most newsworthy incidents of race relations were occurring in the South, where challenges to age-old social practices, originating in the institution of slavery, were taking place.[3]

At first Pulitzer Prize-winning editorial writer Lauren Soth, of the *Des Moines Register*, was typical of those who responded, saying that this southern focus was natural, since "the [race] problem simply did not exist" in the North.[4] Nevertheless, his and a host of other papers subsequently carried stories about their own racial problems, but because the drama in the South was created by the danger of blacks challenging the existing racial order, the *real* story of civil rights was still covered as the southern story.

One casualty of this perspective is that scholarship on many northern aspects of both the civil rights movement and the more aggressive black liberation movement have been neglected. As Howard Zinn was to suggest, after the Montgomery Bus Boycott, the movement for social change in the South moved slowly.[5] The significance of the sit-in movement was that it electrified southern activists as a model for action throughout the South. Besides challenging segregation at lunch counters and restaurants, the movement quickly became elaborated into many other tactics of confrontation, such as "kneel-ins" at churches, "wade-ins" at swimming pools, "stand-ins" at voter registration places, and others.

In perhaps the major scholarly work on sit-in movements, sociologist Aldon Morris stated that despite the Greensboro sit-in's mythic status as the "first," others had occurred in at least fifteen cities between 1957 and February 1960.[6] His study of the linkage between the Greensboro event and other such actions in the South, however, confirmed its quickening effect on the entire movement. He sought to analyze the sit-ins within the context of resource mobilization theory, which posited the importance of preexisting social supports within the black community, such as civil rights organizations and churches. Political scientist Doug McAdams's data also indicates the important function of sit-ins and that student groups associated with the NAACP, churches, or colleges initiated 75 percent of sit-ins or other direct-action tactics in the movement.[7]

Morris's research also revealed that two of the earliest of the modern sit-ins occurred in Wichita, Kansas, and Oklahoma City, Oklahoma, under the auspices of the NAACP Youth Councils.[8] In an early article, Morris, following the seminal work of Martin Oppenheimer, repeated an error in stating that: "the first sit-in cluster occurred in Oklahoma in 1958 and spread to cities within a hundred-mile radius."[9] Later, after considerable primary research, he said in his comprehensive work on the subject: "Less than a week after [the sit-ins] in Wichita, Clara Luper's group in Oklahoma City initiated its planned sit-ins."[10] Thus, one objective of this paper is to establish the correct sequence of events among the chain of early sit-ins occurring in the Great Plains that were precipitating events for social action in that region as well as in the South.[11]

Second, as a result of the journalistic treatment referred to above, as well as early work such as that by Oppenheimer, which appears to divorce the Great Plains movement from the South, scholars have viewed the early Great Plains sit-ins as isolated events. In fact, as a political tactic in confronting segregation based on racial discrimination, they had a historical sequence that had been pioneered by the Fellowship of Reconciliation and the Congress of Racial Equality as early as the 1940s. The importance of the Wichita and Oklahoma City sit-ins, and others in the pre-1960s period, was their proximity to the modern civil rights movement, their linkage to the sit-ins that did occur beginning in 1960, and their engagement of the generation of post–World War II youth in the process of social change.

The Wichita Sit-In

Census data show that between 1950 and 1960 the total population of Wichita, Kansas, grew very quickly, from 168,000 to 255,000, and by 1960 its black population was nearly 20,000.[12] This was a significant pattern of post-war population growth made possible by a developing aircraft industry, which, although it was structured to serve wartime production, rapidly made the transition to commercial markets. Indeed, national publications could write of Wichita as a "boom city" when a house-building frenzy took the city to twice its 1945 size.

Growth was made possible by such giants as Boeing Airplane Company, which became the largest employer, moving from 1402 workers immediately after World War II to 25,855 by 1955, with an annual payroll of $126 million. The city had also become a magnet for companies building popular small commercial aircraft such as Cessna and Beech Aircraft Company, each with about one-third the sales of Boeing.[13]

But although the rising economy incorporated a segment of the black community who worked in aircraft and related industries, the social fabric of the city was distinctly segregated. Although Kansas had "bled" to keep slavery from its territory, Wichita resembled a Southern city in the occurrence of murder and lynching of blacks.[14] Blacks had suffered a long history of discrimination and segregation in Wichita and even by the 1950s, although public transportation was integrated, blacks were not welcome in white elementary schools, theaters, churches, restaurants, parks, or other places of public accommodation. According to Robert Newby, participant in the Wichita sit-in and professor of sociology at Central Michigan University, "In the South, everything was marked 'white' or 'black.' Just over in Kansas City [Missouri] signs were everywhere. But in Wichita there were no signs. Everyone just knew the rules and that you didn't break them."[15] Complaints of discrimination in employment were commonplace as the rising middle class of doctors, lawyers, postal clerks, and education professionals struggled for upward mobility.

As they had in many such communities, Wichita blacks had established a small but active NAACP chapter in the 1920s. The several chapters located in cities throughout Kansas, headed by state conference president Dr. C. A. Rocquemore, defined both racism and its opposition. The Wichita NAACP was headed by a youthful and dynamic attorney, Chester I. Lewis, and the December 1958 issue of *The Crisis*, the magazine of the NAACP, carried pictures of the local and state officers.

The Wichita Youth Council of the NAACP was headed from 1958 to 1960 by Ronald Walters, then a local college student, the author of this article. The Youth Council included high school and college-age youth, the Little Rock generation. The Council was a novelty, since youth had not featured prominently in social change movements until this time. The Council recognized that nowhere in the city could blacks sit down to eat in a dignified manner in white-owned restaurants. The many blacks who worked downtown suffered from this disadvantage as well as the slight to their humanity of being served while standing behind a board at the end of the lunch counters at F. W. Woolworth, Kress and Company, and other stores.

In the spring of 1958, the Youth Council decided to integrate the lunch counters downtown and selected Dockum Drug Store, a Rexall pharmacy located on one of the busiest midtown intersections, at Douglass and Market streets. This idea came from a meeting with attorney Franklin Williams, then west coast regional secretary of the NAACP, who visited Wichita and explained the sit-in tactic used at UCLA to integrate the main dining hall in the 1940s.[16] Once the Youth Council had decided to act, it held workshops on how to conduct the actual sit-in in the basement of the St. Peter Claver Catholic church.

The Council employed a comic book on the method of non-violence, prepared by the SCLC, one of more than 2,500 such books that had been distributed all over the country. Chester Bowles, later U.S. Ambassador to India, wrote about the techniques covered in the comic book in an article about using Gandhi's teachings to achieve civil rights. In the pamphlet:

> a Negro preacher said to his congregation: "Now let's practice it again. I'm white man and I insult you, I shove you, maybe I hit you. What do you do?"

Answer:

> "I keep my temper. I do not budge. I do not strike back. I turn the other cheek."[17]

The Youth Council taught this non-violent method as part of their training for the actual sit-ins. They felt that this method, even though its users were not reflecting a particular religious practice, would give the demonstration both moral authority and discipline.

The sit-in began on Saturday, July 12, 1958, and lasted for several weeks.[18] Each of the twelve to fifteen youths who participated was to march in, sit on the stools at the lunch counter, and ask for service. After being refused the young demonstrators continued to sit silently on the stools.[19] According to a reporter, "On a bright warm Saturday morning in July 1958, young Carol Parks [vice president of the Youth Council] breathed deeply, opened the door to the Dockum Drug Store in downtown Wichita and sat on one of the eight stools at the lunch counter. . . . [She explained,] 'This was my first experience with fear.'"[20] Eventually each time demonstrators arrived the lunch counter put out a sign reading, "This Fountain Temporarily Closed," which told the victorious demonstrators that they were forcing the restaurant to forego income in order to practice racial discrimination. The sit-in pattern was repeated without much conflict, except the usual comments from dissatisfied customers. One potentially serious challenge from a considerable number of young white toughs was thwarted by the presence of the police.[21]

The black community slowly became aware that the sit-in was occurring, but the adult chapter of NAACP in Wichita did not support it because at that time the national office was cool to direct action tactics, favoring legal strategies instead.[22] There was considerable ambiguity and even fear among the adults concerning how whites would react to the sit-in, so a significant number of youths continued to form the support base for the movement.

The sit-in continued until August 7, when Walter Heiger, manager of the Dockum Store, announced that he would serve everyone without regard to race. Carol Parks remembered that it ended without statement or fanfare from the participants because everyone was emotionally drained.[23] It was Chester Lewis, the Wichita NAACP head who had been supportive of the action, who broke with his colleagues and the national office to pronounce the sit-in a victory, indicating that he did not know what "right" proprietors were defining when they asserted the right to do something against the Judeo-Christian precepts of the country.[24]

The Oklahoma Sit-In

Oklahoma City was a somewhat larger city than Wichita, but they shared a similar culture, even though people in Wichita considered themselves more "northern," with all the status distinctions that implied. Oklahoma was more southern in terms of its culture and racial feelings and the barriers constructed against the black community. Oklahoma City had also experienced significant growth between 1950 and 1960, expanding from 244,000 to 324,000, with a black population of 12 percent, or about 35,000, by 1960.[25]

In parts of Oklahoma, including Oklahoma City, the signs that marked a segregated society were occasionally in evidence, but its oil and agriculture sectors sparked economic progress for many, even some blacks. Prosperity, as in other cities, created upward mobility that inevitably led blacks to challenge the racial barriers.

In 1957 the Oklahoma City Youth Council planned to oppose lunch counter discrimination.[26] They selected five stores: John A. Brown Luncheonette, Veazey's Drug Store, Katz Drug, Kress, and Green's Variety Store (ultimately not confronted because the management relented).[27] The Council was led by Barbara Posey, a dynamic fifteen-year-old, and its adult adviser was Ms. Clara Luper, a strong and committed NAACP veteran. The group negotiated unsuccessfully by letter with representatives of the Katz Drug Store chain during 1958, and most attempts to speak directly with the store managers were unsuccessful as well.

Thus, on August 19, 1958, a lunch counter sit-in was launched against the Katz Drug Store, located at 200 West Main, by eight youths from five to fifteen years of age. They requested service and when they were refused, they asked for the store policy on discrimination. The store manager, J. B. Masoner, explained that the store policy was not to serve Negroes, so they remained seated at the lunch counter.[28] When asked by reporters about the sit-in, James Stewart, President of the Oklahoma adult chapter of NAACP said that this "test case" was supervised by the Youth Chapter and added: "I believe there has been one just recently in a drugstore in Wichita, Kansas."[29] The initial Oklahoma City demonstration lasted two days before the store manager decided to serve the youths.

From this successful venture, the youths moved their protest to the Kress and John A. Brown luncheonettes. At Kress they were served,[30] but John A. Brown refused to provide integrated service despite often daily sit-ins. Nevertheless, Barbara Posey evidenced a faith that their movement would ultimately be successful:

> I am convinced that Oklahoma people are strong, eager, and youthful at heart. They have a spirit which is called the Sooner Spirit. This spirit

gives people a firm belief in themselves and in the future. It points with pride to what has already been done in the peaceful integration of buses, theaters, and schools and looks forward to the day when segregation in all public eating places will be abolished. I do not believe that John A. Brown's and other restaurants owners will continue to hold on to a long lost dream of white supremacy.[31]

One may infer from this statement that the youthful leader was driven by a deep religious conviction. Aldon Morris has pointed to the significance of community resources such as churches in the movement, and although, except for one training session, churches were not involved in the Wichita sit-in, Calvary Baptist appeared to be a central organizing place and staging area for the Oklahoma movement. On August 10, 1960, a group of 104 youths went single-file from the Calvary Baptist Church at Northeast Third and Walnut Streets to the Cravens Building, where they mingled in the lobby and asked to be served at the Anna Maude Cafeteria.[32] Other churches contributed both space and funds to the movement. The Reverend Glenn Smiley, a Methodist minister who worked for the Fellowship of Reconciliation (FOR), came to the city and conducted non-violence workshops at Calvary. Journalist Kyle Ragland says that Smiley indicated that "Sit-ins are 'essentially a religious protest and movement. . . .' Although the National Association for the Advancement of Colored People—a secular group—has been active in sit-ins, there frequently is a strong link with church members and leaders."[33] FOR would be an important trainer in subsequent sit-ins occurring in many Southern cities.

The adult leadership of the NAACP strongly supported the youth protestors. Dr. E. C. Moon, Jr., president of the Oklahoma NAACP, led a small group of protesters at Calvary in singing "America" before they went out. In February 1959 Chester Lewis, head of the Wichita branch of the NAACP, had come to Muscogee, Oklahoma, to speak to about three hundred NAACP Youth Council members. He reminded them of the courage it took to fight for freedom and then appealed directly to the adult chapter to support the movement. An editorial in *The Black Dispatch*, a local black newspaper, backed up Lewis:

> We feel that this suggestion is appropriate to the youth movement in Oklahoma City. For several months, members of the local NAACP Youth Council have been trying to obtain first-class citizenship in places of public accommodation. They have been partially successful. But where they have failed it was because of ungiven support of adults.[34]

When the sit-in began in Oklahoma City in 1958, the state executive committee of the NAACP released a statement by the national office stating that they "wholeheartedly endorsed the efforts of the local NAACP chapter to gain first-class citizenship for Negroes."[35] The executive committee also expressed sympathy for sit-ins in other cities *where the national office had not extended sponsorship or support*. The Youth Council acknowledged this endorsement but decided not to substitute adults for the high school and college youth it was recruiting to continue the protest.[36] In any case, the endorsement may have signaled a change in the policy of the national office toward local direct-action tactics like the sit-ins, and in Oklahoma they continued from 1958 to 1961.

One direct effect of the Oklahoma City sit-ins was that a bill was introduced into the state legislature of the adjacent state of Arkansas to prohibit sit-ins. The bill provided for a protester to be fined and imprisoned for refusing to leave any business establishment other than a common carrier.[37] When the Oklahoma sit-ins became national news, they exposed the weakness of the U.S. Civil Rights Commission. The commission held a news conference in September of 1958, to announce its agenda, but when a reporter asked Chairman John Hannah whether the commission would intervene with relief for the Oklahoma demonstrators, Hannah admitted that the commission was powerless to act, since it had been given no mandate by Congress.[38] The Oklahoma sit-ins spread immediately to Enid and Muscogee, which became integral to mobilizing the state NAACP behind the movement.[39] By 1960 the demonstrations were statewide.

Relevance of the Great Plains Sit-Ins

As indicated above, civil rights scholars have tended to view the Great Plains sit-ins as isolated phenomena. For example, Aldon Morris says that "Greensboro would have happened with or without Wichita," and Clayborne Carson, editor of the Martin Luther King, Jr., Papers, has said that the Wichita sit-in had no effect on Greensboro—"the drama of race occurs in every locality."[40]

While these are credible opinions, they are by no means the last word on the matter. Given the links between the Wichita sit-ins and those in Oklahoma and the links between the Oklahoma sit-ins and the rest of the country, while "Greensboro would have happened with or without Wichita," it would likely have happened in another manner and perhaps in another place and time. The NAACP Youth Councils and the nationwide NAACP network would have been different if the Great Plains Youth Councils had not pioneered the sit-ins. Consider these two critical linkages:

The Wichita-Oklahoma Link. The Wichita and the Oklahoma City sit-ins came in close proximity, Wichita in July and August of 1958 and Oklahoma City two weeks after. Although we cannot conclude that one was the cause of the other or that the adaptive response was direct, the Oklahoma NAACP officials, presumably including Clara Luper, and even white store managers, knew of the Wichita sit-in that had recently taken place only two hundred miles away.

The Oklahoma-Greensboro Link. The Oklahoma sit-ins achieved national prominence and lasted for nearly five years. By 1959 the NAACP national office claimed the sit-ins as part of their legacy. The

December 1958 issue of *The Crisis* carried a picture of Oklahoma youths demonstrating at Brown's lunch counter with a story by Barbara Posey and Gwendolyn Fuller, leaders of the movement.[41]

The NAACP *Annual Report* for 1959 carried stories of actions taken by other youth chapters against eating facilities. The Washington University chapter of the NAACP started a protest against discrimination by the off-campus Santora restaurant, later taken up by the St. Louis adult branch. After campus-wide protests and a court decision, the Santora restaurant changed its policy. The University of Chicago chapter picketed the Tropical Hut Restaurant near its campus for advertising for a "white waitress" and forced the restaurant to change its employment policy. The University of Indiana chapter at Bloomington was successful in its campus-wide protest against barber shops that refused black customers, and the Ohio State University chapter successfully challenged the administration to prohibit discrimination in off-campus housing.[42]

Indeed, at the 1959 NAACP Convention, Dr. Martin Luther King, Jr., himself presented citations to the NAACP youth councils of Oklahoma City and St. Louis that had initiated sit-ins.[43] So important had the youth protest movement become within the NAACP that the national organization devoted its fifty-first annual conference in 1960, to an "Accent on Youth," hosting 349 youths from 49 states. The conferees held a special "Youth Freedom Fund Dinner" to raise money for their activities. In his keynote address to the convention, Robert C. Weaver stated that: "NAACP youth units in Wichita, Kansas [sic] and Oklahoma City started these demonstrations in 1958 and succeeded in desegregating scores of lunch counters in Kansas and Oklahoma. The 'sit-in' is not a new tactic for the NAACP." John Morsell restated the same fact at the conference workshops.[44]

In his foreword to the 1960 NAACP *Annual Report*, Executive Director Roy Wilkins, made the direct linkage between the Great Plains sit-ins and the Greensboro event:

The student uprising was spontaneous. No organization, whether new or old, or yet unformed, can claim to have planned and initiated the start of the wave on February 1, 1960. *But of the four original lunch counter sit-in students, two were members of a student chapter of the* NAACP. *Two years before, youth chapters of the* NAACP *in Wichita, Kansas, and in Oklahoma City, Okla.*[sic] *had staged successful pilot sit-in campaigns in those cities* [sic] *winning lunch counter desegregation in sixty or more stores.*[45]

At least in the mind of the NAACP executive director there was a direct link between the "pilot" Wichita and Oklahoma sit-ins and the Greensboro sit-in, in the form of Greensboro participants who were members of the NAACP youth network and presumably had knowledge of the earlier sit-ins. In fact, Joseph McNiel and Ezell Blair, the two students mentioned by Wilkins, had both attended the 1960 Accent on Youth conference and reported on the Greensboro sit-ins.[46]

Nevertheless, by the time the 1960 *Annual Report of the* NAACP was being written, the Greensboro tide had swept the South and the Student Non-violent Coordinating Committee—rather than the NAACP—was receiving the lion's share of the credit. Wilkins's remarks seemed to strike a defensive tone, since the NAACP had been late in throwing its full support behind the activities of its own youth.

This defensiveness suggests the tensions that had begun to unfold among the "Big Five" civil rights organizations and FOR, which had earlier pioneered non-violent methods, including the sit-ins. According to August Meier and Elliot Rudwick, for example:

CORE's advocacy of direct action was by no means a denigration of the NAACP's valuable contribution to the civil rights movement. Privately, however, they recognized that after the southern student movement began in February, "Everywhere under the surface there were conflicts between the NAACP and other race relations organizations. CORE leaders were especially annoyed at the NAACP's claim—based upon [a] variety

[of] store demonstrations sponsored by the Oklahoma City NAACP Youth Council in 1958—to have started the southern student sit-ins."[47]

Rudwick and Meier suggest that the NAACP, the oldest and most venerated civil rights organization, was forced to defend its turf by new organizations that emerged in the 1960s.

It may be that rivalry among the civil rights organizations is one reason the Great Plains sit-ins have received so little notice. Other groups focusing on their own accomplishments have downplayed the linkage between the Great Plains sit-ins and those in the South. This perspective may have been adopted and perpetuated by scholars of the southern movement as well.

In any case, the actions of northern NAACP youth chapters in 1958 and 1959 were not "isolated" from the southern chapters of the NAACP—nor other organizations—and the campaigns of the northern chapters against segregated eating establishments constituted a *national model and network* for change by the time the Greensboro sit-in began. The direct participation of NAACP youth chapter members in the Greensboro sit-in further strengthens the ties between the northern and southern sit-ins.

Thus, it is not only important that the Wichita and Oklahoma sit-ins are linked to each other, and to Greensboro, but as Morris says, to thirteen other cities where sit-ins occurred before Greensboro. Are these actions, which occurred in Great Plains, border, and southern states an unimportant part of the expansion of civil rights activity, or is Morris correct in concluding that "there were important similarities in the entire chain" of sit-ins from 1958 through the mid-1960s?[48] The Great Plains sit-ins and the southern sit-ins occurred within the same environmental conditions and time frame and used the same organizational networks to confront racial exclusion. The northern sit-ins constitute the beginnings of the continuum of action that resulted in the southern movement.

Conclusion

Among the environmental factors leading to the sit-ins, the most significant in the emergence and sustenance of the movement were racism and the race organizations that developed to oppose it.

Racism, of course, was encountered by blacks in the urban environment as the effects of the slavocracy of the rural South extended to the northern cities, resulting in patterns of exclusion of blacks from both public accommodations and private social functions. In both rural and urban environments, the freedom movement has confronted racism's iniquities.

Second, racism provoked various specific responses. The primary cause of sit-ins was the particular discrimination found in a specific restaurant. In the planning stages of both the Wichita and the Oklahoma City movements, however, plans were not directed at only one establishment; instead, protests against one or a series of establishments became a strategy to break down segregation in a variety of eating facilities. More important than the practices of any particular restaurant is the category of racism that expressed itself in discrimination in eating establishments.

Third, there are many ways to interpret the connections among events. Different actors may logically develop the same responses to similar problems. If, however, the actors know how someone else has resolved a similar problem in the past, they may adopt the same style to deal with their own problem.[49] Thus young people in Greensboro may have reacted to lunch counter discrimination with a sit-in not *because* of the Wichita and Oklahoma City sit-ins but because of their own unwillingness to tolerate discrimination. At the same time the style and rhythm of the Greensboro protest seems to have been colored by the earlier sit-ins.

Finally, in order to determine in what ways sit-ins stimulated other tactics in opposition to racism, it is important to discover precisely what *precipitating factor* was responsible. The two sit-ins examined in this study responded to cues in the northern urban environment and became matches that helped to light the modern phase of the southern civil rights movement. The Great Plains sit-ins were not isolated phenomena. Each was linked to the vital process of the entire movement for social justice.

Notes

1. David Levering Lewis, "The Origins and Causes of the Civil Rights Movement," in *The Civil Rights Movement in America*, ed. Charles Eagles (Jackson: University Press of Mississippi, 1986), p. 7, emphasis added; Doug McAdam, *Political Process and the Development of Black Insurgency* (Chicago: University of Chicago Press, 1982), p. 134.

2. See, for example, Warren St. James, NAACP: *Triumphs of a Pressure Group, 1909–1980* (Smithtown NY: Exposition Press, 1980).

3. "Editor Says Press Plays Down Northern Discord," *U.S. News & World Report* 40 (March 23, 1956): 48, 49; "Southerner Says Race Trouble in North Not 'Page One,'" *U.S. News & World Report*, p. 50.

4. "The Negro in the North," *Time* 67 (June 4, 1956): 81–82.

5. Howard Zinn, SNCC: *The New Abolitionists* (Boston: Beacon Press, 1964), p. 26.

6. Aldon Morris, "Black Southern Student Sit-In Movement: An Analysis of Internal Organization," *American Sociological Review* 46 (December 1981): 744–67. See also his comprehensive study of this subject, *The Origins of the Civil Rights Movement: Black Communities Organizing for Change* (New York: The Free Press/Macmillan, 1984), pp. 188–94.

7. McAdams, *Political Process and the Development of Black Insurgency*, p. 134.

8. Morris, "Black Southern Student Sit-In Movement," p. 750.

9. Morris, "Black Southern Student Sit-In Movement."

10. Morris, *The Origins of the Civil Rights Movement*, p. 193.

11. See Ronald Walters, "The 'First' Civil Rights Sit-In," *American Visions* 8 (No. 1, February/March 1993): 20–23.

12. Bureau of the Census, *U.S. Census of Population*, Vol. 1, 1970, parts A and B.

13. "Boom and a City," *Newsweek* 46 (December 12, 1955): 60.

14. E.C. Ford, "A Horrible Blot on the Fair Name of Kansas," *Negro History Bulletin* 19 (No. 2, November 1955).

15. Matthew Schofield, "The Forgotten Sit-In," *Kansas City Star*, January 21, 1991, p. D8.

16. Memorandum, Carol Parks-Hahn to Ronald Walters, December 1990. Carol

Park's mother, the then Mrs. Vivian Parks, served as secretary-treasurer of the local NAACP and was in frequent contact with the national officers.

17. Chester Bowles, "What Negroes Can Learn From Ghandi," *Saturday Evening Post* 230 (March 1, 1958): 19–21.

18. "Negroes 'sit down' in Wichita Restaurants," *Facts on File*, Five-Year Index, 1956–60, 18–21 August 1958; "Oklahoma 'Sit-Down.'" *Facts on File*, Vol. 18, No. 931, August 28–September 3, p. 285. This article erroneously says that the Wichita Sit-in took place over the period August 17–21. See also, a local black newspaper that carried the story of the NAACP Thalheimer Award, Class I, being presented to the Wichita NAACP chapter, in part for the following: "One of the major achievements was the orderly protest made by the NAACP Youth Council *last July* [my emphasis] against discrimination in eating facilities at Dockum Drug Store." "Wichita NAACP Cite for Award," *Enlightener* 2 (July 9, 1959): 1.

19. "Drug Store Picketed by NAACP," *Wichita Eagle*, August 3, 1958, p. C1.

20. Matthew Schofield, "The Forgotten Sit-In," *Kansas City Star*, January 21, 1991, p. 3.

21. "Dockum Fountain Service Now Open to All Wichita Citizens," *Enlightener*, no. 9, August 14, 1958, p. 1.

22. Memorandum, Parks-Hahn to Walters.

23. Schofield, "The Forgotten Sit-In."

24. "Dockum Fountain Service Now Open," *Enlightener*.

25. U.S. Bureau of the Census, *Census of Population, 1970*, Vol. 1, parts A and B.

26. For a comprehensive account of the Oklahoma sit-ins and NAACP politics, see Clara Luper, *Behold The Walls* (Oklahoma City: Jim Wire, 1979).

27. "Negro Drive Spreads to Enid," *Daily Oklahoman*, August 27, 1958, unpaginated photocopy, Newspaper Archives, Oklahoma Historical Society.

28. "Negro Group Sitting at City Drug Store," *Daily Oklahoman*, August 20, 1958, p. 1.

29. "Katz Fountain Gives Negro Group Service," *Daily Oklahoman*, August 22, 1958, p. 1.

30. "Negro Youths Store Sitting in Fourth Day," *Daily Oklahoman*, August 23, 1958, p. 1.

31. "Oklahoma City NAACP Youth Council Speaks," *Black Dispatch*, September 26, 1958, p. 2.

32. "104 Negroes Mill In Cravens Lobby," *Daily Oklahoman*, August 11, 1960, p. 1.

33. Kyle Ragland, "Minister Teaches Art of Non-Violent Protest," untitled photocopy, October 10, 1960, Newspaper Archives, Oklahoma Historical Society.

34. "Today Is For Youth," *Black Dispatch*, February 20, 1959, p. 5.

35. "NAACP Leaders Back 'Sitdowns,'" *Daily Oklahoman*, September 1, 1958.

36. "No Sitdown For Adults," untitled photocopy, September 1, 1958, Newspaper Archives, Oklahoma Historical Society.

37. "Ban Sought On Sitdowns," United Press International, August 27, 1958.

38. Allen Cromley, "U.S. Turns Deaf Ear To City Race Crusade," *Oklahoma City Times*, September 11, 1958.

39. "Enid Restaurants Advised on 'Strike,'" untitled photocopy, August 29, 1958, Newspaper Archives, Oklahoma Historical Society.

40. Morris and Carson quoted in Schofield, "The Forgotten Sit-In," *Kansas City Star*.

41. "Protest Drug Counter Discrimination," *Crisis* 65 (No. 10, December 1958): 612.

42. "The Year of Jubilee," *NAACP Annual Report for 1959, 1960*, pp. 36–37.

43. "The Year of Jubilee," *NAACP Annual Report for 1959, 1960*, p. 86.

44. Gloster B. Current, "Fifty-first Annual NAACP Convention–Accent on Youth," *Crisis* 67 (No. 7, August-September 1960): 407, 418.

45. *NAACP Annual Report for 1960, 1961*, p. 5, emphasis added.

46. Current, "Fifty-first Annual NAACP Convention–Accent on Youth," *Crisis*, p. 414.

47. Meier and Rudwick quote in this statement sentiment from CORE documents from the period in question. August Meier and Elliot Rudwick, *CORE: A Study in the Civil Rights Movement, 1942–1968* (New York: Oxford University Press, 1973), p. 105.

48. Morris, *The Origins of the Civil Rights Movement*, p. 189.

49. Robert C. Carson, *Interaction Concepts of Personality* (Chicago: Aldine Publishing, 1969), p. 5.

CHAPTER 14 | The Omaha Gospel Complex in Historical Perspective

TOM JACK

In this article, I document the introduction and development of gospel music within the African-American Christian community of Omaha, Nebraska. The 116 predominantly black congregations in Omaha represent twenty-five percent of the churches in a city where African-Americans comprise thirteen percent of the overall population.[1] Within these institutions the gospel music genre has been and continues to be a dynamic reflection of African American spiritual values and aesthetic sensibilities. By focusing the research on perceptions and descriptions provided by the music's practitioners, an examination of this genre at the local level will shed insight into the development and dissemination of gospel music on the broader national scale.

Following an introduction to the gospel genre, the character of sacred music in Omaha's African American Christian institutions prior to the appearance of gospel will be examined. Next, the city's male quartet practice will be considered. Factors that facilitated the adoption of gospel by "mainstream" congregations during the 1930s and 1940s will then be addressed. In conclusion, the role of Salem Baptist Church as a focal point and instigator of musical change from the 1950s to the present will be described.

The accepted definition of the word "gospel," as found in the

Oxford English Dictionary, reads, "'the glad tidings (of the Kingdom of God)' announced to the world by Jesus Christ. Hence, the body of religious doctrine taught by Christ and His apostles; the Christian revelation, religion or dispensation." This definition also describes the word as "short for *gospel music* [italics in the original]."[2] Gospel music in the tradition of black Christianity, the subject of the effort at hand, has twice been given articulate and insightful definition by African American scholar Pearl Williams-Jones, who wrote, "The term 'Afro-American gospel music' is used to refer to a particular body of contemporary black religious music which is the sum total of our past and present socio-economic and cultural traditions. Afro-American gospel music is characterized by its use of texts of poetic imagery, poly-rhythms with strong emphasis upon syncopation, melodies based upon the traditional 'blues scales' (which consists of the lowered thirds, fifths, and sevenths) and European harmonies."[3] She elaborated on the cultural ethos a few years later, saying, "Black gospel music, a synthesis of West African and Afro-American music, dance, poetry and drama, is a body of urban contemporary black religious music of rural folk origins which is a celebration of the Christian experience of salvation and hope. It is at the same time a declaration of black selfhood which is expressed through the very personal medium of music."[4]

Gospel music today is the latest stage in a musical continuum whose foundation was in place over one hundred years ago. The first African-American denomination was the African Methodist Episcopal Church (A.M.E.), officially chartered in Philadelphia in 1816.[5] Its bishop, Richard Allen (1760–1831), had earlier compiled *A Collection of Spiritual Songs and Hymns Selected from Various Authors by Richard Allen, African Minister* (1801), the first hymnal designed specifically for use by African Americans.[6] The formal worship service of early African American Protestantism relied on, for the most part, the same repertoire used in the white Protestant church. The works of the English composer, Isaac Watts (1674–1748), for example, were particularly well received, and to this day this body of hymns is simply referred to in the vernacular of the black church as the "Dr. Watts." The performance style was one of "lining-out," also called "surge-singing" or "long-meter," wherein a line of text is recited or sung by a leader and then sung in response by the congregation.[7]

Several of Watts's texts were incorporated for use in the spirituals, improvised hymns born of oral tradition and the first form of African American musical expression to achieve worldwide recognition.[8] Beginning in 1871, black college choirs such as the Jubilee Singers of Fisk University performed programs showcasing "arranged spirituals," formalized for the concert stage, to enthusiastic audiences in the United States and Europe.[9] Professional singing troupes modeled after the college organizations later journeyed as far abroad as Africa, Australia, and Asia.[10]

Concurrent with the appearance of the college choirs, the tradition of male quartet harmonizing was a fixture of many African American communities by the 1870s. "Jubilee quartets" were featured as subgroups within many of the Fisk Jubilee-type troupes, and by 1890 had surpassed these larger ensembles in popularity.[11] Usually performing a cappella, the quartets gradually moved from a polished, homophonic texture toward a less restrained style that reflected vocal and rhythmic independence more characteristic of the folk church aesthetic. The rapid proliferation of these "gospel quartets" at the local level is attested to by the formalized quartet competitions that occurred during the 1920s and 1930s.[12]

It is at this point that the impact of individuals becomes most apparent in the gospel repertoire. Jon Michael Spencer states that the first original hymn collection of the Transitional Period, or Pre-Gospel Era (1900–30), was published by Charles Price Jones in 1899.[13] Philadelphia pastor Charles Albert Tindley (1851–1933) has long been credited as foremost of the early composers in the gospel tradition.[14]

While Tindley compositions such as "Stand By Me" and "The Storm is Passing Over" are standards in the contemporary gospel repertoire, the minister's most significant contribution may be the inspiration he provided as a musical model for the man generally considered to be "the father of gospel music," Thomas Dorsey.[15]

Thomas Andrew Dorsey (1899–1993) was born in the small rural community of Villa Rica, Georgia. As a youth, Dorsey had considerable exposure to sacred music. His father was an itinerant Baptist preacher and his mother a church organist. In spite of this religious background, Dorsey attained initial notoriety in the decidedly secular blues market of Chicago, accompanying and writing songs for such well-known performers as Gertrude "Ma" Rainey and Tampa Red (Hudson Whittaker). By 1929 Dorsey had abandoned popular music to focus exclusively on sacred compositions, imbued with musical sensibilities of blues and jazz, which he called *gospel* songs.[16] Dorsey founded the Dorsey House of Music in 1932 and became the first independent publisher of black gospel. That same year, along with Magnolia Lewis Butts (ca. 1885–1949) and fellow Georgia native Sallie Martin (1896–1988), he established the National Convention of Gospel Choirs and Choruses in Chicago, chartered in 1939 and the first nationwide organization devoted to the genre.[17] Aided greatly by the promotional efforts of Martin, Dorsey's songs were introduced not only into black churches from coast to coast but "by 1939, four of Dorsey's compositions were included in a songbook, printed in d-shape-notes, that was widely distribute in *white* [italics mine] evangelical congregations."[18] Beginning in the forties, "Dorsey" became a generic term for any song in the gospel repertoire.[19]

In addition to the quartet tradition and the composition of new songs, a third element critical to the development of gospel was the musical practice found among the disparate congregations frequently grouped under the rubric of Holiness or Sanctified churches.[20] Historically, the centrality of music within the Holiness service stands in sharp contrast to mainstream Baptist and Methodist practices. Pursuant to Pentecostal interpretation of Psalm 150, Holiness churches routinely incorporated musical instruments in the lifting of praise, a practice too "worldly and secular" for more institutionalized denominations. As George Robinson Ricks has observed, "While the use of instruments was forbidden in the orthodox Negro church, their introduction by Holiness groups gave the music a 'different sound than just handclapping.'"[21] The commonplace piano and organ might be joined by drums, guitar, saxophone, harmonica, or any number of instruments, the whole augmented by the ubiquitous tambourines of the congregation.[22]

Considering the diversified instrumentation, the shadings of jazz and blues that permeated Pentecostal music is not surprising. Sanctified accompaniment was typified by the "stomping" approach of blind pianist Juanita Arizona Dranes of Texas, whose style drew on barrelhouse and other secular traditions.[23] Popular music elements were in fact so pronounced that some saw Holiness music as "essentially the sacred counterpart of the blues, frequently the sacred text being the only distinguishing element."[24] Examining musical change in black religious practice, John Wesley Work singled out the Holiness church as the place where "music is exploited to a degree that probably is not attained in any other denomination."[25] Eventually, the aesthetic preferences of Sanctified musical expression "moved beyond the boundaries of the Holiness-Pentecostal churches into many mainline Black churches, ranging from Baptist to Catholic parishes.[26]

The First Territorial Census of Nebraska, taken in 1854, noted thirteen African Americans among a total population of more than twenty-seven hundred.[27] By 1860 the black population in the new state had grown to eighty-two with roughly one-fourth residing in Douglas County, the location of Omaha.[28] During the fall of 1865, a congregation of five members led by Reverend John M. Wilkerson organized the state's first black church, St. John African Methodist Episcopal.[29] Over the following decades, immigration fueled by job availability in the railroad and meat-packing industries drove Nebraska's African American population to more than ten thousand in 1920.[30] By 1923, the year the foundation of the present St. John A.M.E. was laid, the church that had begun with five people numbered over twelve hundred members.[31]

At the end of the 1930s, Omaha was home to at least forty-three African American churches, most of which supported one choir that relied on a staple of hymns, anthems, and spirituals.[32] Spirituals, in particular, were perceived as both a standard of musical excellence and a source of ethnic pride. A review of a 1940 concert at Zion Baptist judged spirituals "the songs most highly anticipated by the large and enthusiastic audience."[33] The announcement of an upcoming May Day festival that same year requested of the eleven participating churches: "In order that special emphasis may be place on Negro music all choir directors are being urged to consider the use of Negro Spirituals for their individual choir presentations."[34] Commentaries of the period suggest that performances of spirituals in Omaha, as elsewhere, were appraised from a perspective reflective of the Western classical aesthetic. In a prime example, Flora Pinkston's assessment of a local performance by the Fisk Jubilee Singers in 1940 observed, "[The pianist] played with the most artistic melodic expression that only a great artist could produce in tone. The singers sang with trueness of tone from *forte* to *pianisimo*. The *obligato* parts were sung with great control, which in itself produced beauty of tone."[35]

Flora Pinkston was a model music instructor of the time, referred to by the Federal Writers' Project as "Nebraska's foremost Negro teacher of piano and voice."[36] One accompanist who assisted her during the 1930s and 1940s states flatly, "Everybody knew Flora Pinkston was the best."[37] A graduate of the New England Conservatory of Music, she studied privately in Paris before opening the Pinkston School of Music in Omaha in 1908. The Pinkston motto was "Help me and I will help you," which meant they should adhere to a strict diet of European art music.[38] Pinkston sternly discouraged the improvisation and lively accompaniment characteristic to gospel. One current minister of music recalls that when Pinkston found him improvising at a lesson in the 1950s, "She everything but beat me up.... She says, 'You're playing by ear *and I'm not gonna have it!*'"[39] Although for a short time Pinkston directed the choir at Pilgrim Baptist, the bulk of her activities was concentrated in the secular sphere. Her greatest impact came about through the numerous former pupils who continue to influence music ministry throughout the city.

Not surprisingly, the churches most noted for their music in the 1930s and 1940s were the largest and longest established congregations. Among the Baptists, the choirs of Zion, Pilgrim, and Mount Moriah all had enviable reputations. However, no other music program of the time could match the notoriety of St. John A.M.E. The core of St. John's music program consisted of a Senior Choir directed by Pearl Gibson, a Men's Chorus and a Junior Chorus. Since the three sometimes united to perform as a mass choir, the church in effect, featured four choirs.[40] A unique aspect of music at St. John was the instrumental accompaniment furnished by "the orchestral part of the choir," consisting of a full string section, flute, clarinet, trumpet, and saxophone, plus the church's pipe organ.[41]

Pearl Gibson and the Senior Choir gained citywide renown for their performances of anthems, cantatas, and even operettas. Each of the up to eighty singers in the Senior Choir was able to read music. The annual Christmas performance of Handel's *Messiah* filled the spacious church to overflowing, and the reputation of the choir's a cappella renditions equaled that of the orchestral works.[42] Appearing on radio and described in newspaper accounts as "peerless," Pearl Gibson and the Senior Choir set a standard for black congregations throughout the city.[43]

For many years, the single most important annual musical event among the African American community was the Goodwill Spring Musical, an interdenominational extravaganza held annually from 1934 until 1946.[44] Founder L[uther] L. McVay, a Pullman porter and member of St. John A.M.E., saw as the purpose of the musicals "the bringing about of a closer relationship between the churches, the choirs, and the encouragement of the use of musical talents, the realization of which greatly adds to the value and dignity of the church."[45]

The Spring Musical was usually staged in late April, drawing crowds of several thousand to the City Auditorium. With up to fifteen Baptist and Methodist churches participating, the mass choir boasted as many as 350 singers. Programs were devoted entirely to hymns, anthems, and spirituals learned from sheet music and memorized for the performance. In addition to pieces performed by the massed voices, the individual choirs normally rendered one selection each. The soloists, accompanists, and directors for the mass choir were the most well known and respected in the city. Despite the Christian theme of the assembly and the liturgical nature of the music, the Spring Musical was viewed by many who took part as more of a civic or social event than a religious one. In light of the biracial attendance, it also provided the black community a forum for the presentation of ethnic identity.

The path by which gospel music attained the form of a distinct genre owes a large debt to a preexisting, often secular quartet tradition in place by the 1870s.[46] Newspaper accounts of the 1930s attest to the vitality of the quartet practice in Omaha. Popular Southern groups such as the Soul Stirrers from Texas and the Kings of Harmony from Alabama made visits there, influencing the twenty-five or more groups active locally. As one consultant recalls, "churches needing money for expansion programs would bring these various other quartets of renown up and they would put on their programs, and then our quartets would catch on."[47]

Most important of the Omaha quartets was the Loving Four of Mount Calvary Community Church, whom scholar Horace Boyer calls "one of the first gospel groups to use guitar accompaniment."[48] Gospel researcher Lynn Abbott declares the Loving Four "one of the earliest full-time independent professional traveling gospel quartets."[49] Formed by Evlondo Cooper and including two of his brothers, they started out performing secular songs as the Cudahy Quartet. The name is reference to Cudahy Packing Company where all of the members, as well as their musical trainer, were employed. Following their conversion to a gospel repertoire and a name change in the early 1930s, the Loving Four toured throughout the South and from Texas to Illinois, developing a reputation for emotionally charged performances. Bass singer Paul Briggs, a former member of the famous Wings Over Jordan ensemble, recalls, "The famous Cooper brothers were something else. . . . When you'd run into them out there on the road, everywhere a group was appearing, if they happened to be passing through that section of the country at that time and they didn't know who the Cooper brothers were, or the Loving Four, you believe one thing: that when they left there they knew who they were."[50] The group eventually located their base of operations in New Orleans, where Evlondo heeded a call to the ministry and founded the Loving Four Baptist Tabernacle sometime before 1942.[51]

The Loving Four being an exception, most Omaha quartets limited their venues to area churches and meeting halls where quartet programs were held regularly on Sunday afternoons or evenings. Relations between clergy and quartets were frequently contentious, and rarely would a group be asked to sing at Sunday morning worship. Consultants report that some ministers questioned the motivation and moral character of quartets. Financial concerns may have been a further consideration, since services involving a full choir allowed greater participation and thereby larger attendance.

As public appetite for quartet singing led to more elaborate presentations of local groups, church service organizations such as women's and ushers' guilds staged occasional quartet contests or "battles" where eight or ten units would vie for a prize.[52] If the function was held at a church to help raise funds, a conventional collection was generally taken during intermission. Most of the money went to the church, with a nominal amount given to the participating singers. The largest events, called "quartet jamborees," featured over a dozen groups in a single program lasting about three hours and were often held at the YMCA or CIO Union Hall. At these programs, a different procedure was followed. Knowing that each group had their own following, the jamboree sponsors would schedule the most popular quartets toward the end of the program in order to hold the crowd. Audience response was used as an indicator to choose two finalists from among the participants. Two collection tables would then be set up and the audience would file past, donating to the plate of whichever group they preferred. The one that solicited the larger donation was declared the winner.[53]

Throughout the 1950s, quartet promoter Rowena Moore sponsored a series of noncompetitive jamborees know as Musical Fiestas. As a packing-house employee and secretary of the union local, Moore received free use of the CIO Union Hall and thereby benefited from the workplace affiliation characteristic common to the quartet tradition. According to Moore, the name "fiesta" was intended to recognize and appeal to the growing number of Mexican immigrant in the packing plant labor force. The Musical Fiestas featured as many as sixteen quartets, including female groups.[54]

By the 1960s the quartet practice in Omaha was a shadow of what it had been a decade earlier. Consultants blame the changing tastes of youth, whose preference shifted to secular music and entertainers, and the rise of large gospel choirs for the quartets' decline in popularity.[55] At present, the last remaining vestiges of quartet singing in Omaha are found in the city's "male choruses." Most notable of these is the Hub of Harmony II of Sharon Seventh-Day Adventist Church, an ensemble that draws primarily on the traditional quartet repertoire and emulates the a cappella style of performance.

The presentation of gospel music by full choirs took root in Omaha during the 1930s and gathered momentum throughout the 1940s. Appearances by gospel groups from outside the city won converts to the idiom and provided necessary performance models for local church musicians. As accompanist Eleanor Luckey relates, "When a congregation would hear these singers, this is when they wanted to change over to the new gospel. Because it was electrifying. It was ... spirit-filled, and they enjoyed that feeling."[56] Methodist adoption of the gospel repertoire lagged far behind that of their Baptist counterparts. Yet even among the Baptist community, the degree and manner of gospel's integration was often idiomatic to the institution. Initially hindered by the genre's status as an imported commodity and further fragmented by denominational barriers, the acceptance of gospel music into the established liturgy was a multifaceted process that drew upon resources to which a number of congregations had access.

The seminal gospel songs of Thomas Dorsey and others of the 1930s were first demonstrated at the National Baptist Convention and National Convention of Gospel Choirs and Choruses held in Chicago. There, choir directors from throughout the country could learn songs and purchase sheet music for use in their own churches. But few Omaha directors were able to attend these events and area music stores did not stock the new gospel. This need was met at the grassroots level by Reverend Willis E. Fort of Salem Baptist Church and Roscoe Knight of Zion Baptist, each of whom sold gospel sheet music out of his home. Their service made the music available locally and kept the black church community apprised of trends in Chicago and elsewhere. More importantly, by selling to "whosoever will," as one consultant put it, they facilitated the spread of gospel to other Baptist congregations and, notably, across denominational borders.

In the winter of 1938–39, an alliance of four Methodist ministers conceived a community wide worship service that would endure until the late 1950s. The Union Services, as they were known, were held on Sunday evenings from January to April. With attendance ranging from seven hundred to one thousand, the location rotated among the largest churches in the city. Under the format employed, the responsibility for each Union Service was assumed by a church other than the week's host institution, regardless of either's governing affiliation. In other words, a Union Service held at church A must be conducted by the minister and choir of church B, or church C, etc. In an article with the subheading "Denominational Bars Fall as Christendom Move Forward," the *Omaha Star* assessed the impact of this formula, saying, "The Union Services . . . have proved so popular that denominational bars have faded and we now find a harmonious setting of Methodist, Baptist, and Presbyterian worshiping under one roof."[57] Contributors to this research confirm that in addition to communal fellowship, the Union Services were valued as an opportunity to experience the worship music of other congregations. In the context of the city's developing gospel music complex, they represented a temporary bridging of both intra-and, especially, interdenominational differences that opened avenues for diffusion of the genre.

Salem Baptist Church was founded in 1922. Before the mid-1940s, there was little to distinguish Salem from other churches of the community. Attendance in no way rivaled that of St. John A.M.E. or the larger Baptist congregations at Zion, Mount Moriah, and Pilgrim. Never a regular participant in the Union Services, the Salem congregation maintained a schedule of three Sunday services with music furnished by the adult senior choir. A second ensemble, the children's Rosebud Chorus, was added around 1938.[58] The church was led by a series of clergy with the aforementioned music vendor Reverend Fort sometimes serving as interim pastor.

Reverend J. C. Wade came to Salem in 1944, having served the previous nine years pastoring in Memphis, Tennessee. His first sermon was delivered to a congregation of eighty-eight people. At the time of his retirement in 1988, the church boasted more than thirty-two hundred members, making it the largest of Omaha's black religious institutions.[59] The remarks of his daughter, Doretha Wade-Wilkerson, shed some light on this stunning growth. As she explains, "It's kind of like two things that are important in the Black church. That's music and the Word. . . . First of all, is the preacher capable of giving me what the Word says, and then, is the choir capable of giving me what I need to be uplifted? So those two things go hand in hand."[60] Comments obtained in interviews confirm that the content, style, and sheer power of Reverend Wade's oratory certainly held a strong appeal for many. Yet, Wade himself recognized "They come for two reasons. Either . . . they like his preaching, or they like the choir's singing."[61]

The success of Reverend Wade's evangelism was abetted by this cognizance of music's high premium, in particular its potential for attracting and holding youth to the church. A movement to capitalize on this awareness was initiated almost immediately with the establishment of a new teenaged Junior Choir prior to the close of World War II.[62] Salem's next ensemble, the Number 2 Choir composed of young adults, was organized sometime during 1946 or 1947. Although an inspiring and perceptive minister, Reverend Wade was not himself a musician. His efforts to expand the music program benefited greatly in this respect from the vitality of Elma Wells, a musician at Salem since 1934 who chose a fresh and invigorating repertoire. Under her direction, the Number 2 Choir soon established itself as the most contemporary choir in the city.

In 1951 Reverend Wade founded what would become Salem's

premiere ensemble, the Inspirational Choir. His gifted daughter, Doretha, assumed leadership of the group in 1959 at the age of eighteen. The father-daughter ties between cleric and choir director insured a uniquely close communication that freed Reverend Wade from the distraction of extraneous responsibility with the choirs. Elma Wells recalls, "With the pastor approving of it, and her being interested in it, it just took off like wildfire."[63]

Seeking further musical complement to her father's ministry, about 1960 Doretha introduced complex choreography to the choir processionals that opened services. The choir began to tour to outlying communities in Nebraska. Through subsequent programs such as a 1967 concert appearance in predominantly white Crookson, Minnesota, the renown of the choir spread to regional proportions. The conventional instrumentation of piano and Hammond organ expanded with the addition of a drummer about 1971, possibly the first use of a trap set by an Omaha Baptist church. Electric guitar, electric bass, and saxophone were all added over the next few years. A vanity album was recorded in the Salem Baptist Church sanctuary in 1977.[64] Further recording efforts of the Inspirational Choir benefited from Reverend Wade's personal relationship with the late gospel superstar James Cleveland, with whom he had become acquainted in the 1970s. Cleveland was so impressed by a performance in 1978 that he offered to record with them. The collaboration, "I Don't Feel No Ways Tired: James Cleveland Presents the Salem Inspirational Choir" (Savoy DBL 7024, 1978), was nominated for a Grammy Award in 1979.[65]

Stimulated by the example of Salem Baptist, the preference for contemporary gospel was evidenced in an increasingly greater number of congregations throughout Omaha. Speaking of the early 1960s, one prominent minister of music describes the Salem music program as "a focal point, as far as the direction of music at that time. . . . Most people just decided they were either gonna get with it or die."[66]

"Getting with it" might have been especially difficult for music programs such as that at St. John A.M.E., which under Pearl Gibson had built a reputation on the strength of their formal anthems.[67] Perhaps it is only natural that after Gibson's passing in the late 1950s, it was a Baptist, Lester Corbin, who guided them through the transition. Favoring a bolder type of gospel than that to which the church had been accustomed, Corbin introduced the music of James Cleveland and other contemporary composers whose sheet music he purchased from Roscoe Knight.

Of Omaha's historically African American Methodist institutions, one of the last to incorporate modern gospel was Clair Memorial United Methodist Church.[68] As at Salem, where Reverend Wade had been a catalyst, the "conversion" was motivated by a minister who came to Omaha from Memphis in 1971, Reverend Charles Young. Revitalization of the music program became early on a priority of his ministry. Under the direction of Reverend Young's wife, Marlene, a choir christened the Joyful Sounds debuted in 1972, complete with drums and a choreographed processional. Remembering the initial response of many congregants charter member, Carolyn Solomon recalls, "They didn't like it. I think that they were afraid of it.... It was like we were turning the church into a dance hall."[69] In time, however, reservations about the Joyful Sounds' choreography and percussion were abandoned, and both the stylistic practices and expanded instrumentation became permanent fixtures of Clair services.

Over the past two decades, performance of gospel music in Omaha has extended beyond the boundaries of church-specific organizations. Both Creighton University and the University of Nebraska at Omaha have sponsored gospel choirs, as have a few of the city's high schools. A half-dozen or so independent ensembles appear regularly at special events such as church anniversary programs. At present, the city's most conspicuous independent exponent of gospel is the Omaha Mass Choir. Directed by Jay Terrell, the 150 members of this ensemble represent at least twenty-seven congregations, leaving no doubt that gospel music is alive, well, and widespread in Omaha.[70]

Notes

1. "Black Churches Celebrate Their Role," *Omaha World-Herald*, February 16, 1991, 53–54.

2. *Oxford English Dictionary*, 2d ed., s.v. "gospel."

3. Pearl Williams-Jones, "Afro-American Gospel Music: A Brief Historical and Analytical Survey (1930–1970)," in *Development of Materials for a One-Year Course in African Music for the General Undergraduate Student*, ed. Vada E. Butcher (Washington DC: U.S. Department of Health, Education, and Welfare, 1970), p. 202.

4. Pearl Williams-Jones, "Afro-American Gospel Music: A Crystallization of the Black Aesthetic," *Ethnomusicology* 19, no. 3 (1975): 376.

5. Eileen Southern, "Afro-American Music," in *New Grove Dictionary of American Music*, ed. H. Wiley Hitchcock and Stanley Sadie (London: Macmillan, 1986), vol. 1:14.

6. Eileen Southern, *The Music of Black Americans: A History*, 2d ed. (New York: W. W. Norton, 1983), p. 75.

7. Paul Oliver, "Spirituals," in *New Grove Gospel, Blues and Jazz*, by Paul Oliver, Max Harrison and William Bolcom (New York: W. W. Norton, 1986), p. 7; Paul Oliver, "Spiritual, §II, Black," in *New Grove Dictionary of Music and Musicians*, ed. Stanley Sadie (London: Macmillan, 1980), 18:4; William H. Tallmadge, "Dr. Watts and Mahalia Jackson: The Development, Decline, and Survival of a Folk Style in America," *Ethnomusicology* 5, no. 2 (1961): 95–99 passim.

8. Dena J. Epstein, "Black Spirituals: Their Emergence into Public Knowledge," *Black Music Research Newsletter* 8, no. 2 (1990): 5–8 passim; Southern, *The Music of Black Americans*, p. 227.

9. Portia K. Maultsby, "Africanisms in African-American Music," in *Africanisms in African-American Culture*, ed. Joseph Holloway (Bloomington: Indiana University Press, 1990), p. 186; Southern, *The Music of Black Americans*, p. 451.

10. John Lovell, *Black Song: The Forge and the Flame* (1972: reprint, New York: Macmillan, 1986), pp. 402–22; Southern, "Afro-American Music," pp. 13–21.

11. Doug Seroff, "On the Battlefield: Gospel Quartets in Jefferson County, Alabama," in *Repercussions: A Celebration of Afro-American Music*, ed. Geoffrey Haydon and Dennis Marks (London: Century Publishing, 1985), pp. 32–33.

12. Ray Allen, "African-American Sacred Quartet Singing in New York City," *New York Folklore* 14, nos. 3–4 (1988): 10; Horace Clarence Boyer, "Tracking the Tradition: New Orleans Sacred Music," *Black Music Research Journal* 8, no. 1 (1988): 138.

13. Jon Michael Spencer, *Protest and Praise: Sacred Music of Black Religion* (Minneapolis: Fortress Press, 1990), p. 208.

14. Horace Clarence Boyer, "Charles Albert Tindley: Progenitor of Black-American Gospel Music," *The Black Perspective in Music* 11, no. 2 (1983): 103–32 passim.

15. Horace Clarence Boyer, "Tindley, Charles Albert" in *New Grove Dictionary of American Music*, 4: 395; J. Jefferson Cleveland, "A Historical Account of the Black Gospel Song," in *Songs of Zion*, ed. J. Jefferson Cleveland and Verolga Nix (Nashville: Abingdon, 1981), p. 172 [4 pp.]; Arna Bontemps, "Rock, Church, Rock," reprinted in *The Negro in Music and Art*, ed. Lindsay Patterson (New York: Publishers Company, 1942), pp. 78–81.

16. Bernice Johnson Reagon, "Pioneering African American Gospel Music Composers: A Smithsonian Institution Research Project," in *We'll Understand It Better By and By*, ed. Bernice Johnson Reagon (Washington DC: Smithsonian Institution, 1992), p. 15.

17. Horace Clarence Boyer, "An Analysis of His Contributions: Thomas A. Dorsey, 'Father of Gospel Music,'" *Black World* 23, no. 9 (1974): 25–26.

18. Anthony Heilbut, *The Gospel Sound: Good News and Bad Times,* rev. and updated (New York: Harper and Row, 1985), pp. 7–9; Heilbut, "The Secularization of Black Gospel Music," in *Folk Music and Modern Sound*, ed. William Ferris and Mary L. Hart (Jackson MS: University Press of Mississippi, 1982), p. 107.

19. Boyer, "An Analysis of His Contributions," p. 28; Richard Alan Waterman, "Gospel Hymns of a Negro Church in Chicago," *International Folk Music Journal* 3 (1953): 87–93; John Wesley Work, "Changing Patterns in Negro Folk Songs," *Journal of American Folklore* 62, no. 244 (1949): 141–42.

20. C. Eric Lincoln and Lawrence H. Mamiya, *The Black Church in the African American Experience* (Durham NC: Duke University Press, 1990), p. 77. Other denominations frequently considered Holiness churches include Pentecostal, Apostolic, Spiritual, and Church of God in Christ.

21. George Robinson Ricks, *Some Aspects of the Religious Music of the United States Negro* (New York: Arno Press, 1977), pp. 131–32.

22. Oliver, *Songsters and Saints: Vocal Traditions on Race Records* (Cambridge, UK: Cambridge University Press, 1984), pp. 173–197 passim; Southern, *The Music of Black Americans*, p. 448.

23. Oliver, *Songsters and Saints*, pp. 176, 189.

24. Southern, *The Music of Black Americans*, p. 449.

25. Work, "Changing Patterns in Negro Folk Songs," p. 140.

26. Portia K. Maultsby, "The Use and Performance of Hymnody, Spirituals and Gospels in the Black Church," *Western Journal of Black Studies* 7, no. 3 (1983): 168.

27. Dorothy Devereux Dustin, *Omaha and Douglas County: A Panoramic History* (Woodland Hills CA: Windsor Publications, 1980), p. 19.

28. James D. Bish, "The Black Experience in Selected Nebraska Counties, 1854–1920" (thesis, University of Nebraska at Omaha, 1989), p. 16.

29. "St. John A.M.E. Church 125th Anniversary," *Omaha Star*, May 24, 1990, 5.

30. Lawrence H. Larsen and Barbara J. Cottrell, *The Gate City: A History of Omaha* (Boulder CO: Pruett, 1982), p. 168.

31. "Historical St. John AME Church," *Omaha Star*, June 7, 1990, 6.

32. Ida Madonna Rowland, "An Analysis of Negro Ritualistic Ceremonies as Exemplified by Negro Organizations in Omaha" (thesis, Municipal University of Omaha, 1938), p. 25.

33. "King Rich in Artisry" [sic], *Omaha Star*, May 10, 1940, 5.

34. "Fourth Annual May Day Festival to Present Outstanding Youths in Music," *Omaha Star*, April 26, 1940, 1.

35. "The Fisk Jubilee Singers," *Omaha Star*, December 6, 1940, 1.

36. Federal Writers' Project, Works Progress Administration, *The Negroes of Nebraska* (Omaha: Omaha Urban League Community Center), p. 43.

37. Bertha Young Meyers, interview with author, Omaha NE, August 6, 1990.

38. "Assistant Teachers in Normal Department," *Omaha Star*, October 4, 1940, 1.

39. Michael Dryver, interview with author, Omaha NE, July 27, 1990.

40. "Church Notices: St. John A.M.E. Church," *Omaha Star*, September 27, 1940, 3.

41. "Church Notices: St. John A.M.E. Church," *Omaha Star*, November 4, 1939, 3.

42. Dryver interview with author, July 27, 1990; Michael Dryver, interview with author, Omaha NE, July 30, 1990.

43. "Business Support Imperative for Economic Uplift," *Omaha Star*, October 25, 1940, 1; Meyers interview with author, August 6, 1990.

44. Paul Briggs, interview with author, Omaha NE, June 25, 1991.

45. "7,000 Expected to Witness Annual Spring Musical," *Omaha Star*, April 24, 1942, 1.

46. James Weldon Johnson and J. Rosamond Johnson, *The Book of American Negro Spirituals* (New York: Viking Press, 1925–27), p. 35.

47. Raymore Davis, interview with author, Omaha NE, August 17, 1990.

48. Boyer, "Tracking the Tradition," p. 140.

49. Lynn Abbott, "The Soproco Spiritual Singers: A New Orleans Quartet Family Tree," monograph, (New Orleans: Jean Lafitte National Historical Park, 1983), pp. 47–54.

50. Briggs interview with author, June 25, 1991.

51. Rev. J. C. Wade, interview with author, Omaha NE, August 1, 1990; Historical Records Survey, *Directory of Churches and Religious Organizations in New Orleans*, prepared by Historical Records Survey, Division of Community Service Programs, Works Progress Administration (Baton Rouge LA: Louisiana State University, 1941), p. 28.

52. "The Freezers Club," *Omaha Star*, August 5, 1939, 4.

53. Fred Knight, interview with author, Omaha NE, June 28, 1991.

54. Rowena Moore, interview with author, Omaha NE, July 12, 1991.

55. Paul Briggs, interview with author, Omaha NE, July 24, 1991; Dryver interview with author, July 27, 1990.

56. Eleanor Luckey, interview with author, Omaha NE, August 22, 1990.

57. "Union Services to Begin Again Sunday, January 4," *Omaha Star*, January 2, 1942, 1.

58. Pauline Smith, interview with author, Omaha NE, July 11, 1991; Pauline Smith, interview with author, Omaha NE, June 11, 1990.

59. Wade interview with author, August 1, 1990.

60. Doretha Wade-Wilkerson, interview with author, Omaha NE, July 11, 1991.

61. Wade interview with author, August 1, 1990.

62. Wade interview with author, August 1, 1990.

63. Elma Wells, interview with author, Omaha NE, June 27, 1991.

64. "Salem Baptist Church Inspirational Choir History," frontispiece in "Salem Baptist Church Inspirational Choir 40th Reunion 1951–91," commemorative booklet issued at Salem Inspirational Choir's 40th Reunion-Anniversary Concert, July 13, 1991; Mark Poindexter, interview with author, Omaha NE, July 11, 1990; Wade interview with author, August 1, 1990.

65. "21st Annual Grammy Awards Final Nominations," *Billboard*, January 20, 1979, 122.

66. Dryver interview with author, July 27, 1991.

67. Wells interview with author, June 27, 1991.

68. Pauline Smith, interview with author, Omaha NE, October 25, 1991.

69. Caroline Solomon, interview with author, Omaha NE, August 22, 1990.

70. Jason "Jay" Terrell, interview with author, Omaha NE, March 25, 1999.

SOURCE ACKNOWLEDGMENTS

The chapters reprinted here originally appeared as articles in the *Great Plains Quarterly*:

1. "Black Soldiers at Fort Hays, Kansas, 1867–1869: A Study in Civilian and Military Violence" by James N. Leiker, vol. 17, no. 1 (Winter 1997): 3–17.
2. "'Pap' Singleton's Dunlap Colony Relief Agencies and the Failure of a Black Settlement in Eastern Kansas" by Joseph V. Hickey, in vol. 11, no. 1 (Winter 1991): 23–36.
3. "Vengeance without Justice, Injustice without Retribution: The Afro-American Council's Struggle against Racial Violence" by Shawn Leigh Alexander, vol. 27, no. 2 (Spring 2007): 117–33.
4. "Prelude to Brownsville: The Twenty-fifth Infantry at Fort Niobrara, Nebraska, 1902–06" by Thomas R. Buecker, vol. 16, no. 2 (Spring 1996): 95–106.
5. "Black Enclaves of Violence: Race and Homicide in Great Plains Cities, 1890–1920" by Clare V. McKanna Jr., vol. 23, no. 3 (Summer 2003): 147–60.
6. "A Socioeconomic Portrait of Prince Hall Masonry in Nebraska, 1900–1920" by Dennis N. Mihelich, vol. 17, no. 1 (Winter 1997): 35–47.
7. "Diplomatic Racism: Canadian Government and Black Migration from Oklahoma, 1905–1912" by R. Bruce Shepard, vol. 3, no. 1 (Winter 1983): 5–16.
8. "'This Strange White World': Race and Place in Era Bell Thompson's *American Daughter*" by Michael K. Johnson, vol. 24, no. 2 (Spring 2004): 101–11.
9. "The New Negro Arts and Letters Movement among Black University Students in the Midwest, 1914–1940" by Richard M. Breaux, vol. 24, no. 3 (Summer 2004): 147–62.

10. "Great Plains Pragmatist: Aaron Douglas and the Art of Social Protest" by Audrey Thompson, vol. 20, no. 4 (Fall 2000): 311–22.

11. "Frompin' in the Great Plains: Listening and Dancing to the Jazz Orchestras of Alphonso Trent, 1925–44" by Marc Rice, in vol. 16, no. 2 (Spring 1996): 107–15.

12. "Early Civil Rights Activism in Topeka, Kansas, Prior to the 1954 Brown Case" by Jean Van Delinder, vol. 21, no. 1 (Winter 2001): 45–61.

13. "The Great Plains Sit-In Movement, 1958–60" by Ronald Walters, in vol. 16, no. 2 (Spring 1996): 85–94.

14. "The Omaha Gospel Complex in Historical Perspective" by Tom Jack, vol. 20, no. 3 (Summer 2000): 225–34.

SELECTED BIBLIOGRAPHY

Few citations for the African American experience in Texas are included here since other comprehensive bibliographic and historiographic citations on blacks in Texas can be found elsewhere. See works by Alwyn Barr and Bruce A. Glasrud, indicated below.

Age, Arthur V. "The Omaha Riot of 1919." Master's thesis, Creighton University, 1964.
Aldrich, Gene. *Black Heritage of Oklahoma*. Edmond OK: Thompson Book and Supply Company, 1973.
Alexander, Shawn Leigh. "Vengeance without Justice, Injustice without Retribution: The Afro-American Council's Struggle against Racial Violence." *Great Plains Quarterly* 27.2 (Spring 2007): 117–34.
Allmendinger, Blake. *Imagining the African American West*. Lincoln: University of Nebraska Press, 2005.
Anderson, Kathie Ryckman. "Era Bell Thompson: A North Dakota Daughter." *North Dakota History* 49 (1982): 11–18.
Anderson, Robert. *From Slavery to Affluence: Memoirs of Robert Anderson, Ex-Slave*. Steamboat Springs, Colorado: Privately Published, 1967.
Andrews, Thomas F. "Freedmen in Indian Territory: A Post–Civil War Dilemma." *Journal of the West* 4 (July 1965): 367–76.
Armitage, Susan. "'The Mountains Were Free and We Loved Them': Dr. Ruth Flowers of Boulder, Colorado." In *African American Women Confront the West, 1600–2000*. Edited by Quintard Taylor and Shirley Ann Wilson Moore, 165–77. Norman: University of Oklahoma Press, 2003.

———. Theresa Banfield, and Sarah Jacobus. "Black Women and Their Communities in Colorado." *Frontiers* 2 (Summer 1977): 45–51.

Ashley, Velma D. "A History of Boley, Oklahoma." Master's thesis, Kansas State College, 1940.

Athearn, Robert G. *In Search of Canaan: Black Migration to Kansas, 1879–80.* Lawrence: Regents Press of Kansas, 1978.

———. "Black Exodus: The Migration of 1879." *Prairie Scout* 3 (1975): 86–99.

Bailey, Anne J. "A Texas Cavalry Raid: Reaction to Black Soldiers and Contrabands." *Civil War History* 35 (1989): 138–52.

———. "Was There a Massacre at Poison Spring?" *Military History of the Southwest* 20 (Fall 1990): 157–68.

Bailey, M. Thomas. *Reconstruction in Indian Territory: A Story of Avarice, Discrimination, and Opportunism.* Port Washington NY: Kennikat Press, 1972.

Baker, Ben. "Some Aspects of Segregation Law in Oklahoma." Master's thesis, University of Tulsa, 1952.

Baker, June A. "Patterns of Black Residential Segregation in Oklahoma City, 1890–1960." Master's thesis, University of Oklahoma, 1970.

Baker, T. Lindsay, and Julie P. Baker, eds. *The WPA Oklahoma Slave Narratives.* Norman: University of Oklahoma Press, 1996.

Ball, Wilbur P. *Black Pioneers of the Prairie.* Fort Morgan CO: Commercial-PWS Printers, 1988.

Balyeat, Frank A. "Segregation in the Public Schools of Oklahoma." *Chronicles of Oklahoma* 39 (1961): 180–92.

Barr, Alwyn. *The African Texans.* Institute of Texan Cultures. College Station: Texas A&M University Press, 2004.

———. *Black Texans: A History of African Americans in Texas, 1528–1995.* Second edition. Norman: University of Oklahoma Press, 1996.

———. "Advancing from History's Hollow to History's Mountain: Sources on African American History in Texas." *East Texas Historical Journal* 38.1 (2000): 28–34.

———. "African Americans in Texas: From Stereotypes to Diverse Roles. In *Texas Through Time: Evolving Interpretations.* Edited by Walter L. Buenger and Robert A. Calvert, 50–80. College Station: Texas A&M University Press, 1991.

———. "Black Texans." In *A Guide to the History of Texas.* Edited by Light

Townsend Cummins and Alvin R. Bailey Jr., 107–21. Westport: Greenwood Press, 1988.
———. "The Right to Vote." In *Reconstruction to Reform: Texas Politics, 1876–1906*, 193–208. Austin: University of Texas Press, 1971.
Barr, Alwyn, and Robert A. Calvert, eds. *Black Leaders: Texans for Their Times*. Austin: Texas State Historical Association, 1981.
Becknell, Charles E., Sr. *No Challenge—No Change: Growing Up Black in New Mexico*. Kearney NE: Morris Publishing, 2003.
Beeson, Ronald Max. "Desegregation and Affirmative Action in Higher Education in Oklahoma: A Historical Case Study." PhD dissertation, Oklahoma State University, 1986.
Bell, J. D. "A Study of a Negro City." Master's thesis, University of Kansas, 1930.
Belleau, William J. "The Nicodemus Colony of Graham County, Kansas." Master's thesis, Fort Hays State College, 1950.
Bergmann, Leola Nelson. *The Negro in Iowa*. Iowa City: State Historical Society of Iowa, 1969.
———. "The Negro in Iowa." *Iowa Journal of History and Politics* 46 (1948): 3–90.
Bernson, Sara L., and Robert J. Eggers. "Black People in South Dakota History." *South Dakota History* 7 (Summer 1977): 241–70.
Berwanger, Eugene H. *The Frontier against Slavery: Western Anti-Negro Prejudice and the Slavery Extension Controversy*. Urbana: University of Illinois Press, 1967.
———. "Hardin and Langston: Western Black Spokesmen of the Reconstruction Era." *Journal of Negro History* 64 (1979): 101–15.
———. "Reconstruction on the Frontier: The Equal Rights Struggle in Colorado, 1865–1867." *Pacific Historical Quarterly* 44 (1975): 313–29.
———. *The West and Reconstruction*. Urbana: University of Illinois Press, 1981.
———. "William J. Hardin: Colorado Spokesman for Racial Justice, 1863–1873." *Colorado Magazine* 52 (1975): 52–65.
Betts, Robert B. *In Search of York*. Boulder: University Press of Colorado, 2000.
Billington, Monroe Lee. *New Mexico's Buffalo Soldiers, 1866–1900*. Niwot: University Press of Colorado, 1991.

———. "Black History and New Mexico's Place Names." *Password* 29 (Fall 1984): 107–13, 156.

———. "A Profile of Blacks in New Mexico on the Eve of Statehood." *Password* 32 (Summer 1987): 55–66, 90.

———. "Black Soldiers at Fort Selden, New Mexico, 1866–1891." *New Mexico Historical Review* 62 (1987): 65–80.

———. "Civilians and Black Soldiers in New Mexico Territory, 1866–1900: A Cross-Cultural Experience." *Military History of the Southwest* 19 (Spring, 1989): 71–82.

———. "Black Cavalrymen and Apache Indians in New Mexico Territory." *Fort Concho and the South Plains Journal* 22 (Summer, 1990): 55–75.

———. "Buffalo Soldiers in the American West." *African Americans on the Western Frontier*. Edited by Monroe Lee Billington and Roger Hardaway, 54–72. Niwot CO: University Press of Colorado, 1998.

———. "Public School Integration in Oklahoma." *The Historian* 26 (August 1964): 521–37.

Billington, Monroe Lee, and Roger D. Hardaway, eds. *African Americans on the Western Frontier*. Boulder: University Press of Colorado, 1998.

Bish, James D. "The Black Experience in Selected Nebraska Counties, 1854–1920." Master's thesis, University of Nebraska at Omaha, 1989.

Bittle, William E., and Gilbert Geis. *The Longest Way Home: Chief Alfred Sam's Back-to-Africa Movement*. Detroit: Wayne State University Press, 1964.

———. "Racial Self-Fulfillment and the Rise of an All-Negro Community in Oklahoma." *Phylon* 18 (1957): 246–60.

———. "Alfred Charles Sam and an African Return: A Case Study in Negro Despair." *Phylon* 23 (1962): 178–94.

Blake, Ella Lee. "The Great Exodus of 1879 and 1880 to Kansas." Master's thesis, Kansas State University, 1942.

Blakely, Allison. "The John L. Waller Affair, 1895–1896." *Negro History Bulletin* 37 (1974): 216–18.

Bond, Jon. "The Impact of Judicial Policy in a Local Community: School Desegregation in Oklahoma City." Master's thesis, Oklahoma State University, 1973.

Bonner, T. D. *The Life and Adventures of James P. Beckwourth, Mountaineer, Scout, Pioneer, and Chief of the Crow Nation of Indians*. Reprint, edited by Delmont R. Oswald. Lincoln: University of Nebraska Press, 1972.

Bontemps, Arna, and Jack Conroy. *Anyplace But Here*, 53–71. New York: Hill and Wang, 1966.

Boyd, Thomas J. "The Use of Negro Troops by Kansas during the Civil War." Master's thesis, Kansas State University, 1950.

Boyer, James B. "A Voice From the Heart: Gospel Music in the African American Tradition." *Kansas Heritage* 1 (Spring 1993): 11–13.

Brady, Marilyn Dell. "Kansas Federation of Colored Women's Clubs, 1900–1930." *Kansas History* 9 (1986): 19–30.

———. "Organizing Afro-American Girls Clubs in Kansas in the 1920s." *Frontiers* 9 (1987): 69–73.

Breaux, Richard M. "The New Negro Arts and Letters Movement Among Black University Students in the Midwest, 1914–1940." *Great Plains Quarterly* 24.3 (Summer 2004): 147–62.

Brewer, J. Mason, ed. *Heralding Dawn: An Anthology of Verse*. Dallas: June Thomason, 1936.

Broussard, Albert S. "George Albert Flippin and Race Relations in a Western Rural Community." *Midwest Review* 12 (1990): 1–15.

Bruce, Henry Clay. *The New Man: Twenty-Nine Years a Slave, Twenty-Nine Years a Free Man*. New York: Negro Universities Press, 1969.

Bruce, Janet. *The Kansas City Monarchs*. Lawrence: University of Kansas Press, 1985.

Bruyn, Kathleen. *"Aunt" Clara Brown: Story of a Black Pioneer*. Boulder CO: Pruett Publishing, 1970.

Buckner, Reginald Tyrone. "A History of Music Education in the Black Community of Kansas City, Kansas, 1905–1954." PhD dissertation, University of Minnesota, 1974.

Buecker, Thomas R. "Confrontation at Sturgis: An Episode in Civil-Military Race Relations, 1885." *South Dakota History* 14 (Fall 1984): 238–61.

——— "Prelude to Brownsville: The Twenty-fifth Infantry at Fort Niobrara, Nebraska, 1902–06." *Great Plains Quarterly* 16.2 (Spring 1996): 95–106.

———. "The Tenth Cavalry at Fort Robinson, 1902–1907." *Military Images* 12.6 (1991): 118–26.

Bullock, Clifford A. "Fired by Conscience: The Black 14 Incident at the University of Wyoming and Black Protest in the Western Athletic Conference, 1968–1970." *Wyoming History Journal* 68 (Winter 1996).

Burke, Francis D. "A Survey of the Negro Community of Tulsa, Oklahoma." Master's thesis, University of Oklahoma, 1936.

Burran, James A. "Violence in an 'Arsenal of Democracy': The Beaumont Race Riot, 1943." *East Texas Historical Journal* 14.1 (Spring 1976): 39–51.

Burton, Arthur T. *Black, Red, and Deadly: Black and Indian Gunfighters of the Indian Territory, 1870–1907*. Austin TX: Eakin Press, 1991.

Bustamonte, Adrian. "'The Matter Was Never Resolved': The *Casta* System in Colonial New Mexico, 1693–1823." *New Mexico Historical Review* 66 (1991): 143–63.

Butler, Anne M. "Still in Chains: Black Women in Western Prisons, 1865–1910." *Western Historical Quarterly* 20 (1989): 18–35.

Butters, Gerald R., Jr. "*The Birth of a Nation* and the Kansas Board of Review of Motion Pictures: A Censorship Struggle." *Kansas History* 14 (Spring, 1991): 2–14.

Calloway, Bertha, and Alonzo N. Smith. *Visions of Freedom on the Great Plains: An Illustrated History of African Americans in Nebraska*. Virginia Beach VA: The Donning Company, 1998.

Campbell, Lula Lowe. "A Study of the Relations of Negro Churches in Denver to One Hundred Families in the Community." Master's thesis, University of Denver, 1951.

Campbell, Randolph B. *An Empire for Slavery: The Peculiar Institution in Texas, 1821–1865*. Baton Rouge: Louisiana State University Press, 1989.

Carlson, Paul H. *The Buffalo Soldier Tragedy of 1877*. College Station: Texas A&M University Press, 2003.

———. *"Pecos Bill": A Military Biography of William R. Shafter*. College Station: Texas A&M University Press, 1989.

Carney, George O. "Historic Resources of Oklahoma's All-Black Towns: A Preservation Profile." *Chronicles of Oklahoma* 69 (1991): 116–33.

Carper, James C. "The Popular Ideology of Segregated Schooling: Attitudes toward the Education of Blacks in Kansas, 1854–1900." *Kansas History* 1 (Winter 1978): 254–65.

Castel, Albert. "Civil War Kansas and the Negro." *Journal of Negro History* 51 (1966): 125–38.

Castles, Jean I. "The West: Crucible of the Negro." *Montana: The Magazine of Western History* 19 (1969):

Chafe, William H. "The Negro and Populism: A Kansas Case Study." *Journal of Southern History* 34 (August 1968): 402–19.

Chalmers, David M. "Twisting the Klan's Shirttail in Kansas." In *Hooded Americanism: The History of the Ku Klux Klan*, 143–48, 407. Chicago: Quadrangle Books, 1968.

Champion, Laurie, and Bruce A. Glasrud, eds. *Unfinished Masterpiece: The Harlem Renaissance Fiction of Anita Scott Coleman*. Lubbock: Texas Tech University Press, 2008.

Chapman, Berlin B. "Freedmen and the Oklahoma Lands." *Southwestern Social Science Quarterly* 29 (1948): 150–59.

Chartrand, Robert Lee. "The Negro Exodus from the Southern States to Kansas: 1869–1886." Master's thesis, University of Kansas City, 1949.

Chase, Hal J. "Struggle for Equality: Fort Des Moines Training Camp for Colored Officers, 1917." *Phylon* 39 (Winter 1978): 297–310.

Chaudhuri, Nupur. "'We All Seem Like Brothers and Sisters': The African-American Community in Manhattan, Kansas, 1865–1940." *Kansas History* 14 (1991–1992): 270–88.

Chrisman, Harry E. *The Ladder of Rivers: The Story of I. P. (Print) Olive*. Denver: Sage Books, 1962.

Christian, Garna L. *Black Soldiers in Jim Crow Texas, 1899–1917*. College Station: Texas A&M University Press, 1995.

Chu, Daniel, and Bill Shaw. *Going Home to Nicodemus*. Morristown NJ: J. Messner, 1994.

Clark, Carter Blue. "A History of the Ku Klux Klan in Oklahoma." PhD dissertation, University of Oklahoma, 1976.

Clubb, Inez. "A History of the Ku Klux Klan in Oklahoma from 1920 to the Present." Master's thesis, Oklahoma State University, 1941.

Coffin, Nathan E. "The Case of Archie P. Webb, a Free Negro." *Annals of Iowa* 11 (1913): 200–214.

Cole, Kevin L., and Leah Weins. "Religion, Idealism, and African American Autobiography in the Northern Plains: Era Bell Thompson's *American Daughter*." *Great Plains Quarterly* 23 (Fall 2003): 219–29.

Conner, Veda N. "There's a Big We in New Mexico." *Crisis* 61 (January, 1954): 5–8, 62.

Cooper, Arnold. "'Protection to All, Discrimination to None': The *Parsons Weekly Blade*, 1892–1900." *Kansas History* 9 (Summer 1986): 58–71.

Cornish, Dudley Cornish. *The Sable Arm: Negro Troops in the Union Army, 1861–1865*. New York: W. W. Norton, 1966.

———. "Kansas Negro Regiments in the Civil War." *Kansas Historical Quarterly* 20 (May 1953): 417–29.

———. "The Union Army as a Training School for Negroes." *The Journal of Negro History* 37 (1952): 368–82.

Cox, Thomas C. *Blacks in Topeka, Kansas, 1865–1915: A Social History*. Baton Rouge: Louisiana State University Press, 1982.

Crockett, Norman L. *The Black Towns*. Lawrence: The Regents Press of Kansas, 1979.

Cross, George L. *Blacks in White Colleges: Oklahoma's Landmark Cases*. Norman: University of Oklahoma Press, 1975.

Crossley, Mildred M. "A History of the Negro Schools of Oklahoma City, Oklahoma." Master's thesis, University of Oklahoma, 1939.

Cunningham, Roger D. "'A Lot of Fine, Sturdy Black Warriors': Texas's African American 'Immunes' in the Spanish-American War." *Southwestern Historical Quarterly* 108.3 (2005): 345–67.

———. *The Black Citizen-Soldiers from Kansas, 1864–1901*. Columbia: University of Missouri Press, 2008.

———. "Douglas's Battery." *On Point* 11.4 (Spring 2006).

———. "Douglas's Battery at Fort Leavenworth: The Issue of Black Officers during the Civil War." *Kansas History* 23 (Winter 2000–2001): 200–217.

———. "'His Influence with the Colored People is Marked': Christian Fleetwood's Quest for Command in the War with Spain and Its Aftermath." *Army History* 51 (Winter 2001).

———. "Kansas City's African American 'Immunes' in the Spanish-American War." *Missouri Historical Review* 100 (April 2006): 141–58.

———. "Welcoming 'Pa' on the Kaw: Kansas's 'Colored' Militia and the 1864 Price Raid." *Kansas History* 25.2 (2002): 86–101.

Dagley, Asa Wallace. "The Negro of Oklahoma." Master's thesis, University of Oklahoma, 1926.

Dales, David. "North Platte Racial Incident: Black-White Confrontation, 1929." *Nebraska History* 60 (Fall 1979).

Dann, Martin. "From Sodom to the Promised Land: E. P. McCabe and the Movement for Oklahoma Colonization." *Kansas Historical Quarterly* 40 (1974): 370–78.

Davies, Mary Emily and Marsh, Genevieve. "A Study of the Negro in Lincoln." Master's thesis, University of Nebraska, 1904.

Davis, Frank Marshall. *Livin' the Blues: Memoirs of a Black Journalist and a Poet*. Edited by John Edgar Tidwell. Madison: University of Wisconsin Press, 1992.

Davis, James H. "The Ku Klux Klan in Colorado." Master's thesis, University of Denver, 1963.

Davis, Nathan Tate. "Charlie Parker's Kansas City Environment and its Effect on His Later Life." PhD dissertation, Wesleyan University, 1974.

Day, Ava Speese. "The Ava Speese Story." In *Sod House Memories*, edited by Frances Jacobs Alberts, 261–275. Hastings NE: Sod House Society, 1972.

Deacon, Marie. "Kansas as the Promised Land: The View of the Black Press, 1890–1900." Master's thesis, University of Arkansas, 1973.

DeBarthe, Joe. *Life and Adventures of Frank Grouard*. Edited by Edgar I. Stewart. Norman: University of Oklahoma Press, 1958.

Derrick, W. Edwin, and J. Herschel Barnhill. "With 'All' Deliberate Speed: Desegregation of the Public Schools in Oklahoma City and Tulsa, 1954–1972." *Red River Valley Historical Review* 6 (Spring 1981): 78–90.

Dickson, Lynda F. "African American Women's Clubs in Denver, 1890's-1920's." In *Peoples of Color in the American West*, edited by Sucheng Chan, Douglas Henry Daniels, Mario T. Garcia, and Terry P. Wilson, 224–234. Lexington MA: D. C. Heath, 1994.

———. "The Early Club Movement among Black Women in Denver, 1890–1925." PhD dissertation, University of Colorado, 1982.

———. "Lifting as We Climb: African American Women's Clubs of Denver, 1890–1925." *Essays in Colorado History* 13 (1992).

———. "Toward a Broader Angle of Vision in Uncovering Women's History: Black Women's Clubs Revisited." *Frontiers* 9 (1987): 62–68.

Dobak, William A. "Civil War on the Kansas-Nebraska Border: The Narrative of Former Slave Andrew Williams." *Kansas History* 6 (1983): 237–42.

———. "Fort Riley's Black Soldiers and the Army's Changing Role in the West, 1867–1885." *Kansas History* 22 (1999): 214–27.

Dobak, William A., and Thomas D. Phillips. *The Black Regulars, 1866–1898*. Norman: University of Oklahoma Press, 2001.

Driggs, Frank, and Chuck Haddix. *Kansas City Jazz: From Ragtime to Bebop—A History*. New York: Oxford University Press, 2005.

Durham, Kenneth Jr. "The Longview Race Riot of 1919." *East Texas Historical Journal* 18.2 (1980): 13–24.

Durham, Philip. "The Negro Cowboy." *American Quarterly* 7 (Fall 1955): 291–301.

Durham, Philip, and Everett L. Jones. *The Negro Cowboys*. 1965; Lincoln: University of Nebraska Press, 1983.

———. "Negro Cowboys." *American West* 1 (Fall 1964).

Dykstra, Robert R. *Bright Radical Star: Black Freedom and White Supremacy on the Hawkeye Frontier*. Cambridge: Harvard University Press, 1993.

Early, Gerald, et al. *Black Heartland: African American Life, The Middle West, and the Meaning of American Regionalism*. St. Louis MO: Washington University, 1997.

Eick, Gretchen Cassel. *Dissent in Wichita: The Civil Rights Movement in the Midwest, 1954–1972*. Urbana: University of Illinois Press, 2001.

Elahi, Larry. "A History of Boley, Oklahoma, to 1915." Master's thesis, University of Chicago, 1968.

Ellison, Ralph. *The Invisible Man*. 1952; New York: Vintage, 1972.

Ellsworth, Scott. *Death in a Promised Land: The Tulsa Race Riot of 1921*. Baton Rouge: Louisiana State University Press, 1982.

Entz, Gary R. "Image and Reality on the Kansas Prairie: 'Pap' Singleton's Cherokee County Colony." *Kansas History* 19 (1996): 124–39.

Estes, Mary Elizabeth. "An Historical Survey of Lynchings in Oklahoma and Texas." Master's thesis, University of Oklahoma, 1942.

Etter, Earl T. "A Study of Negro Operated Farms in Oklahoma." Master's thesis, Oklahoma State University, 1940.

Fairbanks, Evelyn. *The Days of Rondo*. St. Paul: Minnesota Historical Society Press, 1990.

Farnsworth, Robert M. *Melvin B. Tolson, 1898–1966: Plain Talk and Poetic Prophecy*. Columbia: University of Missouri Press, 1984.

Farrar, Jon. "Black Homesteaders: Free Land for Free Men." *Nebraskaland* 66.6 (June 1988): 12–47.

———. Black Homesteaders: Living Off the Land." *Nebraskaland* 66.7 (August 1988): 16–47.

———. Black Homesteaders: Remembering the Good Times." *Nebraskaland* 66.9 (November 1988): 6–44.

———. "Black Homesteaders: Scratching Out a Living." *Nebraskaland* 66.8 (October 1988): 38–45.
Fedo, Michael. *The Lynchings in Duluth*. St. Paul: Minnesota Historical Society Press, 2000.
Felton, Harold W. *Edward Rose: Negro Trail Blazer*. New York: Dodd, Mead, 1967.
Fisher, Ada Lois Sipuel, and Danney Goble. *A Matter of Black and White: The Autobiography of Ada Lois Sipuel Fisher*. Norman: University of Oklahoma Press, 1996.
Fisher, Mike. "The First Kansas Colored: Massacre at Poison Spring." *Kansas History* 2 (Summer 1979): 121–28.
———. "Remember Poison Spring." *Missouri Historical Review* 74 (April 1980): 323–42.
Fleming, Walter. "'Pap' Singleton: The Moses of the Colored Exodus." *American Journal of Sociology* 15 (1909): 61–82.
Fontenot, Chester J., Jr. "Oscar Micheaux, Black Novelist and Film Maker." *Vision and Refuge: Essays on the Literature of the Great Plains*. Edited by Virginia Faulkner and Frederick C. Luebke, 109–25. Lincoln: University of Nebraska Press, 1982.
Fowler, Arlen L. *The Black Infantry in the West, 1869–1891*. Norman: University of Oklahoma Press, 1996.
Franklin, Jimmie Lewis. *Journey Toward Hope: A History of Blacks in Oklahoma*. Norman: University of Oklahoma Press, 1982.
Frehill-Rowe, Lisa M. "Postbellum Race Relations and Rural Land Tenure: Migration of Blacks and Whites to Kansas and Nebraska, 1870–1890." *Social Forces* 72.1 (1993): 77–92.
Frierson, Eugene P. "An Adventure in the Big Horn Mountains; or, the Trials and Tribulations of a Recruit." *Colored American Magazine* 8 (April 1905): 196–199; (May 1905): 277–79; (June 1905): 338–40.
Frisch, Paul A. "'Gibralter of Unionism': Women, Blacks, and the Anti-Chinese Movement in Butte Montana, 1880–1900." *Southwest Economy and Society* 6 (1984): 3–13.
Fulkerson, Fred G. "Social Forces in a Negro District in Oklahoma City, Oklahoma." Master's thesis, University of Oklahoma, 1946.
Garceau-Hagen, Dee. "Finding Mary Fields: Race, Gender, and the Construction

of Memory." In *Portraits of Women in the American West*. Edited by Dee Garceau-Hagen, 121–55. New York: Routledge, 2005.

Garvin, Roy. "Benjamin or 'Pap' Singleton and His Followers." *Journal of Negro History* 33 (1948): 7–23.

Gaskin, J. M. *Black Baptists in Oklahoma*. Oklahoma City: Messenger Press, 1992.

Gates, Eddie Faye. *They Came Searching: How Blacks Sought the Promised Land in Tulsa*. Austin: Eakin Press, 1997.

Gatewood, Willard B., Jr. "Kansas Negroes and the Spanish-American War." *Kansas Historical Quarterly* 37 (1971): 300–313.

———. "Kate D. Chapman Reports on 'The Yankton Colored People,' 1889." *South Dakota History* 7 (Winter 1976): 32–35.

———. "The Perils of Passing: The McCarys of Omaha." *Nebraska History* 71 (1990).

Gedge, Charles H. "Westward Migration of Blacks in the Nineteenth Century with Special Reference to the Kansas Exodus." Master's thesis, Roosevelt University, 1976.

Gibson, Daniel. "Blackdom." *New Mexico Magazine* 64 (February, 1986): 46–47, 50–51.

Gift, Elmer Birdell. "The Causes and History of the Negro Exodus into Kansas, 1879–1880." Master's thesis, University of Kansas, 1915.

Gill, Loren. "The Tulsa Race Riot." Master's thesis, University of Tulsa, 1946.

Glasrud, Bruce A., ed. *African Americans in the West: A Bibliography of Secondary Sources*. Alpine TX: SRSU Center for Big Bend Studies, 1998.

———. "African Americans in West Texas: A Selected Bibliography." *Journal of Big Bend Studies* 18 (2006): 191–212.

———. "Anita Scott Coleman." *BlackPast Online Encyclopedia* (http://www.blackpast.org).

———. "Black Texas History: A Selected Bibliography." In *The African American Experience in Texas*, edited by Bruce A. Glasrud and James M. Smallwood, 353–76. Lubbock: Texas Tech University Press, 2007.

———. "Buffalo Soldiers in Oklahoma." *Encyclopedia of Oklahoma History and Culture*. (http://digital.library.okstate.edu/encyclopedia).

———. "Enforcing White Supremacy in Texas, 1900–1910." *Red River Valley Historical Review* 4 (Fall 1979): 65–74.

———. "Harlem Renaissance in the United States—Texas and the Southwest." In *Encyclopedia of the Harlem Renaissance*, edited by Cary D. Wintz and Paul Finkelman, 521–25. New York: Routledge, 2004.

Glasrud, Bruce A., Paul H. Carlson, and Tai D. Kreidler, eds. *Slavery to Integration: Black Americans in West Texas*. Abilene TX: State House Press, 2008.

Glasrud, Bruce A., and Laurie Champion, eds. *The African American West: A Century of Short Stories*. Boulder: University Press of Colorado, 2000.

———, and Laurie Champion, eds. *Exploring the Afro-Texas Experience: A Bibliography of Secondary Sources about Black Texans*. Alpine TX: SRSU Center for Big Bend Studies, 2000.

———, and Laurie Champion. "A House Divided: Short Stories and the Civil Rights Movement in the West." *Journal of the American Studies Association of Texas* (2000): 1–18.

Glasrud, Bruce A., and Merline Pitre, eds. *Black Women in Texas History*. College Station: Texas A&M University Press, 2008.

Glasrud, Bruce A., and Michael N. Searles, eds. *Buffalo Soldiers in the West: A Black Soldiers Anthology*. College Station: Texas A&M University Press, 2007.

Glasrud, Bruce A., and James M. Smallwood, eds. *The African American Experience in Texas: An Anthology*. Lubbock: Texas Tech University Press, 2007.

———. "The Texas Tech School of Black History: An Overview." *West Texas Historical Association Year Book* 82 (2006): 102–19.

Glatthar, Joseph T. *Forged in Battle: The Civil War Alliance of Black Soldiers and White Officers*. New York: Macmillan, 1990.

Goldberg, Robert A. *Hooded Empire: The Ku Klux Klan in Colorado*. Urbana: University of Illinois Press, 1981.

———. "Beneath Hood and Robe: A Socioeconomic Analysis of Ku Klux Klan Membership in Denver, Colorado, 1921–1925." *Western Historical Quarterly* 11 (1980): 181–98.

———. "Racial Change on the Southern Periphery: The Case of San Antonio, Texas, 1960–1965." *Journal of Southern History* 49 (1983): 349–74.

Golden, Kevin J. "The Independent Development of Civil Rights in Minnesota, 1849–1910." *William Mitchell Law Review* 17 (1991): 449–60.

Gordon, Jacob U. *Narratives of African Americans in Kansas, 1870–1992*. Lewiston NY: Edward Mellen Press, 1993.

Gordon, Taylor. *Born to be Free*. 1929; Lincoln: University of Nebraska Press, 1995.

Grant, Truett King. "The Negro Exodus of 1879–1880." Master's thesis, Baylor University, 1952.

Graves, Carl. "The Right to Be Served: Oklahoma City's Lunch Counter Sit-ins, 1958–1964." *Chronicles of Oklahoma* 59 (Summer 1981): 152–66.

Gray, Linda C. "Taft: Town on the Black Frontier." *Chronicles of Oklahoma* 66 (1988–89): 430–47.

Green, William D. "Race and Segregation in St. Paul's Public Schools, 1846–69." *Minnesota History* 55 (Winter 1996–97): 138–49.

Greenbaum, Susan D., et al. *The Afro-American Community in Kansas City Kansas: A History.* N.p.: City of Kansas City Kansas, 1982.

Grenz, Suzanna M. "The Exodusters of 1879: St. Louis and Kansas City Responses." *Missouri Historical Review* 73 (October 1978): 54–70.

Griffin, James S. "Blacks in the St. Paul Police Department: An Eighty Year Survey." *Minnesota History* 45 (Fall 1975): 255–65.

Grinde, Donald A., and Quintard Taylor. "Red vs. Black: Conflict and Accommodation in the Post Civil War Indian Territory, 1865–1907." *American Indian Quarterly* 8 (1984): 211–25.

Grow, Stewart. "The Blacks of Amber Valley: Negro Pioneering in Northern Alberta." *Canadian Ethnic Studies* 6 (1974): 17–38.

Guenther, Todd R. "'Y'all Call Me Nigger Jim Now, But Someday You'll Call Me Mr. James Edwards': Black Success on the Plains of the Equality State." *Annals of Wyoming* 61(1989): 20–40.

———. "At Home on the Range: A History of Blacks in Wyoming, 1850–1950." Master's thesis, University of Wyoming, 1988.

Hall, Ella. "The Development of the Kansas City, Kansas, Young Women's Christian Association." Master's thesis, University of Kansas, 1945.

Hall, Johanna L. "The African American Community in Topeka, Kansas, 1949–54: Crucial Years before *Brown*." Master's thesis, University of Kansas, 1993.

Hall, Martin Hardwick. "Negroes with Confederate Troops in West Texas and New Mexico." *Password* 13 (Spring 1968): 11–12.

Halliburton, Janet. "Black Slavery in the Creek Nation." *Chronicles of Oklahoma* 56 (1978): 298–314.

Halliburton, Rudi. *Red Over Black: Black Slavery Among the Cherokee Indians.* Westport CT: Greenwood Press, 1977.

———. *The Tulsa Race War of 1921.* San Francisco: R & E Research Associates, 1975.

———. "Origins of Black Slavery among the Cherokees." *Chronicles of Oklahoma* 52 (1974–75): 483–96.

———. "Black Slave Control in the Cherokee Nation." *Journal of Ethnic Studies* 3 (1975): 23–36.

Hamilton, Kenneth M. *Black Towns and Profit: Promotion and Development in the Trans-Appalachian West*. Urbana: University of Illinois Press, 1991.

———. "The Origin and Early Development of Langston, Oklahoma." *Journal of Negro History* 62 (1977): 270–82.

———. "Townsite Speculation and the Origin of Boley, Oklahoma." *Chronicles of Oklahoma* 55 (1977): 180–89.

———. "The Origins and Early Promotion of Nicodemus: A Pre-Exodus All Black Town." *Kansas History* 5 (Winter 1982): 221–42.

Hansen, Moya B. "'Try Being a Black Woman!': Jobs in Denver, 1900–1970." In *African American Women Confront the West, 1600–2000*. Edited by Quintard Taylor and Shirley Ann Wilson Moore, 207–27. Norman: University of Oklahoma Press, 2003.

Hardaway, Roger D. *A Narrative Bibliography of the African-American Frontier: Blacks in the Rocky Mountain West, 1535–1912*. Lewiston NY: Edward Mellen Press, 1995.

———. "Prohibiting Interracial Marriage: Miscegenation Laws in Wyoming." *Annals of Wyoming* 52 (Spring 1980): 55–60.

———. "William Jefferson Hardin: Wyomings Nineteenth Century Legislator." *Annals of Wyoming* 63 (1991): 2–13.

Hardeman, Nicholas P. "Brick Stronghold of the Border: Fort Assinniboine, 1879–1911." *Montana: The Magazine of Western History* 29 (Spring 1979): 54–67.

Harpole, Patricia C., ed. "The Black Community in Territorial St. Anthony: A Memoir." *Minnesota History* 49 (Summer 1984): 42–55.

Harris, Andrew. "Deerfield: A Negro Ghost Town in Weld County, Colorado." *Negro History Bulletin* 27 (1963): 38–39.

Hart, Charles Desmond. "The Natural Limits of Slavery Expansion: Kansas-Nebraska, 1854." *Kansas Historical Quarterly* 34 (1968): 32–50.

Harvey, James R. "The Negro in Colorado." Master's thesis, University of Denver, 1941.

———. "Negroes in Colorado." *Colorado Magazine* 26 (1949): 165–76.

Hatcher, Ollie Everett. "The Development of Legal Controls in Racial Segregation in the Public Schools of Oklahoma, 1865–1952." Master's thesis, University of Oklahoma, 1954.
Haynes, Robert V. *A Night of Violence: The Houston Riot of 1917*. Baton Rouge: Louisiana State University Press, 1976.
Haywood, C. Robert. "'No Less a Man': Blacks in Cow Town Dodge City, 1876–1886." *Western Historical Quarterly* 19 (1988): 161–82.
———. "The Hodgeman County Colony." *Kansas History* 12 (1989/90): 210–21.
Heath, Jim F., and Frederick M. Nunn. "Negroes and Discrimination in Colonial New Mexico: Don Pedro Bautista Pino's Startling Statements of 1812 in Perspective." *Phylon* 31 (1970): 372–78.
Hebert, Janis. "Oscar Mischeaux: A Black Pioneer." *South Dakota Review* 11 (Winter 1973): 62–69.
Henderson, Judy M. *African-American Music in Minnesota: From Spirituals to Rap*. St. Paul: Minnesota Historical Society Press, 1994.
Hess, Eldora Frances. "The Negro in Nebraska." Master's thesis, University of Nebraska, 1932.
Hickey, Joseph V. "'Pap' Singleton's Dunlap Colony Relief Agencies and the Failure of a Black Settlement in Eastern Kansas." *Great Plains Quarterly* 11.1 (Winter 1991): 23–36.
Hickman, Gerald. "Disfranchisement in Oklahoma: The Grandfather Clause of 1910–1916." Master's thesis, University of Tulsa, 1967.
Higgins, Billy D. "Negro Thought and the Exodus of 1879." *Phylon* 32 (Spring 1971): 39–52.
Hill, Mozell C. "A Comparative Study of Race Attitudes in the All-Negro Community in Oklahoma." *Phylon* 7 (1946): 260–68.
———. "The All-Negro Society in Oklahoma." Master's thesis, University of Chicago, 1946.
———. "The All-Negro Communities of Oklahoma: The Natural History of a Social Movement." *Journal of Negro History* 31 (1946): 254–68.
Hill, Mozell C., and Eugene Richards. "Demographic Trends of the Negro in Oklahoma." *The Southwestern Journal* 2 (Winter 1946): 47–63.
Hine, Darlene Clark. *Hine Sight: Black Women and the Re-Construction of American History*. Bloomington: Indiana University Press, 1994.

Hoffbeck, Steven R. "'Victories Yet To Win': Charles W. Scrutchin, Bemidji's Black Activist Attorney." *Minnesota History* 55 (Summer 1996): 59–75.

Hoffbeck, Steven R., ed. *Swinging for the Fences: Black Baseball in Minnesota*. St. Paul: Minnesota Historical Society Press, 2005.

Holmes, Reuben. "The Five Scalps." Edited by Stella M. Drumm. *Glimpses of the Past* 5 (January–March 1938): 3–54.

Hooker, Forrestine C. *Child of the Fighting Tenth: On the Frontier with the Buffalo Soldiers*. Edited by Steven Wilson. New York: Oxford University Press, 2003.

Horace, Lillian B. *Five Generations Hence*. N.c.: privately printed, 1916.

Hughes, Langston. *The Big Sea: An Autobiography*. 1940. New York: Hill and Wang, 1993.

———. *Not Without Laughter*. New York: Alfred A. Knopf, 1930.

Hulston, Nancy J. "'Our Schools Must Be Open to All Classes of Citizens': The Desegregation of the University of Kansas School of Medicine." *Kansas History* 19 (Summer, 1996): 88–97.

Humphrey, Charles Allen. "Socio-Economic Study of Six All-Black Towns in Oklahoma." Master's thesis, Oklahoma State University, 1974.

Jack, Tom. "The Omaha Gospel Complex in Historical Perspective." *Great Plains Quarterly* 20.3 (Summer 2000): 225–34.

Jackson, Nellie B. "Political and Economic History of the Negro in Indian Territory." Master's thesis, University of Oklahoma, 1960.

James, Parthena Louise. "Reconstruction in the Chickasaw Nation: The Freedmen Problem." *Chronicles of Oklahoma* 45 (1967): 44–57.

Jeltz, Wyatt F. "The Relations of Negroes and Choctaw and Chickasaw Indians." *Journal of Negro History* 33 (1948): 24–37.

Johnson, Michael K. *Black Masculinity and the Frontier Myth in American Literature*. Norman: University of Oklahoma Press, 2002.

———. "'This Strange White World': Race and Place in Era Bell Thompson's *American Daughter*." *Great Plains Quarterly* 24.2 (Spring 2004): 101–12.

———. "Migration, Masculinity, and Racial Identity in Taylor Gordon's *Born To Be*." In *Moving Stories: Migration and the American West, 1850–2000*. Edited by Scott E. Casper and Lucinda M. Long, 119–42. Reno: Nevada Humanities Committee, 2001.

Jones, Lila Lee. "The Ku Klux Klan in Eastern Kansas during the 1920's." *Emporia State Research Studies* 23 (Winter 1975): 5–41.

Jordan, Barbara, and Shelby Hearon. *Barbara Jordan: A Self-Portrait*. Garden City NY: Doubleday, 1979.

Kachel, Douglas. "Fort Des Moines and its African-American Troops in 1903/1904." *The Palimpsest* 74 (Spring, 1993): 42–48.

Katz, Milton S., and Susan B. Tucker. "A Pioneer in Civil Rights: Esther Brown and the South Park Desegregation Case of 1948." *Kansas History* 18 (Winter 1995/1996): 234–47.

Katz, William Loren. *The Black West: A Documentary and Pictorial History of the African American Role in the Westward Expansion of the United States*. Revised; New York: Simon and Schuster, 1996.

King, William M. *Going to Meet A Man: The Last Public Execution in Colorado*. Niwot CO: University Press of Colorado, 1989.

———. "Black Children, White Law: Black Efforts to Secure Public Education in Central City, Colorado, 1864–1869." *Essays and Monographs in Colorado History* 3 (1984): 55–79.

———. "The End of an Era: Denver's Last Legal Public Execution, July 27, 1886." *Journal of Negro History* 68 (1983): 37–53.

Kirschke, Amy Helene. *Aaron Douglas: Art, Race, and the Harlem Renaissance*. Jackson: University Press of Mississippi, 1995.

Klassen, Teresa C., and Owen V. Johnson. "Sharpening of the *Blade*: Black Consciousness in Kansas, 1892–97." *Journalism Quarterly* 63 (Summer 1986): 298–304.

Knight, Thomas. "Black Towns in Oklahoma: Their Development and Survival." Master's thesis, Oklahoma State University, 1975.

Kremer, Gary R. "For Justice and a Fee: James Milton Turner and the Cherokee Freedmen." *Chronicles of Oklahoma* 58 (1980–81): 376–91.

———. *James Milton Turner and the Promise of America: The Public Life of a Post-Civil War Black Leader*. Columbia: University of Missouri Press, 1991.

Lane, Ann J. *The Brownsville Affair: National Crisis and Black Reaction*. Port Washington NY: Kennikat, 1971.

Lang, William L. "The Nearly Forgotten Blacks on Last Chance Gulch, 1900–1912." *Pacific Northwest Quarterly* 70 (1979): 50–57.

———. "Tempest on Clore Street: Race and Politics in Helena, Montana, 1906." *Scratchgravel Hills* 3 (Summer 1980): 9–14.

Laurie, Clayton D. "The U.S. Army and the Omaha Riot of 1919." *Nebraska History* 72.3 (1991): 135–43.

Leckie, William H. *The Buffalo Soldiers: A Narrative of the Negro Cavalry in the West*. Norman: University of Oklahoma Press, 1967.

Leiker, James N. *Racial Borders: Black Soldiers Along the Rio Grande*. College Station: Texas A&M University Press, 2002.

Leiker, James N. "The Buffalo Soldiers at Fort Hays." Master's thesis, Fort Hays State College, 1992.

Leiker, James N. "Black Soldiers at Fort Hays, Kansas, 1867–1869: A Study in Civilian and Military Violence." *Great Plains Quarterly* 17.1 (Winter 1997): 3–17.

LeSure, Lessie Lois Fowler. "Willa A. Strong: An Historical Study of Black Education in Southeastern Oklahoma." PhD dissertation, University of Oklahoma, 1982.

Lewallen, Kenneth A. "Chief Alfred C. Sam: Black Nationalism on the Great Plains, 1913–1914." *Journal of the West* 16 (January 1977): 49–56.

Libman, Gary. "Minnesota and the Struggle for Black Suffrage, 1849–1870." PhD dissertation, University of Minnesota, 1972.

Littlefield, Daniel F., Jr. *The Cherokee Freedmen: From Emancipation to American Citizenship*. Westport: Greenwood Press, 1978.

———. *The Chickasaw Freedmen: A People Without a Country*. Westport CT: Greenwood Press, 1980.

Littlefield, Daniel F., Jr., and Lonnie E. Underhill. "The Crazy Snake Uprising of 1909: A Red, Black or White Affair?" *Arizona and the West* 20 (Winter 1978): 307–24.

———, "Black Dreams and 'Free' Homes: The Oklahoma Territory, 1891–1894." *Phylon* 34 (1973): 342–57.

———. "Negro Marshalls in the Indian Territory." *Journal of Negro History* 56 (1971): 77–87.

———. "Slave 'Revolt' in the Cherokee Nation, 1842." *American Indian Quarterly* 3 (Summer 1977): 121–23.

Littlefield, Mary Ann, and Daniel F. Littlefield. "The Beams Family: Free Blacks in Indian Territory." *Journal of Negro History* 41 (1976): 17–35.

Long, George. "How Albuquerque Got Its Civil Rights Ordinance." *The Crisis* 60 (November 1953): 521–24.

Love, Nat. *The Life and Adventures of Nat Love, Better Known in the Cattle Country as "Deadwood Dick"*. Reprint; New York: Arno Press, 1968.

Lufkin, Jack. "Patten's Neighborhood: The Center Street Community and the African-American Printer Who Preserved It." *Iowa Heritage Illustrated* 77 (Fall 1996): 122–44.

Luper, Clara. *Behold the Walls*. Oklahoma City: Jim Wire, 1979.

Lyles, Lionel Dean. "An Historical-Urban Geographical Analysis of Black Neighborhood Development in Denver, 1860–1970." PhD dissertation, University of Colorado, 1977.

MacMahon, David R. "The Origins of the NAACP in Omaha and Lincoln, Nebraska, 1913–1926." Master's thesis, Creighton University, 1993.

McDaniel, Orval L. "A History of Nicodemus, Graham County, Kansas." Master's thesis, Kansas State College, Fort Hays, 1950.

McDonald, Dedra S. "To Be Black and Female in the Spanish Southwest: Toward a History of African Women on New Spain's Far Northern Frontier." In *African American Women Confront the West, 1600–2000*. Edited by Quintard Taylor and Shirley Ann Wilson Moore, 32–52. Norman: University of Oklahoma Press, 2003.

McGue, D. B. "John Taylor—Slave-Born Colorado Pioneer." *Colorado Magazine* 18 (1941): 161–68.

McKanna, Clare V., Jr. *Homicide, Race, and Justice in the American West, 1880–1920*. Tucson: University of Arizona Press, 1997.

McKanna, Jr., Clare V. "Black Enclaves of Violence: Race and Homicide in Great Plains Cities, 1890–1920." *Great Plains Quarterly* 23.3 (Summer 2003): 147–60.

———. "Seeds of Destruction: Homicide, Race, and Justice in Omaha, 1880–1920." *Journal of Ethnic History* 14.1 (Fall 1994): 65–90.

McKusker, Kristine. "'The Forgotten Years' of America's Civil Rights Movement: The University of Kansas, 1939–1961." Master's thesis, University of Kansas, 1994.

———. "'The Forgotten Years' of America's Civil Rights Movement: Wartime Protests at the University of Kansas, 1939–1945." *Kansas History* 17 (Spring 1994): 26–37.

McMillen, Christian. "Border State Terror and the Genesis of the African American Community in Deer Lodge and Chouteau Counties, Montana, 1870–1890." *Journal of Negro History* 79 (Spring, 1994): 212–14.

Marshall, Marguerite Mitchell. *An Account of Afro-Americans in Southeast Kansas, 1884–1984*. Manhattan KS: Sunflower University Press, 1986.

Massey, Sara R., ed. *Black Cowboys of Texas*. College Station: Texas A&M University Press, 2000.
Masters, Isabell. "The Life and Legacy of Oliver Brown, the First Listed Plaintiff of Brown vs. Board of Education, Topeka, Kansas." PhD dissertation, University of Oklahoma, 1980.
Menard, Orville D. "Tom Dennison, The Omaha Bee, and the 1919 Omaha Race Riot." *Nebraska History* 68 (Winter 1987): 152–65.
Meredith, Howard L. "Agrarian Socialism and the Negro in Oklahoma, 1900–1918." *Labor History* 11 (1970): 277–84.
Mihelich, Dennis N. "A Socioeconomic Portrait of Prince Hall Masonry in Nebraska, 1900–1920." *Great Plains Quarterly* 17.1 (Winter 1997): 35–48.
———. "The Formation of the Lincoln Urban League." *Nebraska History* 68 (Summer, 1987): 63–73.
———. "The Lincoln Urban League: The Travail of Depression and War." *Nebraska History* 70 (Winter, 1989): 303–16.
———. "The Origins of the Prince Hall Mason Grand Lodge of Nebraska." *Nebraska History* 76.1 (Spring 1996): 10–21.
———. "World War II and the Transformation of the Omaha Urban League." *Nebraska History* 60 (Fall, 1979): 401–23.
Mihelich, Dennis N., and Ashton Wesley Welch. "Omaha, Nebraska: Positive Planning for a Peaceful Desegregation." In *Community Politics and Educational Change*, edited by Charles V. Willie and Susan L. Greenblatt. New York: Longman, 1981.
Miller, Timothy. "Charles M. Sheldon and the Uplift of Tennesseetown." *Kansas History* 9 (Autumn 1986): 125–37.
Mitchell, Frank S. "The Development of Facilities for the Education of Negroes in Kansas, 1860–1950." Master's thesis, Northeast Missouri State, 1956.
Mock, Charlotte. *Bridges: New Mexican Black Women, 1900–1950*. Albuquerque: New Mexico Commission on the Study of Women, 1985.
Monhollon, Rusty L. "'Away From the Dream': The Roots of Black Power in Lawrence, Kansas, 1960–1970." PhD dissertation, University of Kansas, 1994.
Moore, Deedee. "Is There Anything Gordon Parks Can't Do?" *Smithsonian* 20 (April 1989): 147–64.
Moore, Jesse T., Jr. "Seeking a New Life: Blacks in Post-Civil War Colorado." *Journal of Negro History* 78 (1993): 166–87.

Morrison, Michael A. *Slavery and the American West: The Eclipse of Manifest Destiny and the Coming of the Civil War*. Chapel Hill: University of North Carolina Press, 1997.

Moten, Rashley B., Jr. "The Negro Press of Kansas." Master's thesis, University of Kansas, 1938.

Mothershead, Harmon. "Negro Rights in the Colorado Territory." *Colorado Magazine* 40 (1963): 212–23.

Murray, Robert A. "The United States Army in the Aftermath of the Johnson County Invasion: April through November 1892." *Annals of Wyoming* 38 (April 1966): 59–75.

Myers, Rex C. "Montana's Negro Newspapers, 1894–1911." *Montana Journalism Review* 16 (1973): 17–22.

Nash, Horace D. "Blacks on the Border: Columbus, New Mexico, 1916–1922." Master's thesis, New Mexico State University, 1988.

———. "Town and Sword: Black Soldiers in Columbus, New Mexico in the Early Twentieth Century." PhD dissertation, Mississippi State University, 1996.

———. "Community Building on the Border: The Role of the 24th Infantry Band at Columbus, New Mexico, 1916–1922." *Fort Concho and the South Plains Journal* 22 (Summer, 1990): 77–89.

Neilson, John C. "Indian Masters, Black Slaves: An Oral History of the Civil War in Indian Territory." *Panhandle-Plains Historical Review* 65 (1992): 42–54.

Nelson, Paul D. *Fredrick L. McGhee: A Life on the Color Line, 1861–1912*. St. Paul: Minnesota Historical Society Press, 2002.

Newgard, Thomas P., and William C. Sherman. *African-Americans in North Dakota: Sources and Assessments*. Bismarck: University of Mary Press, 1994.

Norris, Melvin Edward, Jr. "Dearfield, Colorado—The Evolution of a Rural Black Settlement: An Historical Geography of Black Colonization on the Great Plains." PhD dissertation, University of Colorado, 1980.

O'Brien, Claire. "'With One Mighty Pull': Interracial Town Boosting in Nicodemus, Kansas." *Great Plains Quarterly* 16 (Spring 1996): 117–29.

O'Brien, Patrick G. "'I Want Everyone to Know the Shame of the State': Henry J. Allen Confronts the Ku Klux Klan, 1921–1923." *Kansas History* 19 (1996): 98–111.

O'Connor, Patrick J. "The Black Experience and the Blues in 1950s Wichita." *Mid-America Folklore* 21 (Spring 1993): 1–17.

Painter, Nell Irvin. *Exodusters: Black Migration to Kansas after Reconstruction.* New York: Alfred A. Knopf, 1977.

———. "Millenarian Aspects of the Exodus to Kansas." *Journal of Social History* 19 (1976): 331–39.

Pantle, Alberta, ed. "The Story of a Kansas Freedman." *Kansas Historical Quarterly* 11 (1942): 341–69.

Parkhill, Forbes. *Mister Barney Ford: A Portrait in Bistre.* Denver: Sage Books, 1963.

Patterson, Zella I. Black. *Langston University: A History.* Norman: University of Oklahoma Press, 1979.

Paynter, John H. "Joseph D. Rivers." *Journal of Negro History* 22 (1937): 289–91.

Paz, D. G. "John Albert Williams and Black Journalism in Omaha, 1895–1929." *Midwest Review* 10 (1988): 14–32.

Pelzer, Louis. "The Negro and Slavery in Early Iowa." *Iowa Journal of History and Politics* (1904): 471–84.

Peoples, Morgan Dewey. "Kansas Fever in North Louisiana." *Louisiana History* 11 (Spring 1970): 121–35.

———. "Negro Migration from the Lower Mississippi Valley to Kansas, 1879–1880." Master's thesis, Louisiana State University, 1950.

Perdue, Theda. *Slavery and the Evolution of Cherokee Society, 1540–1866.* Knoxville: University of Tennessee Press, 1979.

———. "Cherokee Planters, Black Slaves, and African Colonization." *Chronicles of Oklahoma* 60 (1982): 322–31.

Perry, Thelma. "The Education of Negroes in Oklahoma." *Journal of Negro Education* 16 (Winter 1947): 397–404.

Pew, Thomas W., Jr. "Boley, Oklahoma: Trial in American Apartheid." *American West* 17 (November-December, 1980): 14–21, 54–56, 63.

Phillips, Edward Hake. "The Sherman Courthouse Riot of 1930." *East Texas Historical Journal* 25.2 (1987): 12–19.

Phillips, Thomas D. "The Black Regulars." In *The West of the American People*, edited by Allan G. Bogue, Thomas D. Phillips, and James E. Wright, 138–43. Itasca IL: F. E. Peacock Publishers, 1970.

———. "The Black Regulars: Negro Soldiers in the United States Army, 1866–1891." PhD dissertation, University of Wisconsin, 1970.

Picher, Margaret. "Dearfield, Colorado: A Story from the Black West." Master's thesis, University of Denver, 1976.

Polk, Donna Mays. *Black Men and Women of Nebraska*. Lincoln: Nebraska Black History Preservation Society, 1981.

Porter, Kenneth Wiggins. "Micheaux, Oscar." In *Dictionary of American Negro Biography*, edited by Rayford W. Logan and Michael R. Winston, 433–34. New York: W. W. Norton, 1982.

———. "Negroes and the Fur Trade." *Minnesota History* 15 (1934): 421–33.

———. *The Negro on the American Frontier*. New York: Arno Press, 1971.

———. "The Seminole-Negro Indian Scouts, 1870–1881." *Southwestern Historical Quarterly* 55 (1952): 358–77.

———. "The Seminole Negro Indian Scouts, Texas, 1870–1914." *The Black Seminoles: History of a Freedom-Seeking People*. Edited by Alcione M. Amos and Thomas P. Senter. Gainesville FL: University Press of Florida (1996): 173–214.

———. "Negroes and Indians on the Texas Frontier, 1834–1874." *Southwestern Historical Quarterly* 53 (October, 1949): 151–63.

———. "Negroes and Indians on the Texas Frontier, 1831–1876." *Journal of Negro History* 41 (July, 1956): 185–214; 41 (October, 1956): 285–310.

Quantic, Diane Dufva. "Black Authors in Kansas." *Kansas English* 55 (December 1969): 14–16.

Ragar, Cheryl R. "Harlem Renaissance in the United States—Kansas and the Plains States." In *Encyclopedia of the Harlem Renaissance*, edited by Cary D. Wintz and Paul Finkelman, 512–14. New York: Routledge, 2004.

Rampp, Lary C. "Negro Troop Activity in Indian Territory, 1863–1865." *Chronicles of Oklahoma* 47 (Spring, 1969): 531–59.

Ravage, Jack. *Singletree: A Novel*. Laramie: Jelm Mountain Publishing, 1990.

Ravage, John W. *Black Pioneers: Images of the Black Experience on the North American Frontier*. Salt Lake City: University of Utah Press, 1997.

Rawley, James A. *Race and Politics: "Bleeding Kansas" and the Coming of the Civil War*. Philadelphia: J. B. Lippincott, 1969.

Reed, Cecil A., and Priscilla Donovan. *Fly in the Buttermilk: The Life Story of Cecil Reed*. Iowa City: University of Iowa Press, 1993.

Reese, Linda Williams. "Race, Class, and Culture: Oklahoma Women, 1890–1920." PhD dissertation, University of Oklahoma, 1991.

———. "'Working In the Vineyard': African-American Women In All-Black Communities." *Kansas Quarterly.* 25 (1994): 7–16.

Rice, Marc. "Frompin' in the Great Plains: Listening and Dancing to the Jazz Orchestras of Alphonso Trent, 1925–44." *Great Plains Quarterly* 16.2 (Spring 1996): 107–15.

Richards, Eugene S. "Trends of Negro Life in Oklahoma as Reflected by Census Reports." *Journal of Negro History* 33 (1948): 38–52.

———. "Negro Higher Education and Professional Education in Oklahoma." *Journal of Negro Education* 17 (Winter 1948): 341–49.

Richardson, Barbara J. *Black Pioneers in New Mexico: A Documentary and Pictorial History.* Rio Rancho NM: Panorama Press, 1976.

Riley, Carroll L. "Blacks in the Early Southwest." *Ethnohistory* 19 (1972): 247–60.

Riley, Glenda. "American Daughters: Black Women in the West." *Montana: The Magazine of Western History* 38 (Spring 1988): 14–27.

Riley, Peggy. "Women of the Great Falls African Methodist Episcopal Church, 1870–1910." In *African American Women Confront the West, 1600–2000.* Edited by Quintard Taylor and Shirley Ann Wilson Moore, 122–139. Norman: University of Oklahoma Press, 2003.

Robbins, Louise S. "Racism and Censorship in Cold War Oklahoma: The Case of Ruth W. Brown and the Bartlesville Public Library." *Southwestern Historical Quarterly* 100 (July 1996): 19–46.

Roberson, Jere W. "Edward P. McCabe and the Langston Experiment." *Chronicles of Oklahoma* 51 (1973): 343–55.

Roberts, Randy. "Heavyweight Champion Jack Johnson: His Omaha Image, A Public Relations Study." *Nebraska History* 57.2 (1976): 226–41.

Rodman, Rosamond C. "Naming a Place Nicodemus." *Great Plains Quarterly* 28 (Winter 2008): 49–62.

Roethler, Michael D. "Negro Slavery Among the Cherokee Indians, 1540–1866." PhD dissertation, Fordham University, 1964.

Rogers, Mary Beth. *Barbara Jordan: American Hero.* New York: Bantam Books, 1998.

Rose, Harold M. "The All-Negro Town: Its Evolution and Function." *Geographical Review* 55 (1965): 362–81.

Russell, Ross. *Jazz Style in Kansas City and the Southwest.* Berkeley: University of California Press, 1968.

Sanford, Jay. "African-American Baseballists and the Denver Post Tournament." *Colorado Heritage* (Spring 1995): 20–34.

Savage, W. Sherman. *Blacks in the West, 1830–1890*. Westport CT: Greenwood Press, 1976.

Saxe, Allan A. "Protest and Reform: The Desegregation of Oklahoma City." PhD dissertation, University of Oklahoma, 1969.

Schubert, Frank N. *Buffalo Soldiers, Braves, and the Brass*. Shippensburg PA: White Mane Publishing Company, 1993.

———. "The Black Regular Army Regiments in Wyoming, 1885–1912." Master's thesis, University of Wyoming, 1970.

———. "Black Soldiers On the White Frontier: Some Factors Influencing Race Relations." *Phylon* 32 (1971): 410–15.

———. "The Suggs Affray: The Black Cavalry in the Johnson County War." *Western Historical Quarterly* 4 (1973): 57–68.

———. "The Fort Robinson Y.M.C.A., 1902–1907: A Social Organization in a Black Regiment." *Nebraska History* 55 (Summer 1974): 165–79.

———. "The Violent World of Emanuel Stance, Fort Robinson, 1887." *Nebraska History* 55 (Summer 1974): 203–19.

———. "Troopers, Taverns, and Taxes: Fort Robinson, NE, and Its Municipal Parasite, 1886–1911." *Soldiers and Civilians: The U.S. Army and the American People*. Edited by Garry D. Ryan and Timothy K. Nenninger, 91–103. Washington DC: National Archives and Records Administration, 1987.

———. "Ten Troopers: Buffalo Soldier Medal of Honor Men Who Served at Fort Robinson." *Nebraska History* 78.4 (1997): 151–57.

Schultz, Elizabeth. "Dreams Deferred: The Personal Narratives of Four Black Kansans." *American Studies* 34 (Fall 1993): 25–51.

Schulz, Harry Richard. "Brown v. Topeka: A Legacy of Courage and Struggle." Doc. diss., Ball State University, 1971.

Schwendemann, Glen. "Negro Exodus to Kansas: First Phase, March–July, 1879." Master's thesis, University of Oklahoma, 1957.

———. "Nicodemus: Negro Haven on the Solomon." *Kansas Historical Quarterly* 34 (1968): 10–31.

———. "Wyandotte and the First 'Exodusters' of 1879." *Kansas Historical Quarterly* 26 (1960): 233–49.

———. "The 'Exodusters' on the Missouri." *Kansas Historical Quarterly* 29 (1963): 25–40.

———. "St. Louis and the 'Exodusters' of 1879." *Journal of Negro History* 46 (January 1961): 32–46.
Scott, Mark. "Langston Hughes of Kansas." *Kansas History* 3 (Spring 1980): 3–25.
Scrimsher, Lila Gravatt, ed. "The Diaries and Writings of George A. Matson, Black Citizen of Lincoln, Nebraska, 1901–1913." *Nebraska History* 52.2 (1971): 133–68.
Seraile, William. "Fort Missoula, 1891–1898." *Voice of Dissent: Theophilus Gould Steward (1843–1924) and Black America*. Brooklyn: Carlson Publishing, 1991.
Sharp, Wanda F. "*The Black Dispatch*: A Sociological Analysis." Master's thesis, University of Oklahoma, 1951.
Shaw, Van B. "Nicodemus, Kansas: A Study in Isolation." PhD dissertation, University of Missouri, 1951.
Shepard, R. Bruce. *Deemed Unsuitable: Blacks from Oklahoma Move to Canadian Prairies*. N.c.: Umbrella Press, 1995.
———. "Diplomatic Racism: Canadian Government and Black Migration from Oklahoma, 1905–1912." *Great Plains Quarterly* 3.1 (Winter 1983): 5–16.
———. "Black Migration as a Response to Repression: The Background Factors and Migration of Oklahoma Blacks to Western Canada, 1905–1912, As A Case Study." Master's thesis, University of Saskatchewan, 1976.
Sheridan, Richard B. "From Slavery in Missouri to Freedom in Kansas: The Influx of Black Fugitives and Contrabands into Kansas, 1854–1865." *Kansas History* 12 (1989): 28–47.
Silag, Bill, Susan Koch-Bridgford, and Hal Chase, eds. *Outside In: African-American History in Iowa, 1818–2000*. Des Moines: State Historical Society of Iowa, 2001.
Sloan, Charles William, Jr. "Kansas Battles the Invisible Empire: The Legal Ouster of the KKK from Kansas, 1922–1927." *Kansas Historical Quarterly*, 40 (1974): 393–409.
Smallwood, James M. *Time of Hope, Time of Despair: Black Texas during Reconstruction*. Port Washington NY: Kennikat Press, 1981.
———. *The Struggle for Equality: Blacks in Texas*. Boston: American Press, 1983.
———. *A Century of Achievement: Blacks in Cooke County, Texas*. Gainesville TX: Gainesville American Revolution Bicentennial Committee, 1975.

Smith, Leland. "Early Negroes in Kansas." Master's thesis, Wichita State University, 1932.

Smith, Thaddeus. "Western University: A Ghost College in Kansas." Master's thesis, Pittsburg State College, 1966.

Smurr, J. W. "Jim Crow Out West." *Historical Essays on Montana and the Northwest*. Edited by J. W. Smurr and J. Ross Toole, 149–203. Helena: Western Press, 1957.

Spangler, Earl. *The Negro in Minnesota*. Minneapolis: T. S. Denison and Company, 1961.

Spann, Dorothy Bass. *Black Pioneers: A History of a Pioneer Family in Colorado Springs*. Colorado Springs: Little London Press, 1978.

Spivey, Donald. "Crisis on a Black Campus: Langston University and Its Struggle for Survival." *Chronicles of Oklahoma* 59 (Winter 1981–82): 430–47.

Stephens, Louise C. "The Urban League of Oklahoma City, Oklahoma." Master's thesis, University of Oklahoma, 1957.

Stone, Robert B. "The Legislative Struggle for Civil Rights in Iowa, 1947–1965." Master's thesis, Iowa State University, 1990.

Strickland, Arvarh E. "Toward the Promised Land: The Exodus to Kansas and Afterward." *Missouri Historical Review* 69 (1975): 376–412.

Strong, Evelyn Richardson. "Historical Development of the Oklahoma Association of Negro Teachers: A Study in Social Change, 1893–1958." Master's thesis, University of Oklahoma, 1961.

Strong, Willa A. "The Origin, Development, and Current Status of the Oklahoma Federation of Colored Women's Clubs." Master's thesis, University of Oklahoma, 1957.

Suggs, Henry Lewis, editor. *The Black Press in the Middle West, 1865–1985*. Westport CT: Greenwood Press, 1996.

Sullenger, T. Earl, and J. Harvey Kerns. *The Negro in Omaha: A Social Study of Negro Development*. Omaha: Municipal University of Omaha and Omaha Urban League, 1931.

Sunseri, Alvin R. "A Note On Slavery and the Black Man in New Mexico, 1846–1861." *Negro History Bulletin* 38 (1975): 457–59.

Suzuki, Peter T. "The Denouement of an Institution in a Black Urban Community: The Jitney Taxicabs of Omaha, Nebraska." *International Bulletin of Urgent Anthropological and Ethnological Research* 23 (1981).

———. "Omaha's Black Vernacular-Cab Driver and His Fare: Facets of a Symbiotic Relationship." *Western Journal of Black Studies* 15 (Summer 1991).

Taylor, David Vassar. *African Americans in Minnesota*. St. Paul: Minnesota Historical Society Press, 2002.

———. *Blacks in Minnesota: A Preliminary Guide to Historical Sources*. St. Paul: Minnesota Historical Society, 1976.

———. "Pilgrim's Progress: Black St. Paul and the Making of an Urban Ghetto, 1870–1930." PhD dissertation, University of Minnesota, 1977.

———. "The Blacks." *They Chose Minnesota: A Survey of the State's Ethnic Groups*. Edited by June Drenning Holmquist, 73–91. St. Paul: Minnesota Historical Society Press, 1981.

———. "The Black Community in the Twin Cities." *Roots* 17 (Fall 1988): 3–22.

———. "John Quincy Adams: St. Paul Editor and Black Leader." *Minnesota History* 43 (Winter 1973): 282–96.

Taylor, Quintard. *In Search of the Racial Frontier: African Americans in the American West, 1528–1990*. New York: W. W. Norton, 1998.

Taylor, Quintard, and Shirley Ann Wilson Moore, eds. *African American Women Confront the West, 1600–2000*. Norman: University of Oklahoma Press, 2003.

Teall, Kaye M., ed. *Black History in Oklahoma: A Resource Book*. Oklahoma City: Oklahoma City Public Schools, 1971.

Terrell, John Upton. *Estevanico the Black*. Los Angeles: Westernlore Press, 1969.

Theisen, Lee Scott, ed. "The Fight in Lincoln, N.M., 1878: The Testimony of Two Negro Participants." *Arizona and the West* 12 (Summer 1970): 173–98.

Thomas, Chleyon Decatur. "Boley: An All-Black Pioneer Town and the Educatiuon of Its Children." PhD dissertation, University of Akron, 1989.

Thompson, Audrey. "Great Plains Pragmatist: Aaron Douglas and the Art of Social Protest." *Great Plains Quarterly* 20.4 (Fall 2000): 311–22.

Thompson, Era Bell. *American Daughter*. 1946; St. Paul: Minnesota Historical Society, 1986.

Thompson, Lucille S., and Alma S. Jacobs. *The Negro in Montana, 1800–1945: A Selective Bibliography*. Helena: Montana State Library, 1970.

Tidwell, John Edgar. "Frank Marshall Davis, 'Ad Astra, Per Aspera'." *Kansas History* 18 (Winter 1995/1996): 270–83.

Tillman, Katherine Davis Chapman. *The Works of Katherine Davis Chapman Tillman*. Edited by Claudia Tate. New York: Oxford University Press, 1991.

Tjarks, Alicia V. "Demographic, Ethnic, and Occupational Structure of New Mexico, 1790." *Americas: A Quarterly Review of Inter-American Cultural History* 35 (1978): 45–88.

Tolson, Arthur L. "The Negro in Oklahoma Territory, 1889–1907: A Study In Racial Discrimination." PhD dissertation, University of Oklahoma, 1966.

———. *The Black Oklahomans: A History, 1541–1972*. New Orleans: Edwards Printing, 1973.

———. "A History of Langston, Oklahoma, 1890–1950." Master's thesis, Oklahoma State University, 1953.

Troper, Harold M. "The Creek-Negroes of Oklahoma and Canadian Immigration, 1909–11." *Canadian Historical Review* 53 (September 1972): 272–88.

Tuttle, William M., Jr., and Surenda Bhana. "Black Newspapers in Kansas." *American Studies* 13 (1972): 44–56.

Truxton, Virginia. "1918–1921: The All-Black Town Phenomenon Re-Visited at a Critical Juncture in its Evolution and Reconstruction of African-American Urban Historical Geography." Master's thesis, University of California, Berkeley, 1989.

Van Delinder, Jean. *Struggles Before Brown: Early Civil Rights Protests and Their Significance Today*. Boulder CO: Paradigm Publishers, 2007.

———. "Early Civil Rights Activism in Topeka, Kansas, Prior to the 1954 Brown Case." *Great Plains Quarterly* 21.1 (Winter 2001): 45–61.

Van Deusen, John. "The Exodus of 1879." *Journal of Negro History* 21 (1936): 111–29.

Vandever, Elizabeth J. "Brown v. Board of Education of Topeka: Anatomy of a Decision." PhD dissertation, University of Kansas, 1971.

Vanepps-Taylor, Betti Carol. *Forgotten Lives: African Americans in South Dakota*. Pierre: South Dakota State Historical Society, 2008.

Van Meter, Sondra. "Black Resistance to Segregation in the Wichita Public Schools, 1870–1912." *Midwest Quarterly* 20 (Autumn 1978): 64–77.

Waddell, Karen. "Dearfield . . . A Dream Deferred." *Colorado Heritage* (1988): 2–12.

Walcott, Rinaldo. *Black Like Who? Writing Black Canada*. Second revised edition. Toronto: Insomniac Press, 2003.

Waldron, Nell Blythe. "Colonization in Kansas from 1861 to 1890." PhD dissertation, Northwestern University, 1925.

Walters, Ronald. "The 'First' Civil Rights Sit-In." *American Visions* 8.1 (February 1993): 20–23.

———. "The Great Plains Sit-In Movement, 1958–1960." *Great Plains Quarterly* 16.2 (Spring 1996): 85–94.

Warren, Hanna R. "Reconstruction in the Cherokee Nation." *Chronicles of Oklahoma* 45 (1967): 180–89.

Wascow, Arthur I. *From Race Riot to Sit-In: 1919 and the 1960s*, 1–11, 105–120. Garden City NY: Doubleday, 1966.

Wax, Darold D. "Robert Ball Anderson, Ex-Slave, A Pioneer in Western Nebraska, 1884–1930." *Nebraska History* 64 (Summer 1983): 163–92.

———. "The Odyssey of an Ex-Slave: Robert Ball Anderson's Pursuit of the American Dream." *Phylon* 45 (Spring 1984): 67–79.

Wayne, George H. "Negro Migration and Colonization in Colorado, 1870–1930." *Journal of the West* 15 (1976): 102–20.

Weaver, John D. *The Brownsville Raid*. New York: W. W. Norton, 1970.

Werner, Brian R. "Colorado's Pioneer Blacks: Migration, Occupations and Race Relations in the Centennial State." Master's thesis, University of Northern Colorado, 1979.

Weston, Jeanette. "In Search of Parity: Coverage of News Events Portraying Blacks in the *Omaha World-Herald* from 1953 to 1988." Master's thesis, University of Nebraska at Omaha, 1993.

Whitson, Edward. "Selected Characteristics of Negro Housing in Oklahoma, 1950." Unpublished Master's thesis, University of Oklahoma, 1957.

Whittlesey, Lee. "A Brief History of Black Americans in the Yellowstone National Park Area, 1872–1907." *Annals of Wyoming* 69 (Fall 1977).

Wickett, Murray R. *Contested Territory: Whites, Native Americans and African Americans in Oklahoma, 1865–1907*. Baton Rouge: Louisiana State University Press, 2000.

Wiggins, Bernice Love. *Tuneful Tales*. Edited by Maceo C. Dailey, Jr. and Ruthe Winegarten. 1925; Lubbock: Texas Tech University Press, 2002.

Wiley, Ben Wayne. "Ebonyville in the South and Southwest: Political Life in the All-Black Town." PhD dissertation, University of Texas, Arlington, 1984.

Williams, Corinne Hare. "The Migration of Negroes to the West, 1877–1900, with Special Reference to Kansas." Master's thesis, Howard University, 1944.

Williams, Murphy Cleophas. "An Ecological Study of the Negroes in Ward Seven." Master's thesis, Municipal University of Omaha, 1947.

Williams, Nudie E. "The African Lion: George Napier Perkins, Lawyer, Politician, Editor." *Chronicles of Oklahoma* 70 (1992–93): 450–65.

———. "Bass Reeves: Lawman in the Western Ozarks." *Negro History Bulletin* 42 (1979): 37–39.

———. "Black Men Who Wore the 'Star.'" *Chronicles of Oklahoma* 59 (1981): 83–90.

———. "Black Men Who Wore White Hats: Grant Johnson, United States Deputy Marshall." *Red River Valley Historical Review* 5.3 (1980): 4–13.

———. "Black Newspapers and the Exodusters." Master's thesis, Oklahoma State University, 1977.

———. "Black Newspapers and the Exodusters of 1879." *Kansas History* 8 (1985–6): 217–25.

———. "United States vs. Bass Reeves: Black Lawman on Trial." *Chronicles of Oklahoma* 68 (1990): 154–67.

Willson, Walt. "Freedmen in Indian Territory During Reconstruction." *Chronicles of Oklahoma* 49 (1971): 230–44.

Wilson, Elinor. *"Jim Beckwourth: Black Mountain Man and War Chief of the Crows*. Norman: University of Oklahoma Press, 1972.

Wilson, Noel. *"The Kansas City Call*: An Inside View of the Negro Market." PhD dissertation, University of Illinois, 1968.

Wilson, Raymond. "Another White Hope Bites the Dust: The Jack Johnson-Jim Flynn Heavyweight Fight in 1912." *Montana: The Magazine of Western History* 29 (Winter 1999): 30–39.

Winegarten, Ruthe. *Black Texas Women: 150 Years of Trial and Triumph*. Austin: University of Texas Press, 1994.

———. *Black Texas Women: A Sourcebook: Documents, Biographies, Time Line*. Austin: University of Texas Press, 1996.

Winks, Robin W. *The Blacks in Canada*. New Haven: Yale University Press, 1971.

Wintz, Cary D. "Langston Hughes: A Kansas Poet in the Harlem Renaissance." *Kansas Quarterly* 8 (Spring 1976): 58–71.
Wood, Roger, and James Fraher. *Down in Houston: Bayou City Blues*. Austin: University of Texas Press, 2003.
Woods, Randall Bennett. *A Black Odyssey: John Lewis Waller and the Promise of American Life, 1878–1900*. Lawrence: University Press of Kansas, 1981.
———. "After the Exodus: John Lewis Waller and the Black Elite, 1878–1900." *Kansas Historical Quarterly* 43 (1977): 172–92.
———. "Integration, Exclusion, or Segregation? The 'Color Line' in Kansas, 1878–1900." *Western Historical Quarterly* 14 (1983): 181–98.
———. "The Black American Press and the New Manifest Destiny: the Waller Affair." *Phylon* 38 (1977): 24–34.
———. "C. H. J. Taylor and the Movement for Black Political Independence, 1882–1896." *Journal of Negro History* 67 (1982): 122–35.
Woods, Randall Bennett, and David A. Sloan. "Kansas Quakers and the 'Great Exodus': Conflicting Perceptions of Responsibility within a Nineteenth Century Reform Community." *The Historian* 48 (November 1985): 24–40.
Woolfolk, George R. "Turner's Safety Valve and Free Negro Westward Migration." *Journal of Negro History* 50 (1965): 185–97.
Wright, Richard R. "Negro Companions of the Spanish Explorers." *American Anthropologist* 4 (1902): 217–28.
Wyman, Walker D., and John D. Hart. "The Legend of Charlie Glass." *Colorado Magazine* 46 (1969): 40–54.
Yerby, Frank. *Western: A Saga of the Great Plains*. New York: Dial Press, 1982.
Young, Brian A. "The History of the Black in New Mexico from the Sixteenth Century through the Nineteenth Century Pioneer Period." Master's thesis, University of New Mexico, 1969.
Young, Joseph A. "Oscar Micheaux's Novels: Black Apologies for White Oppression." PhD dissertation, University of Nebraska, 1984.
Young, Mary E. "Anita Scott Coleman: A Neglected Harlem Renaissance Writer." *CLA Journal* 40 (March 1997): 271–87.
Zavelo, Donald. "The Black Entrepreneur in Lawrence, Kansas, 1900–1915." Master's thesis, University of Kansas, 1975.
Zollo, Richard P. "General Francis P. Dodge and His Brave Black Soldiers [1879, Wyoming]." *Essex Institute Historical Collection* 122 (July, 1986): 181–206.

CONTRIBUTORS

SHAWN LEIGH ALEXANDER, who received his PhD at the University of Massachusetts–Amherst in 2004, is an assistant professor of African and African American Studies at the University of Kansas. His area of concentration is African American social and intellectual history of the nineteenth and twentieth centuries. Alexander recently published an anthology of T. Thomas Fortune's writings entitled *T. Thomas Fortune, the Afro-American Agitator*. He has also published work on early African American civil rights activity in the *Great Plains Quarterly* and other works. Currently, he is completing a monograph on civil rights activity in the post-Reconstruction era.

CHARLES A. "CHUCK" BRAITHWAITE received his master's and doctoral degrees from the University of Washington and has served as editor of the *Great Plains Quarterly* since 2000. A specialist in intercultural communication, Braithwaite has a particular interest in Native American higher education; his publications include *Sa'ah Naagháí Bik'eh Hózhóón: An Ethnography of Navajo Educational Communication Practices*, and he is currently coediting a book, *Communicating Indianness*, forthcoming from the University of Oklahoma Press.

RICHARD M. BREAUX is an assistant professor of Black Studies and History at the University of Nebraska at Omaha. He is currently working on a book manuscript titled "'These Institutions Belong to the People': New Negro College Students in America's Heartland, 1900–1940."

THOMAS R. BUECKER is the curator of the Nebraska State Historical Society's Fort Robinson Museum. He has published numerous articles and pamphlets on Nebraska history, authored *Fort Robinson and the American Century, 1900–1948* and *Fort Robinson and the American West, 1874–1899*, and is coeditor, with R. Eli Paul, of *The Crazy Horse Surrender Ledger.*

BRUCE A. GLASRUD is Professor Emeritus of history, California State University, East Bay (Hayward) and retired Dean of the School of Arts and Sciences at Sul Ross State University (Alpine, Texas). He received his PhD in history from Texas Tech University—one of the early products of the "Texas Tech School of Black History." A specialist in the history of blacks in the West, Glasrud has published thirteen books and more than sixty articles in scholarly journals and works.

JOSEPH V. HICKEY is professor of anthropology at Emporia State University. Among his publications is *Ghost Settlement on the Prairie: A Biography of Thurman, Kansas*, and he is coauthor of *Society in Focus.*

TOM JACK is an adjunct faculty member at the College of Saint Mary, Omaha and Lincoln, where he teaches courses in ethnomusicology and the history of jazz and rock & roll.

MICHAEL K. JOHNSON is assistant professor of American Literature at the University of Maine at Farmington. His primary research interest is the portrayal of African Americans in the literature and cinema of the American West, which is the focus of his book, *Black Masculinity and the Frontier Myth in American Literature* (2002). His other publications include articles in *African American Review, Literature/Film Quarterly, Quarterly Review of Film and Video*, and *Western American Literature*. His current project is a book-length biography of Harlem Renaissance–era singer Taylor Gordon.

JAMES N. LEIKER is an associate professor of history at Johnson County Community College, Overland Park, Kansas. He is the author of *Racial Borders: Black Soldiers along the Rio Grande* as well as numerous articles.

CLARE V. MCKANNA, JR. received a PhD from the University of Nebraska–Lincoln in 1993. He has been teaching American Indian history at San Diego State University since 1985. He is the author of *Homicide, Race, and Justice in the American West, 1880–1920* (1997), *Race and Homicide in Nineteenth-Century California* (2002), *The Trial of "Indian Joe": Race and Justice in the Nineteenth-Century*

West (2003), and *White Justice in Arizona: Apache Homicide Cases, in Nineteenth Century Arizona* (2005). He is currently finishing a book manuscript titled "The Court-Martial of Apache Kid."

DENNIS N. MIHELICH is University Historian at Creighton University, and is the author of a *History of Creighton University* as well as several articles on the Urban League and on Prince Hall Masons.

MARC RICE is an associate professor of musicology at Truman State University and is the area chair of the Perspectives of Music program. He has extensively published on gender and race issues concerning jazz in the Midwest. His work can be found in the journals *American Music, Musical Quarterly,* and the forthcoming *Encyclopedia of African American Music.* He has also conducted fieldwork in Louisiana, tracing the Cajun music revival, and is currently preparing a manuscript on the *Nueva Cancion* movement in Latin America.

R. BRUCE SHEPARD is an administrative analyst for the government of Saskatchewan. Shepard has a special interest in agricultural and immigration history. He has published *Deemed Unsuitable: Black Migration as a Response to Repression*; his articles have appeared in *Material History Bulletin, Canadian Native Law Bulletin,* and other journals.

AUDREY THOMPSON is a professor in Education, Culture, and Society at the University of Utah. Her research includes work on African American philosophy, antiracist and feminist pedagogies, and narrative and visual arts. Among her publications are "Not the Color Purple: Black Feminist Lessons for Educational Caring," "Harriet Tubman in Pictures: Cultural Consciousness and the Art of Picture Books," "Tiffany, Friend of People of Color: White Investments in Antiracism," and "Reading Black Philosophers in Chronological Order." Recently, she served as guest curator for the multicultural exhibition "Cinderella: Masks, Magic, and Mirrors" at the Utah Museum of Fine Arts.

JEAN VAN DELINDER is an associate professor of sociology and director of the women's studies program at Oklahoma State University, Stillwater. She received her PhD in sociology from the University of Kansas. She published *Struggles Before Brown*, and several articles in leading journals.

RONALD WALTERS currently is in the government and politics department at the University of Maryland; he formerly served as professor and chair of political science at Howard University, Washington DC. An activist and a scholar, one of his numerous books, *Black Presidential Politics in America* (1989), won the Ralph Bunche Prize from the American Political Science Association.

INDEX

A. B. Whiting's Subdivision, 60, 62
Abbott, Lynn, 328
Across the Years on Mount Oread (Taft), 219
Adolphus Hotel, 258–59, 263
Africa, black artists and, 237–38
African Grand Lodge of North America, 144
Africanism, 242–43
African Methodist Episcopal Church (A.M.E.), 321
Afro-American Council: activities of, 96–97; the Alexander lynching and, 8, 88–89; Anti-Lynching Bureau, 76; attack on Jim Crow system, 75–76; formation and leadership of, 75; national civil rights and, 71; protest tradition and, 71; rise of local councils, 77. *See also* Kansas Afro-American Council
Afro-American League, 8, 73, 74–75
Age, 74
Agnes City Township KS, 52, 58, 62
Alberta, Canada, 162, 166, 180n2
alcohol: black violence and, 126, 137; during Prohibition, 265; "resorts" in Valentine NE and, 115, 117; soldiers and, 30
Alexander, Albert, 87, 90
Alexander, Alfred, 86, 92
Alexander, Archie, 228n20
Alexander, Fred, 8, 71, 77–86, 90. *See also* Alexander lynching
Alexander lynching: African American response to, 8, 87–95; condemnation of, 86–87; events of, 77–86, 90; Kansas State Afro-American Council and, 90–96
Allen, Charles, 34, 35
Allen, Jap, 259
Allen, Richard, 321
Alliance Lodge No. 7, 158
Alpha Kappa Alpha Sorority, 205, 212, 224, 225
Alpha Phi Alpha Fraternity, 212
Alphonso Trent orchestras: in Dallas, 258–61; in Deadwood, 268–70; during the Depression, 264–65; in Kansas City, 265–68; overview of, 14–15, 256–58; the respectability of jazz and, 261–63; on tour, 263–64
American Art Deco (Duncan), 248
American Bull Dog, 135
American Citizen, 88, 92
American Daughter (Thompson): describing the prairie, 184, 187–93; double-consciousness and the wilderness/metropolis opposition in, 12, 193–202; frontier narratives and, 185; place and race in, 184–85, 186; as a spiritual autobiography, 203n11
American Indian Movement, 25
American Veterans Committee (AVC), 288, 290
Americus Township KS, 52, 58, 62
Anderson, Marian, 213, 229n32
Anderson, Paul Allen, 225

Anti-Lynching Bureau (Afro-American Council), 76
anti-lynching legislation, 76
APHIA, 224
Arkansas, prohibition on sit-ins, 311
Armstrong, Louis, 232n71
army. *See* U.S. Army
art: black university students in, 222–23; Harlem Renaissance and, 14; as social protest, 237–38. *See also* Douglas, Aaron; modernism; primitivism
Art Deco: areas of art explored in, 253n36; Aaron Douglas and, 243–47, 248, 254n45; movement and dynamism in, 254n41
"Art Moderne," 246
Aspects of Negro Life (Douglas), 245
Associated Press, 90
Atchison, Andrew, 54, 55, 58, 62
Atchison, R. B., 55
"At Dawning" (Hill), 216
Athearn, Robert, 51, 53, 56
athletics. *See* sports
autobiographies, 186. See also *American Daughter*

"Baby Won't You Please Come Home" (song), 232n71
Baker, Houston, 216, 225
bands: dance, 14–15, 256; Twenty-fifth Infantry Band, 108, 113. *See also* Alphonso Trent orchestras
Baptist churches, gospel music and, 330–33
Baptist Informer, 172
Barnes, Luke, 36–38
baseball, 112, 118
Bearden, Romare, 239, 245, 248
Beckwourth, James, 3
Bellecourt, Vernon, 42
Bender, Thomas, 208
Bennie Moten Orchestra, 15, 266, 272n29
Berry, Michael J., 296n4
Billington, Ray Allen, 1
Black Bottom (dance), 263
black churches, in Omaha, 325. *See also* gospel music; *individual churches*
The Black Dispatch, 311

black folk culture, artists and, 237–38
"Black Kansas," 4
black migration: to Kansas, 6–7, 127–29; to urban centers, 7–8
Blacks in the West (Savage), 1
black soldiers: Colored Troops, 4; racial violence and, 9; vengeance and, 33–34. *See also* buffalo soldiers; Tenth Cavalry; Thirty-eighth Infantry; Twenty-fifth Infantry
black university students: awards to, 221–22; and the New Negro arts and letters movement, 12, 204–5; in theater and play writing, 218–21; in the visual arts, 222–23; white philanthropy and, 208–11; writers and poets, 214–18
black violence: black population migration and, 127–29; in Coffeyville, 124–25; and defendant conviction rates, 135; "enclaves of violence," 8–9, 126, 129–33, 138; factors contributing to, 126, 137–39; handguns and, 135; and homicide indictment rates, 133–34; measuring levels of, 125–27; and plea bargain rates, 135–36; "southernness" and, 136; urban, 142n37
black women: employment and, 7–8; homicides and, 131; university students and writers, 214–18; wage-earning wives of Prince Hall Masons, 157
Blair, Ezell, 314
Bledsoe, Charles, 288, 292
Block, Opal, 199
blue lodges, 144
blues, 223
Boeing Airplane Company, 305
Boley OK, 175–76
Boley Progress, 164
Bolling v. Sharpe, 296n4
Bonga, George and Stephen, 3
Bontemps, Arna, 217
Born to Be (Gordon), 186
Boston Bull Dog, 135
Boswell Junior High School (Topeka KS), 285–87
Bowles, Chester, 307
Bowman, Alpheus, 110, 114

boxing, 112
Boyd, R. A., 69n29
Boyer, Horace, 328
Brady, Thomas, 84
Braxton, Joanne, 189, 196–97
Brewer, J. Mason, 13
Bridges, J. A., 58
Briggs, Paul, 328
Bristow OK, 176
Bronsema, John, 131
Brown, Ed, 130
Brown, Edward, 76
Brown, Henry, 132–33
Brown, Jess, 130
Brown, John, 112
Brown, Lucky, 132
Brown, Ollie Lee, 210
Brown, Sterling, 94–95
Brown, Theodore, 265
Brownsville incident, 9, 103–4, 120
Brown v. Board of Education, 275, 281, 288, 295, 300n61
Bruce, Maxine, 224
Buchanan Elementary School (Topeka KS), 279, 284, 287
Buchannon, William, 29
buffalo soldiers: commemorations of, 25; complex legacy of, 25, 42; low rates of desertion among, 31; monument to, 24–25; origin of, 5, 24; racism and, 24; reappraising modern perceptions of, 25–26; roles of, 5; vengeance and, 33–34. *See also* Fort Hays KS
buffalo soldiers stamp, 25
Buggs, Charles W., 210–11
Burnett, McKinley, 293, 299n42, 299n45
Burton, Phillip, 289
Butchart, Ronald, 204
Butler, Tom, 38–39
Butts, Magnolia Lewis, 323

Caldwell, George O., 225–26
Caldwell, Harrison, 292–93
Calgary Herald, 177
California, bias in criminal justice, 141n36
Calloway, Bertha, 18

Calloway, Cab, 232n71
Calo, Mary Ann, 211
Camp Mabry TX, 120
Canada, black migration to: Canadian advertising for immigrants and, 163–64; Canadian reactions to, 11, 164–66, 167–72, 177–78, 179–80; G. W. Miller and, 172–77; immediate causes of, 162–63, 166–67, 179; and numbers of immigrants in, 180n2; opposed by the black Oklahoman press, 167–68
Canadian Northern Railway, 171
Canadian Pacific Railway, 171, 177
Cannon, T. R., 56
Carson, Clayborne, 312
Carter, Carrie, 132–33
Carter, Henry, 56, 61
Carter, Robert, 281, 292
Catlett, Elizabeth, 221, 222
cattle farming, 61
cavalry, desertions and, 31. *See also* Tenth Cavalry
census of 1920, 151
Chapman, Kate, 6
Charleston (Douglas), 240
Charleston (dance), 263
Cherokee County KS, 142–43n48
"Cherokee Strip," 51
Chicago arts and letters movement, 207
Chicago Daily News, 303
Chicago Defender, 194
Childers, J. H., 93
cholera, 29
Christian, Charlie, 270
Chudacoff, Howard, 152
"Citizens Committee," 290, 299n42
civil rights, New Negro arts and letters movement and, 207
Civil Rights Act of 1875, 72, 73
Civil Rights Commission, 311–12
civil rights movement: legal challenges to discriminatory state legislation, 15–16; music and, 15; sit-ins, 16–17 universities and, 16. *See also* sit-in movement
Civil War, 4

Clair Memorial United Methodist Church (Omaha NE), 334
Clark, Septima, 297n18
Clark, Thomas, 130
Clarke, Chester, 267
classical music, 224–25
Clearview OK, 175
Clearview Patriarch, 167
Cleveland, James, 333, 334
Coffeyville KS: black in-migration and, 128; black neighborhood in, 128; black violence in, 124–25; "enclave of violence," 8–9, 129–30; and homicide indictment rates, 133, 134
Cohen, Octavius Roy, 218
Cohn, Sarah, 199
Cole, Deliah "Auntie," 115, 116
Coleman, Anita Scott, 14
A Collection of Spiritual Songs and Hymns (Allen), 321
college choirs, 322
Collins, Elmer E., 210
Come Seven (Cohen), 218
Communism, black musicians and, 224
Congress of Racial Equality, 304
Connelly, Marc, 218
The Conquest (Micheaux), 13
Cooper, Evlondo, 328
Corbin, Lester, 334
Cory, W. W., 167
"The Coward" (Johnson), 214
cowboys, 6
Cox, Thomas C., 125, 128, 278
Craig, J. S., 150
Cranston, Joseph A., 82
Creighton University, 334
criminal justice system, racial bias in, 134, 141n36
Crisis, 205, 214, 244, 306
Crooke, Eugene, 257
Cropper, Albert E., 34, 35, 45n32
The Crucifixion (Douglas), 239–40, 252–53n22
Cruse, Harold, 208
cubism, 242
Cudahy Packing Company, 328

Cudahy Quartet, 328
Cullen, Countee, 211–12
Custer, Elizabeth, 31

Dallas TX, Alphonso Trent Orchestra and, 257, 258–61
dance bands, 14–15, 256. *See also* Alphonso Trent orchestras
Daughters of the American Revolution, 229n32
Davis, Frank Marshall, 13
Davis, Marita Burnett, 290
Dawson, William, 233
Deadwood SD, 257, 268–70
DeFrantz, Alonzo, 47
de Olvera, Isabel, 3
depression. *See* economic depression
desertions: from the army, 30–31; Twenty-fifth Infantry and, 109–10
Des Moines IA, 89
Des Moines Register, 303
Detroit Journal, 86
Dewey, John, 237
diarrhea, 29
Dickinson Theater, 289
disenfranchisement, 11, 72, 163
Dixon, Annie, 210
Dockum Drug Store, 306, 307–8
Dodson, Jacob, 3
"Dorsey," 323
Dorsey, Thomas, 323, 330
Dorsey House of Music, 323
"double-consciousness": W. E. B. Du Bois and, 185, 193–94; in Thompson's *American Daughter*, 12, 193–202
Dougherty, Bessie, 77
Douglas, Aaron: Art Deco and, 248, 254n45; the Harlem Renaissance and, 247, 254n44; influences on, 233–34, 250–51n5; Alain Locke and, 233, 234, 235–36; modernism and, 243–47; overcoming the effects of mis-education, 236–37; overview of, 14; pragmatism and, 234–36; primitivism and, 238–43, 248; Rosenwald Fellowship and, 211; "universal" art of, 247–50; as a university student, 222

Douglas, Ann, 208
Douglas County NE, 135, 324
Dove, 211
Doyle, Cornelius, 34, 35
drama, black university students and, 218–21
Dranes, Juanita Arizona, 324
Dred Scott decision, 4
Driskell, David, 247, 254n39
drunkenness. *See* alcohol
"Dr. Watts," 322
Du Bois, W. E. B., 136; "double-consciousness" concept and, 12, 185, 193–94; pragmatism and, 236, 251n8; "the problem of the color-line," 203n12
Dumenil, Lynn, 158
Dunbar club, 261
Duncan, Alastair, 248
Dunlap, Joseph, 50–51
Dunlap Colony: average farm size, 58; decline and death of, 48–49; economic depression affecting, 61–62; failure of, 60–64; the Great Exodus and, 52–57; lands purchased for, 51–52; origins of, 51; overview of, 47–48; physical environment and climate, 49–50; relief agencies and the relocation of Exodusters to, 57–60; social environment, 50–51; success of, 64–66
Dunlap County KS, 7
Dunlap Courier, 57
Dunlap KS, 7, 52; the Great Exodus and, 55–57
Dunlap Reflector, 57, 64–65
DuPree, Ada, 131
DuPree, Joanna, 131
DuSable Museum of Black History, 223

Early, Gerald, 185, 193–94
economic depression, Dunlap Colony and, 61–62
Edmond, Rev. H. H., 170
Edmonton, Canada, 165, 166
educational segregation. *See* school segregation
Edwards, Jeff, 163
elementary school segregation, 277; challenges to in Topeka KS, 290–95

Ellison, Ralph, 1, 262
El Torreon dance hall, 265
Emancipation Day, 65, 107
Emerson, Frank, 130
The Emperor Jones (O'Neil), 218–19
"enclaves of violence," 8–9, 126, 129–33, 138
Enid OK, 312
Enochs, Harvey, 131
Erwin, Thomas "Red," 131
Estevan, 3
Evans, William A., 80
Everhardy, Peter, 82, 83–84, 87, 93, 95
Excelsior Lodge, 149
Exodusters, 7, 27, 52–57, 185, 276–77
Exoduster settlements, 47. *See also* Dunlap Colony

farms, in Dunlap County KS, 58
Fass, Paula, 261–62
Federal Gold Reserve Act of 1934, 268
Fellowship of Reconciliation (FOR), 304, 314
Fenalson, Anne, 220
"field day" exercises, 112
Fielding, John, 257
Fifth Amendment, 296n4
Fifth Cavalry, 40
Fire!!, 241, 252n16, 254n44
Firebird (Stravinsky), 226
"First Black Renaissance," 250n1
Fisk Jubilee Singers, 322, 325
Five Generations Hence (Horace), 13
Fletcher Henderson Orchestra, 266
Flick, Florence, 132
Flinn, Matthew "Red," 34, 35
Flippin, George A., 150
Flowers, Ruth, 8
Floyd, Troy, 15
folk culture, black artists and, 237–38
football, 112
Forbes, John W., 101n45
Forbes, Pearl, 77–78, 81, 84
Forbes, William, 77, 83, 85, 92
Ford, Guy S., 220
Ford, Nick Aaron, 222
For My People (Walker), 221–22

Fort, Rev. Willis E., 330, 332
Fort Bliss TX, 120
Fort Brown TX, 103–4, 119
Fort Des Moines IA, 109
Fort Hays KS: armed confrontations in Hays City and, 39–41; black soldiers and discrimination at, 28; black soldiers and vengeance at, 33–34; black soldiers lynched at, 36–38; black soldiers stationed at, 26; desertions and, 31; disease and, 29; military and social atmosphere, 27–31; physical conditions of, 28–29; racial conflict and, 5–6, 42; relationship with Hays City, 31; shootings of Charles Allen and Cornelius Doyle, 34–35; soldiers' earnings, 29–30; soldiers' retaliation for lynchings at, 38–39
Fortier, L. M., 167
Fort Leavenworth KS, 24
Fort McIntosh TX, 120
Fort Niobrara NE: closing of, 119; desertion rate from, 109–10; establishment and purpose of, 104; morale of soldiers at, 110; regarrisoning of, 105; and relationship to Valentine, 104; soldier life at, 108–11. *See also* Twenty-fifth Infantry
Fort Reno OK, 105
Fort Riley KS, 109, 117–18
Fort Robinson NE, 105
Fort Smith, Arkansas, 264
Fortune, T. Thomas, 74, 75
Fort Washakie, Wyoming, 109
Foster, Howard K., 284–85
Foster, John, 178
Foster case, 280–81
Fourteenth Amendment, 275, 296n4
"The Freedmen's Academy of Kansas," 48, 54, 55, 57, 58, 59, 60, 62, 69n29
Freedmen's Aid Association of Dunlap KS, 54, 55, 56, 57, 59
Freeman, 74
Freemasons, 10, 144. *See also* Prince Hall Masonry
"frontier," 27
frontier narratives, 185
Fuller, Gwendolyn, 313

Fulton, L. P., 55

Gage School (Topeka KS), 285
gambling, 116–17
Gandhi, Mahatma, 307
G.A.R. Memorial Day, 113
Gastil, Raymond, 136
gender, black violence and, 137
General Education Board, 208
General Education Board Fellowship, 209, 210
Gennet recording label, 266
George E. Lee Orchestra, 15, 265
Gerran, Nicholas, 223–24
Gibson, Pearl, 326, 334
Gilded Age, 72
Gillum, Ruth, 221, 224
Gilson, Kate, 84
The Glorious Adventure (Hill), 220–21
Goddard, Aretaf A., 91, 93, 95
God's Great Acres (Lamb), 221
God's Trombones, 239, 244
gold mines, 268
Good Hope Lodge, 157
Goodman, Benny, 270
Goodwill Spring Musical, 327
Gordon, Taylor, 13, 186
gospel music: defined, 320–21; historical background of, 321–24; in Omaha, 18, 324–35
"gospel quartets," 322
Goss, Bernard, 222, 223
Graham, Beatrice, 285
Graham, Oaland, Jr., 16, 285, 286
Graham, U. A., 285, 286
Graham case, 284, 295
grandfather clauses, 11, 15
Great Exodus, 47; Dunlap village and, 55–56; and Exoduster population, 52–53; origin of, 52; prejudice and discrimination against Exodusters, 56–57; relief agencies and, 53–55, 57–60, 63–64; relocations to Dunlap Colony, 57–60
Great Plains, defined, 2
The Great Plains (Webb), 1
Great Plains Black History Museum, 18
Great Plains sit-ins: Greensboro sit-in and,

312–14, 315, 316; Oklahoma City sit-in, 305, 308–12; relevance of, 312–15; scholarship on, 303–4; Wichita-Oklahoma link, 312; Wichita sit-in, 302, 304, 305–8
Greenberg, Jack, 281
Green Pastures (Connelly, Marc), 218
Greensboro sit-in, 302, 303; Great Plains sit-ins and, 312–15, 316
Guinn v. United States, 15
guns. *See* handguns
Guthrie OK, 176
Guy, James H., 91, 278

Hall, Grover, Jr., 302–3
Hall, Prince, 144
handguns: black violence and, 126, 135, 138; types of, 135
Hanna, D. B., 171
Hannah, John, 311–12
Harlan, Louis, 208
Harlem Renaissance, 204; art as social protest, 237–38; black modernism and, 249; Aaron Douglas and, 247, 254n44; Alain Locke and, 247; modernism and, 243; as the "Negro Renaissance," 250n1; overview of, 12–15; photography and, 255n47; primitivism and, 241, 252n16; time boundaries of, 206–7; white patrons and, 252n16. *See also* New Negro arts and letters movement
Harmon, William E., 228n20
Harmon Foundation, 211, 228n20
Harness, London, 48, 58, 61, 63, 65
Harrington and Richardson Company, 135
Harris House, 114
Harvey, James, 38
Hastings NE, 147
Haviland, Laura, 54
Hayden, Palmer, 254–55n47
Hayden, Robert, 217
Hayes, James, 36
Hayes, Roland, 213, 224
Hays City KS: armed confrontations in, 39–41; black soldiers as the town guard in, 33; features of, 31–32; lynching of black soldiers at, 36–38; press coverage of violence in, 35–36;

relationship with Fort Hays, 31; shootings of Charles Allen and Cornelius Doyle, 34–35; and soldiers' retaliation for lynchings at, 38–39; vigilantes and, 35, 37, 40; violence and, 5–6, 32–33, 35, 41, 42
Heading for Harlem (Gillum), 221
Heiger, Walter, 308
Henderson, Harry, 239, 245, 248
Heralding Dawn (Brewer), 13
Heyward, Dubose and Dorothy, 218
Hiawatha KS, 73
Hickey, Joseph V., 7
high schools, 295–96n1
Hill, Ruth Shores, 216, 220–21
Hill, Tony, 222
Hill, Zanzye H., 215–16
Hillyer, Mark and Hannah, 60
Hillyer's Subdivision, 60, 62
Holder, T., 259
Holiness churches, 323–24
Holland, J. B., 287
Holloman, John, 115
home ownership, Prince Hall Masons and, 152–54
The Homesteader (Micheaux), 13, 189–90
homicides: in Hays City, 32–33, 35; indictment rates, 133–34; interracial, 124–25, 132, 137
honor, homicides and, 132
"hookers," 115
"hooks," 115
Horace, Lillian B., 13
Hose, Sam, 75
hotels, black dance bands and, 257
Hoyt, Ralph W., 110–11, 117, 120
Hub of Harmony II, 330
Hudson, William H., 89, 90, 92
Huggins, Nathan, 206, 208, 241
Hughes, Langston, 13, 211, 212–13, 217, 219, 225
Hummingbird nightclub, 258, 259
hunting, 112
Hutchinson, George, 234, 251n7
hymns and hymnals, 321–22

Idlewild club, 261
"I Don't Feel No Ways Tired" (album), 333

illiteracy, 164
illustration, 244–45
Immigration Act of 1910 (Canada), 177
Independence KS, 277
Independent Order of Daughters of the Empire, 166
Indiana University, 268
Indians: criminal justice system bias and, 141n36; Kansa, 50; race relations in Valentine NE and, 108
infantry: duties of on the western frontier, 28. See also Thirty-eighth Infantry; Twenty-fifth Infantry
In Search of the Racial Frontier (Taylor), 2
interracial homicides, 124–25, 132, 137
interracial marriages, 156
Iowa Bystander, 205
Ireland, Hamp, 112
Irwin bill, 96
Iver Johnson Arms Company, 135
Ivy Leaf, 205, 215, 216

Jackson, Eppie, 267
Jackson, Samuel, 291, 292
Jamison, Ann F., 59
The Janitor Who Paints (Hayden), 254–55n47
jazz and jazz bands, 223–24, 256, 261–63. See also Alphonso Trent orchestras
Jesse, Al, 125, 136
Jeter, James, 257
Jewish people, 290
Jim Crow: Afro-American Council's attack on, 75–76; Oklahoma and, 10–11, 163; Supreme Court sanctioning of, 72
Jitterbug (dance), 269
John A. Brown luncheonette, 309
Johnson, Charles S., 213
Johnson, Columbus, 47, 55
Johnson, H. T., 97
Johnson, James Weldon, 213
Johnson, John H., 12
Johnson, Lulu Merle, 210
Johnson, Lulu "Red Top," 116
Johnson, William N., 214
Johosky, Mary, 78

Jones, Charles Price, 322
Jones, John E., 165–66, 169
Jones, Lucille, 130
Jones, S. S., 170
Jordan, Barbara Charline, 17
Journal of Negro History, 209
Joyful Sounds, 334
"Jubilee quartets," 322
Jubilee Singers (Fisk University), 322, 325
junior high schools, 285–87

Kansa Indian Reservation, 50
Kansa Indians, 50
Kansas: Afro-American League in, 74; black migration to, 6–7, 127–29; black population of, 4, 73; Exodusters, 7, 27, 52–57, 185, 276–77; history of race relations in, 274–78; lynchings in, 36–38, 71, 73; notions of "frontier" and, 27; racial discrimination and violence in, 8–9, 73, 137; and reputation among nineteenth century blacks, 26–27; school segregation after 1879, 276–78; slavery and, 4. *See Also* black violence; Fort Hays KS; Hays City KS
Kansas Afro-American Council, 77; formation of, 88–90; response to the Alexander lynching, 90–96
Kansas City: Alphonso Trent Orchestra and, 257; music and, 15, 265–68
Kansas City Call, 262, 265, 266
Kansas City Journal, 94
Kansas City World, 86
Kansas Fever, 73
Kansas Freedmen's Relief Association (KFRA), 57, 58, 64; aid to Dunlap Colony, 48; formation of, 53; the Great Exodus and, 53–54, 55, 63
Kansas Pacific Railroad, 128
Katz Drug Stores, 309
Kellner, Bruce, 206
King, Martin Luther, Jr., 313
Kings of Harmony, 327
Kirschke, Amy, 242
Knight, Roscoe, 330, 334

Knox, Bertha and Lilly, 277
Kolodny, Annette, 190–91
Koohler, Harry W., 78, 85, 86
Kress luncheonette, 309

Labette County KS, 127, 135–36
Lack, Paul, 3
Lacy, Anderson, 266–67
Lamb, Clifton, 221
landscape: sexualization of, 190–91; Era Bell Thompson's description of, 184, 187–93
Lane, Roger, 134, 136, 146
Langston, Carrie, 212
Lawrence, Jacob, 249–50
L. B. Mose Theater, 258, 259
Lead SD, 268
Leavenworth KS: black population of, 127; events after the Alexander lynching, 91; lynching of Fred Alexander, 71, 77–86
Leavenworth Chronicle, 94
Leavenworth County KS: black population of, 127; homicide indictments and homicides in, 133, 135
Leavenworth Times, 77, 78, 79
Leavenworth Vigilance Committee, 82
Lebanon Lodge, 149
Lee, C. Lowell, 220
Lee, Frank, 130
Lee, George E., 15, 259
Legal Redress Committee, 290
Lewis, Chester, 306, 308
Lewis, David Levering, 206, 208, 302
The Life and Adventures of Nat Love (Love), 186
Lindy Hop (dance), 269
"lining-out," 322
liquor. *See* alcohol
literacy tests, 11
literature, the Harlem Renaissance and, 13–14
Little Coney Colony, 64
Locke, Alain, 240; Aaron Douglas and, 233, 234, 235–36; the Harlem Renaissance and, 247; on the moral function of art, 237; New Negro arts and letters movement and, 206, 223; on overcoming the effects of miseducation, 236; pragmatism and, 235–36; the Soviet Union and, 224

"long-meter," 322
Love, Nat, 186
Loving Four, 328
Lowman Hill Elementary School (Topeka KS), 279
Luckey, Eleanor, 330
Luper, Clara, 304, 309, 312
lynchings: Afro-American Council's attacks on, 76; Fred Alexander, 71, 77–86; anti-lynching legislation, 76; on the Great Plains, 8; Sam Hose, 75; and impact on black migration, 127; intimidation of blacks and, 72–73; in Kansas, 36–38, 71, 73; in Oklahoma, 166–67. *See also* Alexander lynching
Lyon County KS, 49, 52, 58, 62

Mandan ND, 197, 198
Martin, Sallie, 323
Marvin Lodge No. 5, 158
Marvin Lodge No. 127, 147
Masoner, J. B., 309
Masons. *See* Freemasons; Prince Hall Masonry
McAdams, Doug, 302, 304
McCoy, James, 131
McDonald, Mike, 80
McDonald, Reddy, 192n52
McFarland, Kenneth, 288, 291–92, 293–94, 299n45
McGechin, Harry, 132
McKay, Claude, 211, 225
McNeil, Joseph, 314
McVay, Luther L., 327
medical exams, black immigrants to Canada and, 165–66
Meier, August, 209, 314–15
Menninger Foundations, 290
Meredith, James, 281
Messenger, 205
Methodist churches, gospel music and, 330
M-H Directory Service, 150
Michaels, Harry, 83, 92–93
Micheaux, Oscar, 13, 186, 189–90
migration. *See* black migration
Miles, William, 132

Miller, G. W., 178, 179
mini-dramas, 220–21
Ministerial Union, 90, 93
Minneapolis Morning Tribune, 303
minstrel shows, 113
miscegenation, 156
missionary groups, the Great Exodus and, 54, 63–64
Mississippi Plan, 72
Missouri Compromise, 4
Missouri Grand Lodge, 144
Mitchell, John, Jr., 74, 76
mob violence, 72–73
modernism: the art of Aaron Douglas and, 243–47; the Harlem Renaissance and, 249
Montgomery County KS: black population of, 127; defendant conviction rates, 135; homicide indictments, 133; plea bargain rates, 135–36
Moore, Miles, 85
Moore, Rowena, 329
Morningside College, 200
Morrill bill, 96
Morris, Aldon, 303, 304, 312, 315
Morris County KS, 49, 58, 62
Morris County Times, 64
Morsell, John, 313
Moscow Conservatory of Music, 224
Mosely, Leo "Snub," 257, 267
Moten, Bennie, 15
Moten, Etta G., 224–25
Motley, Constance Baker, 281
Mott, Frank L., 212
movie theaters, 289–90
mulattoes, Prince Hall Masons and, 154, 155–56
murals, 244–45
Muraskin, William A., 145, 154–55, 157
Murphy, Ed C., 81, 84
Murray, Daniel, 75, 76
Muscogee OK, 312
music: black musicians and the Soviet Union, 224; civil rights movement and, 15; dance bands, 14–15, 256; Harlem Renaissance and, 14–15; jazz, 223–24, 261–63; the New Negro arts and letters movement and, 223–26; spirituals, 322, 325; Twenty-fifth Infantry Band, 108, 113. *See also* Alphonso Trent orchestra; gospel music
Musical Fiestas, 329
Musicians (Goss), 223
Myers, Stance, 84
"My Nantie" (Hill), 215–16

NAACP *Annual Reports*, 313, 314
NAACP Youth Councils: Great Plains sit-ins and, 304, 312; Oklahoma City sit-in and, 309–11; recognized for sit-ins, 313; Wichita sit-in and, 306–8
National Afro-American Council, 73
National Association for the Advancement of Colored People (NAACP): "Accent on Youth" conference, 313; *Brown v. Board of Education* and, 288; McKinley Burnett and, 299n42; challenges to school segregation, 274; challenges to segregation in Topeka and, 289, 290; lynchings and, 8; school integration in Topeka and, 290–91, 292, 293, 295; sit-ins and, 306, 311, 312, 313–15; student productions of *Porgy* and, 220
National Baptist Convention, 330
National Convention of Gospel Choirs and Choruses, 323, 330
National Negro Business League, 88
Native Son (Wright), 218
Nebraska: black population, 148, 324, 325; Prince Hall Masonry in; urban black violence and, 142n37. *See also* Omaha NE; Prince Hall Masonry
Nebraska Fine Arts Council, 222
Neeley, Shaw F., 82
The Negro in Art (Locke), 223
The Negro on the American Frontier (Porter), 1
Negro Renaissance, 250n1. *See also* New Negro arts and letters movement
Nelson, Anderson, 36–37, 38
Neosho River valley, 49
Newby, Robert, 305
"New Negro," 11–12, 206
The New Negro (Locke), 206, 223, 236

New Negro arts and letters movement: awards to black students, 221–22; black militancy and, 205–6; black students in theater and play writing, 218–21; black students in the visual arts, 222–23; black student writers and poets, 214–18; black university students and, 204–5; in Chicago, 207; civil rights and, 207; leading figures in, 211–13; music and, 223–26; *The New Negro* and, 206; overview of, 12–15; white philanthropy and, 208–11
New York Globe, 74
New York Public Library, 244
Nicodemus KS, 27
Nixon, Lawrence A., 15
Nixon, Richard M., 17
Nixon v. Condon, 15
Nixon v. Herndon, 15
nonviolence, 307
North Dakota, Era Bell Thompson's description of, 187–93
Not Without Laughter (Hughes), 13
Novel, Doris R., 224
Number 2 Choir, 332

Oak Cliff pavilion, 258
Ohio State University, 313
Okemah OK, 166–67
Oklahoma: black communities in, 10; Jim Crow and, 10–11, 163; lynchings in, 166–67; segregation legislation and, 162–63. *See* Canada, black migration to
Oklahoma City OK, 176
Oklahoma City sit-in: background to, 308–9; effects of, 311–12; events of, 309–11; Greensboro sit-in and, 312–15; importance of, 304–5; scholarship on, 304; Wichita sit-in and, 312
Oklahoma City Youth Council, 309–11
Oklahoma Guide, 173
Okmulgee OK, 173
"Old Negro," 206
Oliver, Frank, 164, 165, 177
Omaha NE: black in-migration, 129; black population of, 148; black violence in, 137, 138; defendant conviction rates, 135; "enclave of violence," 132–33; gospel music in, 324–35; homicide indictment rates, 133–34; interracial homicides, 137; modern black community of, 17–18; plea bargain rates, 136; Prince Hall Masons, 151, 152–53; racial violence and, 8; red-light district of, 129
Omaha Black Music Hall of Fame, 18
Omaha Mass Choir, 18, 334–35
Omaha Monitor, 205
O'Neal, K. Roderick, 222–23
O'Neil, Eugene, 218
Oppenheimer, Martin, 304
Opportunity, 205, 244
order-in-council, 169, 177, 178, 182n22
Ottawa KS, 277
Ovenshine, Samuel, 34–35
Owens, Sterling V., 210

Painter, Nell, 73, 125
Parent-Teacher Association (PTA), 288, 293
Parks, Carol, 307, 308
Parrish, Alfred, 62
Parsons Weekly Blade, 76
Paseo Dance Hall, 265, 266
Paul Robeson Dramatic Club, 219
Pearson, Ruth, 214
Pendergast, Thomas, 265
Penrose, Charles W., 110
Pentecostal churches, 324
Perry, Regenia, 254–55n47
Philadelphia PA, 134
philanthropy, 208–11, 228n20
Philippine-American War, 5
Philippine Insurrection, 104
photography, the Harlem Renaissance and, 255n47
Phyllis Wheatley Settlement House, 213
Picasso, Pablo, 242
Pillars, Hayes, 264, 267
Pinkett, H. J., 129
Pinkston, Flora, 325–26
Pittsburgh Courier, 107
plea bargaining, 135–36
Plessy v. Ferguson, 72, 280

Plummer, Henry V., 90
pluralism, 242
poetry, 13, 211–12
police brutality, 127
Ponder, James, 36–38
Porgy (Heyward & Heyward), 218, 219–20
Porter, James A., 248
Porter, Kenneth Wiggins, 1
Posey, Barbara, 309–10, 313
poverty, in Omaha, 18
Powell, Colin, 24
pragmatism, 234–36, 251nn7–9
prairie, Era Bell Thompson's description of, 184, 187–93
Prairie View State College, 221
Presbyterian church: aid to Dunlap Colony, 48; the Great Exodus and, 54
Price, Charlie, 114, 117
primary elections, 15
primitivism: Aaron Douglas and, 238–43, 248; the Harlem Renaissance and, 241, 252n16
Prince Hall Mason Grand Lodge of Nebraska, 144, 150–51
Prince Hall Masonry: before 1900, 146–47; early twentieth century membership, 147–50; Grand Lodge of Nebraska, 144, 150–51; and housing patterns of members, 152–54; as a multi-class fraternity, 10, 145–51, 157–58; and occupational status of members, 156–57; origins of, 144; skin color and class issues with, 154–56
Progressive Era, 72
Prohibition, 265
prostitution, 36, 115, 116–17
Puckett, Rev. J. B., 172
Pullman Company, 97
Pythian Temple, 258, 260

"quartet battles," 329
"quartet jamborees," 329
quartets, 322, 327–29

race, early twentieth century notions of, 253n25
Race and Politics (Rawley), 4

race riots, 8–9
racial segregation. *See* segregation
racial violence: on the Great Plains, 8–9; interracial homicides, 124–25, 132, 137; intimidation of blacks and, 72–73. *See also* lynchings
racism: Aaron Douglas's treatment of, 240; sit-ins and, 316
radio broadcasting, 271n7
railroad companies, black migration and, 138, 171, 178
Raines, Simon, 130
Rainey, Gertrude "Ma," 323
Rampersad, Arnold, 212, 223
ranchers, 6
Randolph Elementary School (Topeka KS), 282–83, 284
Rawley, James A., 4
"reinforced segregation," 278
Reiss, Winold, 233, 234, 235, 236
relief agencies, the Great Exodus and, 53–55, 57–60, 63–64
religious groups, the Great Exodus and, 63–64. *See also individual churches*
Rescue Lodge No. 25, 146, 147, 148, 149, 152
"resorts," 114–15, 117
Reynolds, R. J., 289
Reynolds, William, 278–80, 283
Reynolds v. Board of Education, 273, 278–80
Rhapsodies in Black Art, 243
Rich, Blanche, 283
Rich, Maude, 282, 283
Rich, Richard, 283
Rich, Yvette, 283
Richardson, William, 131
Rich case, 280–81, 282
Richmond Planet, 74
Ricketts, M. O., 155
Ricks, George Robinson, 324
Ridley, Ruth, 287
Ringling, John, 186
Rinne, Henry, 257
Ritz Ballroom, 268
Robeson, Paul, 213, 218, 224
Rock Creek Colony, 52, 63

Rockefeller Foundation, 208
Rocquemore, C. A., 306
Rodecker, William, 124–25, 136
Rogers, Joel A., 223
Rogers, W. H., 171–72
Rollins, Nona, 80, 100n22
Roosevelt, Eleanor, 229n32
Roosevelt, Theodore, 103
Rose, Edward, 3
Rosebud Chorus, 332
Rosebud Reservation, 107–8
Rosenwald Fellowship Fund, 208, 209–11
Ross, Clarence, 210
Ross, Cleopatra, 224
Roth, Eva, 79–80
Roth, John, 82
Rough Ashler No. 1 Lodge, 149, 151
Roundtree, Fred, 192n48
Rudwick, Elliott, 209, 314–15
Running Horse, Priscilla, 199
Russell, Ross, 265

Salem Baptist Church (Omaha NE), 331–33
San Antonio TX, 3
Sanctified churches, 323–24
Santora restaurant, 313
Sapulpa OK, 176
Saskatchewan, Canada, 162, 180n2
Savage, W. Sherman, 1
Sawyer, Daniel S., 287
Schneider, Mark R., 207
Schomburg Center for Research in Black Culture, 244
school desegregation: *Brown v. Board of Education*, 288; constitutional perspectives on, 296n4; in Topeka, 290–95
schools, Twenty-fifth Infantry and, 113–14
school segregation: challenges to in Topeka, 280–85, 290–95; controversies in Topeka, 273–74; *Graham* case, 285–87; historical overview of in Kansas, 274–78
Schubert, Frank, 108
Schuyler, George, 107
Scott, Charles and John, 288, 290–91
Scott, Dred, 4

Scott, El Dorothy, 282
Scott, Elisha, 291
Scott, W. D., 170, 171, 172
Sears, Roebuck, 142n39
"Second Black Renaissance," 250n1
segregation: challenges to in Topeka, 288–90; legislation in Oklahoma, 162–63; Supreme Court sanctioning of, 72. *See also* school segregation
Seventh Cavalry, 31
Sexton, James, 86
Shawnee County KS: black population of, 127; defendant conviction rates, 135; homicide indictments, 133; plea bargain rates, 135–36
Shelton, Sam, 150
Shelton Lodge No. 87, 149
Sheridan, Philip, 27
Simms, Shadrack, 131
Singleton, Benjamin "Pap," 6, 47, 50, 51, 52
Singleton's Colony, 51, 64
Sipuel v. Board of Regents of the University of Oklahoma, 16
sit-in movement: environmental factors leading to, 316; "first," 302; Greensboro sit-in, 302, 303, 312–15, 316; overview of, 16–17; precipitating factors and, 316–17; seen as being a Southern phenomenon, 302–3; significance of, 303. *See also* Great Plains sit-ins
skin color, class issues among Prince Hall Masons and, 154–56
slavery, 3–4
Slotkin, Richard, 185
Smith, Alonzo N., 18
Smith, Bessie, 232n71
Smith, Buster, 259
Smith, Ed, 194
Smith, Georgia, 55
Smith, Robert, 131
Smith v. Allwright, 15
"Smoky Row," 130–31
Sneed, Henry, 166
Snodgrass, Rev. John M., 54, 55, 62
social protest, art and, 237–38
Solomon, Carolyn, 334
Song of Tower (Douglas), 245

"Sooners," 185
Soth, Lauren, 303
Soul Stirrers, 327
soundex, 151
"southernness," 136
South Side Community Arts Center, 223
Soviet Union, black musicians and, 224
Spanish-American War, 5, 104
Sparks, Brent, 261, 264
Speers, C. W., 169–71, 172, 179
Spencer, Jon Michael, 216, 225, 322
spiritual autobiographies, 203n11
spirituals, 322, 325
"sporting houses," 114–15
sports, 111–12, 118
"St. James Infirmary Blues" (song), 232n71
St. John, John, 48, 53
St. John African Methodist Episcopal (Omaha NE), 325, 326, 334
St. John's Lodge, 149
St. Joseph Daily News, 87
St. Joseph Gazette, 86
St. Louis MO, 313
St. Peter Claver Catholic Church (Wichita KS), 306
Stalter, Stan, 300n58
stamps, of buffalo soldiers, 25
Stanley, William E., 83–84, 87, 90, 91, 95
Steward, Theophilus, 106, 107, 108, 110, 113–14, 116, 117, 120
Stewart, James, 309
Stewart, Jeffrey, 251–52n14
Stokes, Charles, 221
Stout, A. J., 283, 285, 291
Stovall, Ava and Arthur Lee, 289
Stratton & Kline, 114, 117
Stravinsky, Igor, 226
Student Non-Violent Coordinating Committee, 314
Sumner High School (Kansas City KS), 295–96n1
Supreme Court, sanctioning of racial segregation, 72
"surge-singing," 322
Swayzee, Edwin, 257

Sweatt v. Painter, 16
Sydnor, Clarence, 131

Taft, Robert, 219
Tampa Red (Hudson Whittaker), 323
Tate, Buddy, 259–60
Taylor, Margaret, 223
Taylor, Quintard, 2, 185
teachers, black, 278, 297n18
Tennessee Real Estate and Homestead Association, 51
"Tennesseetown," 53
Tenth Cavalry, 26, 27, 29, 112, 118
Terrell, Jay, 334
"territory bands," 14–15, 256. See also Alphonso Trent orchestras
Texas, slavery and, 3
Texas militia, 118–19
Texas Revolution, 3
The Texas Revolutionary Experience (Lack), 3
theater, black university students and, 218–21
Thirty-eighth Infantry: disease and, 29; drunkenness and, 30; duties of infantrymen, 28; at Fort Hays, 26, 27 (*see also* Fort Hays KS); lynching of soldiers in, 36–38; relocation of, 41; retaliation for lynchings, 38–39
Thoburn, William, 166
Thomasson, Maurice, 210
Thompson, Dick, 194
Thompson, Era Bell, 11–12, 14, 184–203. See also *American Daughter*
Thompson, Mary, 196–97
Thompson, Tom, 188
Thompson, Tony, 187, 197, 198–99, 200
369th Infantry Regiment, 206–7
Tindley, Charles Albert, 322–23
Tinnon, Elijah, 277
Tinnon, Leslie, 277
Tolson, Melvin B., 13
Tomlinson, Joseph B., 82, 84, 85, 87
Topeka KS: Afro-American League in, 74; annexation of outlying areas, 279, 284, 294–95; black employment in, 128; black in-migration, 128; black population of, 127, 128; black response to the Alexander lynching,

88–89; black teachers in, 278; *Brown v. Board of Education*, 288; challenges to elementary school segregation, 290–95; challenges to segregated public accommodations, 288–90; civil rights activism and, 16; "enclave of violence," 130–31; *Graham* case, 285–87; the Great Exodus and, 53; homicide indictment rates, 133, 134; legal challenges to school segregation, 280–85; Lowman Hill area of, 279; racial violence and, 8; red-light district of, 129; *Reynolds* case, 278–80; school segregation controversies in, 273–74, 277–78
Topeka Plaindealer, 92, 93, 94, 95, 102n45, 205
Topeka Railway Company, 128
Townsend, W. B., 88, 91
Trainer Hotel, 75
Trent, Alphonso: career overview of, 14–15, 256–58; later years of, 270. *See also* Alphonso Trent orchestras
Trent, Essie Mae, 258, 259, 260, 261, 263, 268, 269, 270
Tropical Hut Restaurant, 313
Troy Floyd Orchestra, 259
True American Lodge No. 6, 158
Tuneful Tales (Wiggins), 13
Turner, Zatella, 222
"Tuskegee Machine," 208
Twenty-fifth Infantry: arrival at Fort Niobrara, 105–6; arts and entertainment, 113–14; background of, 104; Brownsville incident and, 9, 103–4; desertions and, 109–10; garrisoning of, 105; importance to Valentine, 106–7, 108; interactions with Texas militia, 118–19; life at Fort Niobrara, 108–11; life in "resorts" and "sporting houses," 114–15; on maneuvers, 117–18; morale at, 110; off-duty violence at, 111; and race relations with Valentine, 107–8, 120–21; reduction in strength, 109; relationship between enlisted men and officers, 110–11; sports and, 111–12; transfer to Texas, 119–20
Twenty-fifth Infantry Band, 108, 113
"Twin Territories," 162

Union Pacific Railroad, 29

Union Services, 331
United Farmers of Alberta, 166
United Order of True Reformers, 146
universities, civil rights movement and, 16. *See also* black university students; *individual schools*
University of Chicago, 313
University of Colorado, 8
University of Indiana, 313
University of Iowa: Langston Hughes at, 212; New Negro arts and letters movement and, 204–5; Rosenwald Fellowship Fund and, 210
University of Kansas: black student musicians, 224–25; black women writers at, 216–17; Langston Hughes at, 212; New Negro arts and letters movement and, 204–5; Rosenwald Fellowship Fund and, 210; student theater at, 218–19
University of Minnesota: Langston Hughes at, 212–13; New Negro arts and letters movement and, 204–5, 213; Rosenwald Fellowship Fund and, 210; student production of *Porgy* at, 220
University of Nebraska, 334; black student musicians, 224, 226; black women students at, 214–16; New Negro arts and letters movement and, 204–5; Rosenwald Fellowship Fund and, 210; student production of *Porgy* at, 219–20
University of New Mexico, 16
University of North Dakota, 198, 199
Urban League, 220
U.S. Army: blacks in, 4, 5; Colored Troops, 4; desertions, 30–31, 109–10; drunkenness and, 30; duties of the infantry on the western frontier, 28; Fifth Cavalry, 40; and regarrisoning of old posts, 105; Seventh Cavalry, 31; soldiers' earnings, 29–30; Tenth Cavalry, 26, 27, 29, 112, 118; 369th Infantry Regiment, 206–7. *See also* Thirty-eighth Infantry; Twenty-fifth Infantry
U.S. Civil Rights Commission, 311–12
U.S. Colored Troops, 4
U.S. News and World Report, 303

Valentine Democrat, 119
Valentine NE: cleaning up gambling houses and brothels in, 116–17; importance of soldiers to, 106–7, 108; population, 105; race relations with the Twenty-fifth Infantry, 107–8, 120–21; relationship to Fort Niobrara, 104; "resorts" and "sporting houses," 114–15
Valley Township KS, 62
Van Der Zee, James, 255n47
Vann, Charles, 124, 136
vaudeville shows, 113
venereal disease, 115
Victor recording label, 266
vigilantes, 35, 37, 40
Visions of Freedom on the Great Plains (Calloway & Smith), 18

Wabaunsee Colony, 64
Wade, Rev. J. C., 332–33
Wade-Wilkerson, Doretha, 332, 333
Walker, Bruce, 169
Walker, Margaret, 14, 211, 217–18, 221–22, 222
Wall, Cheryl, 207, 217
Wallace, Daniel Webster "80 John," 6
Walter, Ronald, 306
Walters, Alexander, 75
Washburn University, 300n58
Washington, Booker T., 74, 171, 208–9
Washington DC, 296n4
Washington, John, 34
Washington University, 313
Watkins, Lee, 36–38
Watonga OK, 176
Watson, Maggie, 54, 55
Watts, Isaac, 322
Weary Blues (Hughes), 212
Weaver, Robert C., 313
Webb, Walter Prescott, 1
Webley British Bulldog, 135
Webster, Florence, 216–17, 224
Webster, Lillian, 224
Weleetka OK, 173
Wells, Elma, 332, 333
Wells-Barnett, Ida B., 75, 76
West, Cornel, 251n8

Westover, W. P., 117
Westward Expansion (Billington), 1
WFAA radio station, 259
Wheeler, Beulah, 221
Wheeler, William, 277
White, George H., 76
White, Harry, 131
White, John, 36
White, W. J., 169, 178
whites-only primaries, 15
Whiting's Subdivision, 60, 62
Whittaker, Hudson (Tampa Red), 323
Whyte, William, 171
Wichita KS: population, 305; sit-in, 302, 304–8, 312
Wichita NAACP Youth Council, 306–8
Wichita Searchlight, 71, 88
Wichita sit-in, 302; events of, 305–8; importance of, 304–5; the Oklahoma City sit-in and, 312; scholarship on, 304
Wiggins, Bernice Love, 13
Wilkerson, Rev. John M., 324
Wilkerson, Vernon A., 210
Wilkins, Earl, 221
Wilkins, Roy, 313–14
Willer, G. W., 172–77
William E. Harmon Foundation, 228n20
Williams, Franklin, 306
Williams, Loretta J., 145
Williams, Mamie, 287, 293, 300n54
Williams-Jones, Pearl, 321
Williamson, James, 131
Williams v. Mississippi, 75
Wilson, Frank, 282, 293, 300n59
Window Cleaning (Douglas), 222
Wind River Reservation, 109
Wood, Grant, 221
Woods, C. B., 89
Woodson, Carter G., 209, 236, 240, 251n9
Woodson, George, 89
Work, John Wesley, 324
Works Progress Administration, 248
Wright, Richard, 217, 218
Wright, Wilhelmina, 284
Wright case, 280–81, 282

Yerby, Frank, 4
"Yet Do I Marvel" (Cullen), 211–12
YMCA, 114
York (slave), 3
Young, Rev. Charles, 334

Young, Marlene, 334

Zinn, Howard, 303
Zion Baptist Church (Omaha NE), 325